DIFFERENT EVERY TIME

THE AUTHORISED BIOGRAPHY OF

ROBERT WYATT

DIFFERENT EVERY TIME

EVERY TIME

THE AUTHORISED BIOGRAPHY OF

ROBERT WYATT

MARCUS O'DAIR

First published in Great Britain in 2014 by
SERPENT'S TAIL:
3a Exmouth House
Pine Street
London EC1R 0JH
www.profilebooks.com

3 5 7 9 10 8 6 4 2

Typeset in Minon and Pisak to a design by Henry Iles.

A CIP catalogue record for this book is available from the British Library.
464pp

ISBN 978-1846687594
e-ISBN 978-1847656490

Printed and bound in Great Britain by Clays, Bungay, Suffolk

FSC
www.fsc.org
MIX
Paper from
responsible sources
FSC® C018072

For Charlotte, also terrific when sober

CONTENTS

SIDE TWO: EX MACHINA

INTRODUCTION

by Jonathan Coe

This fine biography will tell you all that you need to know about the story of Robert Wyatt. So, having been asked to write a few words of introduction, I think I'll just say something from a completely personal perspective.

A few minutes ago this page was blank. I was staring at it, not knowing what to write. Then I closed my eyes and waited to see what was the first thing that came into my head when I thought about Robert Wyatt.

It was an image of my desk. A small pine desk I bought in 1991. It stood in the corner of our bedroom in the little flat we rented for a few months just off the King's Road in Chelsea. On it sat a brand new Toshiba laptop, my pride and joy. I used to boast to friends that this laptop had a hard drive with a capacity of 20 MB – big enough to hold the entire novel I proposed to write on it.

And so I began to write the novel. I already had a title – *What a Carve Up!* – and a pretty solid idea of the plot and structure. It was an ambitious book, and the main ambition was to write something intensely political which didn't make readers feel that they were being harangued. To combine anger with warmth and humanity.

Could it be done? For a long time I wasn't sure. I sat at my desk every day and every evening, and wrote what I could, which wasn't much. And then, later that year, pretty much on the day it came out, I bought Robert Wyatt's album *Dondestan*. It was his first proper album since *Old Rottenhat*, some six years earlier, and suddenly, hearing that voice again, entering that soundworld, being welcomed into that lyrical space where political engagement had always co-existed with generosity and humour, a realm of possibility was opened up to me. The inspiration I'd been searching for had been under my nose all the time.

It had been there on Robert's 1974 album *Rock Bottom*, when his extraordinary, wordless vocalising on the playout to *Sea Song* had provided the consoling soundtrack to many an adolescent romantic disappointment. It was there on *Nothing Can Stop Us*: on his sublime cover versions of *Strange Fruit* and *At Last I Am Free* (a less polished but much riskier version than the Chic original, stretching the melody until it becomes almost unbearably fragile and vulnerable). And it had been there, certainly, on *Old Rottenhat*, the album that had, for me, crystallised the emerging ruthlessness of the Thatcherite tendency better than any other, as well as foreshadowing the rise of New Labour ten years before Tony Blair tore up Clause 4 ('If we forget our roots and where we stand / The movement will disintegrate like castles built on sand').

The fact that Robert had managed to make one of his most committed and passionate albums in the mid-1980s is significant, it seems to me now. He began his career, as is well known, as the drummer and vocalist for The Soft Machine, one of the key bands in the early years of the so-called Canterbury Scene.

A distinguishing feature of the Canterbury bands – besides their instrumental virtuosity, English self-deprecation and Dadaist leanings – has been their consistent inability to reach out to a wide audience, to break out from the pages of specialist music magazines and into the mass media and the national consciousness. Too polite? Too obscurantist? Who knows. Mike Oldfield's *Tubular Bells*, a Canterbury record to all intents and purposes (or to all in tents and porpoises, as Hatfield and the North could easily have titled one of their tracks), is one of the two obvious exceptions to this rule. The other is the oeuvre of Robert Wyatt.

In the British musical upheavals of the late 1970s, most of the artists who had emerged from that scene struggled to stay afloat. Their old records disappeared from the shops and no new ones arrived to take their place. But Robert seemed to thrive. With *Shipbuilding*, written for him by Elvis Costello and Clive Langer, he became better known than before. A good deal of artistic longevity and popularity comes down to luck, but in this case I don't think luck had anything to do with it: or with the fact that now, more than forty years after The Soft Machine unceremoniously dispensed with his services, his songs are more widely known, more widely covered and more widely loved than ever.

No, it surely has to be down to the breadth of his vision. After his Virgin albums of the 1970s, something changed: he brought in a wider and more eclectic range of influences, coming from the whole spectrum of world music, while still retaining his unique, instantly recognisable voice and instrumental mannerisms. He developed a new, more overtly politicised outlook, without losing any of his trademark humour or self-mockery. Suddenly, Robert's music was no longer introverted, but outward-looking, inclusive and universal. He began to speak (and sing) for a whole generation. Much as he would recoil from that notion, I'm sure.

I shudder to think what the last few decades would have been like without the continuous, alternative running commentary that has been provided by Robert's music and lyrics. (And when we talk about his lyrics we must also, of course, talk about Alfie's: for theirs is a true creative partnership.) He once said something to the effect that he had no objection to songs not making sense, because when songs do make sense, more often than not he doesn't like the sense that they make. As for his own songs, they can be oblique, certainly; sometimes eccentric. But, to me, they make a better kind of sense than most things that are going on in the world at the moment. More and more, Robert Wyatt sounds like the voice of sanity. Sane songs for insane times. No wonder that I, and countless others, have been inspired and uplifted by them for so long, and will remain forever grateful.

SIDE ONE

THE DRUMMER BIPED

1

THIS IS THE FIRST VERSE

George and Honor, London and Kent

'**My earliest memory**', **says Robert Wyatt**, sitting in a wheelchair that still displays an *Access All Areas* sticker from a rare live performance with jazz double bassist Charlie Haden, 'is looking out the window, and thinking: "I can now look out of this window. I am four, it is my fourth birthday, and I am going to remember this." I decided to remember it and I do.' Six decades on, Robert chuckles into a beard bushier than that of Fidel Castro, if not quite in the league of Karl Marx. A baby grand piano dominates the room, surrounded by trumpet, cornet and assorted percussion instruments. One wall is given over to vinyl, another to a vibrant, if faded, Tunisian rug, a third to books: on music, leftist politics and Pataphysics, the belle époque pseudoscience that paved the way for surrealism, Dadaism and the Theatre of the Absurd. The home studio is in the English market town of Louth, where Robert has lived for close to twenty-five years with Alfie – wife, manager, co-lyricist, and the visual artist responsible for all his solo album covers.

The view filed away by the four-year-old birthday boy, however, was not of Lincolnshire, but rather the South London suburb of West

› 'Blond, pretty and very biddable' – Robert with his mother, Honor.

Dulwich. Robert had actually been born in Bristol, on 28 January 1945, his mother, Honor, a journalist and broadcaster, having followed the BBC to the city during the war. But VE Day arrived when Robert was just three months old and Honor returned with the BBC to London, working first in the Schools Department and then on the new *Woman's Hour* radio programme. Robert and Honor shared a house in Dulwich with another family, the Palmers, and with Robert's half-siblings Julian and Prudence: the two children from Honor's short-lived marriage to the journalist Gordon Glover. 'Robert was a very bright little boy,' recalls Julian, today a successful actor who has appeared with the Royal Shakespeare Company and in a number of blockbusters, from James Bond and *Star Wars* to *Harry Potter* and *Game of Thrones*. 'Not just intelligent. He was a light boy. He *lit*: that sort of light. I wouldn't say the whole room lit up when he came into it, but one was always pleased when he came in. Grown-ups liked him very much.'

Just before his second birthday, the sparkling young boy contracted mastoiditis. Now relatively rare, at least in its acute form, the infection of the bone behind the ear was then a severe condition, and brought Robert so close to death that the hospital advised urgent baptism. Although surgery and kaolin poultices ultimately saw him through, he still suggests, semi-seriously, that the operation might have damaged the left hemisphere of his brain, supposedly responsible for logic, detail and rational thought. 'I do live in a dreamworld,' Robert says, 'and I never haven't done. I wake up just long enough in the daytime to eat lots of food and then try to go back to sleep.'

For the first six years of his life, Robert had an adoring mother and an entirely absent father. George Ellidge was still married to his first wife, Mary Burtonwood. According to Julian, however, it was Honor with whom George was in love. 'My mother used to say that she loved me because I was the firstborn, she loved Prue because she was a girl, and she loved Robert because he was a lovechild. She was a wonderful mother to us, and we all felt we were special in one way. But Robert really was the favourite.' Robert 'was the most enchanting little boy,' recalls his half-sister Prue Anderton. He was blond, he was extremely pretty, and very, very biddable. My mother would say: "Oh darling, go up to the post office for me, would you go and get me some cigarettes?" And he would. He was just so good.'

George and Honor had met in Mallorca in the early 1930s, as part of a circle of literary expats orbiting the poet Robert Graves. At that time still married to Gordon Glover, Honor wrote for *Epilogue*, a literary magazine edited by the poet Laura Riding with Graves as associate editor. George's wife Mary, meanwhile, was working as Graves's secretary, and they possibly had an affair.

During the war, in which George served in Italy and North Africa, George and Honor themselves began an affair. But when the war ended, George returned to Mary, living with her on a houseboat on the Thames at Oxford, where he studied Psychology. The marriage, however, was not to last and after the houseboat sank they decided to separate. Mary went to teach in Hastings, while George moved to Nottingham before, in 1951, securing a job in Watford, which meant he could at last join Honor, Robert, Julian and Prue in Dulwich. He moved in – and Robert acquired two further half-siblings, Julia and Mark Ellidge, older than Robert by ten and six years respectively. Robert also gained an extra surname: having been Robert Wyatt at infant school, he now became Robert Wyatt Ellidge, still the name in his passport.

Wyatt insists he felt no resentment towards his father for those six years of absence, and also takes issue with the general depiction of the post-war era as drab and dreary. 'According to historians now, it was a terrible time, but I had an *idyllic* childhood. We made a thermos flask, a couple of Marmite sandwiches, and we would go and sit on a bombsite with a pencil and paper, drawing. We had loads of bonfires in people's back gardens. Digging holes, pretending you're in the trenches. Playing games where you see how far you can get down the street just by running along the roofs, without ever going onto the ground. It was such fun.'

Julian describes George, Robert's father, as 'an absolutely wonderful man… the perfect bloke to grow up with.' When neighbours complained that, by not having curtains, the family were letting down the tone of their street, Julian responded by placing in the window a message of his own: 'Mind your own bloody business.' George thoroughly approved. 'An Ellidge', as Robert's dad was heard to declare, 'is rebellious against all rules that he has not made himself.'

Robert seems to have inherited his dad's sense of humour, as well as his iconoclasm. 'George and Robert had these silly jokes about sausages,' recalls Prue, shaking her head at the memory. 'They thought the word "sausage" was just the funniest word in the world. Every time the word "sausage" was mentioned, their shoulders shook. One day George came back from work with a bag in which he had what would be the equivalent of about four pounds of pink cotton sausages. He'd got somebody at the workshop to make them. Oh, they fell about, it was the funniest thing. Or George might say, "What mark did you get

> Robert with his parents, sketching at a bombsite.

in your English?" And Robert would say: "Sausages over sausages." It was just ridiculous.'

Robert's sense of humour, in particular his love of word games, also derived from Lewis Carroll and Edward Lear. This pair of Victorian writers – surrealists before their time – helped to inspire Robert's love of fun, puns and nonsense, crucial ingredients in counter-balancing, in Wyatt's adult make-up, what could otherwise be seen as his slightly po-faced politics. To Robert, however, there is not necessarily a distinction. He lists *Alice's Adventures in Wonderland* – along with bubble and squeak, the Spanish city of Granada, the saxophonist Gilad Atzmon and the *Morning Star* newspaper – as one of the five things that make his world a better place. 'People will probably say, "Oh that's his infantilism showing",' he explains, 'but I think it's one of the greatest political satires written. There's an aspect that becomes more meaningful as you grow older, the whole "off with your head"' culture. Very scary.'

Alfie today describes her husband as puerile 'in the non-pejorative sense', and Robert does seem to be one of those lucky adults able to recall precisely how it felt to be a child. The boy's face is still visible behind that grey beard, just as the boy is audible in that frail and fragile voice. Another crucial influence from childhood was A. A. Milne, creator of *Winnie the Pooh*. Robert has described the humble, honey-loving teddy bear as his earliest role model, and to this day he will still sign off an email with Pooh's 'tiddly-pom'. Pooh, like the characters that populate the work of Lear and Carroll, is also a deeply English creation, at least in his original form. Wyatt would later describe its Disneyfication as America's worst crime – 'with the possible exception of the carpet-bombing of Laos'.

The Wyatts and the Ellidges came from very different social backgrounds. Robert's maternal roots are a series of distinguished architects. James Wyatt, known for his Neoclassical and Gothic Revival work, is the most renowned, but he was far from alone. Among the buildings that bear the Wyatt mark, as restorers if not original designers, are Windsor Castle, Crystal Palace, Salisbury Cathedral and Westminster Abbey. Historian John Martin Robinson, in his book on the family, called the Wyatts 'the pre-eminent English example of an architectural dynasty'.

The Wyatt architectural dynasty had ended by the twentieth century, but they remained prominent in other fields. R. E. S. Wyatt was an England cricket captain. Horace Wyatt, Robert's maternal grandfather, was a founding member of the RAC, as well as a writer, noted for his 1917 wartime reworking of *Alice's Adventures in Wonderland* as *Malice in Kulturland*: 'Twas dertag and the slithy Huns / Did sturm and sturgel through the sludge'. 'I really liked him,' recalls Robert, of his very own Lewis Carroll. 'I thought he was great. He taught me about ballet. He said, "pas de deux" means "father of twins". And all these really silly things. I can see that it's not just from my dad that I get some stuff; I can trace some of it to Horace. Apart from being a tragic mistake, life is a mad joke. Well, to him it was.'

Robert had less in common with the most prominent Wyatt of recent times. Journalist and politician Woodrow Wyatt, the father of journalist Petronella Wyatt, was Honor's second cousin. Originally a Labour MP, he lurched to the right in the 1970s, becoming closely associated with Margaret Thatcher and Rupert Murdoch, writing the 'voice of reason'

> Honor Wyatt and George Ellidge at the door of Wellington House, 1950s.

column for the *News of the World*. With his cigars and flamboyant bowties, and snobbish, Little England attitudes, Woodrow represented something close to the antithesis of jazz, socialism and surrealist humour. Robert describes Woodrow, with no little embarrassment, as an 'appalling man' with a 'sadistic sense of superiority', though he can't resist laughing at the story – apocryphal or not – that, when asked by a

Frenchman to confirm the spelling of his surname, Woodrow replied: 'Waterloo, Ypres, Agincourt, Trafalgar, Trafalgar.'

Robert is far more enthusiastic about the ancestors on his father's side. The Ellidges were not, Robert explains, members of the family-tree-keeping classes, but he does know a little of his paternal grandfather: 'My granddad, Sam Ellidge, was a tailor. Apparently he was very nice, drank a lot, always laughing, and never had any money because he was always making people clothes for free. So I'm really proud of him as an ancestor.'

The class gap between Wyatts and Ellidges had narrowed by the time Robert himself was born. His maternal grandfather, Horace, was deemed to have married beneath him when he fell for Robert's Welsh grandmother, Annie Morgan of Glamorgan (who sounds as if she could have stepped straight out of an Edward Lear poem). The Ellidges, meanwhile, had achieved social mobility in the opposite direction. George's father might have been a tailor, but he himself had fought his way into the middle classes through studying at Liverpool, Cambridge and Oxford universities.

Like Honor, George was a committed liberal. They read the *Manchester Guardian*, forerunner of the *Guardian*, and were active members of the Fabian Society. The immediate post-war period was a heady time for the British left, the Labour Party's landslide victory of 1945 having paved the way for the National Heath Service and the whole welfare state, as well as a massive programme of nationalisation. 'My parents certainly thought that starting the welfare state was a wonderful thing,' Robert recalls, 'and that if you expect all the working classes to go and die in the front line for your country, then they do deserve a decent education and healthcare when they come home. That hadn't happened previously.' Yet Robert also points out that, while such changes were enthusiastically supported in the Ellidge household, his parents' political views were relatively moderate. Although introduced to socialism from an early age, he wouldn't join the Communist Party for more than three decades – and, when he did, his family members would be taken aback.

By the time Robert got to know him, George was working as an industrial psychologist, helping to rehabilitate those forced, often as a result of the war, into an abrupt change of career. Yet George had previously worked as a music critic and, as a classical pianist, had even recorded a couple of 78 records. That love of music remained intense and was soon channelled into his son. Robert was taken to the opera well before his tenth birthday and to concerts at London's Royal Festival Hall, built as part of the post-war 'tonic to the nation'

> Robert with his jazz mentors, his father George and half-brother Mark Ellidge.

that was 1951's Festival of Britain. He became familiar with twentieth-century classical composers including Bartók, Hindemith, Stravinsky and Schoenberg, as well as England's own Ralph Vaughan Williams and Benjamin Britten.

Most crucially, George Ellidge introduced his son to jazz. His taste was for the classics – in particular, the pianist Fats Waller and composer and bandleader Duke Ellington – but George's son Mark was a fan of the contemporary scene and passed on his enthusiasm. Even as young as twelve, Robert was delivering talks to the school jazz club. 'The prefects were sniggering,' he laughs, 'because I obviously didn't know what I was talking about. Didn't stop me then, doesn't stop me now.'

There was music on his mother's side of the family, too. Robert says his half-sister Prue 'has a really good voice, miles better than mine', while his grandmother, Annie Morgan, used to sing nonprofessionally. Honor's own influence was no less crucial. Her circle of friends included the novelist Barbara Pym, and she wrote several books of her own, among them a guidebook of sorts called *The Young Traveller in Portugal*.

Honor researched the Portugal book in 1953, travelling on a shoestring with eight-year-old Robert and his older half-sister Prue. 'We travelled by bus a lot of the time,' remembers Prue, 'although sometimes we were lucky enough to get a lift in a truck or cart or something like that. We slept wherever, in blankets that my mother had stitched up – they were old army blankets of George's. We were just camping, but we had no tent. We'd sleep under the stars: in woods, in forests, wherever we could.' Robert also remembers the trip with affection. 'I absolutely loved the place,' he recalls. 'Dirt poor, I now realise, but magical to me at the time.'

Portugal was no one-off. Robert's family enjoyed an unusually close relationship with continental Europe at a time when most British families would simply roll up their trousers at Brighton or Margate.

> The young traveller – Robert in Portugal.

George smoked French cigarettes and, during his military service in Italy, had developed a love of wine, olives and spaghetti.

Robert was also sent on exchange trips, including one, when he was just nine, to a family in Austria. The following year, he paid a solo visit to a Parisian pen friend, spending a term at a French school. Not many ten-year-olds had such experiences in the mid-1950s, but to Wyatt a term in Paris was as unremarkable as his occasional access to some highly celebrated cultural figures. On a later, teenage trip to France he watched the Nouvelle Vague film *Ascenseur pour l'Échafaud*, and was blown away by the Miles Davis soundtrack. On another, he paid a visit to the great Cubist painter Georges Braque.

'Robert told me that when he'd been a kid, about ten, he'd suddenly realised that Georges Braque was still alive,' remembered Mark Boyle (the lighting engineer whose psychedelic show was integral to The Soft Machine's live performances). 'And he told his mother about this, and said, "I think I should meet him, I think I should meet him before he dies." And his mother spoke to Roland Penrose, who was president of the Institute of Contemporary Arts at the time, and he arranged for Robert to spend a day in Braque's studio.' Robert, not in the least overawed, asked a series of questions in schoolboy French – among them, according to family legend, 'Do you believe in God?'.

Robert recalls other formative childhood experiences as visits to South London's Horniman Museum, with its world-class anthropological collections, and being taken to Katherine Dunham's 'African ballet' and a Mexican art exhibition at the Institute of Contemporary Arts. It was, as he says, an idyllic childhood – at least, up until the age of eleven.

→》《← →》《← →》《←

For some time, George had been suffering from various apparently unrelated symptoms: double vision, numbness, clumsiness, slurred speech. To the casual observer, it could seem, embarrassingly, as if he was drunk. Instead, Robert's father was eventually diagnosed with multiple sclerosis, an incurable neurological disease in which the body's immune system mistakenly attacks its own tissue.

At first the condition was relatively mild, and George faced it with remarkably good humour: 'He'd be carrying the coal across the kitchen', recalls Julian Glover, 'when his legs would just give out rather suddenly and he'd go down with a sort of curtsy. We'd all *shriek* with laughter, him too, roll on the floor. And he used to say lovely things like "I can't tell

25

which glass to put down on which table." He lightened the atmosphere, certainly for us.'

Yet, as Honor and George wrote in *Why Pick On Us*, the book they wrote together on living with MS, 'George's sclerosis showed a tendency to get more and more multiple'. By this stage the family had left Dulwich for the commuter-belt town of Egham, in Surrey, in order to be near George's latest job – but, by 1956, he was no longer able to work. With no reason to stay in Egham, and Honor having left the BBC for a career as a freelance journalist, they decided to move to the country using money Honor had inherited from her father. They bought a large but dilapidated Georgian manor house in Kent. Wyatt lore puts it in Canterbury but it was in fact ten miles outside, in the small village of Lydden.

With its sweeping gravel drive, security gates and CCTV, Wellington House is today a grand presence, even if the next-door pub is boarded up and the duck pond opposite half full of rubble. It was rather less stately in 1956. 'Tumbledown, with lots of trees around it, sort of ramshackle', is how Wyatt remembers it. 'It was a Georgian house that was falling to bits. No-one had wanted it for a long time because it had this ivy which had turned into a tree in the middle of the house and was splitting it in half. My parents just sort of whitewashed it and got in there, really. I didn't realise they were thinking: "Well, we don't know how long George is going to live, so the long-term future doesn't really matter."'

Over the years, Wellington House has gained a reputation as a hotbed of bohemianism – and a hothouse for the Canterbury Scene. Wyatt himself plays down the image, insisting it was not 'some sort of international Bloomsbury group. You get people saying, "Oh it was a really different, arty house." I mean, sometimes visiting other people's houses, I would think of the difference: "Ah, my parents have bookshelves with books on. *In East Kent! How weird is that?*" As far as I could work out, it was fairly modest. They had books, they had records, and not just by the Coldstream Guards.'

It may be that Robert doesn't realise quite how unusual his childhood was. Perhaps he is also embarrassed at what could be seen as a relatively privileged upbringing. But Wellington House was by no stretch a wealthy household. In order to make ends meet, spare rooms were rented out to foreign students, and Prue recalls that, when she or Robert went to the shops, they would buy extra cigarettes to hide in the kitchen drawer, anticipating the inevitable moment when George and Honor couldn't

> Robert with George, Honor and his half-sister Prue at Wellington House.

afford even another packet of fags. Yet, however much Robert downplays it, his was no ordinary 1950s upbringing – one minute camping under the stars in Portugal, the next heading off to meet Braque. At Wellington House, he was allowed to paint art of his own directly onto the walls, and Prue still recalls 'these wonderful psychedelic swirls and curls' on a glass window between the hall and the kitchen.

It can be no coincidence that one half-brother, Julian Glover, went on to become an actor, while Mark Ellidge, Robert's other half-brother, became a celebrated *Sunday Times* photographer. Both Julian and Prue describe their upbringing as bohemian. 'I remember Mark once bringing a friend home from school,' says Prue. 'They were always called by their surname in those days. Mark said, "Do sit down, Clarke. The chair is not as dirty as it looks." And my mother said, "Do sit down, Clarke. The chair is *just* as dirty as it looks." This is how we were. Everything was a bit grubby. But we never went without.'

Honor and George themselves seemed to revel in their eccentricity. In *Why Pick On Us*, they speculate on how the neighbours might view the family: 'Those odd but not unendearing types at the Big House who obviously have no money yet smoke like chimneys and are often seen dashing to and from the local with a basket of bottles and she, my dear, though well over forty, goes into Dover wearing neither hat nor stockings, and they leave all their lights blazing, no curtains drawn, even when they're going to bed, and they never lock up a thing!'

–»)《«– –»)《«– –»)《«–

The move to Wellington House coincided with Robert beginning secondary school. The Simon Langton Grammar School for Boys in Canterbury, like Wellington House, looms large in Canterbury music lore, with several pupils going on to become subsequent collaborators.

Hugh Hopper, who would later play bass in The Soft Machine, was actually in the same year. 'The first time I met him, we had a fight in the playground,' laughs Robert. 'His parents were Conservative, mine were Labour, so we had a fight. And a friendship ensued that lasted for ever.'

The bassist and composer was not the only Simon Langton pupil to re-appear in Wyatt's professional life. There was also the spindly prefect who, in a breach of normal protocol, made an overture to the fifteen-year-old Robert: 'He came up to me and said: "Ellidge, I hear you have a Cecil Taylor record. I wondered if I could borrow it?" I was very honoured. I rushed home and got it: it was Cecil Taylor's *At Newport*. And I thought: "Blimey, how about that?"' Cecil Taylor was, and remains, one of jazz's most radical exponents, who even in his eighties still approaches the piano – as writer and photographer Val Wilmer so evocatively put it – like a set of eighty-eight tuned drums. The prefect was Mike Ratledge and, as a first appearance, it is apt. Mike was a headmaster's son – and, to Wyatt, 'very, very straight-laced'. He was also already a highly promising keyboard player, and later a pivotal member of The Soft Machine.

The Langton didn't only boast one entire incarnation of that band. Also among its pupils were Hugh's older brother, Brian, who would go on to play saxophone with The Soft Machine, and Dave Sinclair, who would play keyboards in Wyatt's subsequent group, Matching Mole.

> Robert throwing paint at a canvas. On the back of the photo, he has written: '1. Is the floor on fire? 2. Why are the paints behind me? 3. Why is the palette wiped?'

Music writers have tended to romanticise the Langton, in consequence, as a hotbed of music and art. However, though Robert and Hugh became firm friends after their playground scrap, and Mike Ratledge spent his weekends exploring improvised music and tape loops with Brian Hopper, there was not at the time any sense of companionship binding the future collaborators. In fact, Wyatt dismisses the school's supposedly bohemian ethos as a fantasy. 'I got caned so often, I think this is unique. I don't know anybody else who got caned.'

Wyatt attributes his troubles at the Langton to the fact that he struggled academically in that top tier of state-funded secondary education: 'Being at grammar school just made me feel totally inadequate. Surrounded by clever boys who got 98 per cent in Physics, whereas I would get something like 3 per cent.' Yet Julian insists that Robert was actually

> A teenage Robert (left) at Wellington House with Julian (centre) and his first wife, actress Eileen Atkins (behind), and Robert's friend Marie-Noëlle Chevalier.

'very, very bright'. And Prue recalls that he was streamed into the 'U' class, to his parents' horror – until they found out that 'U' was in fact the top strand, meaning 'university potential'.

If lack of intelligence wasn't the reason Robert didn't fulfil that potential, neither does the blame fall on adolescent recalcitrance. Instead, Robert seems to have been genuinely unaware that the curious and questioning mindset tolerated – even encouraged – in the liberal confines of Wellington House would not necessarily go down so well with his headmaster. 'I'd say things that were alright at home, that really shocked him,' he recalls. 'And I didn't know this. Like, "Jesus's mother can't have been a virgin, obviously, and as far as we know was some sort of equivalent of a geisha girl who got pregnant and couldn't do that job any more and was picked up by some elderly gentleman called Joseph, which is the way things went then." And he said, "*Are you saying Jesus's mother was a prostitute?*"'

It wasn't only that Robert struggled to adjust between Wellington House and his more straight-laced, single-sex grammar school. Robert was also unhappy to find himself stuck out in the country. Lydden today feels a bit twee, entered through ornamental white gates and with more than its fair share of front-garden squirrel statues. In the 1950s, it seemed like the sticks. 'I suffered a bit from a feeling that I'd been dragged out of London at just the age when I really started appreciating it,' recalls Robert, 'because my dad retired to the country. I thought the countryside was unbelievably boring. I couldn't believe it. No girls, nothing. I thought it was a vast open prison. I thought, "Where's the Horniman Museum? Where's the ICA? Where's Soho?" Even as a child I knew about these things; my parents had taken me. You know, the bright city lights.' He did find some distraction, however, in using an old army bugle to confuse hounds on the local hunt – 'an early use of music for political ends'.

Inevitably, Robert was also affected by his father's encroaching MS. George's symptoms varied from day to day, but there was no mistaking the merciless decline. There came a point at which, on bad days, he had to use a stick, then a point at which bad days required a wheelchair. Eventually there were no more good days. The wheelchair became permanent, a pre-echo not lost on Wyatt. 'It is very odd, isn't it? He was in a wheelchair half the time we were in Lydden. And I wish I'd known more about the difficulties he was having. I wish I'd taken him out more, really. He'd be sitting there with his radio and his papers and he looked quite self-sufficient, but I think he would have liked to go out more. Also, I would have been a bit more forgiving. He tried to teach me piano and got very bad-tempered, went all cross-eyed, and he couldn't do it. He got very grumpy with me for not learning properly. But it must have been awful for him.'

⟫⟪ ⟫⟪ ⟫⟪

Lonely in Lydden and frustrated at school, the fifteen-year-old Robert was galvanised by the arrival at Wellington House of the Australian poet and guitarist Daevid Allen. Seven years older and brazenly self-confident, he was a beatnik Christopher Robin to Robert's Winnie the Pooh.

'I think I paid ten shillings a week full board,' remembers Allen, who arrived as a lodger in late 1960 via an advert in left-wing journal the *New Statesman*. Still rangy and energetic, he is today best known for his years at the helm of sprawling space-rock collective Gong. 'I had some

> The first Beatnik in Kent – Daevid Allen outside Wellington House, 1961.
The sign reads: 'Like this gate shutsville. Like really ba-aby, for real.'.

money saved up,' he goes on; 'enough for a year in Europe. I wanted to experiment with Ornette Coleman-style free jazz. So I went down to see the family and I immediately saw Robert, who came beaming up towards me. He was much younger than me, of course: he was only fifteen at that point. But the first thing we did is look at each other's record collections, and they were almost identical. And so I thought: "Go no further."'

At the Langton, even the two-year age gap between Robert and older pupils like Mike Ratledge and Brian Hopper seemed insurmountable. Daevid Allen was twenty-two and already familiar with marijuana and LSD – and yet Allen recalls 'an intellectual equality' with the teenage Robert. 'Either I was way behind,' laughs the Australian, 'or he was way ahead. I think he was way ahead.' Robert and Daevid bonded over a mutual love of music. On café jukeboxes in nearby Whitstable, Robert had listened to Eddie Cochran, Buddy Holly and Roy Orbison, as well as doo-wop group The Platters. He had dabbled in skiffle when the craze swept the country in the mid-1950s, and by the early 1960s was also a fan of soul acts on Detroit's Motown label. But, like Daevid, Robert's primary passion was for jazz.

Although a catastrophic year for rock, with the death of Buddy Holly and the jailing of Chuck Berry, 1959 was for jazz an *annus mirabilis*. Albums from Miles Davis, Charles Mingus, Dave Brubeck, John Coltrane and Ornette Coleman, in particular, still burn with magnesium-flare intensity. It was also the year that saxophonist Ronnie Scott opened his eponymous Soho jazz club. Wyatt no longer had to imagine himself in Harlem. As he got older, Robert was able to escape from rural Kent, going up to see Mingus and 'saxophone colossus' Sonny Rollins right there in London. 'As an atheist,' he declares, 'they're the nearest to gods I've ever had.' When he queued for an autograph from the pianist Thelonious Monk, Robert instead received a pat on the head: a Monk's secular blessing.

Robert would follow the development of jazz, through bebop and hard bop into the radicalism of free jazz – and, later, back to its New Orleans roots, as well. He has a particular affinity, however, with the music of his own era: 'In 1945, the year I was born, Miles Davis made his first record with Charlie Parker. As much as I love everything beforehand in jazz, from Duke Ellington back to Louis Armstrong, I feel that these are my people; this is where I come in. And it *is*, actually, where I come in. Almost to the month, from the moment I'm born, stuff happens. I can trace my life through it, and I still do.'

As well as his love of jazz, Daevid also shared Robert's interest in modernist art and comedy: Scottish poet Ivor Cutler and Spike Milligan's *The Goon Show* were both favourites on the Wellington House radio. Just as important as Daevid Allen's cultural interests, however, was his disregard for societal norms. A real-life dharma bum whose eccentricity extended even to the spelling of his forename, Daevid embodied a life unrelated to academic success. Robert was particularly impressed by his habit of walking around Canterbury with his 'dog' – actually a tin can on a string. 'He made me realise, just by the way he lived, that you could have a life that was nothing to do with anything you'd done at school,' says Robert. 'O levels or geography or arithmetic or any of that. There was a whole other way of having a life that didn't require that. That was really where I got the confidence, or the insight – from seeing Daevid operate on that basis.'

Wyatt claims to have been unaware of any generation gap – he was, he says, a great fan of the modernist music and art of his parents' generation.

But he was, as Julian drily notes, 'something of a non-conformist'. Even before Daevid Allen arrived, Robert was reading Rimbaud, the enfant terrible of nineteenth-century French poetry. What fascinated him, said Honor, was not so much the poems themselves but 'the fact that Rimbaud simply rejected every social standard that existed'. Dave Sinclair still recalls the first time he saw his future Matching Mole bandmate – outside the Langton, in about 1959. 'There was a young lad crossing the road there with very long hair, wearing his school cap back to front and with his jacket inside out. I said to my brother: "Who's that?" And he said: "Oh, that's Bob Ellidge." That was really quite forward for those days, somebody doing that.'

Wyatt doesn't remember the jacket, but does admit to reshaping his school boater into a Stetson, for which he was caned. He was also caned for writing 'Jesus Christ' in the Canterbury Cathedral visitors' book and for smoking behind the bike sheds, a crime of which he insists he was innocent. He protested against this injustice by taking up smoking.

Robert was handsome as well as conspicuous and, as his half-sister Prue recalls, 'very popular with the ladies'. She tells a story of Robert, aged about fourteen, on the bus with pupils from the Simon Langton Girls' Grammar School: 'Robert got on the bus with my mother and they went upstairs. There were a couple of Simon Langton girls sitting there and Robert went by and flicked one of their hats off. And my mother heard the girl say to her friend: "He's always doing that." And the girl said: "He did it to me yesterday." It was sort of a feather in their caps, really, that he actually had taken any notice of them.'

One of the pupils at the Langton's sibling school was Pam Howard – and, if she was on the same bus as Robert, it was very much deliberate. 'I used to walk an extra half a mile to get on his bus,' admits the woman who would become Robert's first serious girlfriend – and, eventually, the first Mrs Wyatt, 'because I fancied him. He was very noticeable. All his shirts were purple. He dyed them all in the same pot. So he'd get sent home from school – "Change that, Ellidge!" – and he'd go home and change it for another one, exactly the same colour. It was the time when we were all pretending to be beatniks, but he really was out there.'

⇢⇠ ⇢⇠ ⇢⇠

The story goes that Robert Wyatt heard about Kevin Ayers before actually meeting him through a Canterbury friend: he was the only other person in East Kent with long hair. A fan of calypso and bossa nova, as well as

> East Kent's only long-haired teenagers: from left, Hugh Hopper, Robert and Kevin Ayers, with schoolfriend (and future Softs roadie) Ted Bing at top.

modernist poets such as Ireland's Louis MacNeice, Ayers already had his famous good looks. Julian Glover recalls him as 'the original denim shirt and medallion man, absolutely gorgeous'. Though born in Kent, Kevin mixed English humour with decidedly un-English insouciance, the result of a childhood spent alternating between Malaysia and British boarding schools. He also had a natural gift for songwriting that would later land The Soft Machine their first management deal. With Kevin's arrival as a regular at Wellington House, the dramatis personae of Robert's early professional life were in place.

Brian Hopper is certain he attended at least a few jam sessions at Wellington House, though Robert himself insists he can't remember any ensemble music-making aside from a few blues duets with Daevid Allen. But the gatherings at Wellington House were, for his friends and associates at least, the stuff of legend. 'It was that time when we all wanted to listen to jazz and be like Allen Ginsberg,' recalls Pam. 'The parties would last all night. To Robert, it was nothing; it was normal life. He'd play his records, listen to his music, hang out with all his mates. But we'd have the windows open, pretentiously sitting there and listening to the music. For a sixteen-year-old, it was a really exciting time.'

Robert – whom Pam recalls as 'a charmer, very charismatic' – was often to be found carrying a trumpet over his shoulder on a string strap. He soon moved onto drums – although initially, since he didn't own a kit, he was forced to make do with a combination of kitchen utensils and cardboard boxes. 'He was always banging,' remembers Julian. 'If he could get two sticks, he would bang them. And he would plonk away on the piano. Music was completely and utterly leading in his life, and we all knew that.'

After one of his trips to Paris, Daevid Allen returned with a Californian jazz drummer, George Neidorf, who also began to lodge at Wellington House. Neidorf was able to give Robert a few lessons – and, since his luggage included a snare drum and cymbals, Robert was also able to graduate from pots and pans. Neidorf recalls Wellington House as the perfect place to be: 'George and Honor were the most supportive people I'd ever met. Whatever we did artistically, they encouraged. They treated Robert as an adult, and me as part of the family. They were highly intelligent, well read and culturally diverse people. If I could have chosen my parents, they would have been George and Honor.'

The impression is of a divided life: that, although school might have been troubled, Robert's home life was happy. In fact, while friends remember the sociable Honor, less tends to be said of George. Perhaps one reason Robert downplays the bohemian aspect of his upbringing is that, although unconventional in many respects, his parents did take a keen interest in his academic success. This was particularly true of George, who had already lost one son, John, who died after being hit in the head by a cricket ball before Robert was born.

'Robert was OK at school for a couple of years,' says Prue, 'but after that he began to get interested in music. And this of course worried George, because he got so interested in music and it was exclusive. He didn't want to work, he didn't want to do exams. And it was the only time I can remember that George really, really got upset and annoyed. Because he would have been so proud of Robert if he'd been to university.'

'My father was dead disappointed,' agrees Robert. 'He had dragged himself up from nothing: he was a Lancashire lad who had worked really hard, gone through the war and done well. He thought: "My son will go further." So when I was drifting further and further down in the dumps at school, completely unable to keep up with anything, he was very disappointed. Both my parents were. And I was mortified on their behalf.'

Though he hides it well behind the beard and avuncular grin, Wyatt is a worrier. When in Portugal with Honor and Prue, he had been so embarrassed at the poverty he witnessed that for a period he refused to wear any shoes. That empathy has remained: it's almost as if he failed to develop the so-called compassion fatigue with which the rest of us slowly become inured. Alfie describes Robert as missing a layer of skin, and that quality is perhaps what makes his music so affecting. But it has also left Wyatt, as a human being, vulnerable, and quick to blame himself when things go wrong. His constant self-effacement is not merely English 'after you' etiquette.

> Robert with Californian Wellington House lodger George Neidorf, who gave him his first drum lessons. .

George and Honor did try to accept that their son's talents might lie outside the classroom. Just as they had encouraged Julian to pursue a career in the theatre, they supported Robert's interest in music, paying for lessons – first on violin, then on trumpet. Surprisingly, Wyatt struggled to progress on this front, despite his obvious musicality. Perhaps the teaching style was to blame. Or perhaps he was progressing perfectly well, but simply fell short of his own – or his parents' – high standards. Robert still talks of the 'curse of the provincial grammar-school boy, brought up with ideas above his station', whose love of Stravinsky and Duke Ellington served only to convince him of just how short of these standards he himself fell.

After his first term of sixth form, the situation reached crisis point. Crushed by the sense of having failed his parents, Robert began to contemplate taking his own life. 'I couldn't understand reading music,' he explains, 'and I wasn't getting better every week. Over the Christmas holidays, I tried to do it and I couldn't do it and I thought: "I can't go back and face it." This was something where my parents had thought, "At last we've found out what Robert can do," and I was fucking even that up. I just felt so ashamed and embarrassed, I decided to kill myself.'

One evening over Christmas 1961, Wyatt took from the bathroom cupboard a bottle of tablets his father used to help him sleep through the discomfort of his multiple sclerosis, and swallowed the lot. He was found unconscious on the floor.

2

MEMORIES

Deià and The Wilde Flowers

Robert made a full recovery from his teenage overdose, after having his stomach pumped in Dover Hospital. But why the desire, after an apparently happy childhood, to eradicate everything? Robert's own explanation is both casual and, for a self-declared dreamer, ruthlessly rational. With rock'n'roll looking more like a fad than a viable career path, and convinced he didn't have the talent to make it as a jazz musician, even had there been opportunities in rural Kent, he simply couldn't picture an adult life that appealed: 'I just thought: "It's such an effort, being a grown-up. Just earning a living, just the daily things that people take for granted, learning to deal with real life." I thought, "I *suppose* I could learn to do that, but I really don't want to. I want to stop right now." So I just decided to try and do that. It was just a practical decision.'

Daevid Allen, who says he and Robert discussed suicide in the abstract in the days before the overdose, also recalls the decision as 'purely philosophical – there was not an ounce of emotion there'. But it was also evidence of the depression from which Wyatt would suffer, episodically, to this day.

Robert is quick to laugh, often with such gusto that his whole torso shakes (he wryly describes himself as a sit-down comedian). Yet it's not hard to see Robert's humour as the tears-of-a-clown flipside of a generally bleak outlook, from which life is nothing more than a cosmic joke. This in part explains the appeal of Lewis Carroll, lonely in his novels and self-loathing in his diaries, and Edward Lear, a fellow depressive whose poems were as sad as they were surreal. Or the life and work of another hero, Pataphysics founder Alfred Jarry, where the division between absurdity and tragedy was often imperceptible.

'I do think life is grim,' Robert asserts. 'You know that saying, the devil is in the detail? I think the devil runs the show, and *God* is in the detail. I think the show itself is devilish but, out of that, little beautiful moments can be plucked with luck and skill. That way round is the only way to make sense of it.'

Robert speaks of a life punctuated by 'cliff-drops into dark places', by moments 'staring into the abyss'. This would not be the last time he tried to take his own life. 'He was suicidal cyclically, ever since that first time,' says Daevid Allen. 'I don't know how many times he actually physically tried, but he was threatening on numerous occasions. He had that tendency.'

⟩⟩⟨⟨ ⟩⟩⟨⟨ ⟩⟩⟨⟨

If the underlying causes of this first suicide attempt are beyond excavation, it was clear that the immediate trigger was unhappiness at school. Following an urgent consultation between parents and headmaster, Robert left the Langton at the start of 1962 and enrolled at the local art college. It could have been a fertile environment. Painting and sculpture had been keen interests since childhood, with the Swiss painter Paul Klee a particular favourite, and for a period Robert saw a future in fine art as more probable than in music.

As a kind of a parallel education system for adolescent non-conformists, art schools offered a path into music too, one followed by numerous contemporaries, such as John Lennon, Keith Richards, Eric Clapton, Ray Davies, Syd Barrett and Pete Townshend. Robert's stint at art school, however, proved little more successful than his time at the Langton: 'I think it was while I was there,' he reflects, 'that I realised I was more interested in music, funnily enough.' He left after a single term.

For some alumni of the Langton, especially those bright young things of the 'U' stream, the subsequent years were straightforward: first sixth form, then university and employment. For Wyatt, it was instead a rudderless time, driven by a kind of existential recklessness. 'I had the youth ideology. I didn't expect to live long. I didn't even learn to do anything properly. I couldn't see the point, since I had no intention of living long enough to need to know anything very much. The 1960s were a vertiginously steep learning curve for me, and I didn't get anything right.'

> Robert Graves talking with musicians at a festival near his home at Deià, Mallorca, 1954.

The drifting began with a journey to Mallorca to stay with Robert Graves, who had remained a family friend since the 1930s; Robert believes he was actually named in the poet's honour. Yet as he and companion George Neidorf made their pilgrimage through olive trees and lemon orchards to Canelluñ, Graves's home in the rural village of Deià, Robert found himself increasingly troubled by his namesake's formidable reputation. Graves had first emerged as a First World War poet, a contemporary of Wilfred Owen and Siegfried Sassoon. By the early 1960s, he had written the historical novel *I, Claudius*; the autobiographical *Goodbye to All That*; *The White Goddess*, a pioneering study of mythology; and various translations of Latin and Greek texts. And he was Professor of Poetry at Oxford.

Robert needn't have felt daunted. Graves, he laughs, 'was very relieved that I was virtually illiterate and hadn't read any of his stuff'. Although born in the reign of Queen Victoria, the puckish poet represented a walking, talking rejection of social and moral restraint. Known for his passionate relationships with muses such as Laura Riding, Graves was not averse to occasional marijuana use and dabbled in hallucinogens. He also retained a physical grace unusual for a man in his late sixties. 'I was completely knocked out by him,' says Wyatt. 'Quite awestruck. A magnificent bloke, bit of a giant. Fantastically handsome. I remember him leaping down the side of the mountain, like a goat, when everyone else was clambering. I thought he was absolutely fantastic. He really, quite obviously, was your proper *great man*.'

Bebop deities aside, Wyatt may consider himself an atheist. But he couldn't fail to be seduced by Graves's idiosyncratic take on spirituality. With its tapestry of folklore, mythology, religion and the muse responsible for poetry of passion, *The White Goddess*, the poet's 1948 'historical grammar of poetic myth', would enchant everyone from Ted Hughes to Thomas Pynchon. 'It gave me a sense of the world,' Robert

> Vinyl choices. 'Now what would that have been – Mingus, probably.'

recalls, 'not just as a geographical place but as an endless story of amazing myths, and different states of mind.'

The classical scholar was also a fan of avant-garde jazz and had embraced Cecil Taylor, no less, at a gig in New York. Graves encouraged Robert as a drummer, soon giving him the nickname 'Batty' from the Spanish word *bateria*, meaning 'drumkit'. Robert even had a few lessons from Graves's future son-in-law, the young Catalan drummer Ramón Farrán. 'Ramón was a young jazz musician,' remembers Robert, 'and both he and George Neidorf taught me things. That was very valuable. In fact, some of my first live gigs ever were at Canelluñ. Robert used to get people to do things. There were always lots of people around, and everybody had to do something at these meals. It was terrifying; you had to sing a song or something. I used to do vocal percussion duets with Ramón Farrán.'

The Deià lifestyle of sangria and beach barbecues was later compared by Graves's son William to the hedonism of Federico Fellini's *La Dolce Vita*. Wyatt recalls paradisiacal afternoons playing conga drums in the open air with Mati Klarwein, whose artwork would later grace Miles Davis and Santana album covers, as the Mediterranean nibbled at fishermen's huts below. It's hard to imagine a more healing environment for the teenage Wyatt to convalescence from an attempted suicide. After five months in this Eden, however, George Neidorf announced that he was moving on: his girlfriend was pregnant, and they were heading to Greece for the birth. Robert too realised it was time to leave and took the ferry to mainland Spain. The journey home brought him back to reality with a jolt. 'I was sleeping on benches in Barcelona because I couldn't afford to go in anywhere,' he explains. 'I came back and had to go to the doctor with malnutrition.'

⤛⤜ ⤛⤜ ⤛⤜

Back home at Wellington House in late 1962, Robert took a job with the Forestry Commission in Kent's Lyminge Forest. The working day began at five in the morning; Canelluñ could hardly have felt more distant. 'It was a very cold winter,' recollects Wyatt. 'They said, "Oh, he's been to a grammar school, he won't stick it out. It's too tough." So I did stick it out until the weather got better, just to prove that I could.'

As soon as he had done enough to defend his reputation, however, Robert left the job and moved to London. Sharing his flat in Belsize Park were Kevin Ayers, Hugh Hopper and Ted Bing, a schoolfriend who later worked as a Soft Machine roadie. 'There were four of us in one room,' Robert remembers. 'It was quite a big room, with a permanent smell of hot curry coming up the staircase and a pregnant prostitute in a little room next door. She used to come and dance for us in her leotard.'

Daevid Allen had also moved to London and soon enlisted Robert and Hugh as the rhythm section of his new group. Inspired by Beat Generation writers of the previous decade, the Daevid Allen Trio set out to combine poetry with avant-garde jazz. Using Daevid's contacts, the trio secured a four-night booking at the Establishment Club in Soho.

The focal point of the early 1960s satire boom, the Establishment Club was co-owned by Peter Cook and hosted jazz gigs by the likes of Dudley Moore: a fine pianist as well as Cook's comedy partner. Yet Robert's first Soho gig did not go well: 'We played there for a night,' he recalls, 'and they said "God, no!" and threw us out. They just wanted foot-tapping jazz, which Dudley Moore was very good at, very good indeed. I completely agree with them, in retrospect.'

The trio's ejection clearly still rankled with Allen the following month, when the trio performed at the Marquee Club on London's Oxford Street. With poor syntax but righteous indignation, Allen introduced *Song of the Jazzman* as 'Something we got fired from the Establishment Club because of'. 'We had a contract for three months supposedly,' he continued, hipster drawl captured on the album *Live 1963*, recorded at the Marquee Club (and released four decades later). 'However, because we did some poetry and some rather strange things there, I'm afraid they gave us the big shove – with a very carefully gloved, immaculate hand.'

Although of interest as his first recording, *Live 1963* offers little insight into Wyatt as a musician, since the trio was dominated by Allen's wry, rambling poems. As a rhythm section, however, Robert and Hugh were already sufficiently robust to withstand Daevid's unorthodox guitar style, which he himself describes with glee as a cross between jazz guitarist Charlie Christian and ukulele comedian George Formby. And in its line-up, at least, this was a proto-Soft Machine, with the trio augmented on a couple of numbers on piano by Mike Ratledge, then studying Psychology and Philosophy at Oxford.

The Marquee show, organised by poet Michael Horowitz, introduced the Daevid Allen Trio to an audience much more sympathetic to its mix of poetry and jazz. Through Horovitz, they also landed a gig at London's Institute of Contemporary Arts, alongside jazz pianist Stan Tracey and Beat Generation novelist William Burroughs – whose novel *The Soft Machine* would provide inspiration for a later Wyatt band.

Despite such prestigious company, however, the ICA show would mark the end of the line for the Daevid Allen Trio. In the liner notes for *Live 1963*, Hugh Hopper attributed the group's failure to the fact that 'as well as being pretty damned challenging, we probably did sound pretty damned awful'. Daevid soon moved on to Paris, where he took a room in the Beat Hotel recently vacated by Allen Ginsberg and Peter Orlovsky; Brion Gysin was in the room next door. Robert and Hugh, meanwhile, stayed on in London. It was there, in a Kensington attic flat, that the eighteen-year-old Wyatt received devastating news from his half-brother Julian.

Since he had left home, Robert's parents had sold Wellington House and set off for a new life in southern Italy. The warmer climate, they explained, might ease George's MS – although Wyatt now believes his father simply wanted to die in the country with which, during his time in the army, he had become so besotted.

> Not quite the Daevid Allen Trio: Robert, Daevid and Mike Ratledge, 1963..

Driven by a friend, George and Honor took the best part of a month to reach their destination, making plenty of stops on the way. 'They'd got right the way down to the town where they were going to live,' says Robert. 'Ariano, near Naples. They were camping, mostly, on the way down, and they got to the very hilltop overlooking the town. He died the night before they went down there.'

According to the autopsy, George had died from cardiac failure, the result of an enlarged heart brought on by the strain of his illness. But since multiple sclerosis is not in itself fatal, Robert had had no sense that his dad was approaching death. Apart from grief at the early loss of the father he had known for just a decade, the news brought with it a crushing sense of guilt. The temporary rupture in Robert's relationship with his father, brought on by academic difficulties at the Langton, had become suddenly, wretchedly permanent. 'My dad had been to three universities,' says Robert, 'got various degrees from Cambridge, Liverpool and Oxford. He'd become a psychologist and he assumed that at last we'd got to a point where university attendance was assumed. And then I'm out there swanning about, working in a forest and hanging about on other people's kitchen floors abroad. Completely *gone* as far as he was concerned. He didn't get it at all. I realised, when he died, that I'd let him down.'

The pity is that George Ellidge, who had taken his son to the opera and played him records by Duke Ellington and Fats Waller, would never see the musical career he helped inspire. Three decades later, Robert would dedicate his compilation album *Flotsam Jetsam* to 'George Hargreaves Ellidge, musician, soldier, psychologist and complete nutcase. I miss him more than I know how to say.' The knowledge that his father died disappointed in him gives Robert nightmares even half a century on.

—»)《«— —»)《«— —»)《«—

Had his father lived, Wyatt would perhaps have bowed to pressure to find regular employment, if not to attend university. Instead, bereaved and bandless, he found himself adrift. Hugh Hopper's return to Canterbury only increased the sense of isolation. 'I hadn't got anywhere to live,' he sighs. 'I just stayed in different places with a big suitcase with my belongings. It wasn't much: toothbrush, change of clothes, and *Porgy and Bess* by Miles Davis and Gil Evans.' A pause. A laugh. 'I don't see what else anybody needs, to this day, actually.'

One unexpected source of solace was a job washing up at the London School of Economics. Founded by Fabian Society members including

George Bernard Shaw, the LSE fitted snugly within the left-wing world Wyatt had known since childhood. Yet the stint in the canteen also helped inspire his slow drift towards a politics in which anti-racism was the fundamental principle. 'There was a staff of about eighty,' he recalls, 'of whom seventy-eight were black women from Brixton. And they were the most wonderful hosts to me. Whereas the people who hired us – who were, of course, white – were very snappy, school ma'am-ish and bossy. But my fellow staff used to tease me something rotten, and I loved it. And they used to take me to their homes at weekends.'

Wyatt insists washing up at the LSE was 'one of my great experiences. I was a lost child in London and they were the ones who made me feel at home. Later on, I thought: "What a paradox." People talk about these aliens in our midst but to me, the aliens were the people I was working *for*. I had nothing against the LSE students and their professors, but to me, they were alien. They were all the people that my dad had wanted me to be, these university people going off to rule the world. It's not inverted snobbery, I was really happier amongst the kitchen staff.'

Robert also made two continental forays. In spring 1964, he headed to Paris to visit Daevid Allen, who was now living on a houseboat on the Seine and hanging out with William Burroughs and American composer Terry Riley. Already developing tape loop techniques inspired by the mesmeric drones of Indian music, Riley would shortly earn himself a position, alongside La Monte Young, Steve Reich and Philip Glass, as one of the four pillars of minimalism. Riley's sense of music as a vast, open landscape, evident on compositions such as *In C*, would influence Robert both as a member of The Soft Machine and as a solo artist. 'One day Daevid brought this young man to my house on Rue Boissonnade,' the composer recalls. 'It turned out to be Robert Wyatt. He had a trumpet with him with a turned-up bell, like the one Dizzy Gillespie played. I had a little spinet piano there and as I remember the three of us spent the afternoon jamming – music and poetry. I felt Robert had an extraordinary, mature, inspired quality that seemed unusual for someone so young.'

After returning briefly to England, Robert set off to Mallorca for a second summer with Robert Graves, this time joined by the sun-worshipping Kevin Ayers. The pair stayed in a fisherman's hut. 'It was very primitive,' recollects Wyatt. 'There were no taps; just this stone hall with a well in the middle. That was where you got your water, pulled up in a bucket. No electricity.'

Graves's son-in-law Ramón Farrán was now running the Indigo jazz club in Palma, and Robert played at the venue on a few occasions. A

> Robert in Deià, 1964, where he had drum lessons from Ramón Farrán at the bottom of Robert Graves's garden.

more prestigious performer at the Indigo was Ronnie Scott, a talented saxophonist better known for his world-famous Soho club – and not, perhaps, the sort of person one expected to meet through Robert Graves. 'You couldn't imagine more difference,' laughs Wyatt. 'This East End Jewish wise guy, really funny and hip, and this patrician classical scholar. But they got on absolutely like a house on fire.' As both punter and performer, Robert would become a regular at Scott's venue. He and Ronnie happened to share a birthday, and their joint birthday celebration would become an annual club tradition. To this day, Robert still defines his ethnic group as 'Soho'.

Daevid Allen soon joined Robert and Kevin in Deià, and they began to play together: it was at this point, according to Ayers, that the music really began to gel. Ramón Farrán sometimes joined them, but recalls that Kevin and Daevid were living 'a different lifestyle'. 'Actually,' says Farrán, 'Deià is a bit dangerous for a person who hasn't got a strong personality. It's really easy to lose yourself in doing nothing, in just having parties, smoking pot and things like that. I used to put them in the right place: "If you want me to work, I'll work. But I don't want nonsense. Work is work and nonsense is nonsense." I was a very strict person.'

Thanks to a peculiarly English embarrassment at breaking the rules, Robert would never get into illegal drugs. 'I was a very provincial grammar-school boy,' he admits, 'in the sense that I was terrified of breaking the law – which is, of course, contemptible in artistic circles. I didn't like dope culture. I wasn't the slightest bit interested in LSD.'

Robert's moderation was perhaps the result of his liberal upbringing: he might have turned his school jacket inside out, but the genuinely wild behaviour at Wellington House had been largely confined to friends unused to the relaxed regime. Also keeping Robert from lotus-eating was his passion for music. He might have shirked schoolwork, but even the exacting Farrán, who provided formal lessons on this second visit to Mallorca, recalls 'Batty' as a joy to teach. Whatever had gone wrong with those early violin and trumpet lessons, Robert clearly lacked neither musical ability nor willingness to learn.

-»)(«- -»)(«- -»)(«-

By the time Robert returned from Mallorca, Britain was in the grip of full-blown Beatlemania, as too was America, with the 'British invasion' spearheaded by the Beatles, Rolling Stones, Animals and Dusty Springfield. By April 1965, the editor of *Vogue* magazine would declare London the most swinging city in the world.

In Canterbury, seventy miles south-east of London, Hugh and Brian Hopper did what teenagers all over the UK were doing: they started a band. Brian contributed guitar and saxophone, while Hugh played bass. Kevin and Robert, upon their return from Mallorca, were installed on vocals and drums respectively. Completing the line-up was rhythm guitarist Richard Sinclair. The cousin of Simon Langton schoolmate Dave Sinclair, he would later make his name as a bassist, vocalist and songwriter with bands such as Caravan and Hatfield and the North.

The young musicians rehearsing at the Hopper family home, known as Tanglewood, called themselves The Wild Flowers but soon added an E in tribute to Oscar Wilde. They made the local paper even before their first performance, having been ejected from a local pub on the grounds that their hair was too long. In Canterbury, at least, the 1960s were not yet fully swinging.

Robert and Hugh Hopper might have been common to both acts, but The Wilde Flowers were a very different proposition to the Daevid Allen Trio: while the trio had been inspired by Ornette Coleman and Beat poet Gregory Corso, The Wilde Flowers were more in the mould of Chuck

Berry. They did play Herbie Hancock and Nat Adderley numbers, but also songs made famous by Wilson Pickett and James Brown – even a couple of Kinks and Small Faces tunes. With the focus firmly on the dancefloor, it was a very different role for Wyatt, who was called upon to provide steady sturdy beats when he had previously been trying, with Daevid Allen, to emulate the free-jazz drummer Sonny Murray. Then and now, Wyatt's ears were as open as his countenance: playing for dancers, he insists, is as noble a profession as is available.

Richard Sinclair describes early Wilde Flowers gigs as: 'Kevin on BBC-shape microphone. Robert on drums, with hat and sometimes shirt. Hugh on flowery-painted Hofner bass guitar. Brian on Rapier maroon guitar, horribly out of tune but with fantastic guitar-hero endeavour. And myself, with limited imagination and large Billy J Kramer quiff, on beautifully in tune, but very out-of-place, rhythm guitar. All through the same amp: in those days, we had one amp and a very small PA. But we did have new band shirts, made by Mrs Hopper.'

> Robert at Tanglewood, Canterbury, with the Hopper brothers, Hugh (left) and Brian, and their mum, Billie.

Sinclair also recalls 'many sexy art-school girls' at Wilde Flowers gigs. One such was Pam Howard, blonde and beautiful and by now Wyatt's girlfriend. That half-mile walk to catch Robert's bus had been worth it. 'I suppose I might have been seventeen when I left school and went to art college,' she recalls, 'and it was round about then that I started to go out with Robert. He had just come back from Deià, and he had nowhere to live because his mum had moved to Italy, so I used to let him stay in my bedroom. I'd sleep on the sofa and put a note on the door. 'My father wasn't very happy about all that, using the place as a hotel, so I left home. I'd just started art college, I'd done the first year. I left home to get a flat so that Robert would have somewhere to live, basically.'

Robert moved into Pam's new flat, in the seaside town of Herne Bay, although they soon moved into Canterbury itself. With only a negligible income from gigs, he took on odd jobs such as hop-picking and life-modelling. Rather conveniently, however, he was barred from conventional employment due to the length of his hair. In order to pay the rent, Pam dropped out of art college and took a job running guided tours of Canterbury Cathedral. 'I was a mouse, I was so in awe,' she admits. 'I must have been bonkers.'

In the late summer of 1965, Pam became pregnant. Suffering morning sickness, she recalls a daily routine of running naked out of the front door to vomit in the front garden, screened from passing pedestrians by only a thin hedge. But she continued to attend Wilde Flowers gigs, Robert improvising a maternity dress by cutting away a circle of fabric to expose her bulging stomach.

-»)(«- -»)(«- -»)(«-

Although The Wilde Flowers never signed a record deal, they have, over the years, become celebrated as the Rosetta Stone of what became known as the Canterbury Scene. The phrase is used most often in relation to The Soft Machine and Caravan, as well as Soft Machine progeny – Wyatt's subsequent band Matching Mole and the solo work of Kevin Ayers and Daevid Allen. Other associated bands include Hatfield and the North, Delivery, Gilgamesh, Khan, Egg and National Health. Wyatt isn't keen on the term. No musician likes to be pigeonholed, and he is not the only one to find something claustrophobic in former schoolfriends forever reenacting the bonds of the past. Robert also makes the point that Canterbury was not a kind of English Haight-Ashbury, but a fairly conventional English cathedral town.

In fact, there did exist a small group of musicians in and around the city whose sound had – perhaps more as the years went on – some shared sense of the English phantasmagoric, slipping between centuries to borrow from folk, modern classical and even church music, as well as contemporary jazz and pop. Caravan are the epitome. At the time, however, it was too small to be properly a scene – in Daevid Allen's words, it was just 'a bunch of middle-class kids from Canterbury grammar, smoking Woodbines and hanging out in front rooms'. And, in any case, Wyatt regards his own output as outside its parameters.

'There were people who lived in Canterbury,' he explains. 'The Hopper brothers, the Sinclairs, Pye Hastings, Richard Coughlan. I *can* see a connection amongst those people. Obviously, the Caravan thing, a very distinctive sound. But I don't think me or Kevin or Daevid were ever really part of that. I went to school in Canterbury, but I'd get the school bus home at four-thirty. I didn't hang around in the evenings with them. I wasn't with them at weekends.'

Maybe it's the term itself that is at fault. Robert has spent far less time in Canterbury than in Lydden, London or Louth – and it was in London, and in Europe, that The Soft Machine made their name. Yet the various acts of the so-called Canterbury Scene did share something specific, which went beyond mere geography. The term has come to represent a style of jazz-tinged, pastoral and very English psychedelic rock: slightly surreal, sometimes slightly silly, and as warm and whimsical as a stoned summer afternoon. Such a description would certainly not encompass Wyatt's entire output, but his music *has*, at times, shared some 'Canterbury' characteristics. There's the jazz influence; the complex time signatures; a preference for keyboards over guitars; and a singing voice that, while contemporaries were posing as Delta bluesmen, remained unapologetically rooted in East Kent.

–》《– –》《– –》《–

Though they sit right at the root of the Canterbury Scene family tree, The Wilde Flowers were very much a part-time concern. Robert was also performing with singer and pianist Norman Hale, the original keyboard player in The Tornadoes – although he somehow managed to leave the band just before they reached number one with the instrumental *Telstar*. With a certain logic, the new duo went by the name of Norman and Robert. 'It sounds extraordinary,' laughs Wyatt, 'like the most effete little thing. But that was good. He was from Liverpool, and we played

> The Wild(e) Flowers' debut, Whitstable, 15 January 1965, in Mrs Hopper's shirts. From left: Hugh Hopper, Kevin Ayers, Robert, Brian Hopper, Richard Sinclair.

rock'n'roll. He was a working rock'n'roll pianist in that tradition: not so much Jerry Lee Lewis as Little Richard. He was a very good pianist.'

Wyatt was merely moonlighting, but Kevin Ayers would soon leave The Wilde Flowers for good, rejoining the similarly itinerant Daevid Allen in Mallorca. It was the first example of Kevin's tendency to disappear at unexpected – and, in career terms, often unsuitable – moments. Kevin was temporarily replaced as singer by his roommate, Graham Flight, although Robert also sang the occasional number from behind the kit. When Graham himself left in the summer of 1965, Robert moved to the front of the stage. For nine months, Wyatt would be, for the only time in his life, a frontman in the traditional sense.

53

> Wyatt fronts The Wilde Flowers, with, standing, from left: bassist Hugh Hopper, drummer Richard Coughlan and guitarist Brian Hopper.

Richard Coughlan, by odd coincidence Pam Howard's step-uncle, was brought in to replace him on drums. 'I was very much in awe of Robert, really,' admitted the man who would himself go on to a successful career with Caravan. 'He was a good drummer – much better than I was.' Even then, Robert was a deeply musical drummer, playing the song rather than merely the beat, while his drummer's sense of rhythm helped to develop his apparently casual vocal phrasing. He was also a promising frontman: charismatic, boyishly handsome and, for all his self-deprecating humour, not lacking in self-confidence.

'He was quite good-looking in his own way,' adds Brian Hopper, who recalls that industry figures at Wilde Flowers gigs would take a particular interest in Robert, 'and he was lively, too. He didn't mind doing a bit of chatting. He didn't hog the mic but he didn't mind saying a few things.' A publicity photo taken at the time, featuring one of the large sewer pipes then being installed near the Hopper family home, supports Wyatt's frontman credentials. Hugh Hopper is leather-jacketed, bespectacled, slightly gawky; Coughlan politely polo-necked; Brian Hopper in suit and tie and neatly trimmed beard. Robert, impressively cheeky for a man sitting inside a sewer pipe, is by some distance the most colourful and least coltish figure, clad in hat and loud floral tie. While the other three look dutifully into the lens, his own gaze is impishly askance.

While his confidence and charisma might have made him a natural frontman, however, Wyatt was no shoo-in as lead singer. His vocals were mournful and high in pitch: 'Jimmy Somerville on valium', as he himself has joked. Robert's voice is as reedy as a soprano saxophone but tremendously affecting despite – or because of – these idiosyncrasies. Knots and grain exposed, it is imbued with the same vulnerable, ingenuous quality he has as a human being: 'Like a poor innocent cast into a complicated world', as friend and collaborator Brian Eno has put it.

Wyatt's first significant vocal on record is *Memories*, a Hugh Hopper composition recorded in the spring of 1966. His singing is resolute and resilient as well as frail and fragile. Already, at the age of twenty-one, Wyatt's voice was a curious combination of choirboy and old man, simultaneously world-weary and innocent as grass.

Memories would be perhaps the most durable of all Wilde Flowers tracks. Later covered by both Wyatt and Daevid Allen, it would also show up on 1982's *One Down* album by Bill Laswell's Material, sung by a then-unknown Whitney Houston and featuring a sax solo by one of Wyatt's heroes, the free-jazz firebrand Archie Shepp. Another Hugh Hopper number recorded at the spring 1966 session was the equally impressive *Impotence*. Wyatt contributed lyrics as well as lead vocal – the subject matter, like the high, hard-won delivery, flying in the face of macho rock'n'roll stereotype. It was such original compositions – primarily by Hugh Hopper and Kevin Ayers – that distinguished The Wilde Flowers from other bands on the dancehall circuit.

Meantime, Pam Howard was waiting around at a Wilde Flowers rehearsal when her waters broke. Sam Ellidge was born on 23 May 1966 in Canterbury hospital.

3

CLARENCE IN WONDERLAND

Mister Head and The Soft Machine

In Mallorca, just as in London and San Francisco, the monochrome shadow of the Second World War was by 1966 giving way to kaleidoscopic colour. After he left The Wilde Flowers, Kevin Ayers joined Daevid Allen on the island, part of a new generation of *étrangers* more interested in psychedelics than sangria. 'I went out of my body completely,' recalls Daevid of an acid trip he took that Easter. 'I basically stepped right out of what we would laughingly call normal reality, into another dimension.' Having previously seen himself as a poet and visual artist as much as a musician, Daevid now recognised, with sudden clarity, that music was his true calling.

'And the moment that I came out of this vision,' he continues, 'I came down from the house and went staggering out into the garden. There's Kevin sitting at a table outside the front of the house with this guy. He looks at me and says: "Well, Daevid, I've found ourselves a patron." This was literally half an hour after the vision. And I looked at him and I just laughed, and I said: "I know." And I did know, I really knew that this guy was going to start the band and that we were on our way.'

Wes Brunson, who had run an optometry business and a nightclub in Oklahoma before arriving in Mallorca, made for an unlikely rock'n'roll

> The Soft Machine's first promotional photo, taken by Robert's half-brother, Mark Ellidge, on a wet Dalmore Road. Daevid Allen is standing above (from left) Robert, Mike Ratledge and Kevin Ayers.

benefactor. Robert Graves's son Tomás has claimed that Brunson not only carried knives and a gun but also believed himself the seventh incarnation of Christ – and would stand in the path of oncoming traffic to prove it. His leap from optometry to svengali, mundane by comparison, would prove short-lived. Yet he did help to kickstart Daevid and Kevin's new band – which, with a nod to the psychedelically enhanced circumstances of its conception, went by the name of Mister Head. Robert, on drums, shared vocal duties with Daevid and Kevin, who alternated on guitar and bass. Completing the line-up was Larry Nowlin, an American guitarist whom Kevin and Daevid had met in Mallorca.

Back in England, Brunson secured Mister Head a house in the village of Sturry, just outside Canterbury, in which to live and rehearse. He

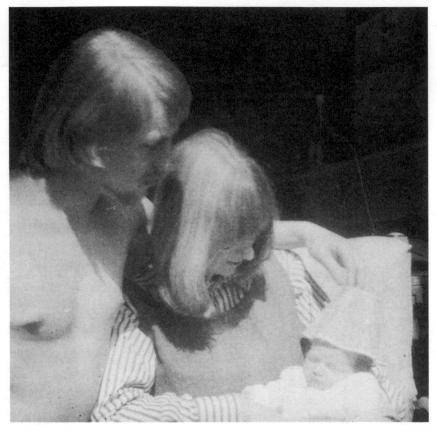

› Robert, Pam Howard and baby Sam in a lampshade hat.

also gave them a budget for equipment. And then, almost as abruptly as he had arrived, he returned to America. The story is that Brunson had abducted his own daughters in Tulsa when denied access by his wife, and he was arrested on a short trip home to the US.

Brunson's disappearance coincided with Robert's departure from Canterbury. Having returned from Italy as a widow, Honor had left Kent for the more familiar environs of Dulwich. Pam soon joined Honor in London, taking Sam with her. Ostensibly, Pam moved away because the Sturry house was no place to bring up a baby. But there was, she says, another woman involved, too. 'Robert was perpetually a bad boy,' she shrugs, mildly amused in recollecting the events of half a lifetime ago. 'To him, it was like having a cup of tea'.

The birth of Sam, says Pam, 'didn't change anything at all'. But with Wes Brunson heading back to the US and the Sturry house soon up for sale, Robert opted to leave Canterbury and rejoin his family in London –

not that he was going to win any dad-of-the-year awards. 'I was crap,' he admits. 'Pam used to carry Sam around in a basket, bring him to gigs. Our only concession to modern health and safety requirements was that we'd put the basket behind the speakers and not in front of the speakers. Poor little bugger. He had an itinerant life, in a basket behind speakers, while we made our racket from place to place.'

–»)) ((«– –»)) ((«– –»)) ((«–

Mister Head's first gig, organised via a Robert Graves connection, was at a Sufi event: the Midsummer Revels, hosted by Idries Shah in August 1966. By this time, they had been joined by Mike Ratledge, who had just finished his degree at Oxford.

'I was starting to miss the keyboard thing that I'd heard in jazz,' explains Wyatt. 'Mike had just finished doing Philosophy at university and I invited him to come and join us on organ and that's when the harmonic possibilities of the band started to open out.'

For Wyatt, leaving Canterbury meant leaving The Wilde Flowers, after only a brief crossover period. With the exception of Larry Nowlin, however, Robert's Mister Head bandmates moved with him to Dulwich. Although Wyatt downplays Wellington House's reputation as a hotbed of music-making, he says 48 Dalmore Road was exactly that: 'That's when I *do* remember musicians piling in. It was semi-detached, just one of a row of identical small houses. And that's where we had Daevid Allen, Kevin, me, Mike, often Brian Hopper, and often my brother Mark, and our girlfriends and my mum. And we played in my bedroom. We had all our instruments out. *That* I remember as being musicians hanging out together. Not Wellington House, but there in a semi-detached in West Dulwich. We had all the walls covered in egg boxes in a totally failed attempt to not disturb our neighbours.'

Honor Wyatt would become the band's most important benefactor. As well as playing a key role in bringing up Sam, she would accommodate a revolving cast of musicians, friends and girlfriends for the next four years. Recently widowed and highly sociable, she may have been glad of the company, but it was quite a sacrifice for a woman in her late fifties. 'She was fantastic,' remembers Pam. 'She was so patient. I don't know how she put up with it. I think she loved it, in a way, but it must have been so intrusive. I mean, she had her moments where she'd get really pissed off with us. You'd hear her out at seven o'clock in the morning, sweeping the stairs rather noisily, and you'd think, "Oh ...."'

Today a red-brick semi-detached on a smart tree-lined street, the front wall of 48 Dalmore Road was in 1966 covered in psychedelic swirls of green and pink paint. The scene inside, meanwhile, sounds almost like a scene from The Monkees' TV shows. 'You never knew quite who you were going to meet when you walked in the door,' remembers Brian Hopper. 'Every square corner was occupied by somebody sleeping or reading or listening to music.'

Fuzzy footage from an Italian TV documentary still exists, showing Sam, as a toddler, bashing drums as beautiful women drift in and out. It seems like the 1960s idyll – and that, says Bill MacCormick, who would later play bass in Wyatt's band Matching Mole but who first visited Dalmore Road as a fifteen-year-old schoolboy, was exactly what it was. 'It was an incredibly welcoming, relaxed place to go to,' he recalls. 'If you have an idealistic view of the mid-to-late 1960s, this was it. You knocked on the door, and instead of somebody going, "Oh, not really, we haven't got time," they'd go: "Come in! We haven't seen you since… yesterday! Drink lots of tea!"'

There's something touchingly innocent about the picture MacCormick paints. Other members of the band might have been dropping acid, but Wyatt was drinking tea, living in the suburbs with his mum, girlfriend and son. Robert himself is adamant that his experience of a London hurtling towards the Summer of Love was domesticated. If he wasn't playing, he laughs, he was at home changing Sam's nappies.

Did he feel part of the counterculture? 'Well, I felt part of it until about half-past ten. Then I had to get the bus or the last train home. Back to the kitchen teabags and the Marmite sandwiches and the little suburban semi-detached.'

Yet even if Robert never took illegal drugs, and was at this stage relatively moderate even in his drinking, he and the rest of Dalmore Road bought in to the free love ethos. Their home, his son Sam recalls, was 'dripping with hippies… full of all these people sitting around and meditating and sleeping with each other'.

Robert's mother, Honor, amazingly, tolerated the whole show. 'I was brought up on Cole Porter,' she recalled. 'I could not understand it at all. But of course hearing this day after day, because they'd rehearse and rehearse and rehearse, although to me it was quite frankly a noise at first, nevertheless it was a noise with a purpose, they knew what they were doing. Well, gradually I got used to it and I began to like it!'

-»)((«- -»)((«- -»)((«-

> Feeding time at Dalmore Road. Clockwise from the top: Daevid Allen, baby Sam, Pam Howard, Mike Ratledge, Kevin Ayers and, pouring Sam's milk, Michèle Heyer (who later married Mark Ellidge).

That Larry Nowlin was the one member of Mister Head not to join his bandmates in Dulwich was a harbinger of things to come: the guitarist would leave the band after only a handful of gigs. 'Culturally, it was a whole different set of references,' Robert explains. 'He came from an incipient American West Coast thing, with Dylan-influenced lyrics. When people like Larry were around, you realised that, yes, we were very English actually.'

By the time Nowlin left, in September 1966, Mister Head had chosen a new name, The Soft Machine. It was a reference to the human body, from the novel of the same title by William Burroughs – the darkly sardonic Beat author who had shared the ICA stage with the Daevid Allen Trio three years previously. Ratledge too had stayed with the author for a brief period in New York, after graduating from Oxford.

On one level, the name was anomalous. While Burroughs' novel is populated by naked boys and noir-ish narcotics agents, The Soft Machine were closer to Wyatt's beloved Lewis Carroll – although later projects like the multimedia *Spaced* applied to audio tape the same cut-up techniques Burroughs employed with text. The name does, however, hint at the band's highbrow reference points. In lyrics and track titles, there would later be nods to Carroll himself, as well as Thomas Pynchon, Alfred Jarry and Samuel Beckett.

Robert might not like the fact, but The Soft Machine were grammar

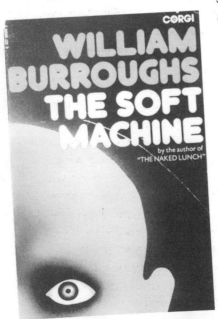

school through and through. They were also peculiarly scrupulous. Deciding they needed permission from Burroughs to adopt the name, Daevid Allen was delegated to seek the writer's blessing. He managed to arrange a meeting in London, near Paddington station. Burroughs 'appeared out of a shopfront, hat pulled over his eyes, looking like a crumpled insurance clerk from the Lower East Side of Manhattan. When I told him the purpose of our meeting, he blinked like an old alligator and drawled, "Can't see wha not!"'

With the name change cleared, and Larry Nowlin gone, Daevid took over guitar duties, while Kevin moved permanently to bass. With Mike

Ratledge on organ and Robert on drums, the first classic Soft Machine line-up was in place. More song-based than the Daevid Allen Trio, less dancefloor-orientated than The Wilde Flowers, the new group was unlike either of Robert's previous bands. However, they borrowed several numbers from Robert and Kevin's old group. 'They hadn't written anything original themselves, as a group,' confirms Brian Hopper. 'So they fell back on what we had been playing for the previous three or four years. *Hope for Happiness* was more frenetic, and quite a few of Hugh's songs were modified or amalgamated or the words were changed. But I think well over fifty per cent of their early set was Wilde Flowers stuff.'

Largely thanks to Kevin Ayers, the band's key writer in these early days, The Soft Machine would soon develop a repertoire of their own. And if their material sounded like nothing that had come before, it was because the band existed at the precise point at which the diverse tastes of its four members overlapped. 'We were four nascent bandleaders,' Daevid Allen recalled, 'who were at war with each other most of the time on the ego level. It was a huge power struggle. We all had very strong opinions.'

Tightly buttoned and thoroughly highbrow, Mike Ratledge represented a pole of The Soft Machine diametrically opposed to that embodied by the carefree Kevin Ayers. Mike was a fan of experimental composers such as John Cage, Karlheinz Stockhausen and Italian electronics pioneer Luciano Berio. He was also, laughs Pam, so intellectual that she hardly dared speak to him. Robert and Daevid, in their different ways, bridged the gap. Both shared Mike's avant-garde tastes, though Robert, like Kevin, was also a committed pop fan.

Personalities within the band were as diverse as musical tastes. Mike and Robert, recalled Ian MacDonald, a friend of the band who later became a respected music journalist, 'would talk entertainingly and informatively for hours on everything from modern art to politics and free jazz. They were by far the most intelligent and educated people on the English rock scene and I learned a lot from them. Daevid was equally amenable and happy to talk, though his interests were more mystic and esoteric... I remember him mystifying me with long discourses on prana and sex-magic. Kevin was the cool, aloof one, always disappearing off to his room with another woman, smiling enigmatically.' With members facing all points of the compass musical ly and temperamentally, the Soft Machine centre would not hold for ever. But, for a while, creative tension within the band resulted in some of the most original and enduring music of the era: an effervescent mix of pop, soul, jazz and incipient psychedelia.

It was Kevin Ayers – ironically, given his later aversion to any kind of career moves – who got the band a management deal, hitching up to London to knock on the door of Anim, a company set up by Mike Jeffery, former manager of Newcastle group The Animals, together with the band's erstwhile bassist Chas Chandler. The introduction had been made through Janey Alexander, a girlfriend of Larry Nowlin, who worked in their office. Chandler and Jeffery were impressed enough with Ayers to sign him up, initially as a solo songwriter, later agreeing to take on his group.

Mike Jeffery was a contentious character – a former Newcastle club owner and an associate of the notorious Don Arden. He and Chandler were, famously, the managers of Jimi Hendrix, who they signed up as much the same time as The Soft Machine. Producer Joe Boyd suggests

> The Management: Mike Jeffery (right) with his Anim number two, Henry Henriod, at London's Speakeasy club.

that Jeffery was uncomfortably close to the mob world portrayed in the Michael Caine film *Get Carter*. There were rumours that Jeffery had worked for British Intelligence, and later that he was responsible for the death of Jimi Hendrix. Such claims may be far-fetched but Jeffery was certainly one of the murkier figures in rock management.

At the time, however, Anim's offer to The Soft Machine of £12 a week per band member seemed too good to turn down. And Anim was a company on the move, as they were soon having huge success with Jimi Hendrix. Wyatt still recalls the 'sheer whirlwind force' of Hendrix, with whom he recorded backing vocals for *Stone Free*, B-side to the guitarist's debut single *Hey Joe*. (His contribution did not make the final cut, though he can be heard on Jimi's version of The Beatles' *Day Tripper*.)

The Soft Machine, too, were soon sent into the studio to record a single. Since Chandler was by now busy recording with Hendrix, the Softs went into the studio with Los Angeles producer and impresario Kim Fowley (who was later to record Jonathan Richman's Modern Lovers and proto-punks The Runaways). At the time, Fowley was best known for a string of novelty hits, though he apparently talked his way into the job on the basis of his involvement with Frank Zappa's 1966 debut *Freak Out*. Chas Chandler, however, was less than happy with Fowley's recording of a Daevid Allen number called *Fred the Fish*, and took The Soft Machine back into the studio to record a replacement A-side. Rather than Daevid's tune, he selected *Love Makes Sweet Music*, written by Ayers after a disastrous gig in Hamburg that September.

It's hard to argue with Chandler's decision. *Fred the Fish* is a ramshackle, goodtime number, an Australian take on a Cockney knees-up. *Love Makes Sweet Music*, featuring a robust lead vocal from Robert, is far more radio-friendly. Exploding into life with scat singing, backing vocals and organ glissando, the track hits its chorus by the ten-second mark and fizzes ever more fiercely before coming to a halt at just two and a half minutes. It remains a glorious piece of carbonated soul-pop.

> Jimi Hendrix, Mike Ratledge and Robert Wyatt at The Speakeasy, at the launch of *Love Makes Sweet Music*, 1967.

This was larval Soft Machine, and The Wilde Flowers' dancefloor influence remained strong. The band even rehearsed for a short period with the soul singer Marsha Hunt, who had worked with Alexis Korner and Long John Baldry. In the end, she didn't join the band – but she did go on to marry Mike Ratledge (the relationship was relatively brief, though they stayed married, and friends, for some years).

The single's B-side, *Feelin' Reelin' Squeelin'*, which *was* produced by Kim Fowley, showed a side of the band that was already more psychedelic than soul. Where *Love Makes Sweet Music* was innocent and upbeat, the B-side (actually a Kevin song, but credited to 'Robert Ellidge' – henceforth he would be Robert Wyatt as a musician) was dark and trippy, although Robert's chorus vocal accompanies a couple of abrupt leaps into sweet, sunny pop. Kevin Ayers delivers the almost impossibly low-pitched verse vocal, in the final minute turning as darkly comic as The Who's *Boris the Spider*. The closing seconds, as rhythm and harmony crumple, could soundtrack a B-movie drink-spiking scene.

'The thing about Kim Fowley was, he was a complete codeine freak,' Daevid Allen later recalled. 'So he never stopped talking. But secondly, he astonished everybody by taking the eight-track master tape, and cutting, splicing the eight-track master tape. Which nobody had ever seen done. It was really wild, to make *Feelin', Reelin', Squealin'*. So he made these huge massive splices, right across all of the eight-track. Because if you fuck it up, that's it, that's the end of the master.'

Love Makes Sweet Music was released by Polydor in February 1967. It was a landmark moment for the 22-year-old Wyatt: since neither the Daevid Allen Trio nor The Wilde Flowers released any records at the time, this was his first commercial release. The band were joined by Jimi Hendrix for a launch show, at London's new Speakeasy club, while Polydor promoted the release with an advert featuring only the label's logo and a handwritten message: 'This waste of valuable advertising spaces comes to you courtesy of The Soft Machine. The Soft Machine have just released a hit record, *Love Makes Sweet Music*, and that will pay for the space.'

Yet even with the endorsement of Hendrix and an interview on leading pirate station Radio Caroline, *Love Makes Sweet Music* failed to live up to Polydor's prediction. Robert has been careful about attributing blame for the flop, but he admits to a hunch that might explain the single's lack of success. 'Chas got involved with some very shady stuff, of which we were casualties,' he sighs. 'I think that he was involved in some payola scams. I think he did that thing that they used to do, with *Love Makes Sweet Music*, of sending people round to buy it in hundreds from the shops, to get it into the charts. At that time, the business decided to do a clean sweep of chart fixing, and he was one of the people they chose to make an example of. And the decision made by, I think, the BBC and people like that, was that any band that had been caught in one of these things, they wouldn't play their records on Radio 1 ever again. I think we then lost the chance to do singles, and we didn't even know why.'

What The Soft Machine did next was equally frustrating – spending three days in the studio with Giorgio Gomelsky. A manager, promoter, producer and impresario, Gomelsky had worked with The Rolling Stones and The Yardbirds and would later work with progressive acts such as Gong and Magma. Due to a dispute over payment, however, Gomelsky retained the master tapes from his Soft Machine sessions, and they only became commercially available a decade later. Although essentially demos, the tracks sizzle with energy. Daevid Allen's guitar playing, as he is painfully aware, is sloppy but the recording shows Robert on superb form as both drummer and singer, particularly on a new version of The Wilde Flowers perennial *Memories*.

In June 1967, The Soft Machine went back into the studio to record a second single: *She's Gone*, written by Ayers back in Wilde Flowers days. The track was produced by Joe Boyd, who had already been in the studio with Pink Floyd and The Incredible String Band and would go on to work with Nick Drake and Fairport Convention among numerous others. For the song, he recalls, the band decided to pay tribute to the author from whom they had taken their name. 'My most vivid memory is just doing that whole thing with William Burroughs' voice under the keyboard solo,' says Boyd. 'You can just subliminally hear it. That was the biggest thing I remember, looping that in, pushing the button to start it

› The original Soft Machine – Daevid, Mike, Robert, Kevin – recording what should have become their first album, with Giorgio Gomelsky (far left).

right at the beginning of the piano solo – because then it all had to be done by hand.'

Wyatt liked the results of the Joe Boyd session but, like the Gomelsky recordings and Kim Fowley's *Fred the Fish*, *She's Gone* would not be released at the time. Whether or not a *Love Makes Sweet Music* payola scandal was to blame, The Soft Machine clearly weren't having much luck with recordings. And with Mike Jeffery and Chas Chandler increasingly distracted by the snowballing success of the Jimi Hendrix Experience, they were left to fend for themselves. They decided to concentrate on playing live – where they found an emerging audience less concerned with pop singles and radio play than with rock and live performance.

–»》《«– –»》《«– –»》《«–

The Summer of Love might be remembered as a phenomenon of 1967, but the arrival of flares, free love and flower power was not quite so sudden. Unnoticed by the mainstream, the constituent parts had been coalescing since 1965, when 8,000 freaks, soon to be known as hippies, turned up to see leading Beat writers at the Royal Albert Hall's International Poetry Incarnation. Confirming the existence of a coherent, if still relatively small, underground scene was an event that took place the following year: the launch of the *International Times*.

Set up to report on the sex, drugs and rock'n'roll ignored by the mainstream press, the *International Times* – or simply *IT* – was the UK's first underground newspaper: the leading fanzine or blog of its day. Its launch, an all-night rave at the Roundhouse on 14 October 1966, was attended by an estimated 2,500, including Paul McCartney (in Arab robes), *Blow-Up* director Michelangelo Antonioni and Marianne Faithfull (who won the prize for shortest dress – a 'nun's habit'). Punters were handed sugar cubes upon arrival – apparently only dipped in 'placebo acid' – and, once inside, rolled around within a giant jelly. Daevid Allen might be pushing it when he declares the night one of the most revolutionary events in the history of English music and thinking, but it was quite a party. The Soft Machine's first gig without Larry Nowlin, their set featured an onstage motorbike and a 'happening' led by Yoko Ono, who came on mid-set and commanded revellers to touch one another in the dark.

The Daevid Allen Trio had emerged, perhaps, at the wrong time; The Wilde Flowers, arguably, in the wrong place. The Soft Machine, however, found themselves right at the heart of London's emerging underground scene. From the *IT* launch onwards, The Soft Machine and Pink Floyd, who also performed on the night, would be, in the words of Floyd drummer Nick Mason, 'the twin house bands of the London underground'.

When the *International Times* staged the 14-Hour Technicolor Dream in April 1967, attended by up to 10,000 revellers and another landmark in London's emerging counterculture, it was a given that Pink Floyd and The Soft Machine would be among the performers, alongside The Move, Tomorrow, The Pretty Things and The Crazy World of Arthur Brown. 'It was breathtaking and uncontrollable,' remembers John 'Hoppy' Hopkins, de facto leader of the underground scene and co-organiser (with *IT* editor Barry Miles) of the Technicolor Dream. 'There were people climbing up the inside of the building, high on acid, hanging off the scaffolding. That was a bit hair-raising.'

Like The Soft Machine, Pink Floyd brought to psychedelia a childlike, neo-romantic quality. Floyd frontman Syd Barrett had, like Robert, grown up reading Lewis Carroll and Edward Lear, while the band's debut album *Piper at the Gates of Dawn* would take its name from a chapter in Kenneth Grahame's *The Wind in the Willows*. The book matched Wyatt's beloved Winnie the Pooh in its cast of anthropomorphic characters, its pastoral English setting and its celebration of simple pleasures: hunting for honey and Heffalumps or simply messing around in boats.

There was musical overlap between the bands too, both of whom sang offbeat but oddly catchy songs in unapologetically English accents. Both Pink Floyd and The Soft Machine also extended and expanded these songs with lengthy improvised sections, heavy on keyboards and cosmic guitar glissandos. The curious hotch potch of musical and literary influences resulted in an entirely fresh sound. 'You could chase the lineage of groups like The Who, The Pretty Things, The Rolling Stones, going back to R'n'B groups and the blues,' asserts Jon Newey, today the editor of *Jazzwise* magazine but then a receptive teenager. 'But, for what The Soft Machine and the Pink Floyd were doing, there was simply no precedent. It was made up of bits of jazz and bits of this and bits of that. But the way they put it all together, and the way they treated the instrument sounds, the sonic palette that they used, was completely new.'

The *International Times* had origins in the London Free School, a community action adult education project set up by left-leaning activists and underground figures including Hoppy, Pink Floyd manager Peter

› Robert drumming at the 14 Hour Technicolor Dream – the Softs' set featured the motorbike as well as a 'happening' by Yoko Ono.

Jenner, and producer and promoter Joe Boyd. The Free School was short-lived but influential, giving birth to the Notting Hill Carnival – and to an unidentified flying object as weird and wonderful as any doughnut in the sky. Set up at the end of 1966 by Hoppy and Joe Boyd, UFO – pronounced 'you-foe' and standing for Unlimited Freak Out – was London's first psychedelic nightclub. Aiming to recreate the spirit of the IT launch on a weekly basis, it took place every Friday and lasted until six o'clock the following morning.

'It hadn't got a focused stage,' says Robert. 'That's what I liked about UFO. It was very dreamlike. You went in, you turned left, there were pillars and columns like you'd get in catacombs. They had a stage there, but the wall went on and on beyond the stage. It wasn't contained. Then there was another place with films and just people sitting about, I think other people played there, and then another bit round the side with people hanging out, being stoned. Some of it was lit, but a lot of it wasn't lit. It was mostly people lying on the floor, people in huddles at the walls. And dense clouds of smoke, of course.'

As well as bands, a typical night in the Tottenham Court Road basement club featured theatre, poetry, mime and dance. Macrobiotic food was on sale, as were velvet trousers and paisley shirts. Films, from W. C. Fields to Kurosawa, were projected from scaffolding at the back of the venue. There were even 'spot the fuzz' competitions to identify undercover police.

'What we tried to create,' recalled Hoppy, co-founder of London Free School as well as the *International Times*, 'was an environment that reminded you of being on an acid trip.' Fundamental to UFO's ethos was the philosophy of the happening, of leaving room for the unexpected. 'For instance, when Arthur Brown put his colander on his head, upside-down, and set fire to it, and leapt off the stage, everybody was very surprised. They didn't think he was going to do that.'

Joining Arthur Brown, self-styled God of Hellfire, were only slightly less incendiary acts like Tomorrow, Bonzo Dog Doo-Dah Band, Procol Harum, Fairport Convention, The Incredible String Band and Jeff Beck. Pink Floyd were synonymous with the club in the early days. When they outgrew it, The Soft Machine took their place.

It was Kevin Ayers' songwriting skills that had originally inspired Mike Jeffery and Chas Chandler to sign the band to Anim. But like the Floyd, whose debut single *Arnold Layne* was released the month after *Love Makes Sweet Music*, The Soft Machine's live sound was fast diverging from that laid down in the studio. UFO audiences – like those at the other key London hippie venues, the Roundhouse and the

Speakeasy, in any one of which the Softs would appear most weeks – were less interested in dancing to tunes they recognised from the radio than in 'head music', extended versions that could be appreciated seated or even prone, more or less psychedelically enhanced.

'We came from being jazz instrumentalists,' explains Daevid Allen, 'so we wanted to have solos and instrumental passages, which of course we did. Even in the midst of all that pop music, we'd have what we called freak-outs. We didn't know what else to call them.'

Kevin and Daevid, the band's twin frontmen, were responsible for many of the core compositional ideas. The audience's gaze, too, tended to fall on Kevin's cheekbones and the equally charismatic Daevid, known

> Soft Machine at the UFO club – Robert just visible on the left, Kevin centre and Daevid right – enhanced by the Sensual Laboratory lightshow.

to perform in miner's helmet or with a cardboard box over his head. The musical impetus for the freak-outs, however, came from Mike and Robert, the band's most talented instrumentalists. 'For a long time, most people just concentrated on Kevin and Daevid,' says DJ and scenester Jeff Dexter, whose memory of the era remains sharp: the drugs, he laughs, didn't work. 'But if you knew about your music, you could see that the source of the drive was coming from Mike and Robert.'

'In all the great jazz acts,' agrees Jon Newey, 'it's the dialogue between the leader and the drummer that creates the massive tension. Miles Davis and Tony Williams. Before that, Miles Davis and Jimmy Cobb. John Coltrane and Elvin Jones. It's always the way: Jimi Hendrix and Mitch Mitchell. That dialogue was Robert and Ratledge, and that dialogue is there in all the greatest jazz acts of all time.'

For all the jazz influence, however, The Soft Machine at this stage lacked the collective technical ability to be a straight jazz group: the obstacle, perhaps, that forced them into originality. 'Looking back on it now I'd say that none of us was technically competent in the way that a session musician would be,' says Robert. 'So, as happens in jazz and lots of music, we simply capitalised on our limitations and made a feature of what we *could* do. Which was, fortuitously enough, called being innovative.'

Even Kevin, less interested in jazz than the rest of the band, pushed towards extended improvisations: his *We Did It Again*, based on a two-note riff close to The Kinks' *You Really Got Me*, was inspired not by the outer reaches of free jazz, but by Sufi whirling dervishes. Live, it could last over an hour.

—※※— —※※— —※※—

Like the punk movement a decade later, the hippie scene looms large in our cultural consciousness but started as a kernel: 'underground', the Floyd's Nick Mason drily points out, was a euphemism for 'unpopular'. Hour-long renditions of *We Did It Again* might have been well received at the UFO club, but outside London, recalls Daevid Allen, audiences would 'boo and shout and throw stuff at us'. The Soft Machine's response was to avoid stopping between numbers, instead running one tune straight into the next. Perhaps it was evidence of their soul roots; this was the technique that gave a Geno Washington gig its relentless momentum.

Crucial to these protracted improvisations were the visuals of Scottish artist Mark Boyle and his collaborator and eventual wife

Joan Hills, together known as The Sensual Laboratory. 'I suppose these bands would all claim they were unique, but The Soft Machine really were,' recalls Joan Hills. 'They were the ones that we felt we best illustrated, or they best illustrated us. There just seemed to be an excitement to it.'

Mark and Joan had stumbled into psychedelia almost accidentally. The pair had emerged from the alternative art world and, by 1968, were working on an epic attempt to recreate small sections of the earth's surface. A decade after that, they found themselves representing Britain in the prestigious Venice Biennale. Their work for The Soft Machine, however, remained close to their scatological *Son et Lumiere for Bodily Fluids and Functions*, notorious for its use of blood, semen, urine, snot, earwax, tears and vomit. 'Mark had a tent,' grins Daevid Allen. 'He used to masturbate and put his sperm in there, all kind of things. It was outrageous. That's why he had a tent, I suppose. Who knows what he was doing in there? He had this incredible power over the movements on the screen to go with the music. You'd swear it had been rehearsed, but it wasn't. He'd explode when we exploded, he'd go quiet when we were quiet. I don't know how he did it.'

The synaesthetic science of the Sensual Laboratory drew on chemistry as much as biology. Dropping acid onto perforated zinc, for instance, created the ideal accompaniment to one of Wyatt's drum solos. 'Robert was absolutely sure that it was his banging of his drum that made things explode,' says Joan. 'But it wasn't – your head makes that connection for you. You see this thing exploding and *you* link it up to him doing that. It was fantastic, it was wonderful.'

Many of the techniques used by Mark and Joan would today have health and safety officers weak at the knees: the band joked that their loud stage volume was necessary to drown out Boyle's screams as he burned face or fingers. 'It was absolutely *lethal* what he was doing up there,' confirms Robert, shaking his head. 'He was burning acid things in coloured frames, none of that was film. If you see stuff burning, that's Mark burning stuff in front of the projector. If you see him burning holes in coloured plastic with acid, he's actually doing that. He was up there on the scaffold doing that with his goggles on.'

The Sensual Laboratory would become an intrinsic part of the Soft Machine live experience for the next eighteen months, the relationship akin to that between The Velvet Underground and Andy Warhol in the US. Mark and Joan followed The Soft Machine to the Speakeasy, as well as UFO. 'The Soft Machine brought psychedelic lighting into the club,'

> Mark Boyle at work on his projections at the UFO club.

recalls Jeff Dexter, 'as opposed to the usual nightclub bump'n'grind-in-the-corner-with-your-bird. They weren't playing as a pop band, they were playing as if it was a *happening*. The people became part of the show as it melted into the lights, and they were much more freeform than anybody else. It was experimental, man.'

The Sensual Laboratory followed the band to Middle Earth, a Covent Garden venue that would shortly inherit UFO's crown as London's leading psychedelic nightclub. By the time The Soft Machine secured a residency there, however, they had lost one of their founding members.

·»)《«· ·»)《«· ·»)《«·

The original plan had been to perform a residency at a beer festival at Saint-Aygulf in southern France: 'Dansez! Freak Out!' screamed the posters. Keith Albarn, today an artist and academic (as well as the father of Blur and Gorillaz vocalist Damon), had designed an extraordinary venue for the performance: as though a multicoloured, retro-futurist igloo had landed amongst the sun umbrellas of the Côte d'Azur.

'The band were great and made a huge impression,' Albarn recalls, 'although most of the beach people were unprepared for the London Sixties invasion and found the combination of music, lightshow and mad venue quite disorientating. We were popular with the punters – although many found it "way out, man" – and very *un*popular with the local clubs. It was a stressful time.'

When the engagement fell through after a few nights, largely due to noise complaints from these clubs, The Soft Machine found themselves stranded in France with no return tickets. Salvation came in the form of artist and poet Jean-Jacques Lebel. Responsible for the first French translations of Allen Ginsberg and Gregory Corso, Lebel was also known for his 'happenings' and art events, such as 1962's *Pour Conjurer l'Esprit de Catastrophe*, in which two naked women, representing Kennedy and Khrushchev, shared a bath apparently filled with blood.

As luck would have it, Lebel was staging Pablo Picasso's surreal play *Le Désir Attrapé par la Queue* (*Desire Caught by the Tail*) in a circus tent near Saint-Tropez. Written during the German occupation of Paris, Picasso's play had first been performed by a cast that included Jean-Paul Sartre and Simone de Beauvoir, with Albert Camus as director. Lebel's version featured performers from Andy Warhol's Factory, while The Soft Machine and the Sensual Laboratory were brought in to provide an hour-long overture of sound and light before each performance.

The production was attended by the great and the good of the Riviera, and The Soft Machine found themselves dubbed 'the new Beatles' by prominent magazine *Le Nouvel Observateur*. It was the first inkling that Wyatt, so often described as quintessentially English, would in fact often find greater success on mainland Europe. Daevid Allen recalls one particular performance, at a private party attended by Brigitte Bardot, as the best concert The Soft Machine ever played. Kevin Ayers later recalled the event in his track *Clarence in Wonderland*: 'Let's go to my chateau / We could have a good time / Drinking lots of sky wine.'

It was in Saint-Tropez that Robert developed his habit of playing without a shirt – or, at times, any clothing at all. 'It started out in France in 1967,' he confirms. 'Jean-Jacques Lebel had us playing one of his happenings, around a swimming pool at night. And the only rule was that everybody had to be undressed, including the band. Completely. If you weren't, you had to stay indoors. It was a very nice feeling, on a warm, breezy, Saint-Tropez evening, to be playing without clothes. That's when I realised you could do it. And being behind a drumkit protected what they call your modesty.' Wyatt insists that the shedding of clothes was practical – 'I sweated like a boxer when I was drumming' – but it was also, surely, evidence of an extrovert streak. Either way, Wyatt's bare torso would become intrinsic to his image as a drummer, occasionally embellished with shirt and tie drawn onto his flesh in crayon.

It was also in France that The Soft Machine won the support of journalist Mike Zwerin, once a member of Miles Davis' 'cool' nonet but by this stage writing for the American jazz magazine *Downbeat*. 'Frankly, Robert is probably the best rock drummer I ever heard,' Zwerin later recalled. 'He was the only rock drummer I'd ever heard play in thirteen and making it sound totally natural. He was also the first one to play without a shirt. That was a big deal, then.'

Zwerin's enthusiastic article about the band also noted Robert's ability to sing note-perfect Charlie Parker solos and his familiarity with the music of Sonny Rollins and Cecil Taylor. They might have looked like rockers with 'their weird hats, long hair, shades, and their funky, bizarre garb', he wrote in October 1967, but the jazz influence was clear too. 'Coltrane died in 1967,' explains Wyatt. 'The giant tree had fallen in the forest and left a clearing for little saplings. Off we went, way beyond our skills. I mean, nobody in the The Soft Machine could play what we were doing, but that was quite exciting. We just seemed to be pulled along.'

> The (semi)-naked drummer. Robert onstage, 'sweating like a boxer'.

The Soft Machine might have missed the Summer of Love in London but they had instead found their very own Wonderland, replete with parties with Brigitte Bardot, naked drumming, and all-night gigs: 'a very grooooovy summer full of sunshine', as Ayers would later put it. Yet the seasons, alas, would soon change. Having finally made enough money for tickets home, the band left France at the end of the summer but they would not all make it back to Blighty. When they arrived at Dover, Daevid Allen was informed by immigration officials that his visa was invalid; his name, he claims, had found its way onto a police blacklist of suspected LSD traffickers and undesirables.

Daevid believes the visa problem that removed him so abruptly from The Soft Machine in late August 1967 probably accelerated an inevitable split. He believes his role in the band was that of catalyst –

and, as he notes, you've got to kill your heroes. Daevid also recalls that his guitar playing was 'so bad that nobody wanted me in the band any more'. Robert vigorously disputes this, insisting that Daevid was not only the focal point of the band both on- and offstage but also a very interesting, innovative guitarist. Inevitable or not, frantic phonecalls confirmed that the split was irreversible. The Soft Machine had lost their Christopher Robin.

Allen, who would not set foot in England for three years, stayed in France for the riots of 1968, and brought together a collection of self-styled pothead pixies to form Gong. The Soft Machine, meanwhile, continued as a trio. Although they were not to know it at the time, Daevid Allen's departure established a precedent: the group's turnover would be rapid, and their sound would evolve at the same brisk pace.

-») («- -») («- -») («-

By the autumn of 1967, London's underground scene had emerged into the light. Even with the loss of Daevid Allen, Kevin's songwriting talent could have taken The Soft Machine towards the mainstream: they had tracks as strong as Pink Floyd's hit single *See Emily Play*, if not yet a debut album to match *The Piper at the Gates of Dawn*. Yet, while the Floyd would become a household name, The Soft Machine – who, Nick Mason happily concedes, were the superior musicians – would remain more or less underground. Maybe it was sheer bad luck that left The Soft Machine lagging behind the Floyd, at least in commercial terms. Maybe they were hindered by the alleged payola scam surrounding *Love Makes Sweet Music*. Maybe their music was harder to package. There was also, however, something wilful in The Soft Machine's sticking to the margins.

Immediately following Daevid's departure, the trio travelled to the Edinburgh Fringe Festival, where they provided background music for Alfred Jarry's *Ubu Enchaîné*, combining the topsy-turvy world of Lewis Carroll with the bawdy humour of a Punch and Judy show. *Ubu Enchaîné* had never been performed in the UK, but the initial performance of sister play *Ubu Roi*, back in 1896, had inspired a riot of *Rite of Spring* proportions. For The Soft Machine, *Ubu Enchaîné* was crucial, not least in introducing them to Alfred Jarry's concept of Pataphysics. The actor and surrealist Simon Watson Taylor, who as a translator played a key role in introducing Jarry's work to Anglophone audiences, recalled that Wyatt embraced the concept of 'ubuesque mayhem', even painting the

> Dancer Graziella Martinez performing *Lullaby for Catatonics* at the Edinburgh Festival, to improvised music from Soft Machine.

spiral logo on his bass drum, although it would be a while before the influence of Jarry's curious, semi-spoof science would fully make itself felt in the band's music.

Henry Henriod, employed by Chas Chandler and Mike Jeffery as The Soft Machine's personal manager, was baffled by the Edinburgh trip. More East End geezer than grammar-school alumnus, the Anim employee saw

> Kevin fronting the Softs on a Dutch TV show in September 1967.

fringe theatre as a distraction. Why weren't the band setting their sights on *Top of the Pops*? They had already turned down the chance to work with producer Mickie Most, who offered a fairly certain chance of chart success, since they weren't keen on the more mainstream material he would have required. As Robert himself admits, 'We kept doing things that were taking us further and further away from being a pop group.'

John Cumming, today a director of jazz and contemporary music promoters Serious but then a young stage manager, saw The Soft Machine's other Edinburgh performance – one equally far from *Top of the Pops*. *Lullaby for Catatonics* featured projections by Mark Boyle and Joan Hills, and an Argentinian dancer, Graziella Martinez, performing a ballet in a bathtub. 'It felt like a very interesting transition, looking back on it,' Cumming recalls. 'On the one hand you had this very grungy organ trio, where Mike was using distorted sounds and they were doing these almost repetitive, very hard-rock things. But every now and then they would break into one of Kevin's songs, a slightly dreamy pop-folk song. It wasn't uncomfortable. It was actually quite nice to have that break. But the two things were very different.'

Without Daevid Allen, each remaining member of The Soft Machine was obliged to shoulder a little more responsibility. Kevin was not only chief songwriter but also literally the frontman, in that Robert and Mike were hidden behind drums and organ respectively. Yet Wyatt began increasingly to share the spotlight with his languidly charming co-vocalist. His high, brittle tenor could have been custom-made as a foil for Ayers' shrugging baritone, but he was happy singing lead vocals too.

'Kevin was the pretty boy, the frontman,' says Pam. 'But Robert would always sing while he was drumming. He was very attractive to women, just everything about him. And he *would* insist on playing without a shirt on. He always had women after him. Always.'

Distant behind rectangular granny glasses, Mike Ratledge was a much more reserved presence. Musically, however, Daevid's departure left him in a crucial role, not only providing harmonic support for the vocals but responsible for all the solos. His relentless style resulted from an instrumental quirk: he played a Lowrey organ, rather than the more common Hammond, and the instrument was prone to feedback if he took his fingers from the keys even for a moment. Mike's frenzied, fuzz-drenched sound, combining technical virtuosity with Hendrix-worthy distortion, would become central to The Soft Machine's sound, helping the band to stand out in a scene dominated by guitars.

After the Edinburgh Fringe came gigs in Europe, including dates with English blues singer and bandleader John Mayall and a show in Paris for which The Soft Machine were joined, for one night only, by Daevid Allen. In December, they played in London alongside Jimi Hendrix, The Who and Pink Floyd at 'Christmas on Earth Continued' – another countercultural landmark but also, as a sign of mainstream popularity, the beginning of the end for what had once been the underground scene. It would be the last time the Softs and Floyd would play together.

The same month, The Soft Machine recorded their first BBC session, for John Peel's *Top Gear* show on the newly launched Radio 1. The *Top Gear* spot was a prestigious one: had next-year's-top-tips features been as ubiquitous in 1967 as they are today, The Soft Machine would no doubt have featured prominently. Their five-song set included credible versions of *A Certain Kind* and *Hope for Happiness*, which would become the core of their first album. In the event, however, the band would play just three gigs in their home country over the forthcoming year, and would have no record release at home, either. Instead, 1968 was dedicated to that rite of passage for every English musician: touring America.

4

LIVING IS EASY, HERE IN NEW YORK STATE

Touring with Hendrix:
the Softs implode in America

Jimi Hendrix might have left his homeland a nobody, but after the immolation of his Stratocaster at 1967's Monterey Pop Festival he came back a star. *Are You Experienced*, the Jimi Hendrix Experience's debut album, made the top five, and Mike Jeffery put together an ambitious US tour for the follow-up, *Axis: Bold as Love*. Hendrix invited The Soft Machine to come along as support. 'He thought we were terribly cute,' recalled a typically self-deprecating Kevin Ayers, 'and absolutely no threat to his sensational stage presence. He was quite right.'

On 30 January 1968, Robert, Kevin and Mike set off for the United States, together with Mark Boyle and Joan Hills of the Sensual Laboratory, and fellow Anim band, Eire Apparent. Hugh Hopper, the schoolfriend who had played bass with the Daevid Allen Trio and The Wilde Flowers, came along as the Softs' roadie.

A 'British Are Coming' welcome party was held for the bands in Manhattan's towering Pan-Am Building: 'They arrived on top of the Pan-Am building,' recalled jazz writer Mike Zwerin, 'which still then had a heli-pad. It's right above Grand Central Station, like a cigar. Anyway,

> Robert with Jimi Hendrix at the Pan-Am Building press conference. Robert is wearing the 'yellow suit that's made by Pam'.

all the music press was up there, in the lounge, and the helicopter lands and they come off. And what a sight that was. First of all, Hendrix by himself, but with Mitch Mitchell, and then The Soft Machine with their big furry coats and long hair. We went, "Fucking Christ, this is a fucking invasion!" That was amazing.'

It would be amazing, too, for The Soft Machine, who were unknown in the US and, indeed, yet to release an album even at home. The tour, clearly, would be on a scale unlike anything they had known. Sharing bills with the Jimi Hendrix Experience, as well as acts such as Detroit proto-punks the MC5 and bluesman Albert King, they were able to reach a huge new audience. When *Axis: Bold as Love* made the US top three, the venues only got bigger: 5,000 on a slow night.

Experience drummer Mitch Mitchell recalled The Soft Machine as more than up to the challenge from a musical point of view. 'Night after night they never lost their impetus,' he wrote in a memoir of the Experience, happily contradicting Ayers. 'They were', continued Mitchell, 'a hard act to follow, every night.' However, the band themselves felt that they struggled in their supporting role. Even Hendrix found that audiences, particularly in the south and the Midwest, wanted only the anthems – *Hey Joe*, *Purple Haze* and the rest – while The Soft Machine had just one obscure UK single to their name (and they didn't even play it in their live set).

The band were also unprepared for the punishing tour schedule. The distances were marathon, the itinerary merciless and chaotic – 47 dates in 66 days, with nearly 20,000 miles of travelling. Hugh Hopper said it was a miracle any of the gigs happened at all; he and the Experience's Neville Chesters were the only roadies for the two bands, criss-crossing America in a single truck. For the Softs, it felt like a very strange accident. 'It was just something we happened to fall into,' recalled Kevin. 'We started playing as friends, then suddenly we were on a stage. And we never really made a conscious decision to sound professional, or appeal to the public. We got on the Jimi Hendrix tour simply because we had the same management. And I think Hendrix happened to like us, because we were weird. But that was it, we were just thrown in there. We were just little amateur musicians from Canterbury, who'd never had a proper soundcheck.'

The pressures of the tour would prove too much for Kevin, and The Soft Machine would not survive in this incarnation. Robert, however, relished his time on the road, partying across the States, enjoying the emerging rock'n'roll lifestyle. As a drummer, too, Wyatt was coming into his own, in part influenced by Mitch Mitchell. Night after night, he watched the Experience bassist Noel Redding stubbornly anchor the groove while Mitchell followed Hendrix as closely as a sidecar – the closest thing in rock to the bond between Elvin Jones and John Coltrane in the saxophonist's 1960s quartet. 'It was a brilliant group,' enthuses Robert. 'I was blown away every night I saw them. Right the way through '68, I thought they were absolutely wonderful. The *band*. I emphasise that because people always talk about how Hendrix was with the wrong people, but Hendrix was very happy to play with those English rock musicians. If he'd wanted to stay in America and play with the sort of musicians you'd expect him to have played with, he could easily have done so – and he did that later on. But that band, with Mitch on drums, I thought was absolutely phenomenal.'

Offstage, different members of The Soft Machine dealt with the rigours of the road in different ways. Mike Ratledge passed the time playing chess with Mark Boyle. Robert went for the rock'n'roll approach. Although too embarrassed at breaking the law to get into marijuana or LSD, he now discovered that 'you could get completely smashed out of your brain on legal drugs' – and embarked upon a 'phenomenal' amount of drinking. It wasn't always a good idea. At San Francisco's renowned Fillmore venue, Wyatt found himself in a drunken argument with impresario Bill Graham, whom he ended up calling a fascist – a provocative use of language for a man who had fled Nazi Germany just prior to the Holocaust. Graham kicked the Softs off the remainder of his dates at the Fillmore.

Later on, the drinking would leave Wyatt alienated within the band, but at this stage he had an accomplice in excess. Kevin Ayers, it is said, has only ever written three types of song: drinking songs, drunk songs and hungover songs. And Kevin, like Robert, spent plenty of the first US tour in one of those three states. 'Girls lining up outside the door, free drink everywhere', is how Ayers recalled the tour, 'so I was drunk every night with enormous quantities of girls at my disposal.'

Glamorous as it might have been within the band-on-the-road bubble, however, the country at large was in places still highly conservative. The dean threatened to cancel one college show in Colorado unless Robert put on more clothes. On another occasion, attempting to fly from Vancouver to Spokane, Washington, the band were refused seats on the grounds of their unconventional appearance.

Mark Boyle and Joan Hills would go through customs separately from the rest of the band. 'I had short hair,' Boyle recalled, 'and we just looked like regular passengers so we'd be straight through customs, and we'd sit for an hour in the coffee bar waiting for them. Robert had, very wisely, painted his suitcase bright yellow, which was funny, but he also had a yellow suit made out of a curtain that Pam had done for him, with red lining. When that got dirty on the outside, he'd just turn it inside out, so it was red with a sort of dirty yellow bit showing, and he would wear it that way. He was picked out all the time.'

The conveyor belt of planes, hotel rooms and limousines was also unhealthily hermetic. Though his drinking only narrowed the blinkers,

Robert couldn't help notice what was happening through the tour bus windows. If 1967 had been the year of peace and love, 1968 was the year of the barricades. Protests against Vietnam were joined by the increasingly militant campaign for African-American civil rights. Hendrix might have been a superstar, but hotels would still mysteriously discover they were fully booked when they saw the colour of his skin. A worse fate awaited some of his fans. 'People were being beaten up in the streets,' recalls Wyatt. 'The police were being violent. I didn't know much about it but my instincts were on the side of our audiences, who were Hendrix fans and had come to see us. And they were getting in trouble from the police. It was pretty obvious whose side one was on.'

Wyatt downplays the Hendrix tour as a turning point in his own thinking. He already knew about the African-American struggle in the abstract, he says, from jazz protest records: Sonny Rollins's *Freedom Suite*, Max Roach's *We Insist: Freedom Now*, Charles Mingus's *Fables of Faubus*, John Coltrane's *Alabama*. Even so, he could hardly fail to be moved by the sort of event he later recalled: 'I witnessed – outside a Hendrix concert in the US – a policeman pick up an excited Hendrix fan, hold the boy's body roughly horizontal and charge at the wall of the concert battering-ram style, then drop him bleeding to the ground.'

Still more shocking news arrived on 4 April, as The Soft Machine sat in a Virginia bar: Martin Luther King had been shot dead in Memphis. To most of us, the assassination of the Gandhi of the civil rights movement is a grenade to the gut even half a century on. But, as Wyatt sat next to Hendrix, a man of African and Cherokee blood, racists at the bar drank the health of King's assassin.

–»3(«– –»3(«– –»3(«–

In the spring of 1968, the Jimi Hendrix Experience began in earnest on their third and, as it turned out, final album. By far their most ambitious record, *Electric Ladyland* would reach number one in the American charts. Yet the recording process was plagued by problems, not least the increasing number of parasites feeding on the guitarist both in and out of the studio. Though bad news for Hendrix, these difficulties worked to The Soft Machine's advantage. Off the back of the American tour, Mike Jeffery had finally secured The Soft Machine a two-album deal with Probe, a subsidiary of New York's ABC Records. By using Hendrix's downtime, the band was able to record the first of these in New York's state-of-the-art Record Plant studio.

On paper, Tom Wilson was the ideal producer for The Soft Machine's self-titled debut. He had worked with avant-garde jazz musicians like Sun Ra and Cecil Taylor, as well as The Mothers of Invention, The Velvet Underground, Bob Dylan and Simon & Garfunkel. For some reason, however, Wilson seems not to have fully engaged with the Soft Machine sessions. 'All I remember about him', Kevin Ayers recalled, 'was that he sat on the phone and called his girlfriends all day long.'

The lack of production input was compounded by the fact that The Soft Machine had only four days in the studio, in stark contrast to the eight *months* Hendrix eventually spent on *Electric Ladyland*. Fortunately, with an intense run of almost fifty shows just behind them, the band could hardly have been more match-fit. *The Soft Machine* was recorded almost entirely live, with overdubs and studio trickery kept to a minimum. Segueing the album's thirteen tracks into just three long suites helped capture the impetus of the live show.

The songs themselves were kept to espresso-shot intensity, with *We Did It Again* lasting just four minutes. As a writer, Ayers also contributed *Why Are We Sleeping?*, inspired by the then-voguish Armenian mystic George Gurdjieff. Kevin's contribution to The Soft Machine's eponymous debut, however, lies largely beneath the surface: as an effective if hardly virtuoso player of the Gibson semi-acoustic bass, and as a writer of effortlessly memorable songs. Aside from blistering solos on *Hope for Happiness, So Boot if At All* and *Lullabye Letter*, Mike Ratledge is also on relatively restrained form, his organ part on *A Certain Kind* almost hymnal.

It is Wyatt, singing the majority of tracks, who comes across as the band's dominant personality. His scatting on *Hope for Happiness* opens the album, a double helix of twin vocal lines twirling almost unaccompanied until the band kicks in after close to two minutes. The delayed drop makes for a strikingly bold opening, reflecting the confidence gained from the US tour. Even Robert himself, who doesn't own the record and has decidedly mixed feelings about his time in The Soft Machine in general, today admits to warm feelings upon stumbling across the album's opening track on a French radio station: 'I thought, "Blimey, what's that?" Someone was saying, "Just listen to the way the voice starts out this record." And I did, and I thought: "I know that" and then, "Blimey, did we do that, on the very first record?"

'I remembered those intros we used to do on *Hope for Happiness*', he goes on, 'before the rhythm kicked in, and all the different ways I did that on different nights. The gigs would start out with this long drone

> Promotional shot of the Softs – Kevin, Robert and Mike – from around the time of the recording sessions for the first album.

in E, with me just doing a free vocal over the top before kicking in with the drums. I remember it being a very dramatic and exciting moment.'

The album's emphasis on songs rather than instrumental jams left less room for Wyatt to demonstrate his increasing virtuosity as a drummer, although there's a musical solo, bouncing between left and right speakers, on *So Boot If At All*. But even when it doesn't draw attention to itself, Robert's drumming was crucial, his fills and accents, for instance, providing the sense of climax so crucial to *We Did It Again*.

'It wasn't so much his technique – although that was formidable – as his *approach* to playing and generating parts that was really unique,' asserts Henry Cow drummer Chris Cutler. 'Robert seemed to be thinking in terms of riffs and melodies. Of course he established rhythms, but the ground was melodic, and that's moderately unusual in drummers, especially in rock. Then he had impressive technique. And his solos! Instead of boring the pants off you by hitting everything as hard and as fast as possible and winding up making dents in his cymbals, he'd either do nothing at all, or play with his fingers, or just play one drum – or a cymbal or his rims. Always something different.'

The Soft Machine also showcases Wyatt's burgeoning writing talent. As a pun-loving drummer and singer, without access to a harmony instrument, lyrics were a natural interest. *Why Am I So Short?* was based on a melody by Hugh Hopper, originally entitled *I Should've Known*. In barely ninety seconds, Robert managed to cover his love of drinking and smoking, his diminutive stature, his garrulous personality and his favourite meal and item of clothing:

> *I'm nearly five foot seven tall*
> *I like to smoke and drink and ball*
> *I've got a yellow suit that's made by Pam*
> *And every day I like an egg and some tea*
> *But most of all I like to talk about me*

The track established a template: simultaneously down-to-earth and mildly surreal, his lyrics would often chronicle minor details of his life, leaving little sense of separation between man and music, between Robert Ellidge and Robert Wyatt.

'It doesn't feel comfortable when I try and pump too much into the delivery,' Robert told Andy Gill of the *Independent* in 1991. 'In my case, what seems to work best is when I sing fairly close to how I talk. When I'm working, I'm basically concerned with hearing myself back: it's me, it's not me pretending to be someone else. You've got to feel at home in your own music, I think – not a tourist.'

Wyatt also wrote the music for *Save Yourself*, one of the poppier tunes on The Soft Machine's debut, although it flirts in its final minute with fast, finger-clicking jazz. *Priscilla*, a short, mid-album instrumental for which all three members were credited as co-composers, also veers close to jazz with its swinging ride cymbal and walking bass. Already, the band was moving away from Kevin's wry psychedelic pop.

> The first Soft Machine album, recorded on the 1968 US tour and released on Probe in November that year. The cover had elaborate cogs that rotated to show photos of the band members (here, Robert in his 'naked suit').

The album's final track offered a clue as to The Soft Machine's future direction. Comprising only a rhythmically complex line played in unison by keyboards and fuzz bass, *Box 25/4 Lid* doesn't sound like anything else on the album, and for good reason. The tune was a last-minute addition, written by Mike Ratledge and Hugh Hopper – and features Hugh, rather than Kevin, on bass. In retrospect, it was less like the last tune on the first album than an early taste of the second.

Kevin Ayers described the album as 'embarrassingly amateur', albeit featuring 'some nice ideas'. But the real 'magic moments', Kevin considered, were onstage. Wyatt agrees that *The Soft Machine* could never capture the power of the band's live show, with Echoplex tape delay on his vocals and, occasionally, even his drums: 'Quite early on, I used Echoplex. And I did drum solos in which Mike would come up and join in on the cymbals with the microphone: a sort of microphone and sticks duet on a cymbal. It was quite theatrical. I now see it would have been thought of as very far out. None of that really gets onto the record. It didn't happen in studios.'

Yet, for all its distance from the live show, and though its final track feels like a bridge to nowhere, *The Soft Machine* remains an incandescent debut. Adventurous yet accessible, it contains a good handful of genuinely enduring songs while also showcasing the instrumental technique of Robert and Mike. Brimming with possibility, it still stands up as one of the era's most enchanting, broad-minded takes on psychedelic pop. And as Graham Bennett points out in *Out-Bloody-Rageous*, his biography of the band, 'uniquely for a rock album at the time, not a single guitar chord can be heard on the album – just organ, piano, bass and drums'.

→» «← →» «← →» «←

Debut album finished though yet to be released, The Soft Machine returned to England in late April 1968. Robert, at last, was reunited with Pam and Sam: while he had been on the road with Hendrix, his girlfriend and son had remained with his mum in suburban Dulwich.

The reunion, however, would be short-lived. When Mike Jeffery secured a second run of American dates for Hendrix, a support slot once again became available – and Robert set off across the Atlantic once again. America was by now in a state of severe civil unrest. Riots had already broken out nationwide in the wake of Martin Luther King's shooting. Then, while The Soft Machine were in the northern city of Dearborn, a second high-profile assassination took place: that of US Senator and Democratic presidential candidate Robert Kennedy. If you saw the news, Bob Dylan writes in *Chronicles*, you would have thought the whole nation was on fire.

As on the first US tour, The Soft Machine were to some extent insulated from such events by the life in limbo of the touring musician. The band, however, had problems of their own. Joan Hills of the Sensual Laboratory opted out of the return trip, unwilling to leave their children for a second stint in the States. Her partner Mark Boyle returned to join her in England after just three weeks – frustrated that the experimentation encouraged in small-scale London clubs seemed to be less welcomed by big-shot American promoters. There would be a handful of other collaborations with the Sensual Laboratory, but visuals would no longer be an integral part of the Soft Machine live experience.

As well as Mark Boyle's departure, the band had to cope with growing musical tensions. On their brief return to England, they had picked up a guitarist: Andy Summers, formerly of soul-jazz group Zoot Money's Big Roll Band and the preposterously named acid-rock act Dantalion's Chariot. Yet friction had quickly developed between Kevin and the new arrival. Robert puts it down to a simple overlap of roles, but there was also a dispute over musical direction. Summers, a technically superior musician, was taking the band further away from the song format with which the bassist felt most at home. 'I could hear Robert and Mike

> A very brief quartet – The Soft Machine with guitarist Andy Summers (front).

getting very carried away,' a candid Ayers later admitted, 'and I thought this isn't what I want to do, partly because I couldn't keep up!'

Wyatt, however, disputes Ayers' rather apologetic self-assessment: 'Kevin enjoyed being avant-garde, he had some of the great avant-garde ideas: *Why Are We Sleeping?* and *We Did It Again* are two of the most far out things we did. So I'm not having him saying he was just the simple one. He was the catalyst for very, very advanced ideas.'

Whatever the cause of the rift, Kevin issued an ultimatum when The Soft Machine reached New York. Either the guitarist left the band, or he himself would quit. Unsurprisingly, given that Kevin was a founding member and the band's core songwriter, it was Andy Summers who got the boot. The third guitarist to leave the band in just two years, he was also the only Soft Machine alumnus to go on to major pop success, emerging almost a decade later – after a stint, ironically, with Kevin Ayers' band – as one third of The Police.

Even the removal of their guitarist in July 1968, however, did not entirely solve The Soft Machine's problems. Hard as it may be to square with his lifelong association with wine, women and song, Kevin had tired of the girls and the booze. Instead, he was spending evenings in his hotel room, cooking simple fish dishes on a portable stove. Pink Floyd's Nick Mason, who spent time with The Soft Machine during the period, recalls him 'more or less standing on his head eating brown rice.'

'I went on a very strict macrobiotic diet,' Kevin recalled, 'and I didn't go out partying. I became alienated from everything that was going on around me – because of the violence and extremity of it. At its worst, it was plane, hotel, gig, hotel, plane, hotel, gig. Mike Ratledge and I would just stay in. He read books, while I used to lie on the floor and stare at the ceiling.' Ratledge was not one for macrobiotics – 'Mike's diet was something like one egg every two days,' recalls Joan Hills – yet he and roadie Hugh Hopper were just as uncomfortable with the monotony of touring life. Eventually Hugh returned to England, leaving schoolfriend Ted Bing, who had come along to share the driving for this second US tour, as the band's sole roadie.

Wyatt, by contrast, continued to bask in life on the road. 'It was gruelling,' he grins, 'but I was what, twenty-three? You're at your fittest at that age. You've got stamina. You can really just live on chutzpah – and I thought it was great.' 'Robert was living the life,' confirms Nick Mason. 'He was playing in his underpants a lot. It was New York in August, and there'd be Robert onstage in his knickers. It was fantastically louche.'

One of Wyatt's favourite watering holes was New York club The Scene. Drinking buddies included fellow drummer Keith Moon of The Who, notorious for driving Cadillacs into swimming pools and blowing up lavatories with dynamite. Moon's drinking game of the moment, alternating shots of Southern Comfort and tequila, was only marginally less explosive. 'Keith Moon really taught me how to get drunk fast,' says Wyatt. 'I'd never thought that was the aim of it before, to drink 'til you dropped. But I'm not blaming him. Everyone over eighteen is responsible for their own actions.' Was he drinking very heavily? 'No, not particularly', replies Robert with a laugh. 'I did stop to eat and sleep.'

There was, said Hugh Hopper, an element of 'lads-on-the-road syndrome' in Robert's drinking. But his boozing was also linked to the insecurity that lay beneath that exuberant exterior. As Robert himself explains, 'It was fun, and it made you brave. Getting on stage in front of 5,000 impatient Texans waiting for Hendrix to come on, you do need a drink. I don't know how else you'd get on stage.'

With Mike and Kevin preoccupied with books and brown rice, Robert spent more and more time with members of The Jimi Hendrix Experience. 'I used to hang out with Noel and Mitch and Hendrix. When we weren't playing, we'd take a busman's holiday, go and see the Buddy Miles Express, which was a great band. We'd go and see Big Brother and the Holding Company, The Velvet Underground, Chicago. On days off, I sat in with [jazz-rock guitarist] Larry Coryell at the Village Vanguard or one of those places.' He grins. 'You know, it was alright, mate.'

So close was Robert to Mitch Mitchell that, by the end of the tour, he received a gift of Mitchell's customised Maplewood drumkit to replace his old Premier kit. He still owns it today. Robert also grew close to the Experience bassist. He had known Noel Redding vaguely since

› The last leg of the Softs' second tour with Hendrix – 8 September in Seattle. There were just five more dates and then Kevin would depart for Spain.

The Wilde Flowers, when Redding – then still a guitarist – had been a fellow Kent musician. Now Noel, like Robert, was having non-musical problems, and would leave the Experience the following year. According to Noel, he and Robert even talked of starting their own band.

Although Robert wouldn't join Noel in taking illegal drugs, they did share a hedonistic streak: 'Noel was a deeply lovely man,' he recalls. 'I shared a room with him on the road. It was very funny, he'd wake up in the morning and go: "Breakfast!" And he'd bring out this great spliff and stick it in his gob. Archetypal, fantastic. An absolutely great man.'

Within The Soft Machine, meanwhile, the cracks were only deepening. With approximately twenty-three hours of waiting around for each hour onstage, the bond created among touring musicians is almost familial, with all the same running jokes but also the same recurring annoyances. Robert's drinking didn't help. 'I drank like a madman,' he admits. 'And I think I must have started to become very difficult to work with from then on. It's very hard to work with drunks, it doesn't matter if they're in a good mood or a bad mood.'

Even aside from what might euphemistically be termed a lifestyle gap within the band, the rest of the trio were burned out by the tour. 'Travel in the States with a pop group is like luxury purgatory,' Mike Ratledge has recalled. 'You stay in Hiltons, then a Cadillac Fleetwood meets you, takes you to the hotel. You wash, the Cadillac Fleetwood takes you to the gig and back to the Hilton. You sleep. It completely destroys your sense of geography. In the end you suffer from depersonalisation, loss of identity.'

There were also genuine musical differences, with Mike pushing towards more technically demanding instrumentals, while Kevin was keen to stay rooted in song. 'I was never particularly into making ugly noises,' he later explained. '*Au contraire*. I was into melody, and I didn't like the free-form things as much as the others did. I was much more into melody and nice sexy rhythms.'

'I don't think either Mike or Kevin enjoyed it that much,' agrees Wyatt. 'By the end of the Hendrix tour, they'd both absolutely had enough.'

After a final show at California's Hollywood Bowl was cancelled due to Robert dropping a cymbal on his foot, The Soft Machine imploded. Mike returned to London, while Kevin sold his bass and headed for the Balearic sun. Robert alone remained in America. Their album had still not been released by Probe, but suddenly it didn't matter: The Soft Machine, it seemed, were no more.

5

ZYXWVUTSRQPON MLKJIHGFEDCBA

Volume Two and a Pataphysical introduction

With The Soft Machine apparently at an end, Mike Ratledge and Kevin Ayers lost no time in leaving America. Robert, however, stayed on with the Jimi Hendrix Experience in a luxurious villa outside Los Angeles: 2850 Benedict Canyon.

For Hendrix, success was starting to turn ugly. Guitars and clothing were going missing, and members of the Manson Family were popping up among the hangers-on. According to Mitch Mitchell, their guard dogs were kidnapped and doped. Robert, however, unburdened by the pressures of fame, found California one long party. Los Angeles also offered a fresh musical start, away from the Canterbury nexus of The Wilde Flowers and The Soft Machine. Robert was asked to join New Buffalo Springfield, a reconstituted version of the West Coast rock act that gave us Neil Young and Stephen Stills – but that, rather crucially, featured neither Young nor Stills. He turned down the offer, citing musical differences, although insists he was happy to have been asked. 'And I'd like that on the record, because I think I wasn't very nice about them at the time.'

Rather than West Coast rock musicians, Wyatt spent time with fellow expats, singing 'girly choruses' for the Irish psychedelic blues act Eire Apparent, who had also been a part of the Hendrix American tours, and recording with Zoot Money, Andy Summers and former Animals frontman Eric Burdon. Yet Robert's time on the West Coast is ultimately of interest less for his session work than as a pre-echo of his solo career.

In Hollywood's TTG Studios, he recorded *Slow Walkin' Talk*, a Mose Allison-style blues by Brian Hopper, featuring Hendrix himself on bass. 'Jimi came in and listened and whispered, "I could try the bass line on that, you wouldn't have to use it,"' recalled Wyatt. 'And he got Noel's bass, and you have to remember he's left-handed, so he's playing bass the wrong way around. Puts down the first take, a fucking Larry Graham bass line. He heard it once, including the changes, the breaks and all that, and it was staggering.' Everything else on *Slow Walkin' Talk* – vocals, drums, piano and organ – was played by Wyatt himself.

Until this point, Robert had largely confined himself to writing lyrics. Yet, though composition would never come easily, access to keyboards in American studios proved a creative spur. He also reworked Daevid Allen's *Chelsa*, later to be recycled as *Signed Curtain* on the first Matching Mole album, and recorded two more musically ambitious pieces: *Rivmic Melodies*, based around tunes by Hugh Hopper, which would become the first side of the Softs' second album, and *Moon in June*, which the band had begun playing on tour and which would become a signature work, featuring on the third Soft Machine album.

Robert's lyrics on *Moon in June* were personal, even confessional: 'Living is easy here in New York State,' runs one of the more literal lines. 'Ah, but I wish I were home again / Back in West Dulwich again'. Like a true Englishman, Wyatt goes on to list the lack of rain as one of the things making him particularly homesick. Also back in London, of course, were his girlfriend, Pam, and two-year-old son, Sam. Robert's failure to join them back in England can in part be justified on the grounds that, with The Soft Machine over, work prospects were better in LA. Yet his reasons were not only musical: 'It was a bit of a shock when he didn't come back with the others,' says Pam. 'I think he was living with some girl in the Chelsea Hotel. I don't know how I found that out. I thought, by then, it's obviously not going to work out. It's obviously over.'

Wyatt, who comments evasively that he remained loyal to Pam 'in my way', admits that his love life at the time was 'a bit of a tangle'. *Moon in June* was frank about the temptations he faced as an Englishman in

New York: 'Between your thighs I feel a sensation / How long can I resist the temptation? / I've got my bird / You've got your man .. . now we're on the floor / And you want more.'

Today embarrassed by the lines, Wyatt feels he should have gone back to England the moment the tour finished. Yet he is adamant that he had remained close to Pam throughout his time in America: 'As far as I was concerned, we were a pair. We were together. I was writing a song about my girlfriend. I didn't feel *not* with her. It was just that my job was to be away for that time – more like a sailor abroad writing about his girlfriend back home. It's only later, realising Sam's schooldays had difficulties and lonelinesses, that I realised I should have been there.'

Wyatt eventually returned to England at the tail end of 1968 – by which time Probe had finally released *The Soft Machine* in America, along with a single, *Joy of a Toy/Why Are We Sleeping*. The album was also released in Europe on the French label Barclay but Probe had no UK distribution and so, bizarrely, it was available at home only as an import until a year later, when it was released as a double album with *Volume Two*.

–»)《«– –»)《«– –»)《«–

The immediate reason for Robert's return to England was that his green card was about to expire, but with offers of work coming in Robert points out that he easily could have had his visa renewed had he wanted to. Instead, he says, he came back for Pam and Sam.

Having assumed that his failure to return at the end of the tour signalled the end of the relationship, Pam was surprised by Robert's return. And she was even more surprised when he proposed marriage. 'He and Noel Redding, they shagged their way across America for all that time,' she recalls. 'The band came back but Robert didn't: he stayed on for another three or four months. I think Honor wrote to Robert and said: "Why don't you marry Pam? She'd be a good wife." He wrote back and said: "I'd be a crap husband and a crap father and she should get on with her own life." And then, having shagged their way across America, they decided, just before they came home, that actually the girls at home were the ones. Noel went back to his girlfriend in Folkestone, and Robert and I got married.'

The wedding took place at Brixton Registry Office on 28 January 1969: Wyatt's twenty-fourth birthday. The bride and groom arrived by bus and Honor made a wedding cake of bread, carrots and cream cheese. The two witnesses were the only guests.

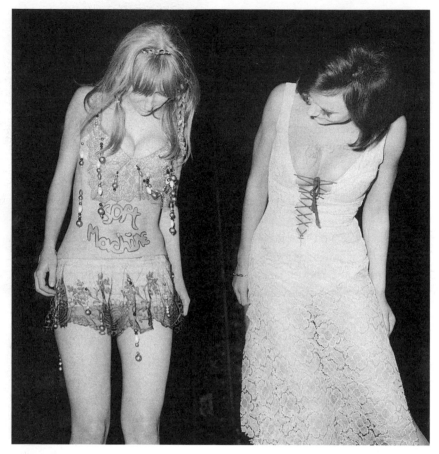

› Pam at a gig with semi-transparent miniskirt and 'Soft Machine' painted on her midriff, with Michèle Heyer.

Perhaps, with The Soft Machine apparently at an end, Robert expected life to become settled. Pam, however, laughs out loud at the suggestion that they could ever have become a traditional nuclear family. The couple remained in Dalmore Road, along with their son, Robert's mum and assorted bandmates. Deep down, Pam admits, she didn't really expect Robert's womanising to stop either. 'By then I knew it was too late,' she sighs. 'It wasn't going to change. I mean, it was all very amicable, we've always been great mates. I would never say a word against him. I knew what he was like, from when he was sixteen. Why would I expect him to change?' In the era of free love, she goes on, 'it wasn't cool to be angry or jealous or any of those things'.

Pam was no conventional housewife herself. And, though she might describe herself as a mouse, she wouldn't stay meek for ever: she remembers 'snogging' Andy Summers, for instance, during his brief stay at Dalmore Road. But it was Pam who bore the brunt of the childcare and cooked many of the communal meals. 'We went to Ronnie Scott's a lot,' she laughs, 'and I've slept through the most amazing jazz musicians you've ever heard of. I'd stay awake for the first set. But we all had to get up with the kids in the morning. The blokes would sleep all day.' Pam recalls that she sometimes went to Soft Machine gigs too, but 'Robert would always go home with somebody else. He'd say: "You go home, see you later. No, don't wait for me." And he'd come home and say he'd spent three days with the Blossom Toes. Well, he probably had.'

A life of quotidian domesticity became a still more distant prospect when Probe, to everyone's surprise, decided to take up their option on a second Soft Machine album. Kevin Ayers was away in Ibiza, on one of his periodic breaks from the music business, and the band's attempts to get him back to London proved fruitless. Hugh Hopper, who had written several numbers still in the repertoire, was the natural replacement. 'Mike Ratledge had definitely given up playing live after the American tour supporting Hendrix,' the bassist recalled, 'as had Kevin Ayers. But there was another album to be done under the original contract, so Robert and Mike asked me to record with them – just to get the record out of the way, you understand, not to do any gigs.'

In fact, Hugh's arrival marked the beginning of The Soft Machine Mark III. Rehearsals began in late December 1968. Six weeks later, they entered Olympic Sound Studios to record their second album, laconically named *Volume Two*.

⟶≫ ⟨≪⟶ ⟶≫ ⟨≪⟶ ⟶≫ ⟨≪⟶

Despite Hugh's makeshift presence, *Volume Two* would be The Soft Machine's most consistent record. Taken as a whole, it is also the record that best represents Wyatt's role in the band. Kevin's departure left Robert as sole vocalist and *Dada Was Here* even found him singing in Spanish, a language he had begun to pick up in Mallorca. Foreign-language vocals would become a recurring feature of Robert's solo career – in part because he's a self-proclaimed xenophile, but also because, on a purely practical level, he liked the fact that different languages forced his mouth to make different shapes and sounds. 'I listen to a lot of foreign records,' he explains, 'and don't know what they're singing about. So I've always got used to the idea of the mouth as an instrument.'

Absurdist philosophy was a feature of the record, too. As well as the namecheck to Dadaism, the opening of the record has Robert introduce the band, in a spoken prologue, as 'the official orchestra of the College of Pataphysics'. On two short subsequent tunes, Wyatt goes on to prove these Pataphysical credentials by singing the letters of the alphabet, first in the usual sequence, then in reverse – just as Pataphysics creator Alfred Jarry had advocated the backwards meal, commencing with brandy and ending with soup. *Ubu Enchaîné*, the ribald, riotous Jarry play The Soft Machine had soundtracked just after the departure of Daevid Allen, was finally leaving its mark.

Pataphysics is concerned with contradiction rather than rational logic, and any attempt at explanation runs the risk of taking a joke too seriously. But, while it never quite coalesced into a movement or philosophy, what *can* be said is that it celebrates anomalies and contradictions: 'Pataphysics will examine the laws which govern exceptions,' declared Jarry, who also defined it as the 'science of imaginary solutions', describing 'a universe

> The introducer of Pataphysics – Alfred Jarry, in Alfortville, Paris, around 1900. He influenced writers like Apollinaire and the surrealist movement, while Picasso, a major enthusiast, was rumoured to own and carry Jarry's revolver.

which can be – and perhaps should be – envisaged in the place of the traditional one'.

Jarry's pseudoscience has often appealed to musicians, from the Softs and their contemporary hippie band Hawkwind to later art punks like Pere Ubu; Paul McCartney, perhaps prompted by the Softs, referenced Pataphysics on *Maxwell's Silver Hammer* on *Abbey Road*. Yet it was The Soft Machine who found themselves officially recognised by France's Collège de Pataphysique, and a well-thumbed copy of Alfred Jarry's collected works still sits on Robert's bookshelf today.

Always interested in modernism, it is no surprise that Wyatt felt an affinity with Jarry, whose play *Ubu Roi* kicked off the whole movement back in 1896. He shares Jarry's interest in the ambiguity of language, and emphasis on childhood memory: the grotesque character of Ubu was modelled on Jarry's unpopular physics teacher, Monsieur Hébert. Jarry's habit of turning up to the opera wearing a paper shirt adorned with painted black tie also inspired Robert's stage costume of a crayon-on-flesh suit. Jarry had a dark side, too. Before his death, at the age of just thirty-four, from TB brought on by alcoholism, the playwright was apparently consuming two litres of wine and three absinthes before midday, and even drinking ether.

Jarry's brutal, irreverent humour, at once bleak and celebratory, continues to influence Wyatt's thinking today. When Robert declares that being funny is a serious business, he comes as close to anyone to encapsulating the Pataphysical philosophy. 'In the long run, it's the only way I can take life,' he shrugs. 'I take it as a joke. It's beyond tragedy.'

⟶»⟩ ⟨«⟶ ⟶»⟩ ⟨«⟶ ⟶»⟩ ⟨«⟶

Perhaps suitably for a science of contradictions, The Soft Machine's most surreal, chimerical days were already behind them by the time they namechecked Jarry's anti-philosophy on record. Robert believes it was the Hendrix tour that knocked the whimsy out of the band, but they were toughened up too by the arrival of Hugh Hopper.

It wasn't just that the band now lacked Kevin Ayers' gloriously indolent voice: Kevin's functional bass lines had also been replaced by Hugh's fuzzed up Fender. Where Kevin had approached the bass guitar from the perspective of a songwriter, Hugh used the instrument for heavy riffs and even lead lines. With Mike, too, using heavy distortion, it wasn't always clear which member of the trio was making any given sound.

> *Volume Two* – the Softs' Pataphysical outing. The cover, like the first Probe album, was by Byron Goto, a Hawaiian-born artist and associate of Willem de Kooning, known mainly for his Abstract Expressionism.

'The bass would take the lead line, or bass and keyboard might riff while the drums took the solo,' recalls Henry Cow's Chris Cutler, a youthful Softs fan, who cites the deconstruction of conventional instrumental hierarchies as one of the band's key innovations. 'I'd never seen that before. I can remember the spark that went through the room at the 100 Club, just after Hugh joined, when he stepped on the fuzz pedal to play the melody line on *Hibou, Anemone and Bear.*'

Right from *Hibou, Anemone and Bear*, the first full-length track on *Volume Two*, it's clear that Hopper's aggressive bass tone and the lack of whimsy aren't the only changes since The Soft Machine's debut. There is also the introduction of brass: Brian Hopper on tenor saxophone, occasionally augmented by Hugh on alto saxophone and Mike on flute. There is also the fact that the opening bass line is in 7/4. With the occasional exception of 3/4 (waltz) time, it remains rare in popular music to use an uneven number of beats per bar. Yet complex time signatures would become a Soft Machine trademark – and something else that impressed Cutler.

'The Soft Machine – especially once Hugh had joined – was one of the first bands to really explore deeply, and more or less exclusively, the use of additive rhythm,' explains the drummer. '5/8, 7/8, 13/8 and so on. There was little precedent, and therefore no rule to apply, no accepted practice. And to make these rhythms fluid and natural meant finding new ways of *thinking* and *feeling* rhythm. That made Robert unique.'

These tricksy time signatures could have felt as cold and awkward as a new squash ball in winter, but Robert made the rhythms feel natural, even danceable, as they ricocheted off the walls. And what would, later in the band's career, begin to feel like a self-conscious flexing of technical muscle was at this early stage saved by a self-mocking humour. 'A few fives to take away the taste of all those sevens,' mutters Wyatt, as *Pataphysical Introduction Part 2* segues into the more freeform *Out of Tunes*. The music, accordingly, leaps nimbly from 7/4 time to 5/4.

The silly and the serious sides of The Soft Machine are balanced on *Volume Two* as they would never be before or since. *Thank You Pierrot Lunaire* references a notoriously challenging Schoenberg song cycle, but also allows Wyatt to gently poke fun at Mike Ratledge: 'In his organ solos, he feels round the keyboard / knowing he must find the nicest notes for you to hear.' Likewise, *As Long As He Lies Perfectly Still* is about Kevin's macrobiotic phase – 'he eats brown rice and fish, how nice' – but still manages to squeeze in a line about Beckett's *Waiting for Godot*, while *Esther's Nose Job*, a suite of Ratledge instrumentals, takes its name from a grisly cosmetic surgery procedure in Thomas Pynchon's novel *V* – a major inspiration for Ratledge at the time.

It was quite a shift in references from the whimsical Lewis Carroll, and that shift was evident in the music itself. *Volume Two* is harder-edged than the band's debut, and far more ambitious. When he recalls the music of this period, Wyatt said later, his immediate reaction is: 'Who is that little clever-dick teenager? Why doesn't someone give him a smack 'round the chops?'

From this point onwards, The Soft Machine would take themselves increasingly seriously – ultimately, perhaps, a little *too* seriously. But Wyatt is being hard on the band here. *Volume Two* represented that wonderful stage at which they were still taking risks, right across the board, with elements of jazz meshing happily with pop songwriting. Indeed, in its musical ambition, and its collision of highbrow references with oddball humour, the album shares something with Frank Zappa and The Mothers of Invention – an acknowledged influence on Hugh Hopper, in particular. Yet *Volume Two* is more charming, as well as utterly English. Breezy and brilliant, it was one of the finest album releases of the year – and all from a record conceived as a contract-filler.

⟶» «⟵ ⟶» «⟵ ⟶» «⟵

Burned out by the US tour, Mike and Hugh were not keen to go back on the road. Shortly before recording *Volume Two*, in February and March, they had done an impressive support slot for Hendrix at London's Royal Albert Hall. More gigs arrived in the spring, including one in Portsmouth supporting jazz saxophonist Roland Kirk, and another at the Paradiso club in Amsterdam. The latter was recorded as a possible live album, and, when the group declined to release it, found its way out as a bootleg release. The set was essentially a heavier, much more aggressive rendering of *Volume Two*.

The band, it seemed, still had reservations about live performance and when artist Peter Dockley commissioned them to soundtrack *Spaced*, a multimedia event at the Roundhouse, they contributed a pre-recorded tape instead of appearing onstage. *Spaced* was very much a fringe event, featuring dancers and gymnasts clad in rubber octopus costumes. The music contributed by The Soft Machine was suitably abstract: their swirling soundscapes, influenced by minimalist composer Terry Riley, could have appeared on an avant-garde film.

It was precisely the sort of project that would have baffled Henry Henriod, the Anim representative, who simply couldn't understand their interest in fringe theatre and Alfred Jarry. In fact, *Volume Two* brought the band's relationship with their management company to an end. Anim's strategy for promoting The Soft Machine had seemed to rely entirely on reflected glory from the Hendrix camp. *Volume Two* had even seen Mike Jeffery thanked for access to the guitarist's coat-tails, tongue firmly in cheek, on *Have You Ever Bean Green?*. The band instead began talks with Sean Murphy and Ian Knight, who had been involved in the band's ill-fated south of France residency the previous year. Knight and Murphy began to manage the band in tandem, although 'Ian and Sean fell out,' recalled Hopper, 'so we were stuck with Sean Murphy.'

> The Soft Machine Mark III – Mike Ratledge, Hugh Hopper and Robert.

According to Wyatt, their new manager promised to extract them from the financial troubles they had encountered with Mike Jeffery. Yet Sean Murphy seems not to have been much better in terms of financial transparency. Robert prefers not to pick over the details. 'Maybe you have to say that it's foolish to be as innocent as we were,' he sighs. 'You know, why can't we find our contracts? Why don't we know what we signed? Why didn't we keep tabs properly on it at the time? All those things. There's a kind of laziness in saying: "Leave it to the manager." But we hadn't got a clue.'

The change of management did mean a revival of live gigs. Soon Soft Machine – now trading without the definite article – found themselves once again huddled in the back of a van travelling up and down the M1, as well as playing shows in Switzerland, France, Belgium and Holland. Then, as now, fees in Europe were far superior. Bill MacCormick, the Dulwich neighbour who would later play alongside Wyatt in Matching Mole, estimates that he saw Soft Machine once a fortnight in the two years after they returned from America. He is adamant that the Hugh Hopper trio represented the band's artistic peak. 'They did one night at the Country Club in London', he recalls, 'when Ratledge was just unbelievable, just incredible. I mean he was *torturing* that poor Lowrey. It was literally tears in the eyes, spine-tingling stuff. They really were, for a while, just absolutely incredible.'

'It was a loud fucking band, it really was,' Hugh Hopper recalled. 'Mike Ratledge was playing through two Marshall stacks and so was I, and Robert Wyatt was blasting away on drums. It wasn't a polite, cerebral band, by any means. The writing was thoughtful but it wasn't presented in a quiet way. You don't actually get that from the studio records, which were a bit dry.'

With Hugh's buzzsaw bass and Mike's screeching organ both going through fuzz boxes and 100-watt Marshall amps, the Soft Machine live experience was now like the Jimi Hendrix Experience meets Lifetime, the jazz-rock organ trio comprising Tony Williams, John McLaughlin and organist Larry Young. It's hard to believe that this was the same band that had released *Love Makes Sweet Music* just two years previously – even if Robert and Mike were in fact the only common members. The new line-up was close to a power trio, although many gigs were played as a quartet, augmented by Hugh's brother Brian on saxophone. 'It was a very powerful set-up,' Brian recalls, 'and to play with them live was quite an experience. It was very loud. Hugh had this famous phrase: "It's like vindaloo between the ears".'

Despite his regular appearances with the band, and an invite from Robert to join the band, Brian Hopper would remain a guest musician as opposed to an official member. He was holding down a job in agricultural science and was reluctant to commit to the nomadic lifestyle of the touring musician. Others in the band had similar misgivings. Bookish, bespectacled and prematurely balding, Brian's brother Hugh was every bit as reserved as Mike Ratledge. The bassist played with his back to the audience or even from an onstage armchair. Brian recalls that Robert, meanwhile, was taking to the stage more and more often

> The fourth Soft: Brian Hopper on sax, alongside his brother Hugh on bass. The stacks were getting bigger, too.

without his shirt, which 'went down quite well with a lot of the audience – particularly the female audience'.

'My brother was very laid-back, very quiet,' Brian continues, 'and Mike was also quite introverted. Mike certainly is not a showman. He was very active when he was playing but he didn't play to the crowd. And Hugh was very content just to sit back and do his walk, this little shuffle. It was all fairly static. But Robert really put a lot into it. And of course he was still singing in those days. He certainly was, if you like, the frontman – although he was sitting at the back.'

It was also his cheeky sense of humour that made Robert the band's focal point. When they performed *Moon in June* on the BBC's *Top Gear* session in June 1969, he sang impromptu new lyrics that poked fun at the division between high and low culture, just as Alfred Jarry had parodied Shakespeare and Victor Hugo in between episodes of Guignol slapstick. 'I remember Robert scribbling away in the control room,' recalled producer John Walters, 'and the result was a new verse in praise of our Maida Vale studios, slightly ironically thanking us for allowing Soft Machine to play as long as they wanted to.'

> *Playing now is lovely / Here in the BBC*
> *We're free to play almost as long / And as loud*
> *As a jazz group / Or an orchestra on Radio Three*

Robert's back-of-an-envelope lyrics also celebrated the BBC's 'tea machine just along the corridor' and with nudge-wink timing worthy of a music hall comedian, he omits the word 'shit', the rhyme with 'hits' instead left mischievously blank. However serious the band's emerging instrumental side, the spirit of Alfred Jarry and Spike Milligan remained undimmed.

⟶»⟨⟨- -»⟨⟨- -»⟨⟨-

Wyatt also took the chance to dedicate the BBC session to 'all our mates like Kevin, Caravan, and the old Pink Floyd'. By this stage, Floyd frontman Syd Barrett had left the band – or rather the band had left him, at first neglecting to pick him up for gigs and then eventually kicking him out on a more formal basis. In the period before he disappeared into mythology as rock's most famous acid casualty, Syd continued as a solo artist. The month before their *Top Gear* session, all three members of Soft Machine had joined him at London's Abbey Road studios to contribute to his solo debut *The Madcap Laughs*.

Wyatt is at pains to point out that the singer-songwriter – infamous in particular for appearing onstage with his hair full of Brylcreem and crumbled up Mandrax tablets – was quiet and polite throughout the sessions, and it does seem that the Barrett legend involves some fairly fanciful myth-making. Yet Syd's taciturnity was eccentric at the very least: he provided no guidance whatsoever as to chord sequences or even key signatures. 'I thought they were rehearsals,' Wyatt later told *Melody Maker*'s Steve Lake. 'We'd say "What key is that in, Syd?" and he'd say "Yeah". Or, "That's funny, Syd, there's a bar of two and a half beats, and then it seems to slow up, and then there's five beats there," and he'd go "Oh, really?" And we sat there with the tape running, trying to work it out, when he stood up and said, "Right, thank you very much."'

Such a slapdash approach could only work with highly talented musicians. Although their contributions went uncredited, Soft Machine contributed to *No Good Trying* and *Love You*, two of the strongest

> Two 1969 maverick albums recorded with Soft Machine backing: Syd Barrett's *The Madcap Laughs* and Kevin Ayers' *Joy of a Toy*.

tracks on *The Madcap Laughs*, which is now recognised as a classic of woozy, wide-eyed psychedelic pop. David Gilmour, who mixed some of the tracks, remembers being impressed by Robert's drumming, in particular: 'I was amazed at how brilliant he was, how he could play along with something that had no real time going on in it.'

In June, Soft Machine returned to Abbey Road studios with Kevin Ayers, who had also been signed up by Harvest Records as a solo artist. *Joy of a Toy* is the wistful, song-based album the Softs' co-founder had always wanted to make, the soundtrack to a summer afternoon idled away with a lover and a couple of bottles of wine. Wyatt played drums on the majority of tracks, while Hugh Hopper and Mike Ratledge came in for *Song for Insane Times*. David Bedford, who played keyboards on the record as well as contributing his considerable talents as an arranger, suggested that Kevin had an umbilical cord still joining him to Soft Machine: 'He hadn't completely broken free. But it was a fact that his ideas were far simpler than where the Soft Machine were going.'

Although he joked that everyone in the band got very good at playing in the key of E, Bedford said that he had the utmost respect for Kevin as a writer. Robert, too, enjoyed the *Joy of a Toy* sessions, partly as a chance to play more direct, song-based music and partly simply because he missed his old mate: 'I loved Kevin. I thought he was great. Very easy-going, good company, made me laugh. He was a terrific songwriter, and I liked singing his songs. And part of the tension in Soft Machine was because I did like his songs, whereas the group itself was abandoning songs in favour of extended instrumental pieces.'

'I think Mike was very uncomfortable with the rest of us,' continues Robert. 'With me and Kevin in particular, and then just with me. He and Hugh had a lot more in common. They were quiet, conventional people. They just were very straight, in the old-fashioned sense.'

As yet, however, that tension – both musical and social – remained in the background. Wyatt was inspired by Soft Machine's new incarnation and delighted to have Hugh Hopper in the band. And by the end of the year Soft Machine would have evolved yet again.

6

ON A DILEMMA

Moon in June and upside-down jazz-rock

On 13 August 1970 Wyatt went for a cigarette outside the Royal Albert Hall. When he tried to come back through the stage door, however, the doorman barred his path. He couldn't be performing, the man insisted: the venue was for proper musicians only.

Despite his unkempt appearance, of course, Robert *was* playing: that night, Soft Machine would become the first rock band ever to perform at the Proms. Some critics sided with the doorman. 'I should like to know', demanded the critic from the classically orientated *Music Review*, 'on what premises I am expected to take seriously a small group of musicians whose range of tone does not exist and whose scale of dynamics is no more than an unvarying FFF.' In fact, the band themselves were unhappy with their performance, which was plagued by technical problems and subject to a strict curfew. Yet to be accepted into the world's most famous classical concert series was quite a coup. True, they played *fff*: an abbreviation of the Italian for 'like vindaloo between the ears'. But, as Richard Williams declared in the *Radio Times*, Soft Machine were as far from *Top of the Pops* as Chopin is from a vaudeville act.

The band had changed considerably since the days in which they would be pelted with bottles if they dared venture beyond Middle Earth or UFO. Music had changed too, with Miles Davis inspired by Jimi Hendrix and Sly and the Family Stone to plug into the mains. Jazz

> The Softs at the Proms, August 1970: Mike, Hugh, Robert and Elton Dean.

purists reacted to what came to be known as jazz-rock fusion with the same horror seen in folkies when Bob Dylan went electric. Yet the trumpeter's new direction, as well as being hugely popular, resulted in imperishable records like *In a Silent Way* and *Bitches Brew*.

If jazz was moving towards rock, rock was fast coming the other way. Wyatt himself was particularly taken by two discoveries from the Hendrix tour: Chicago, then known as Chicago Transit Authority, and Blood, Sweat and Tears. Both acts were using horn sections within what was in broad terms a rock context, something Soft Machine had already explored with guest saxophonist Brian Hopper. Yet, while the rest of the band could hang out at Dalmore Road when not on tour, Brian was still holding down a day job. Eventually the double life became too much: the saxophonist played his last show with the band in October 1969.

A Simon Langton schoolmate who co-founded The Wilde Flowers and even jammed at Wellington House, Brian had been there from the start. But Soft Machine, never sentimental when it came to line-up changes, simply shed another skin. By the end of the month, when they played the rain-soaked, Frank Zappa-hosted Actuel Music Festival in Belgium, the trio had morphed into a septet. 'It gives us a chance to bring out certain things in our music that we have been thinking about for some time, apart from having four extra solo voices,' said Hugh at the time. 'We had some nice powerful sounds with the trio, but when playing for an hour on stage it gets a bit boring.'

Saxophonist Elton Dean, trombonist Nick Evans and cornet player Mark Charig were borrowed from a sextet led by West Country pianist and composer Keith Tippett. 'Robert loved the sextet and I loved the Soft Machine,' says Tippett, recalling a happy period of musical and social crossover. 'Unusually for that time, they were playing in time signatures like 11, 7, 5, 13. But it wasn't academic in any sense. It was music with warmth.'

A fourth new member of the Soft Machine line-up was Lyn Dobson, a flautist and tenor saxophonist who had played with Georgie Fame and Manfred Mann. The stint with Soft Machine, Dobson recalls, was the musical highpoint of his life up to that point. Yet he still shudders at the intricacy of the parts: 'The stuff they were doing when I joined the band was extremely esoteric and incredibly complex. When I went to the first rehearsal, I couldn't play any of it. I bluffed my way through it, then took the parts home and practised for about a month.'

The septet were an act in transition: the two tracks they recorded for BBC's *Top Gear* show in November 1969 could have been by different bands. First came one of Soft Machine's finest jazz recordings, a twenty-one-minute, largely instrumental suite that was an impressive showcase for Wyatt the drummer. The other tune, *Instant Pussy*, was a straight song, featuring Wyatt alone at the piano and lasting less than three and a half minutes. It is hard to think of many other acts that might have recorded both tunes over a whole career, let alone in a single session.

In fact, the *Instant Pussy* side of the band, featuring Wyatt in singer-songwriter mode, was already on the way out. But even the instrumental numbers must have shocked traditionalists when Soft Machine played Ronnie Scott's the same month, supporting bebop pianist Thelonious Monk. With the four-piece brass section, the influence of jazz on the band had become overt. Yet rock – and rock volume – remained integral, too. Nick Evans still winces at the decibel level: 'I used to wear earplugs when I played a Soft Machine gig,' recollects the trombonist. 'I always thought it was like a painter working away while wearing a blindfold.'

Soon, says Robert, it was no longer clear whether Soft Machine were their label's worst-selling rock group or its best-selling jazz act. The septet had plenty in common with jazz-fusion acts, including Miles Davis offshoots like Weather Report, Return to Forever and John McLaughlin's Mahavishnu Orchestra. There was also an affinity with UK jazz-rock acts like Ian Carr's trumpet-led Nucleus, with whom Soft Machine would later trade personnel. But, though straddling jazz and rock, the Softs didn't – yet – quite fit within the sub-genre of jazz-rock. As long as Wyatt still sang, the band maintained links to their psychedelic salad days.

Some categorised the septet instead as progressive or prog rock, but Robert hates the notion of being smugly 'progressive'. 'The whole idea of progress, of getting more weird chords and funny time signatures in itself – a sort of "Ooh, this is better than pop music" – struck me as daft,' he explains. 'What I really liked about pop music, and in fact early jazz, when it *was* a popular music, was the fact that it was intellectual but it was actually visceral and intuitive music at its best.'

> Hugh Hopper and Mike Ratledge put the new horn section through their paces. From left: Nick Evans, Mark Charig, Elton Dean and Lyn Dobson.

Soft Machine certainly took their music seriously; they were interested in unusual time signatures and preferred keyboards to guitars. Yet the band had little in common with bloated, bombastic acts like ELP or the full-blown Yes. They never indulged in Roger Dean artwork or Tolkien-inspired fantasy lyrics, and it's impossible to imagine them attempting anything as ludicrous as Rick Wakeman's *King Arthur on Ice*.

This is where the Canterbury Scene tag is useful, a sub-section or sibling of progressive rock and jazz-rock that fits Soft Machine only because they essentially defined its parameters. Robert, of course, doesn't like that term, either. 'What I liked about Mike and Hugh's playing', he insists, 'was there is no name for their style. You can't really say that what they played is jazz, you cannot say it was rock'n'roll. It was just this *thing* that they explored. And all other musicians I know, in the end, were part of the jazz tradition or the avant-garde tradition or the semi-classical tradition or the sort of proggy thing going on. I just wanted something, I could hear it in my head, but I couldn't pin it down. A kind of music that didn't quite exist yet. It hadn't got a name.'

-»» ««- -»» ««- -»» ««-

They might have changed almost beyond recognition since the summer of love, but Soft Machine had enjoyed a strong following in France ever since their 1967 stint on the Côte d'Azur. And so, two and a half years later, the septet headed across the Channel for a two-week tour.

It was a cold winter, occasionally flecked with snow, and morale in the tour bus dropped with the mercury. With only relatively primitive amplification, the brass instruments were constantly in danger of being drowned out by the distorted organ and bass. There were also financial difficulties. More than doubling the size of the band did not double the size of their fee. Yet suddenly there were four more beds required, and and each brass player had to be paid on a full session basis.

When Soft Machine returned from France in 1967, they had been forced to leave Daevid Allen on the other side of the Channel. This time round, all seven members made it back to the UK – but again, the French tour marked the end of a chapter in the group's history. Nick Evans and Mark Charig left at the end of the year.

Hugh suggested that social tensions were partially to blame for the septet's demise, while Mike cited musical and technical problems: 'With seven musicians it was really becoming too much. Technically speaking, we didn't have the experience to control such a volume. But it was really tiring because with seven people it was either conceptually too rigid or totally chaotic.'

'Nick couldn't get along with the amplified trombone, he was never really happy touring,' Elton Dean recalled. 'Mark got a bit disorientated and eventually he and Nick left to join the Brotherhood of Breath [with South African pianist Chris McGregor]. There were also financial problems – I don't really think the band could afford to run the complete horn section. In the end everyone was quite happy to reduce it to a quintet; it was much more manageable.'

The quintet – the core trio of Wyatt, Ratledge and Hopper plus a two-man horn section of Lyn Dobson and Elton Dean – was equally short-lived, however. Dobson's departure came about in part due to genuine musical differences: the saxophonist and flautist was more interested in Indian ragas than tricky time signatures. But it was also a question of temperament. As Hugh Hopper put it, Lyn was 'on another planet, but a very interesting player'.

The five-piece played a couple of well-received gigs, and did feature, thanks to a live recording, on Soft Machine's next studio album. Yet it is the septet, who never made it into the studio, that was the great lost Soft Machine line-up. *NME* journalist Ian MacDonald would call them 'not only the best-ever line-up in the band's history, but one of the most amazing "live" rock experiences then going'. Wyatt himself hasn't always been so positive, perhaps detecting in the arrival of the horns the beginning of his own decline. 'I was happiest in the Soft Machine when it was an all-electric trio, first with Kevin and then with Hugh,' he said in 1972. 'After that it wasn't quite my dream band any more.'

Today, however, Robert says the septet was perhaps his favourite of the band's incarnations, recalling with fondness their mix of improvisation and set-piece choreography. The sheer number of musicians necessitated a greater degree of discipline, but the tight ensemble motifs were interspersed with moments when they burst the banks with wild improvisation. 'At its best,' he nods, 'I think there was nothing like it. It was an amazing band.'

–»)《«– –»)《«– –»)《«–

With Lyn Dobson's departure, Soft Machine's line-up stabilised and, since it seemed unfair to have only one musician on session status, Elton Dean was promoted to full-time band member. The format had now returned to that of the previous year, when Brian Hopper had regularly joined the band as guest saxophonist, though the tone was different. Elton stood out for his use of the saxello, a relative of the soprano saxophone whose keening is reminiscent of a snakecharmer's pipe. He was also a much wilder soloist, his lines coiling eagerly around Mike and Hugh's melodies.

In April and May 1970, Soft Machine went into London's IBC studios to capture the new line-up on vinyl. With the Probe deal having run its course, the new album would be released internationally by the bigger CBS label, part of Columbia Records, who offered the band a five-album deal. In keeping with tradition, the record was called *Third*.

Far more so than its predecessors, *Third* is the album you would expect from a band that could trace its origins to a borrowed Cecil Taylor record. However much they stretched out live, their recorded songs up to this point had always been pithy. But, though it is a double LP, *Third* contains just four tracks, each lasting approximately twenty minutes and taking up an entire side of vinyl. To those who had followed the band's evolution as a live act, from trio to septet to quintet to quartet in the space of six months, it was a natural progression. Judged by albums alone, however, the shift from *Volume Two* was seismic.

While *Soft Machine* and *Volume Two* have their fans, many regard *Third* as the band's masterpiece. Certainly, it has more sophistication than anything Soft Machine had previously recorded and, in *Moon in June*, the most extended and accomplished piece of work recorded by Wyatt while a member of the group. On the other hand, *Moon in June* aside, the album lacks the coherence, and the charm, of its two predecessors.

Facelift, the opening track, recorded live with the now extinct quintet, is one of Hugh Hopper's finest compositions. The tune demonstrates the band's growing confidence, with five full minutes of tape manipulation and power electronics before the arrival of the monstrous, mountainous main riff. Less hard-hitting but no less complex are *Slightly All the Time* and *Out-Bloody-Rageous*, both credited to the increasingly prolific Mike Ratledge. All three tunes feel of a piece: complex instrumentals that sat somewhere between Terry Riley and electric Miles Davis. *Moon in June*, by contrast, begins like a pop song, Robert's vocal supported by organ and drums, although it twists and turns over the ensuing twenty minutes into something else entirely. The opening nine minutes alone contain enough ideas for an entire album. It is the record's pièce de résistance, and a milestone in Wyatt's career.

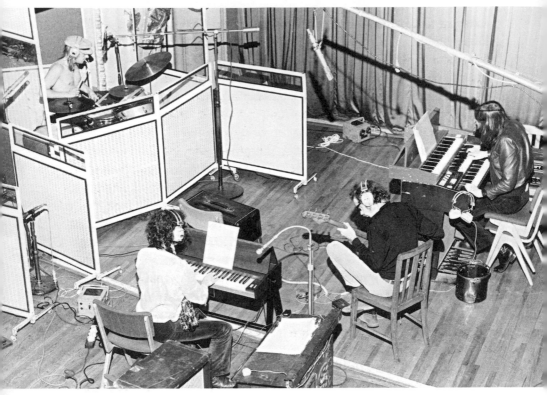

> The Softs quartet in the studio, with Elton Dean (bottom left) adding extra keyboards.

Although there's a forlorn quality to the vocal, *Moon in June* also has a sense of playfulness lacking in the other tracks on *Third*. 'Oh, wait a minute,' Robert mutters at one point, an apparently throwaway line inconceivable on the more solemn numbers by Hugh and Mike, even had they featured vocals. At another moment, he steps out of the song entirely for a spot of metamusical navel-gazing:

> *Music making still performs a normal function*
> *Background noise for people scheming, seducing, revolting and teaching*
> *Well that's all right by me, don't think that I'm complaining*
> *After all it's only leisure time, isn't it?*

With their Pataphysical spirit, these lines make *Moon in June* the only tune on *Third* that has any obvious link to the first two Soft Machine albums. Not coincidentally, it is also Robert's only contribution to the album as either composer or singer. The piece may be made up of pre-existing fragments, and formed a suite that the band had played live over the past couple of years, but he contributed new lyrics and an overarching vision that pulled the pieces into a cohesive whole. Not that he sees it that way. '*Moon in June* sounds very structured,' explains Wyatt. 'But really it was a whole load of unfinished songs where instead of finishing them I just bled them into each other. Literally, actually, all over the studio. What a mess.'

Although more accessible than the other compositions on *Third*, *Moon in June* is, in its way, at least as complex and far more nimble: here hinting at soul, there at swing. Elton Dean doesn't play on the tune at all, and Mike and Hugh appear only briefly. Instead, apart from scraped, squeaky violin played by Veleroy 'Rab' Spall, Robert plays all the instruments himself. It was, he jokes, his first solo record.

'Although it is kind of pop songs strung together into a suite,' Robert maintains, 'it's still very eventful, in the sense that it's changing all the time. In fact, the only bit where it stretches out is where I thought: "Oh, I'm in a group, I'd better have the group on somewhere." So for the second half of the song I graciously invited the rest of the group – some of it, anyway – to come and play a solo on it. That may have been the beginning of the end for me, looking back on it.'

Soft Machine, from Robert's point of view, were holed below the waterline from this point on. But if *Moon in June* is also the point at which Robert essentially parted ways from the rest of the group, it is also the point at which, both literally and metaphorically, he found his own voice. More restrained and more resigned than he'd been on the tune's earlier *Top Gear* version, he could be singing to himself. Yet, like a teacher who has learned to command attention by speaking, counter-intuitively, more quietly, this understated voice is all the more authoritative.

→» «← →» «← →» «←

The way Wyatt recalls it, he didn't want *Moon in June* to be his first solo record; his bandmates didn't play on the body of the track because they were unwilling to do so. When they performed the track live, according to Brian Hopper, Robert thought they did so like unwilling schoolboys picking and fiddling with an unwanted school dinner.

Moon in June signals the end of the old Soft Machine. No subsequent album would feature singing at all and, as the band's centre of gravity shifted towards jazz-rock, even tunes that originally featured a vocal were performed live as instrumentals. For a while, Wyatt persisted in isolated vocal spots, often drenched in tape delay: an attempt to carry on singing even once the band had given up on song. But these passages, part avant-garde improv vocal, part Dada sound poetry, were concerned only with the sonics of language.

Barring a nine-month stint with The Wilde Flowers, Robert has never sung standing up: he couldn't have achieved the swaggering persona, let alone the vocal projection, common to many rock singers even had he wanted to. 'I liked singing,' he explains, 'but I never really concentrated on being a singer. It's just one of the things in the music to me. I wasn't influenced particularly by singers'. Instead, on *Moon in June*, Robert sings as he today plays the cornet – and it is horn players, he says, as opposed to singers, that were the prime influence on his voice.

He makes an exception, however, for the singer Mimi Perrin, whose group Les Double Six set lyrics to horn melodies previously played by artists such as John Coltrane – a style known as vocalese. 'They weren't the first to do it, by any means,' says Robert, 'but they put words to the solos on jazz tunes. And the way they did that, somehow, helped me link instrumental music with singing in a way that's really, really valuable. I've often said I'm more influenced by the way Coltrane plays ballads than by the way anybody sings, and people might think it's a bit unlikely. But if you hear Mimi Perrin sing *Naima* you'll think, "Oh yeah, I can see why." It's not how I think anyone else should sing, but how *I* should sing.'

While Wyatt was finding his voice, however, the rest of the band were becoming committed to instrumental music. Robert's vocal spots were usually unaccompanied – and soon felt as awkward as a room in which all conversation has suddenly dried up. 'My role got narrower and narrower and narrower,' Robert recalls. 'I would come up for air in the middle of sets with embarrassing vocals, rather like a whale comes up and does a spout. But you notice that the others virtually stopped playing when I did that. Everyone else's solos, they would get backup. When I started singing, everyone else just sat quietly in the corner and waited until I stopped. Gradually I got the hint and stopped singing.'

Arguably, the material Mike and Hugh were now writing was too technically demanding to allow Robert to sing and drum simultaneously. But the decline in vocals also reflected, and exacerbated, a broader change in band dynamics, with Robert now increasingly boxed off. 'It's hard to work out exactly what the differences were,' Mike Ratledge reflected, 'but they existed for quite a long time. For instance, Robert has always preferred playing straight 4/4 – he's never really enjoyed or

> Soft Machine's *Third* – the gatefold revealing a band not in obvious high spirits.

accepted working in complex time signatures. But I never got a specific picture of what he does want to do.'

'Hugh, myself and Elton', Ratledge has also said, 'were pursuing a vaguely jazz-related direction. Robert was violently opposed to this, which is strange looking back on it because he was passionate about jazz. But he had defined ideas about what pop music was and what jazz was.' To some extent, Ratledge's confusion is understandable: it had been Wyatt's own idea to introduce the brass section that ultimately limited his own role as vocalist. Robert acknowledges the irony: 'I was sort of hoist on my own petard, because I'd been such a jazz fan at school and I was very fascinated by jazz development. You can't really have it both ways.'

Yet it's not quite accurate to say that Wyatt only wanted to play in 4/4: he simply didn't see complex time signatures as intrinsically superior. Neither is it correct that Robert thought jazz and popular music should stay separate. He simply didn't like the particular combination that became codified as jazz-rock fusion. 'To me, fusion jazz was the worst of both worlds,' explains Wyatt. 'It was rock rhythms, played in a rather effete way, with noodling, very complicated solos on top. I rather fancied the reverse: the light fluidity of a jazz rhythm section, but keeping the almost folk simplicity of popular songs.'

125

Apart from a dislike of off-the-shelf jazz-rock fusion, Wyatt also wanted to sing because that's what he'd always done – long before Hugh and Elton had even arrived in the band. Robert was spectacular behind the kit: he was, for instance, John Peel's favourite drummer. But, as the man who had put together *Moon in June*, he had far too many lyrical, melodic and harmonic ideas to be satisfied with rhythm alone.

Wyatt's interest in vocals is also explained by his resentment of what he calls the aristocracy of high culture. To Wyatt, there was something condescending in the way some jazz musicians were jumping onto the jazz-rock bandwagon. 'What pissed me off a bit about jazz musicians', he elaborates, 'is that there was a resentment of rock. And they said, "If we can get into a rock context, play in front of rock audiences, we can do what they do better than they do it." They really resented the fact that jazz was still being played in little clubs and they weren't stars, when all these people who couldn't play as well, who were just playing louder and with long hair, *were* doing it. So there was a side of sheer opportunism: they were just doing it because they wanted the money and the high profile and the lifestyle they assumed went with it.'

'Virtuosity is very useful stuff', Wyatt continues. 'It gives you a wider range of things you can do. I still listen to bebop trumpeters like Dizzy Gillespie in awe and wonder. But they *use* their technique. With that technique, they can really say stuff. What you get with Lee Morgan, all those trumpet players, is just the opportunity for an emotional discharge of immense, exhilarating power. It's all *in the service of*. And, to that extent, it's neither better nor worse than Johnny Cash, who can hardly sing a note in tune. Johnny Cash, to me, is just as good as Lee Morgan.'

So as Soft Machine moved from carefree whimsy to the serious and cerebral, Robert, if anything, was moving in the opposite direction. 'There was a bit of a misunderstanding with the avant-garde rock scene', he later explained to Richie Unterberger, 'because I think I was sort of swimming the wrong way, really. A lot of the rock thing came out of people who'd started out doing covers of versions of the English scene and the American scene, The Beatles and Dylan and so on, and then got more and more involved in instrumental virtuosity and esoteric ideas. I was going the other way. I was brought up with esoteric ideas and modern European music and Stockhausen, Webern, avant-garde poets, and all the kind of avant-garde thing in the 1950s, before pop music – the Beat poets, the avant-garde painters at the time, and so on. To me, the amazing thing was to discover the absolute beauty of Ray

Charles singing a country and western song or something like that. So my actual journey of discovery was I discovered the beauty of simple, popular music.'

The growing schism within Soft Machine was also rooted in the different personalities. 'Robert was the opposite of Mike and me', explained Hugh Hopper; 'extrovert, exhibitionist, promiscuous, given to speaking in aphorisms and saying things apparently mostly for effect.' Onstage, Mike and Hugh might have been content to let their music do the talking, and to allow Robert's more exuberant performance to command audience attention. With his bare torso and long hair swinging across his face, he provided a much-needed focal point. Offstage, however, he was causing friction. Photographs of the era show the rest of the band hunched over sheet music, while Wyatt hammers away on drums with no manuscript paper – or shirt – in sight. He refused to learn to read music, he later suggested, so the rest of the band couldn't tell him what to play.

In retrospect, even Wyatt is a little embarrassed by the memories: 'Look at him waving, flashing his arms about, hair waving in the wind,' he sighs, looking back from such a distance that he lapses into the third person. 'I mean, proper drummers, they just sit there and play. They don't suddenly get the microphone and start screaming down it. I can see how the others were frightfully embarrassed. As happy and successful Canterbury grammar-school boys, they must have thought: "*This is not what we meant.*" I can see that. And I'm sort of on their side. If I could have left me, I'd have left me. That's very damning.'

Robert is so quick to put himself down that he isn't an entirely reliable witness; continuing to sing hardly disqualified him from being a 'proper' drummer. Yet Lyn Dobson says Robert's deep unhappiness was obvious even during the band's earlier septet and quintet phases: 'I recall him crying in the dressing room. He was too professional most of the time to fuck up onstage, but yeah, I remember him being very unhappy. I *know* he was very unhappy. And he did become more and more ostracised.'

Lyn Dobson has a soft spot for Mike, but found Hugh unapproachable. That Robert's friend and future bandmate Bill MacCormick found the opposite – that Hugh was easy to talk to, whereas Mike was monosyllabic – serves as a useful reminder that the two were not, to borrow the title of another Canterbury Scene band, in cahoots. Yet the bassist and organist did, increasingly, have more in common with one another than they did with their old friend behind the drumkit. Or, as Mike Ratledge recalled, 'Although the so-called conspiracy between Hugh, myself and Elton covered a lot of actual differences between us, we had sufficient similarity to define ourselves against Robert.'

Third would become Soft Machine's best-selling record, in part due to the move from Probe to CBS. Behind the scenes, however, the group was disintegrating. From about the time of *Third*, Robert says, Soft Machine became 'a descent into hell'.

7

AT LEAST I WON'T BE SHOT FOR SINGING

The End of an Ear and moonlighting
with The Whole World

'Mike and I couldn't stand Robert's singing,' recalled Hugh Hopper. 'His vocals had been elbowed and he was becoming less and less happy with the way Mike Ratledge, Elton Dean and I were disregarding his ideas. By then we simply couldn't stand him and he became very discouraged – he wouldn't have dared present a piece of music because it would be a song, so he started doing other things.'

Looking for an escape hatch, Wyatt began moonlighting with Kevin Ayers' new group, The Whole World. Rather than a return to the old Soft Machine, it was a taste of what that band could have been: free jazz meets happy-go-lucky, hallucinogenic pop. It was a remarkable band, with the composer David Bedford on keyboards (he was notorious for placing a brick on the keys to create a discordant drone); saxophonist Lol Coxhill, a bald, boiler-suited impish improviser who seemed to have at his fingertips the entire history of jazz, from tender ballads to the squawks of free blowing; and the seventeen-year-old Mike Oldfield, initially playing bass, but moving to guitar after issuing an ultimatum to Kevin Ayers and exchanging instruments. Oldfield was a precocious

> The Whole World playing Hyde Park with, from left, Kevin, Lol Coxhill, David Bedford (obscured), Mike Oldfield and Robert.

talent, playing solos that illuminate Ayers' albums *Shooting at the Moon* and *Whatevershebringswesing* and that anticipated elements of his own work-in-progress, *Tubular Bells*.

Wyatt joined The Whole World for European dates alongside Pink Floyd, Joan Baez and Eric Clapton's Derek and the Dominos. He still recalls a particularly joyful, chaotic and 'very drunk' show in London's Hyde Park, now released as *Hyde Park Free Concert 1970*. Listening to the CD, Robert laughs that his playing sounds like jazz-rock powerhouse Jon Hiseman of Colosseum: 'I love it but it's mad, my drumming is completely bonkers. Just smashing through everything.

We're doing a bossa nova and I'm doing the whole thing like a Jon Hiseman solo. They just keep bobbing along, don't take any notice. "Oh, the drummer's off…"'

Seemingly always on the edge of collapse, the band were carried through by phenomenal musicianship and an infectious sense of carnival. It's very hard to be in a bad mood whilst listening to Kevin Ayers and The Whole World. 'Kevin had this song,' recalls Robert. 'I loved doing it. It went: "You say you like my shirt / You say you like my hat / You never say that you love me / Or anything nice like that / What about me / What about me." He started off singing it very slowly and we'd just get faster and faster until we were all sort of falling off. It was such fun.'

From a commercial perspective, the band sabotaged Ayers' songs. With his lack of interest in self-promotion, however, Kevin was more than capable of destroying his own career prospects. And, from a musical point of view, The Whole World were crucial, introducing the sound of surprise into these catchy, well-crafted compositions. It is no small testament to Kevin's writing ability that his songs could stand firm even as the scaffolding was kicked from under them.

In September, Wyatt joined Kevin Ayers and members of the London Sinfonietta at London's Queen Elizabeth Hall, to perform Bedford's setting of the William Blake poem *The Garden of Love*. At a certain point, the score called for 'six beautiful girls' to take over the instruments, while the band stop for an onstage beer break. By the time Kevin read the poem itself, the calm after the wildly improvised storm, the musical director of the London Sinfonietta had walked out in disgust.

—»)(«- —»)(«- —»)(«-

It was not only The Whole World that offered temporary respite from Soft Machine.

Keith Tippett, who describes Wyatt as 'a wonderful, warm drummer/ percussionist and also a wonderful guy to work with', asked Robert to play on his 1971 album, *Dedicated to You But You Weren't Listening*. Then came a request to join the pianist in a far more ambitious project. Named for its mammoth line-up of fifty musicians (and thus 100 legs), Centipede was an avant-garde big band, the closest England came to the outlandish Arkestra of Sun Ra.

'It was a real breakthrough,' says Robert. 'There were a lot of people in London who were doing experimental things and mixing all different stuff, but as a kind of cottage industry. Keith Tippett just did it writ large. And it was wonderful. What a happy band of people we were.'

As with The Whole World, the prevailing spirit was celebratory: when the band toured France and Holland, in autumn 1970, there were jam sessions in hotel rooms and aeroplane aisles. Centipede also allowed Robert to meet subsequent collaborators, notably South African jazz trumpeter Mongezi Feza. Having fled the apartheid regime following the Sharpeville massacre in 1963, Mongezi and his fellow Blue Notes helped to create a golden era in British jazz, epitomised by Anglo-South African big band the Brotherhood of Breath.

Robert was closest to Mongezi of all the exile South African jazz musicians. Small and wiry, the trumpeter was the baby of The Blue Notes: Dudu Pukwana said he was dwarfed by his own sandals. Yet Mongs compensated with tremendously energetic playing, sharing something with Don Cherry but more obviously rooted in the South African township tradition. 'It doesn't surprise me that Robert Wyatt fell in love with Mongs,' says Louis Moholo-Moholo, the sole surviving Blue

> Keith Tippett's jazz-rock big band Centipede, at London's Lyceum Theatre, 15 November 1970. The sharp-eyed might be able to identify Robert (central of the

Note. 'I'm happy to have fallen in love with him before Robert Wyatt. He was a fantastic trumpet player, as little as he was. His structure was so small but he had such a big sound.'

The following year, Wyatt joined Centipede in Wessex Studios to record *September Energy*, a double album stretching from fragments of song to tender brass to driving jazz-rock. Robert wrote the sleevenotes, describing the group as an insane travelling circus – and the happiest group he'd ever been in. There were other freewheeling jazz projects, too, including The Amazing Band, a free jazz collective led by cartoonist and trumpeter Mal Dean, and Symbiosis, in which Robert alternated on drums with Louis Moholo-Moholo; the group's line-up also featured Gary Windo and Mongezi Feza, both important future collaborators, as well as Soft Machine's former trombonist Nick Evans and future bassist Roy Babbington. Keith Tippett, who played electric piano with Symbiosis at first, recalls the gigs as: 'Wonderful. It was very free. We had a few tunes, which we'd refer to, but it was just a very upbeat, joyous ensemble. That would vary in size from five to twelve.'

three drummers), Robert Fripp, Elton Dean, Keith Tippett, Julie Tippetts, Gary Windo, Ian Carr, and future Softs Roy Babbington and Karl Jenkins.

Away from jazz, Robert also collaborated with Daevid Allen, who had finally been allowed back into the UK. Allen's debut album, *Banana Moon*, saw Wyatt drumming on tracks including *Fred the Fish*, the Soft Machine single that never was, and *Stoned Innocent Frankenstein*, a tribute to the band's early benefactor Wes Brunson. Robert's main contribution to the album, though, was to sing Hugh Hopper's *Memories*, a weightier and more elegiac version than the demos recorded by The Wilde Flowers. He would revisit the song in later solo work.

By far Wyatt's biggest side project, however, was his own debut solo album. CBS had offered each member of Soft Machine the chance to record an album without their bandmates, and Robert, frustrated by his narrowing role within the group, jumped at the opportunity. *The End of an Ear*, however, was not quite the record his label was expecting.

'It was a sort of aberration,' grins Wyatt. 'CBS very foolishly said we could do a record each, thinking I would do a pop record, more like *Moon in June*. But I did *The End of an Ear*, which flummoxed them – and, I think, appalled them.' Which was pretty much the case. 'Most people in the company thought I was nuts when I played them that record,' CBS A&R David Howells later confirmed. 'CBS was a big record company, and a lot of people may perhaps have misunderstood where Robert was coming from. *The End of an Ear* wasn't the album they anticipated after the success of *Third*.'

Given Wyatt's frustrations with Soft Machine, it's no surprise that CBS were expecting an album of songs. The cover artwork even declared Robert an 'out of work pop singer'. But *The End of an Ear* – the pun more prescient than perhaps he realised – is, indeed, an aberration, at least in the sense of deviating from an expected course. Wyatt didn't want only to play drums in Soft Machine jazz-rock instrumentals. But neither, it turned out, did he want to sing songs. Even the few vocals on his solo debut were voice-as-instrument scats, akin to his vocal solos with Soft Machine – albeit with more sympathetic backing. With the exception of *Las Vegas Tango* by Gil Evans, Robert composed all the music on *The End of an Ear* himself. Yet the album took its reference points from beyond pop, even beyond music: 'I wanted an aural wildlife park,' says Robert, 'an apparently self-generating soundscape, subsequently edited, rather than a predesigned one.'

Wyatt has spoken of the influence on the album of visual artists, such as Picasso and Marc Chagall, and we can just about envisage Chagall's folksy, fantastic figures floating past through the inky wash. Turbid and murky, favouring texture over melody, *The End of an Ear* is music under muslin. Yet it is also the sound of Wyatt casting off the corsets.

> 'While the cat's away, the mice will play piano': Robert Wyatt's first solo album flummoxed CBS.

'There's a word "play"', says Robert, 'which has to do a lot of different kinds of work. I tend to put them together. Play as in children playing, almost the opposite of working, and then musicians play instruments. To me, playing is playing and all the different versions of what that word can mean tend to coincide when I'm working – or playing, whatever we're going to call it.'

Although *Moon in June* was in some ways more indicative of his future direction, *The End of an Ear* also anticipated Wyatt's subsequent work. As on *Moon in June*, he used the multitracking possibilities of the studio to lay down piano and organ as well as drums and vocals – and this time there were no guest appearances from Hugh Hopper or Mike Ratledge. 'While the cat's away,' as Robert puts it, still delighted at the temerity of recording his own keyboard parts, 'the mice will play piano.'

The End of an Ear does, however, feature Soft Machine guests. Wyatt's original choices for trumpet and saxophone, Mongezi Feza and Gary Windo, were unable to make the date; instead, Elton Dean came in on saxello, while erstwhile septet member Mark Charig contributed cornet. Neville Whitehead, from Keith Tippett's group, plays bass. Other guests came from beyond jazz. On organ is the self-proclaimed 'song man' Dave Sinclair, ex-Wilde Flower and future member of Matching Mole. By far the dominant personality, though, is Wyatt himself.

To Mark Everywhere is named after Robert's half-brother, who plays piano on the record, just as *To Saintly Bridget* was named for Bridget St John, the singer-songwriter signed to John Peel's Dandelion label. Other tunes are dedicated to ex-Soft Machine trombonist Nick Evans; to Caravan; and to Daevid Allen and his girlfriend, the poet and 'space whisperer' Gilli Smyth. 'The record isn't anti-Soft Machine,' Robert explained shortly afterwards; 'it's anti-me for not being able to think clearly what I wanted to do. The dedications on the cover are no-pride-left, anybody-out-there-help type ones, claiming people by writing down their names. It was absurd. I look back on it as being a feast for some second-rate psychiatrist.'

This unhappiness might be evident to Robert only with hindsight, but to others it was obvious at the time – pervading even high-spirited projects like The Whole World. Mike Oldfield, in his autobiography, called Wyatt 'the world's most innovative drummer' and praises his humble, human vocal delivery. Yet Oldfield also recalls Robert was sinking into the quicksands of despair: 'I looked up to him tremendously; he was my hero. The downside was that he was always so depressed and unhappy, and so full of angst and misery. Occasionally he would perk up, but not very often. Being on tour with him for a few weeks at a time, I have never seen such an unhappy person.'

It wasn't only within Soft Machine that things were going wrong for Robert. Pam had spent 'a lot of time sobbing, gazing out the window, waiting for him to come home, clutching his slippers in pathetic fashion'. Now, having finally had enough of playing the passive wife, she admits to one or two 'dalliances' of her own. 'I got my own back,' she laughs. 'I had my moments. Once I sussed what life was like, and that no matter how much I stayed at home and brought my baby up and was the faithful, loving, wonderful woman it still didn't make any difference, I thought: "Well, I might as well join in."'

Pam met Pip Pyle during a run of Soft Machine shows at Ronnie Scott's in April 1970. Pip's band, Delivery, were playing upstairs. He would soon establish himself, with bands such as Gong, Hatfield and the North and National Health, as a leading drummer of the Canterbury Scene. 'There were a few months when Pam disappeared for longer and longer periods of time,' recalls Robert. 'She was being picked up by a bloke called Benj, who was a roadie for the band that Pip Pyle was in. And it turns out he was taking her back to see Pip. For a while I didn't know, and then eventually it turned out she was leading a double life. I was quite impressed really. I thought, "Blimey – that's my Pam! Go, girl!" Not one to let life pass her by.'

That it was, in fact, Pam who left Robert is perhaps surprising given the balance of power within the relationship, but Pam sees the split as inevitable: 'It was obviously just pathetic, playing at being married,' she smiles. 'I loved it, it was great, but he was away a lot of the time and

> Sam Wyatt with Pip Pyle, near Sens, France, 1971, in a photo used on the cover of Gong's *Camembert Electrique*. Daevid Allen is next to them, with the staff.

137

neither of us was being particularly true to the other – to put it politely. And I think I'd just had enough by then. So I moved in with Pip.'

Wyatt, who agrees that the split was entirely amicable, points out that he and Pam had married young: he was only in his mid-twenties when they separated. He seems genuinely untroubled by the fact that his son, Sam, was at least partially brought up by Pip Pyle. But then this was the era of free love, and within a scene in which it was not only the musical relationships that were promiscuous.

'Robert's my father but Pip was my dad,' chuckles Sam, 'because Pip was the one who brought me up.' Life with Pip – sleeping on beer barrels and washing in streams – was hardly more conventional: witness the classic hippie photo, which includes Sam alongside Pip, on the cover of *Camembert Electrique* by Gong. 'It was just a very bizarre childhood, to be honest,' Sam continues. 'I was brought up by a complete bunch of

> Robert's children, Alice (left) and Sam (right), with their half-sister Jojo.

loonies. It gave me a wonderful understanding of certain aspects of life. But it left me completely unprepared for *real* life.'

Many years later, Robert learned that he and Pam had also had a daughter. 'She wrote to me,' he recalls, 'and said, "Don't be frightened, I'm not asking you for anything, but I think you're my dad. Hello."'

Alice Pyle had been born after Pam left Dalmore Road, so everyone had assumed her father was Pip. A DNA test, however, proved otherwise. 'I knew really, I suppose,' smiles Pam, 'because she looks so like him. But we didn't think of the consequences. We just thought it was all cool, it will be fine. You think of those times, how many babies have not been brought up by the parents who conceived them? And Alice always thinks of Pip as her daddy. They all had their daddy and their *spare* daddy.'

'So,' concludes Robert, 'there's Sam at the beginning of the relationship with Pam, and a girl called Alice, who now lives in Canada, at the end. We did have, I thought, a very nice marriage, but it was hopelessly flawed by my lifestyle. And by the fact that I was meeting other people, and so was she.'

⤜⤛⤜ ⤜⤛⤜ ⤜⤛⤜

The penultimate tune on *The End of an Ear* was *To Carla, Marsha and Caroline (for Making Everything Beautifuller)*. 'Carla' was Carla Bley, the pianist, composer and bandleader best known for her extraordinary jazz opera *Escalator Over the Hill* and her work with the double bassist Charlie Haden. 'Marsha' was the American singer, actress and model Marsha Hunt who had briefly rehearsed with Soft Machine in the early days and married Mike Ratledge. She later starred in the hippie musical *Hair*, and had a child, Karis, with Mick Jagger.

The third member of the triumvirate was artist and activist Caroline Coon. One of the dedicatees of Germaine Greer's *The Female Eunuch*, she already appeared regularly on television and magazine covers. Later, for a period, she would manage The Clash. To fans of Wyatt's later band Matching Mole, however, her most intriguing role is as the subject of the lovelorn *O Caroline*.

'Caroline had an organisation called Release,' recalls Robert, 'which dealt with advice and help for people who were busted with drugs. I'd been given the impression of a brilliantly effective operation, casually improvised and spontaneous; that Caroline's strategy was simply that she and a bunch of posh girls would go and blind the police with their stilettos and get their lads off; that she'd storm into the copshop, the incarnation of Rita Hayworth, saying, "Release them at once!" But in a vertiginous learning curve, I soon realised that this initial observation was about as accurate as a tabloid headline. What Caroline's very hard-working network of lawyers and other specialists were putting into action was in fact heartwarmingly ethical and rigorously conscientious. Release was my introduction to real grassroots activism.'

It was the prospect of a benefit show for Release that first brought Robert and Caroline together, but their relationship was soon more than merely professional. 'We'd go to Ronnie Scott's,' says Caroline. 'And because Rob is very modest he won't like me saying this, but when he went into Ronnie Scott's there was an absolute buzz. Everyone loved him being there. And that, for me, was a kind of holiday because I could hide behind him. So that's how our friendship developed. Soft Machine were on the road all the time, but sometimes when Rob was in town, he would ask, "Would I like to come to Ronnie's?" Then he began inviting me to come away for the weekend – to Oslo, for instance. And for me to have a weekend off was wonderful, because Release was a twenty-four-hour enterprise.'

It is common today to paint the 1960s as naïve. Yet Release – like Shelter, Centrepoint and Crisis, all set up to fight homelessness – represented genuine socio-political advances that remained long after the pot smoke cleared. (Not that Coon herself did drugs; she didn't even drink alcohol.) At its peak, Release, a twenty-four 'underground welfare service', was dealing with a third of all drug busts in the country, as well as broader issues of civil liberties and human rights.

What linked Caroline with Carla Bley and Marsha Hunt? 'Robert invited me to Ronnie Scott's to hear Carla Bley,' replies Caroline. 'He wanted me to hear her not only because she was a performer but because she was a *composer*, too. That was Carla Bley's significance, apart from the fact that she was stunningly beautiful – but maybe that also. Marsha Hunt was stunningly beautiful, too. If he did put the three of us together, it was because he liked women with beauty and brains!'

Even nights at Ronnie's with his brainy and beautiful new girlfriend, however, couldn't distract Robert from the problems with his day job. With Centipede, The Amazing Band and The Whole World, he had been attempting to tunnel his way out of Soft Machine, yet none offered a permanent alternative. He soon found himself overwhelmed.

Bill MacCormick recalls the night, at a party in central London, when he realised how bad things had got: 'We all turned up fairly jolly, but Robert sat in a corner and within half an hour, nobody wanted to talk

> Robert with Caroline Coon, Greenwich Village, 1971.

any more. He was just oozing depression, it was terribly, terribly sad. We just didn't know what to do. I was really worried about him. He came across almost as suicidal. He just sat and didn't say a word, and slumped. I thought, "Shit, what is going on here?" Because it's so unlike him, he's usually so exuberant and bouncy and positive. And he really was in a very, very bad state.'

Although Robert tends to deflect serious discussion of his emotional lowpoints with self-deprecating humour, he now believes he was having a breakdown, brought on by the feeling that he was being squeezed out of his own group in a jazz-rock coup d'état. On one occasion, he recalls walking up and down Holland Park Avenue, banging his head against each tree he passed. 'I'd go up to each tree and whack my skull into it. And, looking back on it, that's quite odd.'

'When you form a band like Robert did,' suggests Caroline Coon, 'you are in love with your band, you *are* the band. It is your identity. And when the band fractures, your heart breaks and your identity is pulverised. It can feel like the most crucial, fecund years of your life are reduced to nothing.'

'Unlike Mike,' she goes on, 'Rob wanted to make music that was sensual, that you could dance to, that was popular, that was romantic and also intelligent and broad. The whole of Rob's personality was to rush out with open arms into the abundant musical world, rather than narrowing the musical world down.'

⊸» «⊸ ⊸» «⊸ ⊸» «⊸

In October 1970, just six months after the sessions for *Third*, Soft Machine went into London's Olympic Studios to record a new record. Named, naturally, *Fourth*, it was the first Soft Machine album to feature the same core line-up as its predecessor. Yet it was clear, almost from the opening waft of wah-wah, that they had taken another step towards jazz-rock even since *Third*. *Fourth* features two Hugh Hopper numbers, including the four-part suite *Virtually*, while the highlight is Mike Ratledge's ambitious opener, *Teeth*. Completing the tracklist was Elton Dean's first composition for Soft Machine, the free-jazz indebted *Fletcher's Blemish*. The one member not named in the writing credits is Robert Wyatt.

Not coincidentally, the album is entirely instrumental: Robert's battle to maintain an element of song, and the Pataphysical spirit of 1967, had finally been lost. 'Soft machine', when William Burroughs used the term, had been a reference to the human body. Shorn of Wyatt's vocals and compositional input, however, the humour and humanity of the band's early days is nowhere to be found.

Released in February 1971, *Fourth* was judged by *Rolling Stone* magazine 'both better and no better than *Third*' – which is not only nonsensical but, with the benefit of hindsight, plain wrong. Tellingly, while Hopper, Dean, 'the amazing Ratledge' and even Roy Babbington, the Symbiosis bassist who had come in as a session player, are referred to by name in the *Rolling Stone* review, Wyatt is not mentioned once.

By this stage, the two sides of the band even *looked* different. Mike, Hugh and Elton each sported a handlebar moustache. Mike wore dark glasses, even in the studio at times, and onstage wore an overcoat with upturned collar: he could have been an undercover agent in a 1970s cop

> The odd man out: the Softs line up for *Fourth*, Robert's last album with the band.

show. Wyatt, with his five o'clock shadow, was by contrast every bit the unkempt rock star.

'I think there were two quite explicit charismatic masculinities on display in Soft Machine,' says Caroline Coon. 'There was the charisma of Rob and his nakedness and long hair flowing, and the charisma of Mike Ratledge, wearing a jacket and his hair longish but like a helmet – a steel helmet. Mike Ratledge was in front, this rigid, steel pole. And Robert, in another spotlight, in the background, was weaving and flowing like a golden river.'

For all the problems that already existed with Mike and Hugh, Robert identifies the end of the septet as the tipping point for him with the band: the moment that Elton Dean was promoted from session musician to full band member. To the already deepening divide between Mike and Hugh, more or less in one camp, and Robert, forlornly clinging to his role as a vocalist in another, was then added a *third* camp, pulling towards free jazz.

'Elton decided to assert himself at that point and start to say how things should go,' sighs Robert, clearly uncomfortable discussing the subject. 'If you ask somebody to be a fourth member, that's perfectly reasonable, that's presumably what it means. But actually, musically, I didn't think he had anything like Hugh or Mike's acuity, or understanding of what that particular group's potential was. It was unique, it wasn't some group you could just turn into any other group.'

Of course, others might argue that was exactly what defined the whole history of The Soft Machine. Graham Bennett, in *Out-Bloody-Rageous*, muses over the existence of five distinct bands, even before Elton joined the band: the 'freak-out quartet, the 1967/68 psychedelic trio, the 1969 power trio and the big-band septet.' None of the bands, none of the records, really sounded alike.

That acknowledged, Elton was, in a sense, the first outsider to join the band. Born in Nottingham and brought up in South London, he had developed as a musician during the British R'n'B boom, playing with Long John Baldry's Bluesology before moving into jazz alongside Keith Tippett. (As trivia fans will know, Bluesology keyboard player Reg Dwight would borrow the forenames of both Dean and Baldry to reinvent himself as Elton John.)

Wyatt is keen to point out Dean's strengths: 'Elton was a fanatic, elastic, gymnastic, everything-else-tic player of difficult music. Fast, with a lively, vibrant, vibrating tone. Playing solos over difficult chord sequences and time signatures: he was virtuosic at that, absolutely brilliant.' Yet though he might have been expected to sympathise with the saxophonist's attempts to move away from rigid composition, Robert saw free jazz as a strictly extracurricular activity. Within Soft Machine, he wanted to combine hints of free improvisation with a solid foundation in song, roughly along the same lines as Kevin Ayers and The Whole World. Simply emulating a Miles Davis drummer like Billy Cobham or Jack DeJohnette had little appeal.

'Elton would write a tune,' Robert recalls, 'and I'd start improvising on it. He'd say, "Why can't you just play like Jack DeJohnette? That's this kind of tune." I'd say, "That's *exactly* why I can't play like Jack DeJohnette on it – *because it is that kind of tune*. It's the one thing you know I'm not going to do." And it really pissed him off.' Wyatt was very much familiar with pioneering free-jazz drummers such as Milford Graves and Sunny Murray. Yet, as Elton Dean pushed towards free jazz, Robert moved in the opposite direction, adopting the raw, pile-driver power of Led Zeppelin's John Bonham.

Perhaps what Wyatt calls his 'reckless counter-playing' was evidence of a recalcitrant streak. It was also evidence of his technical prowess. Mike and Hugh's melodies may twist and turn like a skier in a mogul field, but Robert's playing is not that of a man desperately counting barlengths in his head. More than anything, though, the counter-

144

playing was a musical decision. By combining Bonham's punch with the adroitness of Dave Brubeck drummer Joe Morello, Robert was refusing to choose between pre-existing pigeonholes. 'There's got to be this tension between what you know and what you don't know, all the time,' he explains. 'If you're doing a free thing, it's got to be in a context where it's going somewhere, or it's going against something else. Otherwise it's just flaccid. To play free jazz drums over a cockney rhythm, then *that's* something! You don't just let go all the reins and see where the horses go. That's not the point. You take them over difficult rocks and crannies, but you don't just let go of the reins.'

This tension is what would keep Robert's own music unique. Soft Machine, on the other hand, were moving towards the generic. The band's collective technical abilities had increased beyond measure since the days of UFO club, and that virtuosity had, for a period, produced some of the most enduring music of the era. By *Fourth*, however, they were starting to rely on technique more than ideas – and were for the first time producing music that could have been played by a band other than Soft Machine.

'My trouble with Soft Machine at the end was that the possibilities, as it was so-called "becoming more advanced", were actually narrowing right

>John Peel's Christmas *Top Gear* programme for 1970 assembled a choir of rock musicians, including various members of the Softs, The Faces, T. Rex and Curved Air, and Lol Coxhill. Robert duetted with Ronnie Wood on *Good King Wenceslas* – 'achingly beautiful,' Peel recalled; 'I can't listen to it dry-eyed.'

145

down,' says Robert. 'Less and less actual stuff could come in, the format was getting tighter and tighter. That was the problem. So my vanity bridles a bit when people say, "Did Soft Machine get too intellectual for you?" I did understand what they were doing, and I could have carried on doing it, I think – well, had I sobered up.'

To some extent the result of his sense of alienation, Wyatt's increasingly heavy drinking only alienated him further. He says the rest of the band found his lifestyle 'vulgar'. 'We are talking about people from a fairly straight-laced background. As hip as they were in terms of intellectual ideas, the idea of living the degenerate life did not appeal. I think they were right in the end. I regret my great wallowing in degenerate behaviour.' In fact, Robert was hardly a typical lager lout – and not just because, to use his own term, he was always more of a wino. They might have hit the tequila and Southern Comfort together but, according to Hugh Hopper, Robert didn't have much in common with the drummer in The Who. 'He wasn't like a Keith Moon or anything like that,' said the bassist. 'Nothing at all like that. Because he still had that very civilised intelligence. So he wasn't that wild. He was sort of a civilised person, Robert, I think. He was kind of ambushed by alcohol, really.'

Hugh's brother Brian says Wyatt's boozing hadn't been too bad back when he had been playing saxophone with Soft Machine, but it got worse and worse – from about the time when Elton Dean joined the band as a full member. It may not, he agrees, have been a coincidence: 'Robert, musically, was getting increasingly frustrated,' he explains, 'and maybe that was one of the reasons he took more to the drink. He was still wanting to do songs, basically. He's very much a song man, which is the original reason he moved from drums to vocals in The Wilde Flowers. He never really wanted to give that up.'

'I think that led to disillusionment on the part of Mike and Hugh,' continues Brian. 'He wasn't always performing up to his best. In fact, he often was late getting onstage and this sort of thing. He just wasn't *there* all the time, properly.' Journalist Michael Watts, who accompanied Soft Machine on a short tour of Holland during the recording of *Fourth*, reported that Wyatt actually broke down in tears after a show in Rotterdam, 'storming into one dressing room at the interval while the rest of the band went into another.'

What is remarkable, however, is how little of the tension was evident onstage. The journalist Steve Lake recalled the atmosphere at a typical gig of the era as follows: 'The place is packed, tense with heightened sense of expectation that you still had at rock gigs in 69/70/71. (A sense of: "Wow, I wonder what amazing new things I'm about to hear." You weren't there for the "hits".) Tape loops play as the lights dim – like the *Out-Bloody-Rageous* intro – tape loops continue to play... and play... and play... People look at their watches. Finally the Soft Machine wander onstage, usually direct from the pub across the road, with all their outdoor gear on. Coats, scarves, hats. They're laughing, Wyatt and Dean continuing to share a joke while Ratledge arranges his leather coat on the back of his chair and Hopper fiddles with amplifier knobs and foot pedals. Wyatt pulls his T-shirt off, shakes his hair over his face, takes a last gulp from a bottle of beer and then – blam! – they're off, deadly serious as they steer the enormous sound of this band through the demanding charts... the room vibrates with the sheer, exhilarating power of it.'

This painfully English passive aggression was reminiscent of the split between Syd Barrett and the rest of Pink Floyd. 'Robert swallowed his unhappiness a lot,' Elton Dean later recalled. 'There were things going on within that trio, barely spoken but felt. Robert's pieces were dropped one by one until he would just try and incorporate his voice into the improvisation, which probably wasn't enough for him.' 'Because we were sort of middle class white chappies from England,' explained Hugh Hopper, 'we didn't hit each other – which probably would have got it over with much quicker.'

For those who share Wyatt's belief that the band was at its best when it featured vocals, it is tempting to take Robert's side in the rift. The fact that all three bandmates ultimately took against him, however, is a reminder that Robert must, as he readily admits, have become almost impossible to work with. The period can't have been a barrel of laughs for the rest of the band, either. Mike Ratledge later said that Soft Machine's peak, in terms of human relationships, was around the time of their debut album. *Third*, he asserted, a little ironically, was 'probably the last time I enjoyed what I was doing'.

Today, not untypically, Wyatt lays much of the blame on his own shoulders. 'In retrospect, I feel sorry for Mike,' he sighs. 'They'd sort of moved on musically, and I had regressed. But at the same time, they did know – I assume they remembered – that I had actually got them together. In fact, my best contribution to Soft Machine, I think, was that I got Hugh playing with Mike, and then I got Elton helping play Mike's tunes. And they wouldn't have met, they don't come from the same background at all. I was the common bond, which worked very well. Except that the only bit that didn't work properly was me.'

'I'm reminded of this,' he goes on, 'because someone showed me an old film of our rehearsal for Soft Machine *Fourth*. They're working away at this thing and Mike's saying: "It's got to be so many microseconds per beat, and it's varying slightly, slightly faster here and there." They're all working on it. And I wander in from the drumkit with a suggestion for Elton, and they all look away, embarrassed, until I've stopped, and then they carry on their conversation. You can see they're just thinking, "Fucking hell…" But they couldn't just say, "Let's get another drummer straight away," because I *had* got them together.'

⊷⊶ ⊷⊶ ⊷⊶

After a handful of UK shows, including a headline slot at the Royal Festival Hall in April 1971, Soft Machine went to America for the first time since the Hendrix tour three years previously. Relations between Wyatt and the rest of the band had deteriorated to the point that manager Sean Murphy asked Caroline Coon to come, too: quite an ask for a non-drinker.

On paper, the three-week tour was a triumph, a run of shows at the Gaslight club in New York going so well that early hero Ornette Coleman invited the band to a party in his loft. On 20 and 21 July, Soft Machine went one better, supporting Miles Davis at New York's Beacon Theatre. The band were, in many ways, playing the right music at the right time. Elton Dean recalled that 'it was a fabulous time to be in New York. We gigged opposite Miles's last good band – with Keith Jarrett – and there was Herbie Hancock's new sextet, Mahavishnu's first gigs…'

Behind the scenes, however, the American dates were disastrous. Caroline, who recalls Robert as 'drinking but keeping it together', remembers 'an undercurrent of strife' within the touring party. According to Elton Dean, 'Robert started to walk offstage in the middle of gigs. Then he'd wander back on later. He'd had enough.'

Things only got worse when they got back from the States. 'There were nights when we would make fun of Robert behind his back,' Hugh Hopper later admitted. 'It really had got that bad. Mike and I couldn't stand Robert and he couldn't stand us. We were very cool and calculated whereas Robert was very open and impulsive.'

'During one evening of drunkenness at Ronnie Scott's,' the bassist continued, 'he said to someone, "I wish I could find another band." The rest of us leapt on it and said, "Right, go on then." Robert was definitely pushed out of what he felt was his own group.'

> The man without shades – Robert Wyatt's last European tour with Soft Machine in Oslo, 1971.

By autumn, the split was official, with *Melody Maker* carrying the front page headline 'Wyatt quits Softs'.

-»)(«- -»)(«- -»)(«-

For Soft Machine, Wyatt's departure was only another twirl of the revolving door. Elton's friend and collaborator Phil Howard initially took Robert's place on drums, although he was soon replaced by John Marshall from Nucleus. Elton Dean left in 1972 and was replaced by Karl Jenkins, another Nucleus alumnus who soon became the group's driving force. His incarnation of the band was easy to admire but, for fans of the early material, hard to love.

Wyatt quits Softs

R OBERT Wyatt, drummer and singer with the Soft Machine, has left the band.

The reason for his departure is believed to be a difference of musical opinion, apparent for some months, which crystalised during the band's recent and highly-successful American tour.

A member of the Softs since their very earliest days in Canterbury, Wyatt left them for a short period last year when, for the same reasons, he went to play with Kevin Ayers and The Whole World. He returned when he found that Ayers' outfit came no closer to realising his musical ambitions.

Wyatt's replacement in the Soft Machine will be Phil Howard, who has for some months been a member of the part-time quartet of Soft's altoist Elton Dean.

Hugh Hopper left Soft Machine in 1973 and was replaced by Roy Babbington. 'I was starting to get bored,' he explained. 'The band weren't exciting enough – we weren't getting on anymore – particularly when Karl joined. I didn't particularly like him personally and I found his music third-rate and third-hand.' Mike Ratledge, too, finally left in 1976. 'Mike couldn't say no,' said Elton Dean. 'He told me once that he should have left the band three or four years earlier. He let it peter out. He was still there and he wasn't enjoying it. He didn't do anything about it, so it affected his musicality until he hated performing.'

Despite the loss of all its founding members, a band calling itself Soft Machine continued until 1984, long after the departure of all founding members. Highly talented musicians continued to join the band, including guitarists Allan Holdsworth, John Etheridge and former Cream bassist Jack Bruce. Yet, like the proverbial axe that's had three new heads and two new handles, the latter incarnations of the band qualified as Soft Machine in name only.

Looked at from the outside, and in retrospect, Robert seems lucky to have been shot of the group by 1971. Perhaps the only pity is that he didn't jump ship a little earlier in favour of hedonistic tours with Kevin Ayers and The Whole World. We know now that he would go on to a solo career that to most ears surpassed his stint with Soft Machine – and which is without a doubt superior to anything released by the Softs without Wyatt.

Despite the *Melody Maker* headline, however, Wyatt wasn't really quitting the Softs. He was, at best, half-pushed – and the sense of rejection, that 'even having given up vocals, I was still not good enough for them', was crushing. Though he might have talked of leaving the band, the circumstances of his departure led to feelings of ineptitude, which he himself links to those he had felt as a sixth-former: 'I'd first of all had this "not good enough for grammar school", he sighs, 'and the consequence was, I should have realised, not being good enough for bands run by grammar-school boys.'

Band splits are notoriously contentious, bringing to a sudden end the intimacy of collective creativity and the shared history of successes and failures both large and small. For Wyatt the difficulties were particularly intense, having known Mike and Hugh since school, and having lived with his bandmates in Dulwich even when not on the road.

'I was orphaned in a way,' he reflects. 'My dad died and I hadn't got a home to go to. My mother was still alive, but Soft Machine, I felt, was my family. And, of course, that's almost unhealthy in a way. It's not fair on other grown adults, with their own families and their own lives, to assume that they're family.'

'When Soft Machine dumped me,' Robert goes on, 'I totally agreed with them, and I thought, "Can I come too? It's not fair, I agree with you, can I come? This is crap. I'm not allowed to leave me." And the same with anything like that, with any girlfriend or my first wife or whatever it might be. I always sort of agreed with them. I thought, "I am doing the best that I can, actually, and I do agree it's not good enough." And that's been a constant theme.'

Robert insists that being thrown out of Soft Machine was more traumatic than breaking his back two years later – and it is the band, rather than his legs, that caused the lingering phantom pains. 'It's still painfully embarrassing to deal with,' he confesses. 'I still have nightmares about it, which is extraordinary after this number of years. Nightmares all veering around getting onstage with them and not being able to play, not knowing what to play, or I can't remember the names of the tunes or what order they're in. And all the audience coming in, and panicking. Or I'm there with my drumkit and they don't know who I am. Things like that, endless variations.'

8

I MAY PLAY ON A DRUM

Matching Mole – and Robert meets Alfie

At the time he was kicked out of Soft Machine, Robert – who had left Dulwich shortly after the split with Pam – was living in a house on Hampstead Way with record producer Ian 'Sammy' Samwell, DJ Jeff Dexter and singer-songwriter Linda Lewis. Dexter describes the house as full of people 'tripping and getting stoned'. But, while everyone else was getting high, he adds, Robert was getting low.

'In those last few weeks that we were lovers,' Caroline Coon recalls, 'evenings would end with Rob very, very unhappy, extremely distressed, extremely drunk, saying he wanted to kill himself. And I couldn't stop the drinking. I believed there were two things going on to cause Rob to drink to excess and feel suicidal. There was the heartbreak at the band breaking up, and his personal lack of self-confidence and self-worth.'

Wyatt might have been too puritanical for drugs, but his self-destructive streak manifested itself in drinking. The booze also provided a shield against anxiety. 'I find that an unblinking look at reality sears the eyeballs,' Robert explains. 'Drink and drugs is an escape route. If you really want to wallow in angst, the way to do it is to be drunk. Set 'em up, Joe, one more for the road, all that. It's a time-honoured and famous way, isn't it? And I completely understand – I have to and I do – addicts of various sorts who drown their sorrows with artificial stimuli. Putting a light on at night is artificial but it keeps the dark away.'

The artificial stimulus was required, perhaps, to overcome his break-ups from both Soft Machine and Pam. But there were difficulties in his new relationship, too: used to calling the shots in previous relationships, Robert had met his match in Caroline Coon. 'He had his private life and I had mine,' says Caroline. 'We were seeing each other, we were lovers, but he's a rock'n'roller! I am absolutely not going to ask what he is doing when he is not with me. I wanted nothing from him except good love and good company.'

Judging by the lyrics to *O Caroline*, the song Robert would later write about the relationship, Robert had anticipated their becoming 'man and wife'. Yet Caroline was adamant that, however much she loved him, she was never going to get married – to Robert or to anyone else. 'I didn't realise until a few years later,' she asserts, 'that if I were to avoid men the embarrassment of me refusing to marry them, I'd have to announce to the world that I was a confirmed spinster.'

Perhaps Robert, only human, wasn't quite as happy at the idea of Caroline seeing other people as he was with the freedom to see other people himself. Caroline says it would be 'best to assume' that they were both seeing other people during their relationship, and even recalls being introduced to an 'exquisitely beautiful' French woman whom she assumed was another of Robert's girlfriends. (This was Cyrille, Kevin Ayers' ex-wife, who had played percussion on *The End of an Ear*). 'Robert wasn't monogamous,' shrugs Jeff Dexter. 'But none of us were monogamous in those days, not really. It was free love, man.'

Like his ejection from Soft Machine, difficulties in the relationship with Caroline only dented Wyatt's already fragile sense of self-worth. Eventually, in an echo of his adolescent bout of depression, Robert proved that talk of attempting to take his own life was entirely serious. 'I remember the evening when I finally had enough,' says Caroline. 'We'd gone back up to Hampstead from Ronnie Scott's and Rob was in a terrible state, having to be restrained. I think there was sick and blood – he might have cut his wrists. I stood back from the melee and this big black hole opened up before my eyes. It was really horrific.'

Though candid in discussing his teenage suicide attempt, Robert is less willing to talk about trying to take his own life in the early 1970s. Instead, he simply points to the scars that still mar the inside of each wrist. 'I got very drunk,' he says, quickly and quietly, 'and slit my wrists in a bath somewhere. And was woken up in a cold bath and rushed to hospital and stitched up again.'

Following Robert's suicide attempt, Linda Lewis recalled, the women in the commune 'drew straws to decide which of us was going to comfort him. I was chosen. It was supposed to be a cuddle, a life-saving cuddle. One thing led to another and I can only say that if life-saving is always as good as that, I want to volunteer for the St John Ambulance.'

The suicide attempt marked the end of Robert's relationship with Caroline Coon. She makes it clear, though, that she 'stepped aside not for lack of love for Rob – actually, quite the opposite. I felt that if I couldn't argue any more with Rob about suicide, I was a dangerous person for him to be with. I wasn't going to be any help to him. He needed somebody to be with him who still had the energy and time to argue against suicide. And not only that – there were my feelings and safety to consider. Being around someone suicidal was dangerous for me. I was battling with my own bad family experiences, my own depressions and insecurities.'

With what he admits was a lack of sensitivity, Jeff Dexter asked Wyatt to move out of Hampstead Way. Robert describes the period after this as torment. 'I just dossed at people's houses – at Mark Boyle and Joan Hills's place, and at Steve and Jenny Peacock's. I was in such a state, I can hardly remember – although they probably do, because it must have been nightmarish. Gone. I had nothing, absolutely nothing.' Robert's half-sister Prue agrees that Robert 'went completely to pieces' at this time, becoming acutely anxious. His drinking remained heavy, too, perhaps one reason why he himself says there are plenty of things during this period of which he has 'no memory at all, none whatsoever'.

'We have an alcohol problem in our family,' states Prue, adding that their mother, Honor, liked a drink – 'how she stayed upright sometimes, I do not know ' – and that Robert's maternal grandmother actually died as a result of alcoholism. It is, she says, a family failing.

–»)(«– –»)(«– –»)(«–

Although foundering desperately in his personal life, offers of work continued to arrive. The 'Wyatt quits Softs' headline appeared on 4 September 1971. Before the end of the year, Robert had played the Royal Albert Hall with Centipede and performed, at the suggestion of Annette Peacock, with Canadian avant-garde pianist Paul Bley. In November, he played several dates at the Berlin Jazz Festival alongside vibraphone player Gary Burton, guitarist Terje Rypdal and violinists Jean-Luc Ponty and Don 'Sugar Cane' Harris.

Wyatt also remained on good terms with fellow Soft Machine refugees, his celestial backing vocals gracing the chorus of Kevin Ayers' *Whatevershebringswesing*: 'Let's drink some wine / And have a good time / But if you really want to come through / Let the good time, good time have you'. In terms of a more permanent role, some expected Robert to start playing drums with Gong, led by Daevid Allen. Karl Jenkins suggested that he join his band, jazz-rock act Nucleus, after their drummer John Marshall moved to Soft Machine in January 1972. There was even a possibility that Robert might play drums with Stone the Crows, the Glasgow blues band fronted by vocalist Maggie Bell.

No existing band, however, could fully accommodate Robert's desire to be both singer and drummer, to play both simple songs and extended instrumentals. Instead, he began to work on material of his own.

'I had to put something together,' Robert later explained. 'Because it's very difficult to find bands to work in. I mean, very often if you're a drummer or a singer, there's some opportunity to join this band or that band. But the particular way in which I like to operate – which is, you know, I might want to do songs, but I might want at least as much instrumental, and I might want to have a few very accessible pieces, and a few pieces where we try everything we can think of on them – there wasn't any band to join where you could do that in. So the only way was to find some sympathetic friends and carry on. But people who, even if they didn't like you singing, didn't have the power to stop you.'

In later years, Robert would become known for taking long gaps between records. At this stage, though, he remained driven, bordering on manic. Still on the rebound from Soft Machine, and smarting from their continuing use of the name, he must have found the new project a welcome distraction. When naming his new act, he couldn't resist a punning two fingers to his former bandmates: the prime audience for Soft Machine had been France, and the French for 'Soft Machine' was '*machine molle*'. Dave Sinclair, who had played on *The End of an Ear* and until recently been a member of Caravan, joined Matching Mole on keyboards. Phil Miller, who had played alongside Pip Pyle, Lol Coxhill and Roy Babbington in Delivery, was invited to play guitar. Completing the line-up, on bass, was Robert's former neighbour, Bill MacCormick.

> The original Matching Mole line-up, clockwise from top: Dave Sinclair, Phil Miller, Bill MacCormick and Robert Wyatt.

Wyatt rented the band a flat in West London as rehearsal space – and, if mattresses on the floor deserve the term, band dormitory. Just as Soft Machine had made Dulwich their HQ, this so-called Canterbury band was in fact based in Notting Hill. Wyatt remembers the St Luke's Mews flat warmly, aside from the fleas in the carpet: 'It was a bit like walking through a piranha river.'

Once Dave Sinclair's piano had arrived from Canterbury, the band tried out one or two Sinclair compositions, as well as *Moon in June*, George Harrison's *Beware of Darkness* and Gil Evans's *Las Vegas Tango* from *The End of an Ear*. Now and again, they would swap instruments.

'We were playing around with all sorts of things,' recalls Bill MacCormick. 'It really was pretty vague at the time. There was no real this-is-what-we're-going-to-do vision at all.'

Even so, Wyatt had accrued enough of a following during his five years with Soft Machine for CBS to offer his new band a deal. And so, in late December 1971 and January 1972, mere weeks after their formation, Matching Mole found themselves in CBS studios recording their self-titled debut album.

--» «-- --» «-- --» «--

After leaving Caravan, Dave Sinclair had hitchhiked to southern Portugal. He arrived there to find a telegram from Robert: 'Come back, your country needs you.' Having lured him home with the Lord Kitchener telegram, Robert visited the keyboard player in Wraik Hill, near Whitstable, to hear his recent compositions.

'I just kept playing through songs,' recalls Sinclair. 'We got to one song and he said: "Oh, can you play that one again?" And I played it again. He said: "Have you got lyrics?" I said: "Well, I've got partly written lyrics." He said: "Would you mind if I wrote lyrics for it, and we record it?" I said: "No, that's alright." And that was, of course, *O Caroline*.'

It is sometimes suggested that Wyatt's particular emotional timbre – that sense of thin-skinned vulnerability and pained sincerity – arrived with his paraplegia. But one need only listen to *O Caroline* to hear that it predated the fall; the track squeezed into just five minutes all the emotion missing from Soft Machine's *Fourth*.

'I remember putting the piano and organ parts down,' recalls Dave Sinclair, 'and by then it was evening, time to pack up. But Robert worked through the whole night. When we came back the next morning to carry on recording, he was still there. We walked in and he said: "Have a listen to this." And then played it to us. He'd put the Mellotron on, the vocal, everything, through the night. I thought it was magic, it was really great. And it was so honest as well, because it was coming from inside him. It was pouring out.'

Songs reputedly about Caroline Coon include Bob Dylan's *She Belongs to Me* and The Stranglers' *London Lady*. Yet, where The Stranglers are caustic and Dylan enigmatic, Wyatt approaches his love song with a combination of candour and English understatement – and just enough self-awareness to admit that the whole piece may be dismissed as 'sentimental crap'. The chorus – 'I love you still, Caroline / I want you still, Caroline / I need you still, Caroline' – could hardly be simpler, but it hits home like a Chinese burn to the heart.

Caroline Coon has understandably mixed feelings about Wyatt's song, and even Robert is uncomfortable about *O Caroline*. 'Old records are like old tattoos,' as he would later reflect. His concern with this particular tattoo, he admits, is that 'it just seems to me a bit rude to my other girlfriends at the time.' It's hard to fathom quite what Robert wanted from his relationship with Caroline and, even today his comments can be contradictory. At times, he claims that the tune was really about his separation from Soft Machine – 'it's a totally metaphorical song' – while at others he admits what is, given the title, tricky to deny: that it is an open love letter to his ex-girlfriend. It can, perhaps, be both: the sound of a man dumped twice over.

As an album opener, the straightforward *O Caroline* made for quite a statement after the complexity of Soft Machine's *Fourth*. The song was even deemed sufficiently poppy to release as a single. And it has endured, in the Wyatt canon and beyond.

The B-side to the single was another album track, a deconstructed pop song named *Signed Curtain*. Lyn Dobson remembers Wyatt jamming this tune back in the days of the Soft Machine septet, and a version of the song appears on a recording back in 1968, where it is named *Chelsa*. The new title was intended to convey closure: 'I liked the idea of a curtain coming down,' explains Wyatt, 'like at the end of a show. And signed, like the signature at the end of a painting. They're both like, *that's it. Signed Curtain* was meant to be my final pop song. 'You know how Johnny Rotten says, "I'm making the last ever rock record?" That was the feeling. I wanted to write the absolute bare bones, terminal pop song. Just, what is it? It's a verse and a chorus and a bridge, another verse. The pursuit of a kind of authenticity, really, just trying to say something that was true.'

Like *O Caroline*, *Signed Curtain* was musically simpler than anything released by Soft Machine, even in the era of Daevid Allen and Kevin Ayers. Also like *O Caroline*, the song's lyrics are fundamental, with Wyatt breaking down the fourth wall to draw attention to the song's very construction: 'This is the first verse, this is the first verse, this is the first verse,' he sings. 'And this is the chorus / or perhaps it's the bridge / or just another part of the song / that I'm singing'.

Finally, with the joke wearing thin, Robert abandons the distancing devices for the disarmingly frank closing lines: 'Never mind, it doesn't hurt / It only means that I / Lost faith in this song / Because it won't help me reach you.' The listener is free to decide whether that 'you' refers to

Caroline or his erstwhile bandmates. Either way, the sense of despair, mingled with the Pataphysics, is palpable. *Signed Curtain* is saved from triteness by the same thing that rescues *O Caroline* from being sentimental crap: Robert's unimpeachable sincerity.

-»)) ((«- -»)) ((«- -»)) ((«-

Journalist Steve Lake recalls the impact of tunes such as *O Caroline* and *Signed Curtain* during early Matching Mole performances: 'On the last Ratledge/Hopper/Wyatt/Dean shows I'd seen, Robert's vocal contribution was shrinking from gig to gig. 'This was a source of regret, although I still thought the concerts were fantastic. But when Matching Mole started their debut show with *Signed Curtain*, that was a big emotional moment. More than I'd hoped for – a song! For the first time in how long?'

Had they heard only those two tunes, CBS would finally have had their Robert Wyatt pop album. However, *O Caroline* and *Signed Curtain* were far from representative. Although Robert had at first envisaged an album of love songs, Matching Mole's debut in fact unfolds as a predominantly instrumental, full-band record. *Part of the Dance*, the only piece on which Wyatt has no composer credit, was a nine-minute rock jam bookended by a monster Phil Miller riff. *Immediate Curtain* called to mind the ambient strains of Tangerine Dream, while Robert's voice-as-instrument contributions to *Instant Pussy* and *Instant Kitten* were reminiscent of *The End of an Ear*.

With its combination of more or less solo songs and full-band instrumentals, the album lacked coherence – a weakness exacerbated by the fact that the band had gone into the studio before they had played a single gig. Recording sessions for the album were also fraught with problems. 'All sorts of things went wrong,' sighs Bill MacCormick, who, to make matters worse, had his Fender bass stolen just before the sessions, forcing him to find his way around a short-scale Gibson. 'The studio was very, very cold, and because of that, tuning the instruments was difficult. The tape machine was running at varying speeds – that wasn't by design, that was by mistake. Equipment kept breaking down, things kept dropping out. It was terrible. It really was a disaster. And of course, to add to the fun, it was one of those Heath-inspired industrial crises where there were power cuts all the time.'

'It was a very big studio,' recalls Dave Sinclair, who had to wear gloves to record his keyboard parts, 'and as far as I remember, there was a

> The first Matching Mole album, released in April 1972, just months after Robert had put the band together.

little one-bar electric burner. One bar, about a foot long, of heat in the building. We were all huddled around that before doing takes, warming our hands, and then we'd rush off to our instruments and do the take. It was a little bit bizarre.'

Matching Mole, which featured two bespectacled – and, naturally, identical – moles on its cover, was released on 14 April 1972. 'What we have here, ladies and gentlemen,' announced Richard Williams in *Melody Maker*, 'is a band on the first rung of its creative ladder – and already they could cut to ribbons almost any band you could think of.' Ian MacDonald noted in the *NME* that, although musically shaky, the album 'devastates anything by the corporate cool smoothie the Soft Machine has become in the last two years sheerly in terms of musical engagement.' It's worth remembering that MacDonald was the elder brother of Matching Mole bassist Bill MacCormick and had changed his surname precisely to avoid charges of nepotism. Yet his critical instincts here are spot on. So was his claim, in the same review, that 'the album is primarily about misery'.

Wyatt himself admits that he was very insecure during the period: 'lacking a sense of being anchored', as he puts it. That unmoored quality is most obvious on *O Caroline*, but even the instrumental numbers are saturated with personal and professional heartbreak. *Dedicated to Hugh But You Weren't Listening* is a clear allusion to Hugh Hopper's almost identically titled track on Soft Machine's *Volume Two*. Swirling and immersive, with the occasional screech but also a seductive sense of surrender, *Instant Pussy* could be the sound of a man drowning.

One problem was that Matching Mole remained in the shadow of Wyatt's former band. 'It's worse than it was in the early days of the Softs,' complained Robert, 'because then we could live with my mum and practise in the front room, with slightly less panic about rent or food.'

Each member received a weekly retainer from Sean Murphy, although the relationship is not recalled with fondness. Bassist Bill MacCormick, who describes their manager as 'a fucking shit', insists that they never saw a penny from either album – at least until long after the group's demise. 'The finances of the band were appalling from start to finish,' he recalls. 'I actually had jobs from time to time. I worked in the civil service as a temporary clerical officer for six months. I wasn't paid a huge deal of money, but it was a good deal more than anybody else had. I actually paid the rest of the band for quite a period of time during the early weeks, because there was no money coming in. I was paying Phil Miller's rent. It was ridiculous.'

It wasn't just the finances that were getting Wyatt down. Musically, Matching Mole were struggling to find a direction, in part due to Robert's own restlessness. The line-up, originally assembled to play songs, was ill-suited to instrumental jams. Dave Sinclair was a talented songwriter, rather than a virtuoso soloist. Bill MacCormick, meanwhile, had only been playing bass guitar for one year, and freely admits that he was 'the least musically experienced and knowledgeable of anybody in the band by a very, very long way'. Robert, however, insists that he was 'a terrific bass player, athletic and imaginative'.

Further complicating matters was the fact that Robert, though essentially the leader, was not finding it easy to stamp his authority on his bandmates. And, while the social aspect of Matching Mole worked far better than it had in the latter days of The Soft Machine, no new band could easily attain the sort of creative dynamic built up over almost a decade with musicians such as Hugh Hopper. On a personal level, too,

Wyatt had yet to fully recover from his multiple break-ups: from Pam, from Caroline, from Soft Machine. Yet the *annus horribilis* of 1971 would soon be over – and there were clearer skies beyond the arrow shower.

—»)(«— —»)(«— —»)(«—

Matching Mole's first gig was at Hydraspace in Watford, northwest of London, on 22 January 1972. 'I could not stand up,' recalls Bill MacCormick. 'My legs had gone completely. I literally got off stage and collapsed, I'd been so nervous.'

The bassist's nerves were only slightly less frazzled the following night, for the band's London debut. It was a benefit gig at the Roundhouse, organised – a full decade before Wyatt released his *Shipbuilding* single – in support of the Upper Clyde Shipbuilders. Wyatt's mind, however, was not on the politics. 'I saw this beautiful girl,' he recalls. 'She wasn't doing the hippie thing of waving your arms round in the air. She was doing smart little foot moves: how you dance if you're in a crowded soul club. She had a fringed jacket and those rather Asiatic cheekbones, which I now realise are Slavic but I didn't know she was East European. Just completely something else. Very cool, very hip and very beautiful.'

The girl was Alfreda Benge, known to all, after the Michael Caine film – and, more importantly, its Sonny Rollins soundtrack – as Alfie. Both personally and professionally, Robert's relationship with Alfie would be far and away the most important of his life. Although they are both resolutely unsentimental on the subject, it was one of rock's more unusual, more honest and – against all odds – more enduring love stories.

'You know how you can share the world with somebody?' asks Wyatt, rhetorically. 'It just completely doubles what you see, everything opens out and you're not alone? That's what I felt: I'm not alone any more. I didn't want to be anywhere where Alfie wasn't. I'd found my soulmate, and I knew it. It doesn't mean to say I behaved appropriately, or was good for her in any way. I just knew that I didn't want to ever, ever, lose this girl.'

Born to a Polish mother and Austrian father, Alfie had lived in England since the age of seven. Like Robert, she talks of the relationship with unmisty eyes, though the strength of feeling is unmistakable. 'The minute I met Robert,' she recalls, 'it was like magnets. I couldn't bear the idea of going anywhere for a day where he wasn't. Wherever we went,'

> Robert with Alfie in her Notting Hill tower block flat, 1972.

she goes on, 'we had to sit right next to each other, glued next to each other. I was older than him, thirty-one or thirty-two, and I felt like I'd finally found a person who was going to stop me feeling lonely.'

Alfie's flat, on the twenty-first floor of the now demolished Hermes Point tower block, wasn't far from Notting Hill and Robert's flat in St Luke's Mews. 'A couple of months into 1972,' remembers Bill MacCormick. 'Alfie started coming along to things… and suddenly it was Rob and Alfie. She was great, she was very funny, and she did have a distinct effect on Robert.'

'The first time I saw Robert with Caroline Coon,' Bill continues, 'I thought I was looking at somebody completely different. He'd had a haircut, he was wearing perfectly pressed clothes – no, this isn't right! She'd obviously had an effect on him, he looked a completely different man. With Cyrille [Ayers], it was tempestuous. She could be just as easily baking you a cake or throwing teacups at you – and sometimes, within a few seconds, she was doing both. I think it was perhaps a physical relationship more than it was an emotional one. Whereas clearly with Alfie it covered all the bases.'

Alfie herself was aware that Robert had some 'quite fancy women' at the time. 'He seems to think I looked alright,' she continues, 'and I probably did. But I wasn't glamorous, and I had seen him with extremely glamorous looking women like Caroline and Cyrille. I was more of a hiding-in-the-shadows sort of person.'

Whatever she says about hiding in the shadows, Alfie was also luminously beautiful – and hardly lacking in style. On at least nodding terms with a whole host of Swinging Sixties faces, she counted two icons of the era as genuine friends: Jean Shrimpton, arguably the world's first supermodel, and actress Julie Christie. Long before she made the A-list with *Darling* and *Doctor Zhivago*, Christie had been a neighbour – so close, as Christie tells it, that they conversed via string telephone. 'Alfie was always more fashionable than anybody else,' recalls Julie Christie: quite an accolade from this most glamorous of British screen stars. 'She always wore absolutely the latest gear. I couldn't believe it, the way she looked. I looked out of the window once, before I met her, and saw this vision: long blonde hair, wonderful colours, just a little bit ahead of everybody else, walking up the street. I thought, "Oh wow." Somebody turned around and said, "There's somebody looking absolutely smashing out there, I wonder who they are?"'

In fact, Alfie was penniless at the time and making all her own clothes. When she met Robert, she had just emerged from a decade of study at three consecutive art schools. She had made in-house films for IBM and had worked on Robert Altman's *McCabe and Mrs Miller*, where she contributed to Julie Christie's dialogue. At the Royal College of Art film school, she had also edited the film loops used by designer Sean Kenny at Expo 67 in Montreal, and had written and edited a number of short films, including *Lone Ranger* by Richard Stanley, which featured a soundtrack by The Who's Pete Townshend, and she had written and directed a film celebrating the bicentenary of the Royal Academy for BBC2. She had also been teaching film part time at art college but gave that up to join Matching Mole in the tour bus. 'She came on the road with us and made us pumpernickel sandwiches, central European that she is,' grins Robert. 'And that was a fine thing. She also knitted us

> Alfie on the set of *McCabe and Mrs Miller* with Warren Beatty (right).

woolly hats – I've still got mine somewhere. So that was very good. And just sort of joined us, really.'

By spring 1972, Robert had moved in with Alfie. They had a deep natural affinity and their paths had come close to crossing for some years. Alfie had worked behind the bar at Ronnie Scott's, and Robert is touchingly proud of the fact that she knew what all his favourite jazz musicians drank. She also knew various musicians who were, or who would become, members of his extended musical family. One ex-boyfriend was Pip Pyle, by this point living with Robert's first wife Pam, although Robert insists the situation was not as 'free love' as it might sound. 'On the surface,' he acknowledges, 'the Pip and Pam thing may look excruciatingly embarrassing. In fact, at the time, as far as I remember, it was a very amiable thing. Alfie was with Pip for a while, and Pam, of course, had been with me. And in a roundabout way they did a swap. But, I mean, we were all friends, we were working with each other's bands. I don't remember any big problem about it. In fact, I think Pam had suggested it to Alfie, saying, "You'd probably get on with Robert," or something like that.'

'We got Robert and Alfie together, me and Pip,' confirms the magnanimous Pam. 'We decided they were made for each other, they'd be perfect for each other. Alfie and Pip, that was finished. But Pip was still great friends with her and we used to go and see her in her tower block. I always thought she was wonderful. I didn't know what a feminist was, but she was like that. He'd say, "Oh, Alfie, can you do…?" And she'd say, "Mend your own fucking jeans, who do you take me for?" And I thought, "That's great!" I'd always done everything, I never dared talk back. But she'd say it in a funny way. She was very feisty, she was very arty, she was very clever, she was very attractive. She was into her films and all that. So much more suitable than me for Robert!'

9

FIGHTING FOR A SOCIALIST WORLD

The *Little Red Record* and
calling time on Matching Mole

In August 1972, Matching Mole went into the studio to record their second album, *Little Red Record*. Politics, it seemed, had arrived with a bang. Not only was the title a direct reference to Mao Zedong's 'little red book' but the front cover also exactly echoed a Chinese propaganda image of granite-jawed military personnel, originally captioned: 'We are determined to liberate Taiwan!' The iconography was provocative to say the least, although less so in 1972, when the mass deaths of Chinese at the hands of the despotic Mao had not been widely revealed. The image was actually chosen by the CBS art department, like the moles on the first record, though Robert had selected the title.

Robert would not have been the only one of his generation who saw only what he wanted to see in Mao: a man on the side of ordinary people who, like Trotsky or Che Guevara, represented an alternative to Soviet communism. Yet, though he today regards Marxism as 'the least silly way of analysing world events', Robert himself would never be a Maoist – and his slow drift from liberal, Fabian Society background to the hard left was by no means complete by 1972. There would be no explicit politics

MATCHING MOLE'S
LITTLE RED RECORD

> Matching Mole as Maoist revolutionaries for the second album.

on his next two albums, and it was not until the end of the decade that he would finally join the Communist Party of Great Britain.

'Matching Mole had participated in the shipworkers' benefit concert at the Roundhouse,' Robert explains, 'but it was like cultural empathy. "The workers are having a hard time, good blokes, up the union." There wasn't a big picture in my mind, just cultural empathy, which is totally inadequate in the end. It's like fighting for animals but only cuddly ones, so you fight for the koala but not the rhinoceros. You haven't quite got it yet if you're only doing that.'

At this stage, perhaps, Wyatt was simply casting around for a framework that was harder-edged than the peace and love of the hippie generation. Alfie, an anarchist at heart, was engaged in politics to an extent Robert had not witnessed in contemporaries except Caroline Coon. While his own parents were left-wing moderates, Alfie's stepfather had been a member of the Communist Party. Although she never set out to influence Robert politically, the memes, she says, couldn't help but transfer, particularly when he started reading her copies of the *Workers Press* (published by the Workers Revolutionary Party). 'If you hadn't thought about things that way, that in fact somebody has control over people's lives, there is somebody responsible for making people's lives miserable, you suddenly see *everything* like that,' Alfie recalls. 'It was Robert's first encounter with Marxism.'

That *Little Red Record* coincided with Wyatt's introduction to the *Workers Press* is surely no coincidence. Yet Robert shrinks from too literal a reading of the album cover: 'I saw these things from the perspective of an artist,' he insists. 'I was very interested in politics from that point of view. I really warmed to, and was very touched by, socialist imagery. I thought, "Well, that is a dream I can understand having, even if it's only a dream." Whereas the right-wing art, as it were, I did in fact find alien, and not invoking worlds that I wanted to imagine.'

More Pataphysician than pedagogue, Robert also had a mischievous aspect in his adoption of Maoist imagery; the same instinct that would later lead him to cover pop tunes disparaged by some of his rock and jazz contemporaries. Had he not seen something genuinely appealing in the Marxist dream, just as in acts like Chic or The Monkees, this would have been mere posturing. But he does seem to have enjoyed arguing his way off the ropes. 'All those ideas where anybody puts socialism into practice,' he explains, 'were considered to be hell on earth and proof that this won't work. So I started to enjoy the imagery, in a perverse way. I just took this imagery of what seemed to me a perfectly reasonable idea, of which the failures were being highlighted so as to discredit the whole idea.'

Robert says he didn't like the *Little Red Record* cover artwork at all, though Bill MacCormick recalls the concept as 'a hoot'. However, the album is nowhere near as partisan as its title – nor the CBS artwork – might suggest. In fact, its only real political moment arrives during *Gloria Gloom*:

> *Like so many of you*
> *I've got my doubts about how much to contribute*
> *To the already rich among us.*
> *How long can I pretend that music's more relevant than fighting*
> *For a socialist world?*

There's a hint here of Mao Zedong thought: nothing as bourgeois as music should be allowed to get in the way of the revolution. But even back on *Moon in June*, Robert had been worrying over music's humble role as background noise: 'after all, it's only leisure time, isn't it?' With the first stirrings of true political awareness came a more powerful sense of guilt at the frivolity of the artistic existence – what the Germans call *Kunstlerschuld*. 'To me, culture is pudding,' says Wyatt today. 'It's lovely, and I'll always eat one. But to me, on its own, it's not a full life's diet for the brain. And the politics, to me, is indeed the protein.'

Robert may be reverent towards his jazz heroes but, in general, he finds the Romantic notion of the artist as tortured genius embarrassing. Instead, he sees something almost indulgent in attempting to earn one's living through music, and prefers to celebrate those professions making a practical contribution to society. Politics, he says, is 'the actual meat and potatoes of life'.

A sense of guilt pervaded other tunes on the new album, most obviously *God Song*, a composition by guitarist Phil Miller for which Wyatt contributed playfully irreligious lyrics: 'What on earth are you doing, God? / Is this some sort of joke you're playing?' run the opening lines, before Robert passes on some advice to the man upstairs: 'Next time you send your boy down here / Give him a wife and a sexy daughter / Someone we can understand.' But, for all its apparent irreverence, *God Song* was not anti-religion. (Marx's famous description of religion as the opium of the people, Wyatt points out, is widely misunderstood: 'That whole paragraph is actually very touching.') Rather, insists Wyatt, 'it is about the impossibility of actually living in the way that religion prescribed, and therefore spending your whole life in a state of guilt'.

Wyatt still describes himself as 'a secular Christian, if there is such a thing'. What does he mean by the phrase? 'It means that I like the New Testament,' he replies. 'The Old Testament is a bit fascist for my tastes, but I think the New one is very good. You can separate the advice, the rules for living and how to behave, from the metaphysics quite easily.'

Marxism, perhaps, is a natural home for someone with religious tendencies but incapable of making the leap of faith. And Robert happily describes politics as his 'secular religion'. 'I don't believe in the supernatural,' he explains. 'So the idea of most religions is, "It doesn't matter what happens in this life, there's another life awaiting you." That to me was nonsense, as was the idea of a virgin birth. But the Marxist idea was great. The old idea was that most people suffer in this life, a few people have it good, but all the people who suffer have a good life after they die. And I thought, "Well, that's really silly. Obviously they'll be dead then, won't they? That's not on the cards."'

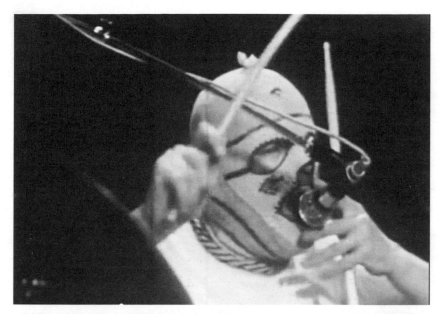

> Robert appearing with Matching Mole, enigmatically clad in a balaclava, on French TV show *Rockenstock*.

'But I liked the Marxist idea of, "How about the rewards for the masses, for their toil and suffering, being during their own lives, instead of just investors and owners of things getting all the rewards?" It didn't seem to me a particularly outrageous thing, it seemed a perfectly reasonable thing. That seemed to be called socialism. And so I said, "Right, that's obviously what I am."'

Bill MacCormick says that, while the *Matching Mole* sessions had been miserable, he had a great time recording *Little Red Record*. For one thing, it was summer: none of the musicians had to play wearing gloves. But the situation was also improved by the fact that CBS had a brand new studio, with equipment that actually worked.

'It went better,' recalls the bassist. 'It came out, in my view, sounding like a band album, whereas the first Matching Mole album sounds like a Robert album with some other guys in there to fill in some bits and pieces. Also, in some respects, the first Mole album is looking back and the second Mole album is looking forward.'

That Wyatt's interest in Marx and Mao did not come at the expense of his sense of humour was clear from the album's opening track. Had

> A friendly context: Matching Mole's second line-up: Robert, keyboard player Dave MacRae, Bill MacCormick, Phil Miller.

Monty Python dreamed up a Ministry of Silly Voices, it could happily have featured Robert's ludicrous, lugubrious, vocal on the opening track, *Starting in the Middle of the Day We Can Drink Our Politics Away*. Though recorded barely half a year after *Matching Mole*, the absurdist streak largely absent from the band's debut album had by *Little Red Record* returned to full strength. The musicians are listed in the liner notes in order of beard length, Dave MacRae just pipping Robert to the top spot. The sleevenotes also include a surreal essay by Alfie's friend David Gale on the subject of 'Gasphetti', and an admission from Wyatt that his own vocal parts are 'extremely silly'.

Nearly a year after leaving Soft Machine, Robert had also regained enough confidence to allow others into his creative world, allowing him to concentrate on the drumming. 'One thing I'd say about Matching Mole', he reflects, 'is that, maybe because of the more relaxed social atmosphere, I really got the hang of drumming: a synthesis of various things I'd been trying to do. So, just for that alone, I'm terribly grateful for that last year with Matching Mole. I really got to play how I had always wanted to play, without the paranoia and conflicting requirements and pressures around me. It was a friendly context.'

As well as being more upbeat and more of a collective effort, *Little Red Record* differed from *Matching Mole* in that – *God Song* aside – it represented a move away from song into longer, more improvised pieces. Dave Sinclair, less musically restless than Robert, was unhappy with the change in direction. 'Dave was uncomfortable the further we strayed from tunes,' says Robert. 'He'd written the tune for *O Caroline*, and he wanted to just do lots of records like that, I think. And I didn't want to. There was no way I'm going to find a formula and just stick with it. I couldn't keep awake.'

The solution lay in the form of heavyweight session keyboard player Dave MacRae. 'Dave MacRae is probably the best pianist I've ever worked with,' enthuses Wyatt. 'He came on because I wanted that fleetness and lightness of harmonic athleticism that, it seems, only really jazz musicians have in the end.'

A New Zealander, MacRae had worked with big band drummer Buddy Rich but he had also been a member of the jazz-rock act Nucleus and was a regular at Ronnie Scott's. It wasn't long before he ran into Wyatt. 'Robert came across as a man of immense enthusiasm and energy,' remembers MacRae, 'and this alone was enough for me to want to get involved with him in the creation of interesting music drawn from several different musical areas. It was a time of experiment, and the attitude "let's try it and see what happens" prevailed. A really exciting time to be in London, probably the central place where the musical melting pot was on the boil.'

MacRae had appeared on the first Matching Mole album as a guest, but he was now asked to join the band on a full-time basis. His rippling electric piano, reminiscent of Weather Report's Joe Zawinul, introduced a new element of electric jazz – a step back towards Soft Machine, although Matching Mole stayed rooted in 4/4 and continued to feature guitar in place of saxophone.

Matching Mole continued for a period as a quintet, recording a BBC *Top Gear* session for John Peel. (The broadcaster supported Matching Mole with all the enthusiasm he had shown Soft Machine, and for years kept a photo of Robert on his kitchen wall, sharing pride of place with Liverpool football manager Bill Shankly.) Yet, by the next BBC session, a *Sounds of the 70s* recording in March 1972, Sinclair had left the band. An almost entirely improvised gig in Brussels had been the final straw.

Dave Sinclair's departure reflected a central duality within Wyatt: the man who, back in Soft Machine, had responded to the request to play jazz fusion in the style of Jack DeJohnette by moving towards Led

Zeppelin's John Bonham. 'I've always had this problem, right from the time I started playing music,' explained Robert in 1974. 'Right back to schooldays, actually, and The Wilde Flowers. I've always worked with two kinds of musician – some that were into improvisation as a process, and some that weren't. And I've always kind of played the devil's advocate to all of them. Y'know, talking about Cecil Taylor to Dave Sinclair and taking the exact opposite stance with some jazz musician.'

Yet just as he resists the tag of 'born rebel', which implies a mere pose, Robert insists he is not simply a contrarian: 'If something is alright, being well looked after, I don't feel the need to nurture it,' he explains. 'Whereas if something is OK but it's somehow more marginalised or threatened, I will try and redress the balance by saying, "Hang on, there is this to it." But that doesn't seem to me to be perverse. It seems on the contrary an attempt to address an imbalance.'

Perhaps Robert's impulse is better seen as an example of *antimony*, the 'plus–minus' central to Pataphysics – or of the musical concept of counterpoint. 'When it goes into a mass tabloid-led thing, I just pull back,' he explains. 'So, actually, I see myself, strictly speaking, as a reactionary, to the extent that I respond to events.' Typically, he uses the term in the opposite of its usual sense; as usually defined, a reactionary is more likely to be waving the *Daily Mail* than the *Little Red Book*.

The 'reactionary' impulse might have led Robert towards Marxism, as well as to champion both straight songs and complex instrumental music. One lesson from jazz, however, was carried through into almost all Robert's music, regardless of genre. From bandleaders like Duke Ellington and Charles Mingus, he had learned that individual personalities could and should remain distinct within the group's overall sound. 'You had Bill MacCormick; the two Daves on keyboards, Dave MacRae and Dave Sinclair, alternating, one eventually taking over from the other; and Phil on guitar,' Robert recalls. 'I didn't want to subsume their contribution into a kind of soup. I wanted to enhance it, really, enhance their uniqueness. So the second album is different because the people are different. On the first Matching Mole record, there are no jazz musicians. So there's no jazz. On the second one, there's Dave MacRae, so there is some. It's as simple as that.'

Alfie conceived several track titles, including *Gloria Gloom* – a reference to her own inscrutable face. 'I don't smile a lot,' she explains, 'because Poles don't smile unless there's a reason. Not like the English.' She also performed spoken word skits with David Gale and Julie Christie, under the name of Der Mütter Korus. Although the collage

> Alfie – 'I don't smile a lot' – going against the grain.

effect obscures many of the words, Gale's 'I very rarely work naked for that reason' stands out on *Gloria Gloom* like a deliciously timed line of overheard conversation.

Christie, billed in the credits as 'Ruby Crystal', was by now a major star, having followed early roles in *Billy Liar* and *Darling* with *Doctor Zhivago*, *The Go-Between* and, most recently, *McCabe and Mrs Miller*. Her presence in the studio, recalls Bill MacCormick, was more than a little distracting. 'Julie Christie was my teenage heartthrob,' admits the bassist, not the only one of Robert's friends to go weak at the knees when recalling the Hollywood star. 'So when it turned out that Alfie was one of Julie's best friends, it was – ah! And then, of course, it turns out that she's absolutely lovely, to make it even worse. You wouldn't mind if she turned out to be an absolute bitch, but she was delightful. She was very, very sweet. So you've got absolutely no excuse for not falling deeply in love with the woman.'

Dave MacRae and Der Mütter Korus were not the only new arrivals on *Little Red Record*. Credited as 'this summer's guest superstar' was Brian Eno of Roxy Music, who contributed the synth soundscapes that open *Gloria Gloom*. 'They were very jazz-derived,' remembers Eno. 'I was very anti-jazz, in that I thought jazz was a bit easy. I also thought it was a music of faith – and I still do, in some sense. I think, especially with free jazz, how much you enjoy it depends entirely on how much you believe in it.'

The link to Eno was Phil Manzanera – who had played alongside Bill MacCormick in the Dulwich College band Quiet Sun and was by this stage the Roxy Music guitarist. The band's image, a glittery explosion of fashion, art and pop, was a long way from the earthy Matching Mole. Eno, typically clad in silver gloves or a feather boa, seemed particularly remote. Despite the superficial differences, however, Robert and Brian in fact had much in common, from a panoramic view of pop to a fascination with fine art. They would work together on several occasions over the ensuing decades.

Eno picked up a second future collaborator during the *Little Red Record* sessions: King Crimson's Robert Fripp. Perhaps realising that *Matching*

> *Little Red Record* producer Robert Fripp with Brian Eno. The pair would go on to record together, on joint albums and most famously on Bowie's *Heroes*.

Mole had lacked coherence, Robert asked the Crimson kingpin (and producer of Centipede's *Septober Energy* album) to produce the band's second album. Fripp was a phenomenal musician, and Bill MacCormick admits that both he and Phil Miller were somewhat in awe. As guitarist, the pressure on Phil was particularly intense. 'Phil's a guy with his own sound and his own musical ideas,' recalls Bill. 'And that was thwarted to a certain extent, in my view, by the presence of this character in the control room.' As a virtuoso, Fripp, for his part, may have wondered why Wyatt was working with relatively inexperienced musicians like Bill MacCormick and, to a lesser extent, Phil Miller. Yet Wyatt is reluctant to discuss any problems – and, diplomatic as ever, shoulders the blame himself. 'I think it was a duplication of roles that was uncomfortable for Robert Fripp. A producer is someone who says, "Do it like this or like that" – and I didn't really want to be told.'

The statement captures, in miniature, the broader problem within Matching Mole: although more than up to the job musically, Wyatt was simply not cut out to be a bandleader. In Soft Machine, Robert hadn't liked receiving orders; in Matching Mole, he found himself equally uncomfortable *giving* them. 'Robert couldn't be a dictator,' says Alfie. 'When he was with a group, he would give them freedom despite the fact that they were doing things he wouldn't have done. Even though Robert was the leader, he wasn't able to say, for fear of hurting anybody, "That's not exactly what I meant."'

'I found there's two things I wasn't being very good at,' Wyatt agrees. 'One was being in somebody else's band, and the other one was running my own band. I couldn't work for anybody else, and I wasn't comfortable with anybody else working for me. I was completely stuck.'

Little Red Record was, nonetheless, more robust than the band's debut, not least because this time the material had been road-tested before they went into the studio. Vocal and instrumental passages were also much more convincingly integrated: tunes such as *Nan True's Hole* and *Gloria Gloom* explore a molten middle ground where Wyatt the jazz drummer and Wyatt the singer could begin to co-exist.

Although more coherent than *Matching Mole*, however, *Little Red Record* didn't entirely do the band justice. Phil Miller comes to the fore on only a minority of tracks, while the relatively straightforward *God Song* shares almost nothing with the complex jazz-rock instrumentals Wyatt could explore now that Dave MacRae was on board. Always hard on himself, Robert still felt that he had not quite achieved his goal: a fusion of jazz-inspired instrumentals and song-based rock that was somehow different to jazz-rock fusion. Wyatt professes himself happy with a lot of ideas on *Little Red Record*, but it is the collected Matching Mole BBC radio sessions, rather than either studio album, that he regards as the finest representation of the band.

–»)(«– –»)(«– –»)(«–

Although there had been clear progress since their debut, Matching Mole, true to their name, remained underground. Lack of money was still a problem, and Robert was increasingly uncomfortable with the sacrifices he was demanding from his bandmates. 'Although Mole was good fun,' he says, 'it was a hard time for the lads. I couldn't really look after them as a bandleader should do. It doesn't matter if it's your own initiative, but if you take people out of their lives, take them with you somewhere, you take responsibility for that. They were very friendly, never complained, but I know it was difficult for them.'

> Matching Mole on tour in France with Soft Machine. From left: Daevid Allen of Gong, Karl Jenkins, John Marshall, Bill MacCormick, Mike Ratledge, Robert Wyatt, Elton Dean and Francis Monkman.

One option for a bandleader too embarrassed to issue orders to his musicians would have been to let the band run on interminably, forever waiting to muster the courage to call it a day. Instead, Robert opted for a single, drastic decision. By the time *Little Red Record* was released, at the end of October 1972, he had broken up Matching Mole. 'I'm a bit suicidal like that,' Wyatt later admitted. 'I left the previous band just as they were starting to break even as well.'

Yet there is self-deception here as well as self-destruction, since the split from Soft Machine had not been entirely of his own choosing. Oddly for someone still traumatised by the split from his previous band, let alone someone with a growing interest in egalitarian politics, Robert doesn't seem to have anticipated the effect on his bandmates of pulling the plug on Matching Mole. 'None of us had the first idea that this was coming,' says Bill MacCormick, still adamant that, having put in the groundwork, the band's prospects were about to improve. Matching Mole had just beaten Genesis in the *Melody Maker* 'brightest hope' poll and there were a further fifteen gigs already in the diary.

While Dave MacRae could confidently return to session work, the demise of Matching Mole left the less experienced Miller and MacCormick facing a highly uncertain future. 'It actually made Phil and myself very, very angry,' continues the bassist. 'Robert wouldn't have been safe at one point because both of us were so angry about what had happened. We had frankly been put through the mincer for seven or eight months, not made money – I say not made money; I was *owed* money because I was paying for other people's food and fags and God knows what else.'

Robert explained his decision to disband Matching Mole as being 'because I don't have the qualities of leadership. I don't want to run things... I just wanted to be a quarter of the group. I just couldn't handle it.' He was, perhaps, temperamentally unsuited to leading a group, as well as musically frustrated as he struggled to find a truly coherent direction. There's little doubt, however, as to the immediate trigger: a September 1972 tour of Holland and Belgium in support of Soft Machine. Signed to the same label and sharing a manager, the Soft Machine/Matching Mole billing had a certain logic, and an obvious attraction for fans. Yet, to find himself relegated to warmup act for a full fortnight, as his old group continued to trade on the reputation he himself had done so much to establish, was, for Robert, a humiliation too far.

10

FOLLY BOLOLEY

Venice and the fall

The demise of Matching Mole in September 1972 left Wyatt without a band for the second time in a year. Robbed of the vindication he might have felt had his new group achieved the same prominence as Soft Machine, Robert seemed for the first time in his musical life to lose momentum. Submerged in self-doubt, he talked, not for the last time, of giving up music altogether. One option he discussed with Alfie was becoming a postman: at least, she says, he would have had the energy for the early starts. 'He was up in the morning long before me,' Alfie recalls, 'going out for walks. He was incredibly hyperactive, a workaholic. There was a sense that he did have a manic edge – and the contrasts, which were depressions.' Alfie recalls fearing that '*something* was going to happen to him. He was going to do something to himself, or something was going to happen to him. He was so scarred by the experience of Soft Machine. He was having post-traumatic stress disorder.'

It was, nonetheless, a creative and productive time. Towards the end of the year, Robert sang backing vocals on *Bananamour*, perhaps Kevin Ayers' finest solo album, and guested on vocals with Phil Miller's new band Hatfield and the North (which also featured Dave Sinclair, Richard Sinclair and Pip Pyle). Then, in December, he recorded a *Top Gear* session for John Peel accompanied only by Francis Monkman from the art-rock group Curved Air.

The duo performed three songs: *We Got an Arts Council Grant,* an old Broadway number called *Little Child* and a version of *God Song* that

> Robert and Alfie in Paris, on the way to Venice. Note Pataphysical hat badge, Gong sticker and Matching Mole T-shirt.

incorporated an early Hatfield number, *Fol de Rol*. The former, with its high warble, pig snorts and ludicrously rolled Rs, owed something to both *The Goon Show* and Gilbert and Sullivan. *Little Child*, previously recorded by Danny Kaye and his daughter, Dena, had Robert singing Dena's part (as well as Danny's), showing his ability to make affecting even a whining head voice that should, by any conventional standard, have been more ridiculous than sublime.

Alfie's career, meantime, was picking up momentum. She had already worked with Nic Roeg, of *Performance* fame, on the documentary *Glastonbury Fayre*, and he now offered her work on another movie, *Don't Look Now*. Her role, as second assistant editor, would get her the crucial union card then required to work regularly in film. The job also involved several weeks on location in Venice, which would allow her to spend time with her friend Julie Christie, who was to co-star opposite Donald Sutherland. At first, Robert was reluctant to join Alfie in Italy. 'I didn't understand holidays,' he admits. 'What is a holiday? It just means you have to stop working. That just seemed a complete delay in life. The whole concept struck me as utterly perverse.' Even a workaholic, however, could see that a couple of months apart could prove fatal to the relatively new relationship with Alfie – especially since Robert was, in her words, 'absolutely a totally weak weed when it came to any kind of female attention'. And so, just after Christmas 1972, he and Alfie joined Julie Christie in a villa on the Venetian island of Giudecca.

With its canals and crumbling masonry, Venice might be the paradigmatic city of romance, and *Don't Look Now* would feature some of cinema's most convincing sex scenes. Yet the real love story, recalls Julie Christie, was played out offscreen. 'They used to go round, Alfie and Robert, as if they were in a three-legged race. Always together. Three-legged person sitting, three-legged person walking, and so on. I remember them sitting at the end of the garden, with their backs to me. The two of them just sitting on a bench for hours and hours and hours, just looking out. I remember thinking, "How nice, just the two of them, they can talk and talk and talk and talk, obviously... or maybe just sit and sit and sit, and look at the water, while Robert got – as Alfie said – watery ideas."'

These watery ideas came together like so many tributaries on a cheap Riviera keyboard, bought by Alfie from a local music shop. The organ was small, almost a toy, but it allowed Robert to begin working on a new batch of material – and its slow, shimmering vibrato seemed to mirror the dull slap of wave against *vaporetto* station.

'I was very influenced there by the water, really,' remembers Wyatt. 'Not the little canals, but the big open ones. And the feeling, staying in this house, that you'd go down this path and, instead of a road, there'd be water. Venice in winter: when the tide goes down, there are all these tiny little crabs scuttling around in the moss, at the waterline. It's very evocative and strong.'

Wyatt still owns the Riviera, which appeared on several subsequent recordings. Perhaps as much of a catalyst as the keyboard itself, however, was the enforced idleness of Giudecca after a decade of constant activity. While Julie and Alfie were on set, Robert spent his days alone – and *O Sole Mio* singing contests with off-duty gondoliers provided only brief diversion. 'I think that period in Venice was incredibly important,' says

❯ Robert accompanying a gondolier on *O Sole Mio*, 'which seemed to fit the chords of *It's Now or Never*'.

Alfie, who believes Robert's manic energy hindered his creativity as much as it helped. 'You can't go rushing off, doing this, doing that. You're here, you've got nothing else to do except twiddle about on this keyboard.'

Eager to put together a band to work on this new material, Wyatt returned to London in February 1973, a fortnight earlier than Alfie. But she remained the inspiration for tunes such as *Alifib* and *Alife* – even if, at the time, the link wasn't so obvious. 'When he started working on the lyric "Alife my larder,"' says Alfie with a wry smile, 'he was singing "*Polly* my larder". I said, "Who's this Polly?" The next time I heard it, he was singing, "Alife my larder". I thought, "Well, I've just somehow forced a name change that wasn't intended."'

–»)«– –»)«– –»)«–

While Robert was in Italy, Bill MacCormick had been meeting up with Francis Monkman to discuss the prospect of a revived Matching Mole. Yet the *NME*'s announcement, in March, that the band was re-forming proved premature. It was true that Wyatt was trying to put together a band. But, pulled in conflicting directions by his diverse tastes, he couldn't decide on a line-up. 'I was doing stuff with Francis Monkman, with whom I'd done the John Peel session. He had a whole other kind of keyboard brilliance, a whole other area that Dave MacRae could have done but wasn't interested in. And I couldn't think which to use. I thought Francis would be more up for working on songs and getting the most out of that, in ways that really suited me, using prepared pianos and synthesiser things. But Dave MacRae makes everything sound alive and full of beans and joyful.' Henry Cow's guitarist Fred Frith was another possibility considered for the new band.

Although on the one hand moving towards song, Robert was also pulled towards the freer end of jazz. In March and April he played a series of entirely improvised gigs, both in a trio with Dave MacRae and bassist Ron Mathewson, and with the exuberant British tenor saxophonist Gary Windo in the WMWM (Windo-MacRae–Wyatt–Matthewson) quartet. Windo had played alongside Wyatt in Keith Tippett's Centipede and in the free improvisation ensemble Symbiosis. 'The combination WMWM I think produced some astounding music in its short life,' recalls Dave MacRae. 'Gary Windo had a similar energy to Robert, boundless enthusiasm, and Ron Mathewson is without doubt one of the most amazing bass players ever heard. I felt privileged to be involved.'

Two tracks by WMWM survive, both recorded live in April 1973. The instrumental *Carmus* is close to free jazz. *Spiderman*, named after the figure Gary Windo used to doodle on his manuscript paper, is also impressionistic at first. Yet Robert's mid-tune vocal arrives, for fans of his later work, with a jolt: it is clearly recognisable as an interlude from *Rock Bottom*. Although there is good reason for seeing the accident as the fundamental divide in Robert's musical, as well as personal, life, the reality was not quite so clear-cut. More singer than drummer, he was already closer to his solo guise than to the role he had played in Soft Machine or even Matching Mole.

Another new project, Wyatt's soundtrack for *Solar Flares Burn for You*, a short film composed by Alfie's friend Arthur Johns, also suggests that he was tipping from drummer to singer. Johns would go on to work on Hollywood blockbusters, but he was then an underground filmmaker. *Solar Flares* had no obvious narrative, and Wyatt's soundtrack, recorded in a basement owned by Floyd drummer Nick Mason, was appropriately abstract. The tune would reappear, in more focused form, on his 1975 album *Ruth Is Stranger Than Richard*.

The *Solar Flares* soundtrack helped establish the drone-based palette that would recur throughout Wyatt's career. At this stage, however, Robert was not thinking as a solo artist. Instead, he had finally settled on a line-up for the revamped Matching Mole: Francis Monkman on keyboards and Gary Windo on saxophone, plus bassist Bill MacCormick from the band's original incarnation. There were two or three meetings in late May 1973, when Robert played through draft versions of his new material. Robert even sent a note to Nick Mason, to ask if he would produce the band's third album. Yet, almost as soon as he received the note – possibly, says Mason, the very same day – the Floyd drummer also received calamitous news that meant, at the very least, that the recording would never take place.

⠀➤ ⠀ ➤ ⠀ ➤⠀

June Campbell-Cramer – better known as Lady June – was an artist and poet today best remembered for her west London flat. Her nickname was not a mark of nobility but an abbreviation of 'landlady', and her tenants were artists and musicians. She had become friends with Robert and Kevin Ayers through living in Deià, near Robert Graves, and over the years rooms in her Maida Vale flat were rented to members of Gong, The Whole World, Henry Cow and Hawkwind.

On 1 June 1973, Robert and Alfie attended a birthday party at June's flat. The evening, Alfie recalls, was portentous from the start. That she had not finished working on the foreboding *Don't Look Now* added an ominous spin. Alfie still remembers Nic Roeg reiterating, over and over, the film's underlying theme: we are not prepared. 'What was so awful was, we really didn't want to go to that party,' Alfie goes on. 'And when we got there, it all started going weird, the whole thing. In the lift, Robert said – not about the party – he said: "Oh, I'm so happy." Ever since then, whenever he's said he's happy, I've thought, "Oh no, no. Don't say that, something horrible is going to happen. Don't ever be happy!"'

Some assumed, after what happened next, that Wyatt had taken LSD. In fact, he'd stuck to legal intoxicants, albeit consumed, even by his own standards, in unusually large quantities. 'I don't know how drunk you know "really drunk" can be,' he sighs. 'But however much you know it can be, that was my *normal* state. So I was really drunk *for me*. I was hallucinating, out of it, I was somewhere else. I was having a dream.'

Robert talks openly about the earlier stages of Lady June's party, when he knocked back wine, whisky and punch. Ask about anything after that, however, and the reasons why he came to fall from a fourth-floor window, and his eyes turn hunted. 'I have to say this is one point I really don't like talking about,' he says, 'except to say that I did get incredibly drunk and it's not anybody else's fault. I did fall out of a window. I know it spoiled the party. It must have been awful for the people there, and terrifying for Alfie.'

Wyatt's accounts of his fall have actually varied slightly over the years. At times, he has spoken of it as a suicide attempt, the consequence of his forced departure from Soft Machine two years previously: 'I really admired them,' he said in 2003, 'so I thought they must be right. That's why I threw myself out of the window, if I'm honest. They threw me out, so I threw myself out. Literally.' In fact, it seems that he attempted to leave the bathroom by climbing down the drainpipe, in an attempt, as *Melody Maker* journalist Vivien Goldman explained euphemistically, 'to evade a typical party tangle'.

'There's no concept of falling,' Robert recalls. 'You have no idea. It was a terrible thing – not for me, but for everyone else. Me, I just fell. You immediately lose all feeling. I didn't lose consciousness. I didn't fall on my head, I fell on my left heel – although the rest of me obviously followed quite quickly, not having become detached *en route*. I remember hearing, in the distance, a scream like a wolf's howl. I mentioned this later to somebody and they said: "That was you." But

I remember it as though it was distant, across the traffic. So I heard my own scream as a wolf, echoing in the distance. I was quite detached from it. I remember being bundled into an ambulance. Anyway, then six weeks later – because apparently, you're put on so many drugs in hospital that you're completely out of it – I wake up and I'm in a hospital bed, and that was a whole new world.'

–»)(«– –»)(«– –»)(«–

Robert survived the fall, the doctors told him, only because the alcohol had kept his body relaxed upon landing. The impact had broken his twelfth vertebra – technically, T12 L1 – and, as a result, he was paralysed from the waist down. In a sombre echo of his father's multiple sclerosis, he would be in a wheelchair for life, at the age of twenty-eight. Robert's half-sister Prue still has a photo, inherited from their mother, that bears the chilling caption, 'The last picture I have of Robert standing.'

'The accident was a horrifying time,' recalls Prue. 'I was actually expecting one of our boys, and I nearly miscarried, it was such a shock. I had to go to bed for a week. I was bleeding and everything. When that child was born, and it was a boy, we called him Robert. We call him Robbie now, because we've got the other Robert. But we nearly lost Robert.'

Honor said it was the worst thing that ever happened to her, after George's death, though she remembered Robert's gallows humour: 'The first thing more or less he said to me in hospital when he was conscious was, "Don't worry, Mummy, I always was a lazy bastard".'

Warren Beatty, Julie Christie's partner on and sometimes off the screen, offered to pay for private health care. Yet Robert opted to remain in the NHS Stoke Mandeville Hospital: the oldest spinal injuries centre in the world. Alfie, who stayed for much of the period with Lol Coxhill in Aylesbury, in order to be close to the hospital, remembers: 'I didn't think he'd live for a week. And then another week. And then another. But he was incredibly brave. I've never heard him whinge about it, even at the time. He seemed to accept it straightaway.' Sam, Robert's son, visited, too. 'I was about seven,' says Sam, 'and it was a big shock, obviously. I made him a little pamphlet. It had crossword puzzles in it and it had a story about a spaceman whose cutlery was floating away so it had to be tied down with string.'

John Peel, 'rendered almost inarticulate' by his friend's accident, asked his listeners to send postcards to Robert at the BBC for him to pass on.

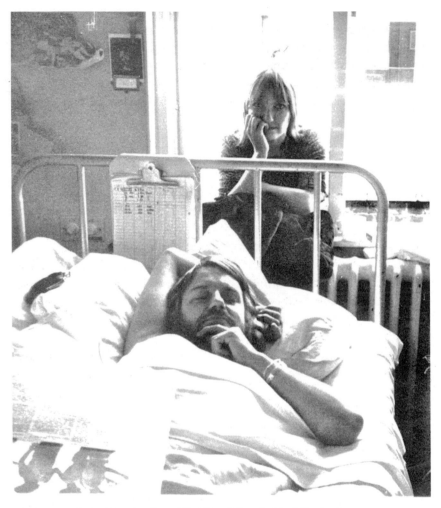

> Robert at Stoke Mandeville, with Alfie sitting behind the bed.

He noted that 'Robert's whole philosophy as far as his accident went was "hum, bloody typical!" It's a memory shared by many of his family and friends: that Robert was philosophical about the accident from the off, that it seemed to calm him down. Perhaps his years of self-confessed recklessness meant he had long been living under a Damoclean sword. 'When he had his accident,' recalled former Wilde Flower and Caravan drummer Richard Coughlan, 'I wasn't really surprised. He was the sort of bloke you always knew *something* was going to happen to. He was very reckless, in a way. He was a very fit, very fine, tanned bloke in those days. He used to drink a lot and run about, jump around in front of cars and things.'

'I didn't really know him very well before,' says Brian Eno, on the subject of the accident. 'But it seemed to me that he almost embraced it, in the sense of saying: "Yup, this is what you could have expected, given the life I was leading. I've made my bed and now I'm going to make the best of it." I never saw any sense of anger in him about it. It was more that sort of melancholy about him, which I think has always been there.'

'I remember him, when I met him first, as being hyperactive,' Eno continues. 'A very, very active person, like drummers often are, always tapping: a huge amount of physical and nervous energy. And what I also remember is that afterwards, he smoked very heavily. I talked to him about that one day. And he said: "I've got a theory about smoking. I think people smoke in order to reduce their health to match their circumstances." I thought that was an absolutely brilliant theory.'

There is, in fact, a curious sense in which Wyatt actually became *less* sorry for himself once he had become paraplegic. He claims to have actively enjoyed hospital – 'People bringing me breakfast, making my bed like Little Lord Muck... this is the life!' – and is adamant that he was able to focus his mind elsewhere during the various operations. 'I think, if God had invented wheelchairs,' Robert insists today, 'he would have presented them as a natural alternative to legs for those who preferred the choice.'

–»》《«- -»》《«- -»》《«-

To hear Wyatt's Pataphysical take on paraplegia is heartening. But his relentlessly upbeat take on the accident can also stretch credulity. The fact that Robert goes as far as to describe breaking his back as 'an incidental detour' in his life has led some to suggest that he is attempting to suppress the trauma. Alfie is one of them – and, she says, it's a thoroughly good thing: 'There are huge losses that he's had,' she explains. 'He's somehow coped with it by being in denial, which I think is a pretty good strategy. People say, "Oh, you're in denial." "Yeah, well this is how I cope! Please let me be in denial, don't let me have nightmares about this terrible loss, the fact that I'm never going to be able to run down the road or get on the bus on my own, I'm always going to be relying on other people, won't be able to reach the top shelf, won't be able to run and drum and chase women and things." Although,' she adds with a dry chuckle, 'it didn't entirely stop him.'

As regards the huge losses, it's hard not to conclude that Alfie is articulating what Robert himself will not. One area in which he has *not* downplayed the impact of the accident, however, is in terms of its effect on Alfie. Otherwise, the only consequence of the accident by which Robert will admit to being troubled was its effect on his ability to make music. No longer able to operate bass drum and hi-hat pedals, paraplegia seemed to have brought to an abrupt end his career as a drummer. There were suggestions that he might re-form Matching Mole, playing hand percussion, after leaving hospital, but he flatly rejected the suggestion: 'I didn't want to be, "He used to be a drummer, now he plays bongos", he explains. 'It didn't sound right; it would get the pity audience. I wanted to do something just as well as I could before, but different.'

After three months staring at the ceiling, Robert began to glimpse a possible musical future when he was allowed to take short trips around the hospital in a wheelchair: 'First of all you get to see what the people you've been talking to look like,' he recalls, 'because you're not allowed to move your head, you just look at the ceiling. So you get to know people quite well in the bed either side but you don't know what they look like. And then you have an hour – or just twenty minutes, I think, on the first day – in a wheelchair. I found, after a couple of days, that there was a visitors' room with an upright piano in it.'

Using the visitors' room piano, Wyatt began to develop the material he had first sketched out in Venice. An album began to take shape, split into two twenty-minute sides. Without access to recording facilities, he committed the whole thing to memory. 'Forty minutes of stuff I was carrying round in my head,' he recollects, 'so I was never bored in hospital.'

Robert, who can't read music, instead conceives of music in visual terms – and the image to which he kept returning was that of a seabed. 'I was very affected by reading about the abyssal ooze at the bottom of oceans,' he recalls. 'There are things at the bottom of oceans as strange and weird as anything people imagine on Mars. And, musically, my landscape seemed to be more and more underwater. You can't make direct analogies between music and visual stimuli, but I do have physical landscapes in my head. That's how I remember things, by picturing them. So it was a sort of a wildlife garden – not a land garden, an underwater one.'

There was a sense in which Robert's problem had always been that, as a singing drummer able to turn his hand to anything from pop to jazz, he had simply had too many choices. Now his options had been cruelly narrowed – but, he realised, he could still play any instrument that required only the top half of the body. 'You'd think that was hard,' he says, 'but in a way it was fantastically liberating. Maybe that's one of the reasons why I don't have a problem in a wheelchair. Paradoxically, it was truly liberating. I suddenly couldn't be all the different things I'd been trying to be: a drummer for other people, a singer of things. I had to sit down and think, "Stop depending on other people." Do your own thing, that's the point.'

Had he died in the fall, Wyatt's posthumous reputation, despite *Moon in June* and *The End of an Ear*, would have been largely as a drummer. From this point on it would be, more than anything, as a solo artist and singer. 'That's my year zero, really: breaking the back, and Alfie, and working out this stuff. Suddenly the freedom with those tunes, not having to fit these into a band and thinking: "What would the bass player do? What would the pianist do?" I could just do it myself. So to me it was a great breakthrough after years of trying things upside down – but always from the point of view of the drum stool, where you're not in control of the chords, or the tunes, or solos, or anything, really. How could anybody else play what was in my head? I had to do it myself.'

SIDE TWO

EX MACHINA

11

DIFFERENT EVERY TIME

Rock Bottom and
marriage to Alfie

Robert came out of Stoke Mandeville Hospital in January 1974, an occasion he and Alfie – who has herself, in Robert's words, 'fallen off many a bar stool in her time' – celebrated by heading straight to the pub.

In the longer term, however, their prospects seemed as bleak as those of the country at large, which had just introduced the three-day week. With its broken lift and cramped bathroom, Alfie's twenty-first floor flat was hopelessly inaccessible for a wheelchair user. Neither did they have an obvious source of income: Robert had no band, and, in these early days of his paraplegia, Alfie was obliged to provide full-time care.

It was the generosity of friends that saw them through. Pink Floyd, boosted into the A-league with *The Dark Side of the Moon*, played two benefit shows and raised £10,000. The support act for the gigs was Soft Machine. Such was the pace of the band's evolution, however, that only Mike Ratledge remained in the line-up from Robert's era.

Recognising that public transport was now out of the question, the model Jean Shrimpton donated her old car to Robert and Alfie (who had taught herself to drive while Robert was in hospital). Julie Christie bought them a flat in Lebanon Park, Twickenham, just north of the Thames. Robert and Alfie would live in the London suburb for a decade and a half. Before they got the keys to the flat, however, they holed up in Wiltshire, on a farm estate owned by Spanish philanthropist Delfina Entrecanales. Robert, who knew Delfina through his half-brother Mark, regards her to this day as his 'fairy godmother'.

It was at Delfina's farm, in the village of Little Bedwyn, that Wyatt began to adjust to life in a wheelchair. 'When you come out of hospital,' he explains, 'they have to sign you out. They have to say you can do certain things. You can cross roads, get in and out of the bath, all those things – so you'll be all right in the world. But the reality of it is, there are a lot of things you just don't know how to handle at all. So Delfina's was a place to get used to it.' It was also at Little Bedwyn that, in February 1974, Robert began to record the music he had written in Venice and Stoke Mandeville. It should have been the third Matching Mole album. Instead, the music would be released as *Rock Bottom*, the true start of Robert's solo career.

It was an album that would demand new methods of working, different from anything Robert had done before and, as he acknowledges, these were at the heart of its originality. 'I did think, "I'm having to invent a way of doing things without any particular reference to any way of doing things that I could have learned from someone else." So I knew I had to make it a different way. And, as a consequence of that, it wouldn't be in any known genre, quite. I did know that. But what value that would be to anyone else, of course, you have no idea.'

The most obvious change was that Robert could no longer play the drums. Instead, he contributed hand percussion, using a tea tray and a toy drum borrowed from Delfina's son, James. On *Alifib*, he constructed a subtle percussion part simply from the sound of his own breathing. Otherwise, apart from a little guitar on *A Last Straw*, Wyatt restricted his instrumental contributions to piano and the Riviera organ. No keyboard virtuoso, Robert adopted an impressionistic style inspired by Pink Floyd's Rick Wright – and the Northern Lights: 'I'm not a keyboard player in the sense of the spectacular keyboard players I'd worked with, like Dave MacRae and Mike Ratledge and David Sinclair. But I thought that the way Rick created a sort of aurora borealis of harmonies around the Floyd was a very underestimated feature in what made them so distinct. He gave this wonderful backdrop to play on.'

The restrained percussion and keyboard parts left Wyatt free to concentrate on singing. On *A Last Straw*, Robert did his best impression

> A watery microcosm: Alfie's original cover for *Rock Bottom*.

of a horn solo, complete with opening and closing mute. 'There's two or three inspirations for that,' he recalls. 'One is, funnily enough, the brass instruments on Ellington records, where they use a lot of wah-wah. Then I noticed that Sly and the Family Stone were doing these wah-wah things – and between Ellington and Sly Stone, that was it. But then, with *Rock Bottom*, the whole end of the first song, *Sea Song*, was actually also encouraged by Indian classical singing.'

197

There were straight lyrics as well as voice-as-instrument scats, at times hinting at Wyatt's artistic rebirth. The line 'Dead moles lie inside their holes', on *Little Red Robin Hood Hit the Road*, is surely a reference to his previous band, and there is a quality to *Rock Bottom* that is childlike, even foetal. 'It seems to me', says Robert, 'that – unless you're a Creationist – we go through human evolution. In the early stage, a baby has gills. Later on it has a tail, which goes, and so on. And all this is done in a watery microcosm. We start our life underwater and our first development is underwater – before we are called a human. And it strikes me that maybe some kind of art actually taps into that, which is not available by conscious, rational means. You know, people think art transcends daily life. It may do the opposite. It feels like it's more about re-finding the animal inside the sophisticated human. That is more like my idea of what artists maybe do – or of what I am doing, if I'm an artist.'

Robert delights in 'the beauty of the thing badly done', and a childlike quality runs through his favourite music, literature and visual art. 'The way that Paul Klee and Picasso started doing infant-like scrawls when they got older,' he explains. 'I thought that was so moving and interesting. This abandonment of technique. The history of jazz was a bit like that too, in the sense of Ornette Coleman playing a violin – which he couldn't do. I find that really brave. Or Ivor Cutler drawing with his left hand because he found he was too facile with his right.'

Yet this instinctive approach was combined with a decade of experience as a professional musician, and a sense of absolute focus ran through the whole writing and recording process. For all its childlike qualities, *Rock Bottom* was also Wyatt's first mature record. Where his writing contributions to The Soft Machine and Matching Mole had been largely as an arranger and lyricist, *Rock Bottom* represents Robert's first consistently brilliant statement as a songwriter. At times, the album has the miry feel of *The End of an Ear*; at others, elements of the avant-garde jazz Wyatt had played with Centipede and The Amazing Band. Going back to The Wilde Flowers, the songs were also linked by what Robert calls 'trance sections'. The disparate strands of his career were twisted for the first time into a single thread.

-»)((- -»)((- -»)((-

It is often supposed that *Rock Bottom*, as a title and an album, reflected Wyatt's wretched emotional state following the accident. In fact, the title emerged, simply, from the 'rocky bottom' line on the second track, *A Last*

Straw. Indeed, the majority of tracks had been written when Robert was still, in his own words, a 'drummer biped'. He denies, for instance, that the fall inspired lines such as 'Oh no, no I can't stand it / Stop please' or the wonderfully English 'Oh blimey' on *Little Red Riding Hood Hit the Road*: 'I don't remember that song having anything to do with the accident,' he insists. 'In fact, I find the tradition of singer-songwriters working their way through their mental neuroses in public a bit limited.'

It is a fair point, and Wyatt, for all his insecurities, is less needy and narcissistic than many singer-songwriters. Even if we should be wary of reading too much into specific lyrics, however, it is impossible to believe that the accident did not to some extent colour Robert's treatment of even those songs written before the fall. 'Even though the *Rock Bottom* lyrics predate the accident,' says Henry Cow's Fred Frith, who played viola on *Little Red Riding Hood*, 'there's a sense that this record is a whole new beginning, and I'm sure that the combination of survival and starting afresh has a lot to do with it. It's a very emotional record.'

That emotion was complex and bittersweet. Robert's voice, as bassist Richard Sinclair puts it, expressed 'pain and joy all at the same moment'. Robert himself gives a slightly different complexion, describing the mood during the recording as closer to euphoria.

Certainly, the anguished *Little Red Riding Hood* showed only one end of the album's emotional spectrum. Representing the opposite extreme was the lovers' nonsense speak of *Alifib* and *Alife*. Some lines, such as Robert's 'Burlybunch, the water mole / Hellyplop and fingerhole', could have come straight from Edward Lear or Lewis Carroll. When Robert sings of 'Alife my larder', itself an arrestingly mature image in the maybe-baby world of rock'n'roll, Alfie actually puts in a brief appearance. 'I'm not your larder,' she replies, 'jammy jars and mustard / I'm not your dinner / you soppy old custard.'

'I was pissed,' Alfie remembers, 'and I was listening to this: "Oh, you're my this and my that." And I said, "No I'm not." And Robert said, "OK, answer me then." So I went away and wrote this thing. Then Steve Cox recorded me saying this little verse, and he stuck it on. It was a slightly tiddly response: "I'm not your larder..."' The set-up at Little Bedwyn was unusually intimate: Robert and Alfie were often joined at the cottage only by Steve Cox, the engineer, whose mobile studio was set up on the other side of the field. The braying of a distant donkey is, Robert insists, still audible in the final mix.

Although Robert and Alfie might not speak of it in such terms, *Rock Bottom* is in some senses a love album, yet that most familiar of musical subjects is approached from a startlingly fresh perspective. *Sea Song*, the album's most widely covered track, contains evocative lines such as 'your lunacy fits neatly with my own'. Yet it also finds Robert describing his beloved as 'partly fish, partly porpoise, partly baby sperm whale'. It's hard to imagine any other singer sounding as tender while comparing his girlfriend to a mutant fish.

Already more surreal than soppy, *Sea Song* is also saved from sentimentality by a heart-on-sleeve candour. The line about 'foam-crested brine' was inspired by the fact that Robert found Alfie rather

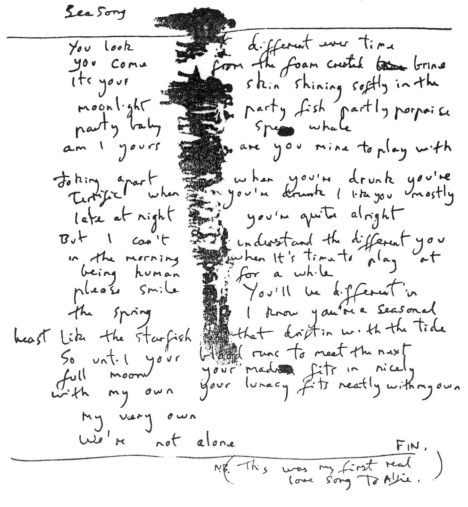

> *Sea Song* – 'my first real love song to Alfie' – handwritten by Robert for *MW*, a book of his lyrics published by Jean-Michel Marchetti.

more 'salty and practical' in the mornings than when drinking together the previous night. Instead of glossing over such temperamental differences, *Sea Song* addressed them head-on: 'I can't understand / The different you in the morning / When it's time to play at being / Human for a while / Please smile'. The final line of *Sea Song*, the simple but uplifting 'We're not alone', echoes something both Robert and Alfie say about their relationship: that their meeting brought an end to feelings of solitude. It could hardly have been lost on Wyatt that not every woman would have stayed with him after the fall. The 'party tangle' circumstances of the accident add a tremendous poignancy, too, to the apparently simple lyrics of *Little Red Riding Hood Hit the Road*: 'You've been so kind / I know I know / So why did I hurt you? / I didn't mean to hurt you / But I'll keep trying / And I'm sure you will too.'

When he left Delfina's farm, Wyatt had recorded a solo album in the strictest sense. A *Top Gear* session Robert recorded alone in September 1974 gives some idea of the sparse beauty these versions might have achieved. For *Rock Bottom* itself, however, he wanted other musicians to colour in the black and white outlines. He left Little Bedwyn for a second phase of recording at the Manor, an Oxfordshire manor house converted by Richard Branson's Virgin Records into the UK's first residential studio, with Nick Mason as producer.

Being in a wheelchair had not only forced Wyatt to change his primary instrument. By rendering all but impossible a career as regularly gigging musician, it freed him from the obligation to make an album he could recreate live – as well as from having to use the same musicians on every track. Seeking a guest musician, rather than full-time bandmate, Robert even felt comfortable enough to invite Hugh Hopper to put down three bass parts. Lingering tensions were eased by the fact that Hugh himself had now left Soft Machine, but also by the fact that Robert was only asking him into the studio for a matter of hours.

'The big difference with *Rock Bottom*', explains Wyatt, 'was that, not being in a group, you could choose particular guests to come in on particular tracks. I mean, there's two bass players. Hugh Hopper played on certain things I thought he'd be comfortable on and Richard Sinclair, another friend from East Kent, played on other tracks. You can't normally do that without causing friction.'

The choice of guests reflected Robert's panoramic musical tastes. Both sides of *Rock Bottom* closed with offbeat incantations from the Scottish poet, singer and storyteller Ivor Cutler, a marvellously eccentric character despite his protestations to the contrary ('I'm not an eccentric. Everybody else is an eccentric'). Cutler, who had taught for a period at A. S. Neill's progressive Summerhill School, was known for his singular wardrobe – plus fours, fez – and his epigrams, written on cards and distributed to strangers from his bicycle. Among them were such gems as 'Never knowingly understood', 'True happiness is knowing you're a hypocrite' and 'Add 15 inches to your stride and save 4 percent of insects'.

Ivor Cutler's Home Service broadcasts had been highlights of the week in Wyatt's adolescence, at Wellington House, and subsequently Cutler had been adopted by the counterculture: as John Peel's poet in residence and acting as bus conductor Buster Bloodvessel in The Beatles' *Magical*

> The insistently un-eccentric Ivor Cutler, *Rock Bottom*'s concluding voice.

Mystery Tour. Cutler brought to *Rock Bottom* a droll humour – and, on *Little Red Robin Hood Hit the Road* – the record's closing track – a final sense of resolution.

Musically, *Little Red Robin Hood* is remarkable for two guest contributions. Henry Cow's Fred Frith contributed improvised viola, building from double-stopped drone to screeching overtones reminiscent of The Velvet Underground's John Cale. And the track reaches its summit with an epic, multitracked guitar solo by former Kevin Ayers and The Whole World bassist Mike Oldfield.

David Bedford says it had long been clear that Oldfield was 'a genius', and his guitar playing was as crucial to *Rock Bottom* as it had been to The Whole World. Even more important to the album was Oldfield's suggestion that Robert multitrack the Riviera organ to create a more full-bodied, shimmering effect. The simple, portable combo organ Alfie had picked up in Venice sounded scrawny next to the more popular Vox and Farfisa brands, let alone the growl of a Hammond. Yet the Riviera would define the album's sound. 'You only have to get one of these things,' laughs Robert, 'put three fingers on it, and you'd say, "Oh, that sounds like Robert Wyatt's *Rock Bottom*."'

Jazz-rock fusion had been, to Wyatt, the worst of both worlds. Freed from the band format, Robert was finally able to combine rock and jazz – plus the absurdism of Ivor Cutler and Alfie's spoken word interlude – in the 'upside down' fashion towards which he'd been stumbling for years. South Africa's Mongezi Feza appeared on *Little Red Riding Hood*, which concludes the album's first side, single-handedly creating what the *NME* called a 'fierce forest of trumpets'. The squeaking tenor saxophone of Gary Windo, on *Alife*, provided the album's other flirtation with free jazz. 'The looseness of jazz, and the rhythm section of jazz,' was the intention, explains Wyatt, 'but with a folk song element to what happens on top. Then bursting through into Gary Windo or Mongezi Feza. I wanted landscape contrasts like that.'

The results sounded like nothing and no-one else. 'I haven't ever deliberately tried to be either different or the same,' shrugs Wyatt. 'It just so happens that, when I am doing my own thing, what I hear in my head doesn't seem to me to be very much like anything else. What I do, it's not even in a category that I could name. And this is not some attempt to be different. It just *isn't*: it isn't rock'n'roll, it isn't jazz, it isn't modern classical music, it isn't folk music. It doesn't exist as a genre. It's like a Galápagos Island animal, some kind of underwater duck. Just some sort of *thing* that I turned out to be.'

Laurie Allan, from Delivery and Gong (and an old boyfriend of Alfie's), played drums on two tracks. Both of these were recorded – like those featuring Richard Sinclair – not at the Manor, but at CBS studios in London. Like Mongs and Gary Windo, Laurie was a versatile musician, technically impressive but content to serve the song rather than his own ego. 'Laurie was a free-jazz enthusiast,' recalls Nick Mason, 'and when we sent him the track, he went completely bananas, playing free over the whole thing. Robert and I looked at each other, trying to work out who was going to have to start telling him how to do it. But it then transpired that he hadn't actually been hearing the track, he'd just been fiddling around setting up. It's a great story in a way, because when you hear that track, it's just the opposite – this absolutely fantastic light touch.'

Wyatt won't admit to any frustration that he was unable to play the drum parts himself, instead paying tribute to Laurie as the only person capable of doing it properly. He is not only being big-hearted. One of the reasons Robert was able to morph so effectively into a solo career was that, for a virtuoso drummer, his musical perspective had always been unusually broad. 'What I was interested in was the *music*,' he maintains. 'Most of my contributions to the bands I'd been in had been in terms of organisation: the trajectory of the concerts, how to begin, how to end, what shape it would be. What I didn't like was the habits in jazz and rock'n'roll of where solos would come and where vocals would come. I liked to try to arrange it so it was a moving, changing landscape all the way through the set. Drumming was part of that, almost like being a conductor. You think: "Well, we've just had ten minutes of ferocious business; let's have a nice open space here and then go somewhere else." Just thinking in terms of the whole set rather than each tune. The very fact that I'd written *Moon in June* – drums have a fairly modest role on that. I was thinking about the overall music.'

Prog rock might have been at its peak in 1973 but, says Alfie, it had become 'too much playing your instrument and not enough music, just so clever-dick with the time signatures'. Instead, the arrangements on *Rock Bottom* were inspired by John Coltrane, Indian classical music and *Astral Weeks*, Van Morrison's sublime amalgamation of Celtic soul and jazz. Released in 1968, *Astral Weeks* was Morrison's first significant solo statement after breaking free of a regular pop band; with its 'childlike visions leaping into view', the record shares with *Rock Bottom* a combination of maturity and wonder that seems closely linked to artistic rebirth. Morrison's record also mixed elements of jazz and rock

> Mike Oldfield, guitarist and multitrack visionary on *Rock Bottom*.

without sounding like the established template of jazz-rock fusion, and seems equally poised between hope and despair.

Rock Bottom shared the unhurried spaciousness of *Astral Weeks*: the willingness, in Robert's words, to just let things unfold. For his piano solo on *Sea Song* he seemed almost to slow time, a basketball player hanging in the air a second or two longer than his opponents. Key to this sense of pause and poise was the man in the producer's chair, who came into his own once Wyatt moved from Delfina's farm to the Manor. 'Nick Mason had that wonderful Floyd sense of space,' remembers Wyatt. 'They made a new architecture, the Floyd. That was their great contribution, and that's why I got Nick in. There was always a tendency for me to bunch things up and get lost in dense detail. He just said, "All good stuff, but space it out. Give the listener time to breathe. Go with the flow." And he used to crack dry British jokes, to stop everyone getting too hubristic.'

For his part, Mason describes *Rock Bottom* as 'probably the most satisfying bit of production I've ever done – and great fun. The way I've always approached production is not to bring very much to it, but just to try to help the artist do whatever they want. Occasionally try to find some sort of idea if they're a bit stuck, but Robert was rarely stuck for

> Producer Nick Mason working with Robert on *I'm a Believer*, which followed on from *Rock Bottom*.

anything. With so much recorded music, the tendency – particularly if you're a good musician – is to want to put all your brilliance down. I think it should absolutely be the space between the notes and all that stuff. You want less rather than more.'

Mason was also familiar with what were then advanced editing and multitrack recording techniques. *Little Red Riding Hood*, for instance, was flipped halfway through, so that most of the instruments played backwards throughout the second half of the song. Richard Sinclair, however, was required to play his part in real time, an experience he likens to taking an acid trip.

⇢⟐⇠ ⇢⟐⇠ ⇢⟐⇠

She may have inspired several songs on the album, but Alfie's involvement in *Rock Bottom* went far beyond mere muse: even before she went on to become Robert's co-lyricist, her role was hardly passive. As well as contributing the spoken word section of *Alife*, it was Alfie who suggested the album title, Alfie who suggested *Astral Weeks* as a reference point and Alfie who suggested that Richard Sinclair perform over the tape join on *Little Red Riding Hood*.

Her influence on Robert's career from this point on parallels that of another husband-and-wife team on the other side of the Atlantic: Kathleen Brennan and Tom Waits. Brennan helped her husband from brilliant but hardly groundbreaking Beatnik barfly into a strikingly original artist, drawing on influences from Captain Beefheart to microtonal composer Harry Partch. She would go on to co-write several songs with her husband, to help get his finances in order and to give him the confidence to work without a producer. Eventually, again like Alfie, she helped the once heavy drinker become teetotal.

Also like Brennan, Alfie played a key part in negotiating a new record deal. *Rock Bottom* would be released on the new Virgin label – whose owner, Richard Branson, also owned the Manor studio. Hard as it may be to believe, given the contemporary associations with everything from airlines and trains to mobile phones, Virgin was in those days an alternative, slightly underground, operation, its very name an allusion to their lack of business acumen.

'I don't think Richard Branson was ever anything remotely like a hippie,' says Peter Blegvad, whose band Slapp Happy were also signed to Virgin. 'He had the trappings of a hippie, but I think he was always a hard-nosed businessman with his eye on the main chance and making money. That's what drove him. But of course it was bad manners to be a breadhead in those days. And it was a very casual, open set-up. You could just walk in to Richard's office and he'd be sitting there on the phone: a very tolerant guy, at least in those days. After business hours, everyone would cross Portobello Road and sit in the pub, and it would just be long-haired ne'er-do-wells hanging out together and dreaming. The roster of acts in those days was definitely leaning towards the alternative, the experimental. That seemed pretty damned wonderful at the time.'

Robert was attracted by the fact that Virgin seemed more interested in albums than singles, and by the fact that the label, together with its subsidiary, Caroline, was signing a whole fistful of related acts: Henry Cow, Gong, Slapp Happy, Hatfield and the North, Lol Coxhill, Lady June, Ivor Cutler. Virgin, Robert told a journalist at the time, was where all his mates were.

That Virgin signed so many musicians associated with Wyatt was no coincidence. Most agree that Richard Branson, for all his entrepreneurial talents, never seemed interested in the creative side of running a label. Instead, he left the music policy to his cousin Simon Draper and his assistant, Donald Vanrenen, known to all as Jumbo.

'It seemed as if Richard had decided to try to corner the market in a field small enough to dominate, rather as Island had done,' says Chris Cutler. 'I don't think he particularly liked the kind of music the label wound up supporting. But he trusted Simon Draper and Jumbo Vanrenen, who did like – and knew well – this music, and he gave them their head. They in turn went, more or less, after anybody who had ever had anything to do with The Soft Machine: first Kevin, who they didn't get, but then Mike Oldfield, David Bedford and Lol Coxhill, who were all in Kevin's band at the time, who they did. They also signed Daevid and went after Robert. Even Henry Cow was recommended to Virgin by Daevid Allen, Ian MacDonald and Robert Wyatt – all Soft Machine connections.'

As South Africans, Draper and Jumbo were also very much aware of their exiled compatriots, and used the Caroline subsidiary to release jazz albums such as Dudu Pukwana's *In the Townships*, featuring fellow ex-Blue Note Mongezi Feza. Virgin also signed reggae acts like U-Roy, and distributed Carla Bley's avant-garde Watt label. But Simon Draper had a particular weakness for the musicians of the Canterbury Scene. 'When I was at university in South Africa,' he recalls, 'I was avidly reading the *Melody Maker* and *NME*, but also *Downbeat* and American stuff. And I remember reading an article about The Soft Machine by Michael Zwerin. And I was so taken with the idea of them that I bought the first Soft Machine album from an import shop in Johannesburg without ever hearing it. And it lived up to my huge expectations. I became a huge fan.'

Draper remained a Kevin Ayers fan, which is how Virgin came to pick up *Tubular Bells* – the debut solo album by Mike Oldfield which all the main labels had turned down. '*Tubular Bells* had huge significance to me,' Draper explains, 'because he had been in the Kevin Ayers band. I loved his solo on *Whatevershebringswesing*, and his playing on *Shooting at the Moon*, where he mainly played bass. I was interested in what he was doing because of his association with Kevin.' Somehow managing to be both middle-of-the-road and genuinely avant-garde, *Tubular Bells* was, if nothing else, a dazzling technical achievement. Beginning life on a tape machine borrowed from Kevin Ayers, Oldfield played twenty instruments on the final album, which comprised two lengthy, almost entirely instrumental pieces.

> Fellow Virgin band Hatfield and the North was virtually family, comprising (from right): Richard Sinclair, Dave Stewart, Pip Pyle and Phil Miller.

It was hardly an obvious cash cow. Yet the album would reach number two in the UK charts and, after featuring on the soundtrack for *The Exorcist*, made the US top three. The record launched not only Virgin Records but the entire Virgin empire. Branson's five-billion-dollar fortune can, bizarrely, be traced back to Simon Draper's fondness for Soft Machine.

The Wyatts do not have particularly fond memories of Branson, although Robert remains grateful that he visited the hospital with an invitation to join his new label. And it was, in fact, Alfie's dealings with the emerging tycoon that set her on the path towards becoming Wyatt's manager. Unhappy with Virgin's contract, and especially the suggestion that Robert should incorporate his publishing rights into the record deal with Virgin (cutting off its potential income), she set up a meeting with Branson. 'We went to see Richard,' she recalls, 'and I said, "That clause has got to come out." And he said, "I don't speak to women about these kind of things. Get a lawyer." So we paid what was then a fortune, four hundred quid, to get a lawyer to speak to his lawyer and cross it out. But our lawyer turned out to be worth every penny, because he put a time limit on the ownership. Which is why Robert is the only person on Virgin who owns his back catalogue. So that was lucky that he wouldn't listen to women.'

It was force of circumstance that pushed Alfie into managing Robert – that forced her, in her own words, to become a grown-up. 'It's like, if two people are scared of mice, and there's only two people, one of them will have to overcome their fear of mice and deal with it.' Alfie would make a highly effective manager, understanding that, more than knowing the ins and outs of copyright law, the key job requirement is simply to maintain and deserve the artist's absolute trust. Despite her success in the role, however, it was not the path she would have chosen. She had, after all, been on track for a career in film until Robert's accident – and she never did get that union card.

Aware of that untapped art school background, Robert asked Alfie to design a front cover for *Rock Bottom*: the final element in an album of rare conceptual coherence. Alfie's image, inspired by a Victorian book cover, depicted a beach scene: seagulls, sandcastles, distant steamer. The bottom third of the picture was given over to the flora and fauna beneath the water's surface, as strange and weird as anything on Mars. Her muted pencil drawing was a reflection of the music and its Venetian inception. It was also a deliberate attempt to distance *Rock Bottom* from the dazzle of competitors such as Roger Dean, who designed famously elaborate covers for Yes: 'It was prog-rock time,' recalls Alfie, 'and all the covers were getting more and more complicated, competing with each other with pizzazz. I thought the only way to counter that, to stand out, was to be absolutely minimal and quiet, which you didn't get. You got things with doors that opened, and dragons.'

Alfie would be responsible for the artwork of every record Robert released from this point on. Journalist Vivien Goldman would later compare her relationship with Robert to jazz trumpeter Don Cherry and his painter wife Moki, her sleeves providing 'such a deep-pile context for the music that it's almost impossible to think of one without the other floating into your mind.'

―✺⟨⟨― ―✺⟨⟨― ―✺⟨⟨―

In advance of the release of *Rock Bottom*, Robert managed a few live appearances. In April and May 1974, he appeared with Hatfield and the North, for whose eponymous debut album he had recorded a wordless version of Phil Miller's *Calyx*. When Wyatt later added lyrics, the tune would become a Canterbury Scene standard: 'Poetry in motion is what you've become...' The following month, he was asked to take part in an all-star concert at the Rainbow, devised as a live album for Island's key artists, Kevin Ayers, Brian Eno, John Cale and Nico. As well as various Ayers numbers, and a couple of Eno songs, the supergroup brought a sense of disembodied dread to covers of *Heartbreak Hotel* and *The End*. Offstage, things were less harmonious. The story goes that Ayers seduced Cale's wife at the show, apparently inspiring a line in Cale's song *Guts* ('the bugger in the short sleeves fucked my wife'). There was no further collaboration between the two musicians.

In July, Robert took part in a concert at the ICA, a benefit for the family of the illustrator, jazz critic and Amazing Band trumpeter Mal

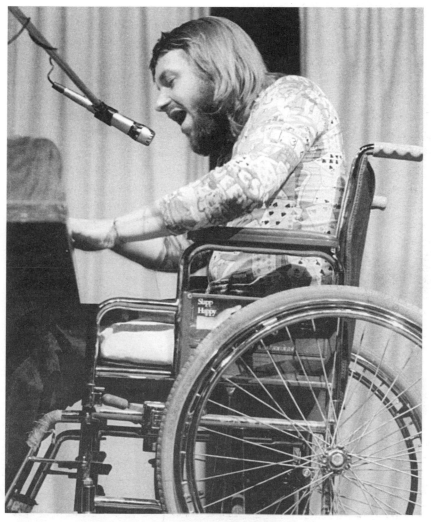

› Robert's first solo performance, previewing *Rock Bottom* at the Mal Dean benefit at the ICA, 25 July 1974.

Dean, who had died from cancer at the age of just thirty-two. According to *Melody Maker*'s report, Wyatt seemed 'naked and alone' during the performance, which previewed songs from *Rock Bottom*, though the audience reportedly responded warmly – particularly when Gary Windo joined him mid-set on tenor saxophone. Wyatt himself recalls the gig as terrifying, which was hardly surprising. Quite apart from the new logistical challenges posed by being in a wheelchair, this was his first ever solo performance.

Whether or not the audience picked up on Wyatt's nerves, they didn't have long to wait before hearing the album proper. *Rock Bottom* was released by Virgin the following morning: 26 July 1974 – a day Robert chose because it was the anniversary of the opening salvo of the Cuban Revolution.

As if the occasion wasn't momentous enough, Robert married Alfie the same day. 'I don't remember the details,' says Alfie, 'but it was probably my idea. All that was on his mind was this live thing at the ICA the night before. He was worrying about that the whole time. You could have said anything to him, "I'll cut your legs off on Wednesday night," and he'd have said, "Yeah, yeah." So I just said something like, "*Rock Bottom* is coming out, let's get married the same day."'

'Charming and extraordinary' is Wyatt's own, equally played down, recollection of Alfie's proposal of marriage. 'Whether she regrets it or not, you'd have to ask her. But I'm very grateful.'

The wedding took place in Sheen Registry Office. Robert wore a green gingham shirt, Alfie an Indian dress. Apart from the registrar, who stayed seated throughout on Wyatt's behalf, the only people present were his half-brother Julian Glover, Julian's wife Isla Blair and the *NME* photographer Pennie Smith.

Having finally moved into the flat bought for them by Julie Christie, the newly-weds held a reception party in Twickenham. 'We didn't decide to get married until as near as you can get,' recalls Alfie. 'I thought, "Well, we'll have a party at our house. It's such short notice and it's a Friday, nobody's going to be available." So I rang up 70 people and said, "By the way we're getting married if you want to come round." And they *all* came. So it was quite a lot. But it was summer and we had a garden…

'My mum made some things to eat. I made some sausages. We had some Smarties, sausages, "teenage pudding" [raspberry cheesecake] – various unhip items. Some giant bottles of incredibly cheap and probably dreadfully horrible Italian wine. The whole thing cost £70 and that included my wedding dress, which was £14. Because it was the

> A Wyatt wedding. Robert and Alfie sign up, witnessed by Julian Glover and his wife Isla Blair, at Sheen Registry Office, 26 July 1974.

same day as *Rock Bottom* was released, people at Virgin came, including the beastly Branson.'

As well as Richard Branson, those present included *Rock Bottom* contributors Fred Frith, Richard Sinclair, Ivor Cutler, Gary Windo and Mongezi Feza, as well as old musical associates and friends Lol Coxhill, Pip Pyle and John Peel.

Richard Branson held a separate event to mark the album launch, at which Wyatt performed extracts from *Rock Bottom*. Reviews of the album were by this stage starting to appear, and were unanimous in their praise. 'Robert Wyatt was probably the most creative and individual drummer in British rock,' declared the *NME*'s Ian MacDonald, 'and his enforced retirement from that activity is a great loss. Fortunately, he is also one of the most creative and individual singers/composers in British rock, as you can hear on *Rock Bottom*, the title of his new album.' Steve Peacock of *Sounds* was equally enthusiastic: 'Not only is *Rock Bottom* the album you've been hoping Robert Wyatt would make for years, it is one hundred per cent better than you dared hope it would be. Welcome to critical overkill – bear with me – but for once I think it is justified… Strong without being arrogant or overbearing, melodic without being fettered, it embodies all the things that make Robert a musician, singer and composer with no rivals and few equals.'

That Christmas, *Rock Bottom* appeared among end-of-year highlights in both the *Melody Maker* and the *NME*, who ranked it with Bob Dylan's *Blood on the Tracks*, while critics in France awarded it the prestigious Grand Prix International du Disque as an album of the year. It is still widely considered one of the finest albums ever made.

For Robert, *Rock Bottom* represented a new dawn. 'People think I must have problems talking about my accident,' he later explained. 'But I don't; what I have problems talking about is what happened *before* the accident. *Rock Bottom* and beyond, that I see as me. But my adolescent self, the drummer biped, I don't remember him and I don't understand him… I see the accident now as being a sort of neat division line between my adolescence and the rest of my life.'

Wyatt still insists that breaking his back, marrying Alfie and releasing *Rock Bottom* represent his 'year zero'. Few fans would share the casual dismissal of his decade with The Soft Machine and Matching Mole, nor his dismissal of his drumming as mere adolescence. Robert was in fact twenty-eight when he broke his back. It is absolutely true, however, that his life splits, LP-like, into two distinct halves. Side One sees him married to Pam and primarily a drummer. He is also walking. On Side Two, Wyatt is paraplegic, married to Alfie, and a solo artist, primarily a singer. Unlike most albums, it is not front-loaded: the second half is even finer than the first.

12

I'M A BELIEVER

Drury Lane, *Top of the Pops* and Henry Cow

'**For Robert Wyatt of Twickenham, opportunity knocks!**' announced compere John Peel in his typically off-kilter introduction. Robert had chosen to premiere *Rock Bottom* with a full band at the Theatre Royal, on London's Drury Lane, and the warmth of feeling was unmistakable.

Robert would learn later that the theatre had been designed by Benjamin Dean Wyatt, one of the architects on his mother's side of the family. But, even without the historical rhyme, this would have been an extraordinary show. Wyatt's first headline gig since the fall, it earned him the front cover of the *NME*, and a standing ovation before he had sung a note. Characteristically, Robert was petrified. 'I thought it would be a disaster, quite frankly,' he concedes. 'I just thought, "I can't do this, it's going to be ridiculous. Just get it over with."'

The nerves showed at first. But from the moment the opening vocal of *Sea Song* was recognised with applause, Wyatt's fists began to unclench. The set featured every number from *Rock Bottom*, each more extended and exuberant than its studio counterpart. Eventually, Robert relaxed enough to start making jokes: 'With a bit of promotion he could do very well,' was his deadpan comment on Mike Oldfield, whose *Tubular Bells* was already well on its way to selling twenty-five million copies.

For the live show, the *Rock Bottom* band, including both Nick Mason and Laurie Allan on drums, were joined by Dave Stewart (the one from

Hatfield and the North rather than Eurythmics). Vocalist Julie Tippetts, a friend since Centipede, offered support on a couple of the ensemble numbers and also performed solo tracks from her album *Sunset Glow*, which Robert regards as a *Rock Bottom* companion piece.

> The cast of Robert's Drury Lane Theatre line-up in wheelchair solidarity, an image used for the the concert poster and on the cover of the *NME*.

As well as *Rock Bottom*, played in its entirety and in order, Robert played versions of Hugh Hopper's *Dedicated to You But You Weren't Listening* and *Memories*. He concluded with Matching Mole's *Instant Pussy* and *Signed Curtain*, and *Calyx* by Hatfield and the North. It was a perfectly judged set, driven by a flawless performance from the rhythm section, and the critics, from both the music and daily papers, were enraptured. 'There was more genuine originality in Robert Wyatt's concert at Drury Lane Theatre last night than I have heard for a long time,' raved Maurice Rosenbaum in the *Daily Telegraph*. 'It is a variety of pop music for which there is no neat pigeonhole but it is as creative and satisfying in its own way as the music of the so-called "serious" avant garde.'

Even Wyatt admits to warm memories of the show. 'I was surprised at the elastic energy that sustains the whole thing,' he says, after listening back to the live recording, issued many years later as *Theatre Royal Drury Lane 8th September 1974*. 'Not just me, but the way the whole group gelled. Laurie Allan and Hugh as a rhythm section. Dave Stewart, I thought, was brilliant on keyboards. These lovely guitarists, Fred and Mike Oldfield. This lovely team of Mongezi and Gary Windo. And then Julie coming in halfway through. I get a nice warm feeling from that record, I really do.'

–»)《«– –»)《«– –»)《«–

The encore at Drury Lane was a jubilant version of Wyatt's first solo single, released by Virgin two days previously: an offbeat cover of *I'm a Believer*, written by Neil Diamond and made famous by The Monkees. Robert maintains that the whole thing was a misunderstanding: 'Simon Draper at Virgin saw an interview with me in one of the music papers, where somebody asked me, "If you had to do some songs, just pop songs, which ones would you do?" I listed a few. And he actually called my bluff and said: "Would you do one?"'

It was not the most predictable move from the man who had just released *Rock Bottom*. Yet rueful cover versions of popular tunes, from Chic's *At Last I Am Free* to *What a Wonderful World*, most famously sung by Louis Armstrong, would become a Wyatt trademark.

Like these later reworkings, *I'm a Believer* allowed Robert to express his contrarian side. 'Sometimes I am having a laugh,' he admits. 'I was doing like a "what if" thing, which can actually come from the visual arts, the sort of juxtapositions you might get in what used to be called

> Robert at Drury Lane, flanked by Mike Oldfield and Fred Frith.

surrealist art. I just thought: "What if, in some deranged moment, Neil Diamond, who wrote *I'm a Believer* – what if actually McCoy Tyner had written it? What would the chords be like?" I do like to have fun with things like that.'

I'm a Believer also reflected Wyatt's genuine conviction that pop was as valid as the more technically complex music played by McCoy Tyner, a virtuoso pianist best known for his work with John Coltrane. To Robert, who had loved playing for dancers with The Wilde Flowers, the growing dichotomy between 'disposable' pop and 'authentic' rock seemed absurd. Even if they later learned to play their instruments, The Monkees were the ultimate 'manufactured' group – yet Robert saw their popularity as part of their appeal. 'It's amazing to hear myself saying this,' he told *Sounds*, 'and five years ago if I'd heard myself I'd have been shocked to the core, but a lot of innovative music is like Esperanto. We make this incredible new language… but who the fuck's going to use it?'

For all that, Wyatt's foray into the lingua franca of pop was a long way from The Monkees' original, closer in spirit to the covers of 1960s tunes that emerged in the aftermath of punk: Devo's *Satisfaction*, The Slits' *I Heard It Through the Grapevine*, Magazine's *Thank You (Falettinme Be Mice Elf Agin)*, *Money* by The Flying Lizards. It wasn't just the wonderfully skewed violin solo by Fred Frith. Whether Robert anticipated it or not, a line about disappointment haunting his dreams had a very different resonance when delivered from a wheelchair.

I'm a Believer was released on 6 September 1974, with The Wilde Flowers' enduring *Memories* as the B-side. To the surprise of everyone involved, it reached number twenty-nine in the charts, one of only two hits in Wyatt's entire career. John Peel made it record of the week in *Sounds*; Charles Shaar Murray, likewise in the *NME*. *Melody Maker* got particularly carried away, declaring it 'the best single for many years… an all-time great'.

On 18 September, Robert and friends mimed *I'm a Believer* on *Top of the Pops* to a reported audience of five million: a startling development for those who had followed his career since the days of UFO club. Yet this was no conventional bid for chart success. Nick Mason, who produced the studio version of the track, played drums for the performance, and chuckles that, 'in terms of trying to interest an audience in new music, it's probably the wildest thing that's ever been on *Top of the Pops*'. According to Wyatt, Mason broke into a sweat at having to play faster than 'Pink Floyd tempo' of 70 bpm. 'My doctor told me never to play faster than my pulse rate,' countered the drummer.

Dave MacRae, formerly of Matching Mole, pounded out the piano part, while Richard Sinclair, by this stage a member of Hatfield and the North, played bass. Sinclair still recalls the artificiality of the experience: 'We had to mime three times: once for a sound rehearsal, once for a dress rehearsal and again for the real show. So not a note was played by these wonderful musicians for a whole day.'

Wyatt himself, draped in what looked like a hospital gown, could hardly have looked further from the airbrushed world of pop. Eyes screwed shut rather than making love to the camera, he rocked backwards and forwards in his chair, pitching and rolling like a ship

Side One

Screen Gems

I'M A BELIEVER (3.30)
(Neil Diamond)
ROBERT WYATT
Produced by NICK MASON
© Virgin Records Ltd

VS.114
V-ÞII·SA
℗ 1974

in a storm. With his beard and shaggy hair, he would later liken his appearance on the show to that of an ageing bear.

Sadly, there was friction between the ursine singer and the show's producer – and it wasn't caused by sartorial differences. Instead, the squabble centred on Robert's wheelchair, apparently deemed unsuitable for family viewing. 'The BBC were astonishingly stupid about it,' says Fred Frith, who recalls the disagreement lasting throughout the day. Richard Sinclair even remembers having to prop Wyatt up in his chair at one point, when someone insisted upon removing the arms. The BBC did eventually allow him to perform from his wheelchair and, reluctant to become a spokesman for disabled politics, Robert often downplays the incident. Certainly he won't hear of his role as a paraplegic musician being in any sense trailblazing. When pushed, however, he does admit *Top of the Pops* was a nasty surprise: 'It was the first time anybody had made me feel unsightly. And it was a shock. I thought other people must think that, but they don't say it. It did upset me.'

> The band assembled for *Top of the Pops*; from left, Richard Sinclair, Dave MacRae, Andy Summers, Nick Mason, Robert and Fred Frith.

There was a happier TV experience on Granada's *Forty-Five* show the following month. Overall, however, Robert found his flirtation with the pop industry deeply unsettling and was not enthusiastic for more. 'I wasn't making a jump for the charts,' he sighs, 'but it turned out Virgin *were*. I didn't know. Who knew that they were actually desperate to be exactly the same as every other record label? Simon was thinking, "Let's have some hit singles." The whole point of that record company was that bands *didn't* have to have hit singles.'

Wyatt thought *I'm a Believer* was a curveball. For Virgin, it was the future – although, as Simon Draper admits, they were still very much feeling their way. 'You have to remember also that we were novices, really, in the business of marketing singles,' he concedes. 'The Virgin stores never sold singles. Our stance was that we were going to release singles as radio tracks, we never actually expected to have hits. Then we started to realise that, if we had hits, we would sell more albums. So we learned how to do it. But it wasn't really until the late 1970s, with punk, that we got any good at it. We were learning how to run a record company. There was no-one to teach us: we had to do it ourselves. We didn't employ people who had worked at other record companies. We saw their experience at other record companies as being a distinct disadvantage. We were', he laughs, 'quite arrogant, to say the least.'

As a follow-up, Wyatt recorded another cover version, *Yesterday Man*, a top three hit the previous decade for the English singer and songwriter Chris Andrews. Like *I'm a Believer*, Wyatt's version dug beneath the original's feelgood surface to expose the song's melancholic underbelly. But, although Robert was happy with the result, some at Virgin apparently considered it too lugubrious. Given a delayed and low-key release, it marked the beginning of the end for Wyatt and Virgin, although he remained with the label for one more album and continued to work with other Virgin artists, notably Henry Cow.

-»)(«- -»)(«- -»)(«-

In October 1974, the month after the triumphant Drury Lane show, Wyatt was asked whether he expected to be back onstage any time soon. 'No, absolutely not,' he replied. 'I'm not being responsible any more for half a dozen other people's food and rent… If I stop working now, I can just sit about for a year if I want and have a think, something that you're never free to do with a band.'

It wasn't that Wyatt desired an idle twelve months. The problem, rather, was that he refused to take responsibility for running, as an ongoing project, the sort of band he had assembled for the Drury Lane show. Robert's horizons were also expanding beyond popular music – and he was now rationalising his discomfort with showbiz in socialist terms. 'Very often you will find there's a class thing in it,' he explained to *Sounds*, 'and that groups from what [reactionary journalist] Auberon Waugh calls the lower orders are desperate to get into the charts, because the alternative is not being successful and it's not much fun. Comfortable gents like Slapp Happy and myself are going to lead nice, pleasant lives, with nice social lives, whether we're successful or not.'

Slapp Happy were an art-pop trio, comprising American-born musician, writer and cartoonist Peter Blegvad, English avant-garde composer Anthony Moore and German vocalist Dagmar Krause. Originally based in Hamburg, they signed to Virgin and moved to England, later merging for two albums with Henry Cow. Peter Blegvad

> Art-pop trio Slapp Happy: Peter Blegvad, Dagmar Krause and Anthony Moore.

says Wyatt had been a hero ever since *Third*: 'I never dreamed that I would actually *meet* the guy.' But when Blegvad and his bandmates arrived in England, Robert soon invited them round to his house in Twickenham – where they were impressed to find him a certified devotee of Alfred Jarry's science of imaginary solutions.

'I remember being completely blown away that he had a certificate on his wall from the Collège de Pataphysique in Paris,' says Blegvad, himself later president of the London Institute of Pataphysics. 'I was a very keen Alfred Jarry fan, and fan of French surrealism. So, to add to all his other qualities, that he was also recognised by the Collège – that just made him a god! But his friendliness, his generosity, and this kind of clear honesty about the guy; there's something so soulful, just the bedrock. So a kind of awe-inspiring figure. But he broke that very quickly. He just wanted direct, no bullshit. So that was great.'

Wyatt joined Slapp Happy for a *Top Gear* recording in June 1974, sharing vocals with Blegvad and Krause. *A Little Something*, preserved for posterity on the *Flotsam Jetsam* compilation, is a skewed, bossa-tinged pop song, with Dagmar singing lead and Wyatt and Blegvad on backing vocals – and, as the latter concedes, getting rather carried away with the Noël Coward accents.

More significantly, Robert joined Henry Cow – now incorporating Slapp Happy vocalist Dagmar Krause – for three gigs the following summer. It was a characteristic Wyatt pendulum swing: from playing Neil Diamond on *Top of the Pops* to a group who had toured with Faust and Captain Beefheart and were every bit as uncompromising. A character in the Jonathan Coe novel *The Rotters' Club* describes Henry Cow as 'The Yardbirds getting into bed with Ligeti in the smoking rubble of divided Berlin'. In fact, the band's influences were broader still: from Coltrane to Captain Beefheart via Varèse, Schoenberg, Mingus, Sun Ra, Syd Barrett, and Eisler, Weill and Brecht.

The collaboration with Henry Cow was a natural step. The band was signed, like Wyatt, to Virgin; Fred Frith had played on *I'm a Believer* and *Rock Bottom*, as well as almost joining Matching Mole, while Robert had collaborated with Dagmar Krause in Slapp Happy. There were friends in common, too, including Lol Coxhill, Ivor Cutler and the South African trumpet player Mongezi Feza. Just as important as this musical common ground was a broad ideological affinity. Henry Cow's background, chuckles bassist John Greaves, was 'very much heart-on-the-sleeve, left-wing, fairly radical… a rainbow of lefty weirdos'. A proposed *Melody Maker* advert, never actually published, made the band's politics still more overt: 'This is where our music comes from: from a disgust with Capitalism & its degrading of everything into money relations...'

Chris Cutler, however, points out that this political affinity was more assumed than overt: 'We had something of a political reputation,' he recalls, 'and so did Robert. To a degree deservedly – because, given half a chance, we would all make semi-outrageous political statements in interviews. But we weren't living and breathing the ideology. Somebody might say, "That's bourgeois crap," and we'd all nod because that was a language we all understood. But that would be the end of it. A commonality was accepted. I don't think we ever had any heated ideological discussions, much less debates.'

Wyatt joined Henry Cow for dates in Paris, London and Rome. 'Hugely exciting, vast crowds of people,' is how Fred Frith recalls the shows. 'In Paris they smashed a window of the theatre trying to get in, when it was sold out.' 'I think the one in Paris is the most legendary,' agrees John Greaves. 'Perhaps it's because I live in France. I must have personally met at least 40,000 people who claimed they were at that gig.'

The London show was recorded, with two tracks subsequently appearing on Henry Cow's *Concerts* album. Wyatt duetted with Dagmar on *Bad Alchemy* and added lead vocals to a driving *Little Red Riding Hood Hit the Road*. As well as the musical and political common ground, part of the reason the collaboration worked was that he and Dagmar had such different voices: his English, intimate and colloquial, hers Germanic and theatrical, recalling the Weimar Republic world of Hans Eisler and Kurt Weill.

In June came the third and final show, a huge open-air gig in Italy – Wyatt's first performance in the country that had so captured his father's heart. 'We played in the Piazza Navona, which used to be a chariot-racing arena,' recalls Fred Frith. 'Robert did a circuit in his wheelchair, which was very entertaining. More than 20,000 people came out. It was also a free concert publicising a campaign to legalise marijuana, which we hadn't known before we got there.'

From a musical point of view, Wyatt seems to have enjoyed singing with a band: 'During these rehearsals I remember Robert telling me that singers in a band are often quite misunderstood,' recalls Dagmar. 'Because we carry our instrument inside our body, it is part of us. Our voice is integral to who we are, directly connected to our core.' Yet, though she recalls the concerts as 'a great success', Dagmar was also aware that Robert found the concerts physically challenging.

> Henry Cow at the Piazza Navona, Rome, June 1975. From left, Lindsay Cooper, Robert, Dagmar Krause and Chris Cutler.

'He tried this one concert in Italy with Henry Cow,' explains Alfie, 'and it was just a disaster. He had to be carried up the stairs, because there wasn't a hotel in Rome with a ground floor lavatory he could get into. Consequently, he didn't keep asking to be carried up the stairs. So he was out in the boiling heat, dying to go to the loo, backing up, getting iller and iller, and then had to perform. It just wasn't practical. He was up for going and doing concerts, but it was just such a drain on him.'

The ignominy hit a spot still bruised by *Top of the Pops*. Provision for wheelchairs has improved dramatically since 1975, yet Robert has performed a mere handful of times since Rome – and even then only as a guest. 'I've done it a couple of times,' he later explained, 'and I'm just passing out with fear. I'm so knotted up with anxiety.' Rather than the physical challenges and minor humiliations, though, Robert says he is kept from the stage by a terror of not being good enough. 'I see a line of people outside,' he says, 'and they've all combed their hair and bought tickets and I've got to entertain them for that evening. I just feel so awful. I think: "I'm so sorry, I don't know if I can do it tonight." I just feel the responsibility is appalling. So I'd rather do what painters do, which is do my painting in the studio, then chuck it out. Somebody else can go and see it when they want to see it, in their own time, or not. I don't have to be there.'

Even if it had sometimes taken Dutch courage, Wyatt – shirtless and exuberant behind his static bandmates – had relished being onstage with Soft Machine. But a kind of dread had now descended. He still has nightmares about live performance, including one in which Miles Davis laughs at him as he plays: an extraordinary revelation from someone who really did support the trumpeter, to no obvious sneers, in 1971. The chronic stage fright – Robert prefers the French term *'le trac'* – would make his Drury Lane performance still more momentous: not only his first proper solo performance, but almost certainly the only one he will ever play.

-»)(«- -»)(«- -»)(«-

Though retreating temporarily from the record industry, and more permanently from the stage, Robert continued to appear as a guest, singing high-pitched backing vocals on Brian Eno's second solo album, *Taking Tiger Mountain (by Strategy)*. His contribution on *Put a Straw Under Baby* created a tender, if off-kilter, cradlesong on an otherwise chilly record.

Eno had left Roxy Music after the band's second album, 1973's *For Your Pleasure*, and Robert identified with his friend's new solo status. 'Elephants separated from the herd, rogue elephants, hang about with each other,' he explains. 'We were free, early on, from the more totalitarian aspects of having to be in a rock group and all that involved, and were able to try out different things.'

Playing guitar on *Taking Tiger Mountain* was Phil Manzanera, himself on sabbatical from Roxy Music and working on a collection of sunny Latin rock tracks that would be released in 1975 as *Diamond Head*. Back in the 1960s, as a pupil at Dulwich College, Manzanera had befriended Bill MacCormick and his older brother Ian (MacDonald), who would arrive at school each morning with news of Soft Machine, picked up on their regular visits to Dalmore Road. 'Vicariously,' he laughs, 'we lived every moment of their lives.' When it came to vocalists for his debut solo album, says Manzanera, Robert was 'number one on my list'.

Wyatt played percussion on *Frontera*, the opening track, and also sung the vocal in Spanish – more or less. '*Frontera* was a track that me, Bill MacCormick and Ian MacDonald had written,' recalls Manzanera, who is half-Colombian and speaks flawless Spanish, 'and it had some pretty limp English words on it. I wanted a different version. I picked out the chords and we kept the same melody, but I said to Robert: "Can you write some Spanish lyrics?" He proceeded to open a dictionary, and just pick out a whole load of words. And mispronounce a few of them, which I didn't bother to change. Of course, it's led to a lifetime of Spanish people saying: "What's that all about? It's meaningless! Or does it mean something? Is it abstract?" It is truly very Robert, in that it has lots of different meanings, and in a funny way can mean about three different things.'

As well as these side projects, Wyatt was working towards a follow-up to *Rock Bottom. Ruth Is Stranger Than Richard* was recorded at the Manor in March 1975, shortly after Robert's thirtieth birthday. Although actually his third solo record, *The End of an Ear* had been more of a prologue than a first chapter. It is *Ruth*, rather than *Rock Bottom*, that was the Difficult Second Album. Intimidated by the need to live up to *Rock Bottom*, yet determined not to simply repeat the same tricks, Wyatt did not compose a single new piece of music for the record. The only tune for which he was credited as sole composer was *Solar Flares Burn for You* – which he had written two years previously for the Arthur Johns short film.

Like *Rock Bottom, Ruth Is Stranger Than Richard* divided neatly into halves. *Side Richard* featured *Solar Flares* and *Five Black Notes and One White Note*, which reinvented Romantic composer Jacques Offenbach in warm, undulating electronics. Dominating that side of the album, however, were the three sections of *Muddy Mouse* and the full-length *Muddy Mouth*: finally, Wyatt had a name for his voice-as-instrument approximations of Duke Ellington and Sly and the Family Stone. Fred Frith, who wrote the *Muddy Mouth* music, was on unusually lyrical form, his piano part 'written out on paper and everything'.

Side Ruth opened with *Soup Song*, a boogie-woogie reworking of Brian Hopper's *Slow Walkin' Talk* with new lyrics by Wyatt. *Sonia*, up next, featured a Mongezi Feza trumpet solo over a vamp played by Robert and Henry Cow bassist John Greaves. Originally intended as the B-side for *Yesterday Man*, the township feel and Caribbean-influenced, offbeat bass drum pointed to the growing influence on Wyatt of what would later be called world music.

Not all the musicians were happy with the album's combination of song and jazz-influenced instrumental sections. Matching Mole's Bill MacCormick, who played bass on several tracks, recalls tension between

› Alfie sets the tone again, for *Ruth Is Stranger Than RIchard*.

George Khan and Gary Windo, in the jazz camp, and Brian Eno, the self-declared non-musician, on the other. Thankfully, help was at hand in the form of Oblique Strategies, the *I Ching*-like divination system ('over one hundred worthwhile dilemmas') devised by Eno and the artist Peter Schmidt. It is one of MacCormick's most treasured memories:

'George and Gary were going at it, about the mix of the brass on this track, and you could see Robert was just like, "Whose fucking album is this?" And Alfie was going, "Robert doesn't need this." Eno had just given up. So eventually I said, "There's only one solution. I think what we'll do is Oblique Strategies."'

'Brian's eyes lit up. George and Gary went, "What's this?" I said, "Basically, you take a card out, and you interpret what it says. It depends on the circumstances, therefore it is open to interpretation, but in most cases it's pretty definitive. And whatever it comes out, we do. OK?" "Alright." [MacCormick mimes pulling out a card and reading it.] "Tape your mouths." Alfie almost fell off her chair laughing. Perfect! Right, we're all now not going to say a word. Robert: over to you. Eno was going: "That's it! I am a genius!" It was absolutely brilliant.'

The album credits Eno with 'direct inject anti-jazz raygun', which he still describes as his favourite ever credit. Yet *Side Ruth* did, in fact, finish on a jazz note: a cover of *Song for Che* by bassist and composer Charlie Haden. Once a key member of Ornette Coleman's pioneering free-jazz quartet, Haden had gone on to found the Liberation Music Orchestra, releasing instrumental protest songs at the height of the Vietnam War. With its martial snare drum and brass, Wyatt's version of *Song for Che* was every bit as stirring and stoic as the Carla Bley-arranged original.

The inclusion of the Charlie Haden track also pointed to Wyatt's increasing immersion in politics. The first communist state in the history of the Americas, Cuba in the years after the 1959 revolution was an inspiration to radicals all over the developing world. Castro had come to power in an indigenous revolution against a corrupt and unpopular dictatorship. Treatment of political prisoners by the new regime was harsh but usually stopped short of physical torture, and prisoners of conscience were few by the standards of Latin American states. Under Castro, there were spectacular improvements in both health and education; ongoing problems, meanwhile, could be blamed on the long blockade by the USA.

Although executed in 1967 by Bolivian authorities assisted by the CIA, the legacy of Castro's comrade-in-arms Che Guevara – the revolutionary physician ready to kill or die for his ideals anywhere in Latin America – has proved remarkably enduring. For Wyatt, Guevara represents a psychological, if romanticised, sanctuary. 'My country retreat is in the jungle with Che Guevara,' he smiles. 'Then back to town, which is Harlem in 1940. But when city life's got too much for me, I decide to go off into the jungle and live with the monkeys and the lads around a campfire, with a beret and a gun on my lap and minimal provisions. Just tough it out in the mountains with the *compañeros*.'

Charlie Haden may not have worn a beret or carried a gun but, for Wyatt, the bassist and composer is every bit as heroic as the Argentinian-born revolutionary: 'He represents the voice of the oppressed, to put it crudely. I share with him an idea that you must take the bean out of your own eye before you take them out of other people's.' So I'm in tune with him both metaphorically and as a musician.' The bassist's notes, says Robert, run through his life like a string of pearls.

-»)⟨⟨- -»)⟨⟨- -»)⟨⟨-

The release of *Ruth Is Stranger Than Richard* in May 1975 brought to an end a remarkable two years for Wyatt. Since his fall in June 1973, he had married Alfie, appeared on *Top of the Pops* and released two solo albums. But, although it featured many of the same musicians, *Ruth Is Stranger Than Richard* is a very different album to its predecessor. The number of composers robbed the album of quite the same singularity of purpose. The record also differed in its sonics: if *Rock Bottom* had been painted in diffuse watercolours, *Ruth*, based around piano rather than organ, showed the individual brushstrokes.

Wyatt would grow increasingly fond of the album over the years, despite – or because of – the fact that it didn't win quite the same acclaim as its predecessor. At the time, however, he professed himself less than happy with the album, blaming the pressure of high studio fees: unlike *Rock Bottom*, the bulk of which had been recorded at Delfina's farm, *Ruth* had mainly been recorded at Virgin's studio, the Manor. Robert even claimed to be horrified by the sound of his own voice.

Soup Song and *Sonia* were as vivid and vibrant as Alfie's surreal cover image. At other moments, however, Wyatt sounded helpless. The album's bleakest moment is *Team Spirit*: the standout track, and not only for George Khan's scorching tenor sax solo. Like *Soup Song*, it was an adaptation of an existing number – Phil Manzanera's *Frontera* – but featuring new lyrics by Wyatt. The title, which might have been a tribute to the record's collective spirit, was in fact ironic. Opening by mangling Admiral Nelson's famous last words, 'Kick me, Hardy', Wyatt continued with the same sense of dejection: 'I'm the best football you have got.'

The music journalists found it a tough record to review, after all the superlatives endowed on *Rock Bottom*. Peter Erskine of the *NME* conjectured that, for the first time, Robert seemed to be referring 'to the agony that thus far he has managed to be appearing to shrug off... he seems to be despairing a little, at his physical semi-helplessness.' *Melody Maker* too found it 'a most disturbing record... harrowing in its reflection of helplessness', made bearable only by a façade of humour.

Although he continues to insist that he's perfectly happy in a wheelchair, even a short period in Robert's company will reveal some of

> Robert with Alfie, a promotional shot for *Ruth Is Stranger Than Richard*. Alfie claims she had just been cutting onions in the kitchen.

the more mundane consequences of the accident. He can get trapped by a fallen tray or the edge of a rug. He is prone to backache and, since he can't feel his legs, can be slow to notice a drop in temperature. Horribly for an internationalist, foreign travel became difficult – and, far from improving over the years, says Alfie, it's got worse and worse.

231

A wheelchair affects even basic social interaction, since there is only so long for which the rest of us can comfortably squat. Parties are worse. 'It's terrible when you go to somebody's house,' says Robert, 'and you find a place in the corner, and it suddenly becomes your home and you feel you have to stay there for ever. I get put somewhere and then that's it for the rest of the evening. And then eventually I'm stuck, because I get used as an all-purpose coathanger and handbag guard. I get really hemmed in. And then, if I was drunk, I'd say, "I want to get out of here!" and I'd go *whoosh*' – he makes a wild arm movement – 'trampling god knows what in my wake to get out. Those are the kind of things that upset Alfie, that drunk people do.'

Friends reluctantly and briefly allude to 'awkward' episodes during the period, or 'tensions' evident in Robert's relationship with Alfie. Robert himself admits to smashing all the door handles in his flat in a fit of inebriated rage. It's impossible to know how much to blame paraplegia for such episodes, although Wyatt himself rejects the excuse: 'I was drinking too much beforehand and, to be honest, losing my temper too much. So, much as it would be nice to say that, I cannot with my hand on my heart.'

Instead, Robert says his confidence plummeted during the period 'not because I'd broken my back, but because I'd been rejected with the group I'd put together: Soft Machine'. Even releasing *Rock Bottom*, surely superior to any album released by his former band, and certainly more critically acclaimed, had not tempered the sense of inadequacy. According to Alfie, the full extent of the damage caused by the split emerged *after* the first two records of Robert's solo career: 'There was too much going on before for him to get miserable. He then had these terrible dreams about Soft Machine. I'd have to wheel him up and down the road in the middle of the night, he was so hurt. He was really damaged by it, confidence completely blown.'

The rising tide of depression reached its high-water mark with another drunken accident. 'The wheelchair collapsed,' sighs Alfie. 'We were going to Ronnie Scott's – with Branson, actually. Anyway, both legs were broken. He had to go back to Stoke Mandeville. There he had an explosion of anger with a private patient who was being horrible to a nurse, and immediately got pounced on and injected with all kinds of tranquillisers. They told me that he'd had a breakdown.' Robert was sent home with a supply of Largactil, used for schizophrenics, but Alfie wouldn't let him break the seal.

At the same time, Mongezi Feza was also admitted to hospital, suffering from pneumonia. Mongs had played in Keith Tippett's Centipede, and had joined Robert both on record and at Drury Lane. Robert regarded the trumpeter as an increasingly valuable musical foil, but the bond was not only musical. In part because they were exactly the same age, Robert saw him almost as a twin brother.

Mongs was only thirty when he was admitted to hospital, and his pneumonia was not expected to prove fatal. Yet he died that December, his body apparently lying in a bare room all night before it was noticed.

Wyatt was devastated, in particular by a conviction that his friend's death would have been avoided had his skin been of a different colour. 'Mongezi Feza died a quite unnecessary death of double pneumonia whilst he was in a psychiatric hospital,' he later told *Pulse*, 'and he was only in a psychiatric hospital because he just couldn't handle whether he was allowed to deal with white people or not.'

That claim is not as over the top as it might sound. Maxine McGregor, the wife of former Blue Notes leader Chris McGregor, says there is 'a large question mark' over the circumstances of Mongezi's death. The trumpeter had a history of fragile mental health, she goes on, but 'somehow got into a hospital that knew nothing of his history and where they seem to have neglected him shamefully'.

> Mongezi Feza.

The account of trumpeter Dave DeFries, who saw Feza two days before he died, uncomfortably echoes the treatment Wyatt himself received during the same period: 'They had drugged him with Largactil, which I knew, because I had worked with mentally handicapped people, makes one super-sensitive to heat and light. Well, the nurses had the strip-lighting on full and they said Mongs wouldn't talk. He was hiding under the bedclothes, so I switched off the lights and he greeted us with great warmth. But two minutes later the nurses switched on the lights again and he went straight back down into the bed.'

The loss of Mongezi cut Wyatt to the quick. 'It was very important for me,' he acknowledges. 'Everyone had got so used to having the South Africans around, and I suddenly realised how fragile they all were. I got terribly angry about why they were in this situation. They were having a great time in Europe as celebrated jazz musicians, but they'd lost their roots. They weren't attached to anything. They hadn't got homes to go back to. They were really floating, they were like gypsies, and I just thought how incredibly unfair it was. And, indeed, they did sort of disintegrate. Johnny Dyani went to Scandinavia and died. Dudu Pukwana died. The casualty rate was very high. But it was Mongs that hit me because I'd worked with Mongs and he was fantastic on *Rock Bottom*. For me, he's the cherry on that.'

⟶»〉〈«⟵ ⟶»〉〈«⟵ ⟶»〉〈«⟵

Problems with Virgin were also coming to a head. 'The difficulty with Virgin', explains Wyatt, 'was that the records cost so much to make. You had to spend the money at Virgin studios, and Virgin also wanted the publishing. The contracts were such that you couldn't really get any money because you were contracted to make a certain number of records, and the cost of each record was taken out of the profits from the last one. It's almost like the Third World debt situation. You keep piling on the debts so they keep owing the owner. Later on, this got called Reaganomics, but Richard Branson was sort of there first.'

The profit-driven world of the music industry was hardly the natural habitat of a subscriber to *Workers Press*. Yet resentment of his indentured status was combined, for Wyatt, with a crushing sense of creative failure. Although slow to write material, Robert could have met Virgin's demand for new albums by doing cover versions, such as *I'm a Believer*, or by inviting bandmates to contribute compositions, as on *Ruth Is Stranger Than Richard*. That album, however, had triggered a crisis of confidence from which *Rock Bottom* – recorded with the adrenaline rush of a man just brought so violently face-to-face with his own mortality – had been free.

The label's new interest in hit singles was symptomatic of broader changes. 'The first six to eight months of working at Virgin,' says Simon Draper, 'I can remember being stoned all day every day. Everyone was.

But gradually, with the demands of getting bigger, expanding, all that stopped, because you couldn't work like that really. And we became a lot more professional.'

'We had a lot of success with avant-garde music,' Draper continues. 'Whatever people think about *Tubular Bells*, it did appear to me to be quite an adventurous and original piece of music. And then Tangerine Dream, similarly, we had lots of commercial success with that. All the other interesting things we did – Henry Cow, Slapp Happy, Faust – gave us a good reputation, particularly in Europe. But we were learning what every record label has to learn, which is that you can't survive on two commercial artists. You need to have lots. Then you can give people breathing space, let them release a record every two years or three years, rather than wanting them to release a record every year because you needed it for your turnover. So we had to change. We desperately wanted to have more mainstream music.'

In its early days as a record shop, Virgin had been synonymous with Che Guevara posters and beanbags, or selling experimental records such as *The Faust Tapes* at bargain-basement prices. Yet by the time punk exploded into the mainstream, the label would have parted ways with the likes of Faust and Henry Cow.

Wyatt himself took a highly irregular step: he asked Richard Branson to stop his retainer. He has a certain pride that, unlike some of his peers, he left the label of his own volition. 'I didn't get pushed off, funnily enough,' he recalls. 'A slight reverse of the Soft Machine situation. I was the only person ever to have been fired from The Soft Machine. However, I was the only person *not* to be kicked off Virgin Records. Make of that what you will. I left, and Branson was very cross about that – not because I was economically important, but he didn't like somebody else deciding whether they were on Virgin or not.'

13

SILENCE

Other people's records and the CPGB

In the first half of the 1970s, Wyatt had recorded seven albums as a solo artist or full-time band member. In the latter half of the decade, he released nothing at all under his own name. Robert had felt the pull of Marxism ever since Matching Mole but now, disillusioned with the music business and overwhelmed by Mongezi Feza's death, he could no longer pretend that music was more relevant than 'fighting for a socialist world'. 'People would ask me who I thought the best vocalist I'd heard that year was,' Robert recalled, 'and I'd say Dennis Skinner. His gigs were a lot better than most rock gigs.'

Increasingly interested in politicians such as Skinner, a miner turned left-wing Labour MP, Robert also felt left behind by a dramatic change in musical climate since *Ruth Is Stranger Than Richard*. In spring 1977, Virgin released *Kew.Rhone* by John Greaves and Peter Blegvad. With its mix of jazz, deconstructed song and word games, Blegvad describes the album as 'as a kind of love letter to influences like Robert', and that love was requited: Robert bought two copies of the album, in case the first wore out. Yet, within a few months, Virgin were focusing their activities on the release of the Sex Pistols' *Never Mind the Bollocks*: a symbolic jumping of ships from progressive rock to punk.

Wyatt shared John Peel's avuncular enthusiasm for the genre and would go on to work with several post-punk musicians, including, on

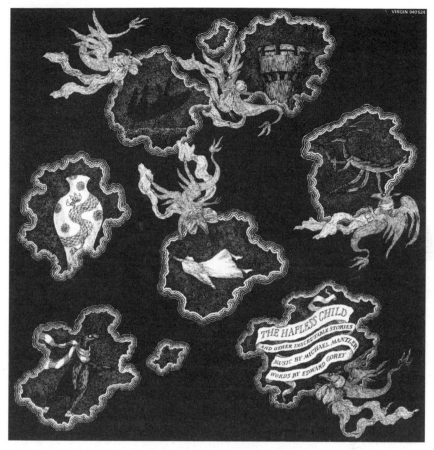

VIRGIN 940 524

> Edward Gorey's artwork for the cover of Michael Mantler's *The Hapless Child*.

one occasion, Johnny Rotten. At the time, however, he assumed that he was seen as a dinosaur and was happy to make way for the arrival of a new generation.

Yet punk did not prevent Robert from entering the studio as a guest. He recorded one of his finest albums with Michael Mantler, an Austrian trumpeter and composer who had played with Cecil Taylor and in Charlie Haden's Liberation Music Orchestra. For *The Hapless Child*, based on a book by American author and illustrator Edward Gorey, Mantler needed a vocalist with the facility of a classical singer but the edge of an untrained voice. Gorey was an admirer of Hilaire Belloc, whose 1907 *Cautionary Tales* poked fun at the admonitory children's literature of the Victorian era. Robert, himself a Belloc fan, was able to bring out the darkly comic aspect of the American's macabre tales, his vocal tone casual yet unsettling.

Pink Floyd drummer Nick Mason compares the experience of working on a Mike Mantler record to going to the gym: challenging, if ultimately rewarding. Yet Robert – who, as a drummer, had negotiated the fiendish time signatures of Soft Machine with an offhand ease – was able to bring a natural feel even to Mantler's formidable vocal parts. And, rather than relying on vibrato to make subtle adjustments to pitch, Wyatt risked hitting his notes like a pianist: right on the nose. 'He had extremely good ears,' says Mantler, 'but he couldn't read a note of music. He just worked until he had it. He was a tireless worker to get something right, to study it and memorise it.'

The Hapless Child could be the score for a gothic horror film, written by an opera composer for jazz musicians – among them bassist Steve Swallow and drummer Jack DeJohnette. Credited to composer rather than vocalist, the record is easily overlooked by Wyatt fans. And yet, let down only by Mantler's penchant for wailing rock guitars, it could be the great lost Robert Wyatt album. There is a thrill to the opening track, *The Sinking Spell*, that recalls *Little Red Riding Hood*.

By the time *The Hapless Child* was released, in March 1976, Wyatt and Mantler were already working on the follow-up, this time using text by Harold Pinter. Like the Gorey project, *Silence* was undercut with menace, and Robert, contributing vocals as well as percussion, made the superficially banal lines appropriately disturbing. *Silence* was another remarkable record, featuring Carla Bley and Kevin Coyne alongside Robert, and it would mark the beginning of an ongoing partnership with Mike Mantler. However, the composer was moving into an instrumental phase; it would be a decade before he and Robert would work together again.

> The cast of *Silence* – Kevin Coyne, Carla Bley and Robert Wyatt.

Still, Robert continued to enter the studio, recording two pieces by John Cage for *Voices and Instruments,* released by Brian Eno's Obscure label. *Experiences No 2* featured words by the poet e. e. cummings, while *The Wonderful Widow of Eighteen Springs* was based on a passage in James Joyce's final novel, *Finnegans Wake.* Robert's vocal parts staked out a previously unexplored middle ground between innocent chorister and the battered but irrepressible tramp of Gavin Bryars' *Jesus' Blood Never Failed Me Yet* – the first release on Obscure and the tune that proved minimalism could win hearts as well as minds.

Although the *Voices and Instruments* album remains dear to Eno, he admits with a chuckle that sales figures were as low as the label name implied. 'Yes. It remained obscure. It's a shame because I thought that was so good.' The e. e. cummings tune is, for Eno, a particular highlight. 'I've heard that song done by classical people,' he explains, 'and it's deadly. Robert just brought such tenderness to it. He took what was meant to be an exemplary piece of diagrammatic modern music and he turned it into something so sensitive and beautiful.'

Still suffering the crisis in confidence that had plagued *Ruth Is Stranger Than Richard,* Robert did not share Eno's enthusiasm for his voice. He turned down the chance to sing a second e. e. cummings lyric, *Forever and Sunsmell,* asking Carla Bley, best known as a composer, arranger and pianist, to take his place. 'He said he couldn't do it,' Bley recalls. 'And I said, "What do you mean, you can't do it?" He said, "I don't want to do it, I can't do it, I don't feel like doing it. You have to do it for me." So I did it for him. But I couldn't understand his sudden lack of self-confidence in his voice.'

There were two other records with that rogue elephant Eno. Credited as Shirley Williams, the then Secretary of State for Education, Robert played percussion on *Before and After Science,* Eno's 1977 album of playful but pensive pop. The following year, he recorded for his friend's landmark *Ambient 1: Music for Airports.* Eno had been exploring serene loop landscapes with guitarist Robert Fripp ever since their meeting during the *Little Red Record* sessions. It was *Music for Airports,* however, that launched ambient as a codified genre: music that was expressly environmental and, in Eno's own words, as ignorable as it was interesting. Wyatt's ruminative piano part formed the backbone of the cocoon-like opening track, unfurling like an ink-drop in water.

'Apart from the fact that I really like him as a person, and I liked his company,' says Eno, 'part of my experiment in those records was to see: what happens if you mix this, with this, with this? It was being a little bit like a chemist. Can you get an interesting reaction out of that? I knew Robert was a very unusual ingredient. But I also knew he has no ego in the studio at all. It's very easy to work with him. He always seems enormously grateful that you would think of asking him, which is funny because I always felt the other way around: enormously grateful that he'd think of accepting.'

Wyatt's final project of the 1970s, although not released until 1981, was *Fictitious Sports*. Credited to Nick Mason, it was, as Mason freely admits, a Carla Bley album in all but name. *Fictitious Sports* featured musicians Wyatt knew from the jazz scene, including Mike Mantler (by this stage Bley's husband as well as musical partner) and Gary Windo. Several of the songs, however, had been originally written for Bley's

> Robert with Carla Bley, who 'shamed' him back into music, to work on her album with Nick Mason, *Fictitious Sports*.

punk band, Penny Cillin and the Burning Sensation. The result was an eccentric mix: meticulously arranged post-punk, peppered with jazz saxophone solos and powered by Nick Mason's straight, sturdy beats. The drily humorous lyrics covered everything from unappreciative audiences to failing car motors – an impotence metaphor – and flying saucers. Wyatt's underplayed delivery and highly developed sense of the absurd were crucial to the record's success.

It was a rare venture into the studio for Robert, who for the past three years had hardly recorded any music – of his own or with anyone else – aside from those guest spots with Brian Eno. He was grateful for the push. 'Carla Bley made me work when I wasn't working,' he recalled. 'She said: "Come on, who do you think you are? Some fucking pop star? You've never had a hit record, you're not good-looking enough. You're just a musician like the rest of us, so get on with it!" So, she shamed me back into the studio and I enjoyed it.'

It was a timely jolt and brought a fallow period to an abrupt end. Within a few months, Robert would have signed up to Rough Trade and started recording the first of a string of remarkable singles. But perhaps the time out from the music scene had been equally important. Thanks to the generosity of Julie Christie in buying them a flat and the money raised by the Pink Floyd benefit concert, Robert and Alfie had, for a while, been able to get by. Meanwhile, the time and energy Robert had previously spent on the road or in the studio had gone into catching up on the education he had missed by leaving school at sixteen.

With music no longer the axis on which daily life turned, Robert's perspective, suddenly, became panoramic. 'For ten years I did gigs,' he explains, 'but my life after that was so much bigger. It opened out in the 1970s and 1980s, at the time when people think I didn't do anything. In fact, me and Alfie, we got into stuff – film festivals and politics – instead of going round with four geezers.' They read books, too, by the likes of linguistics professor Noam Chomsky and investigative journalist John Pilger, both outspoken critics of Western foreign policy. Another favourite was the psychiatrist and anticolonial theorist Frantz Fanon, whose most famous book, *The Wretched of the Earth*, covered in chilling detail the French occupation of Algeria. Titles such as *Writing in Cuba Since the Revolution*, *Cuba: the Second Decade*, *The Poverty Brokers: The IMF and Latin America*, *The Chilean*

Revolution and *Women and the Nicaraguan Revolution* piled up on the shelves. It would have taken a snowplough, says Robert, to shift them all.

He and Alfie also watched Open University programmes, particularly those related to international politics, and became regulars at the London Film Festival. 'I'd say that, for me, that was one of the most really mind-expanding periods,' comments Robert. 'The film critics at the time, on the rare occasions that they even mentioned the films we saw, would talk about how well they were made: "That was a very badly made film from the Congo." But the quality of the film, in that sense, was of no interest to me. I wanted to get out of this endless cultural claustrophobia and just get a chance to feel the rest of the world. This is a paraplegic thing, not being able to travel, finding this other way. And it was absolutely wonderful. As much of a blindingly wonderful, squashed-up, psychedelic thing as the discovery of jazz, in a way.'

Another stimulus was the Notting Hill Carnival, the annual African-Caribbean street festival that originated from the same London Free School that spawned the UFO club and the *International Times*. 'Hanging out at Carnival was extraordinary,' says Robert. 'If you followed it right from when it starts out, with the children's parades, right to the end with the booming bass bins and littered, tattered streets, at four o'clock in the morning, it was an amazing journey. And we watched things, saw evidence of stuff. The papers would always say: "Black mob on rampage, police have trouble holding it back." But we would watch police provoking people who weren't doing anything. *They* were the maniacs...'

Together with the books and films, such experiences dragged together previously disparate thoughts like so many iron filings. Until this point, says Robert, he had more or less accepted the status quo. Now, his instinctive anti-racism started to become part of a broader ideology: 'I'd never thought of the direct relationship between capitalism and colonialism and therefore racism. I thought racism was just an attitude problem.'

The rise of the National Front in the 1970s, on the street and even at the ballot box, made racism a particularly urgent issue. But in an era in which Margaret Thatcher could speak of the country being 'swamped' by immigrants, and teacher Blair Peach could die at an anti-racism demonstration, almost certainly at the hands of the police, the problem went far beyond the boot boys. Alfie had adopted siblings from Trinidad and Ghana, her stepfather having set up library schools in those countries that stocked books by indigenous writers, rather than dead white males – heady stuff, she now reflects, in the days of Empire. The period in which her Ghanaian brother stayed with them in Twickenham made the bigotry suffered by black and minority ethnic residents all the more apparent. 'It was heartbreaking, the experience he had,' remembers Alfie. 'Going to pubs, he'd come back and say he'd waited twenty minutes to be served. All these little things. So the effect that racism had on people's lives was very apparent to us.'

Alfie wrote an outraged letter to *Melody Maker* following Eric Clapton's notorious 'Enoch was right' speech, in which the guitarist claimed that Britain was in danger of becoming 'a black colony'. 'Eric Clapton says he loves dancing,' it began. 'I know because he used to dance with me a lot at the Scene Club. This was in 1963 when he was working on a building site. I don't suppose he noticed that I was an immigrant because I'm white and I don't talk funny.' Meanwhile, comments around the dinner table, of the sort that began 'I don't mean to sound racist but…', caused Robert to throw wine over at least one fellow diner. 'When I stopped drinking,' he smiles, 'I thought, "Gosh, I could have drunk that. What an awful waste."'

Robert and Alfie initially joined the Labour Party, but found themselves increasingly disappointed by the lack of attention to foreign affairs. 'We were just there to get people elected,' says Alfie. 'Occasionally, people would come out with fairly dodgy opinions: some members talked about council residents as if they weren't taxpayers. It felt uncomfortable to be with anyone who regarded themselves as "us" and the working class as "them". Being in the Communist Party was much more fulfilling and educative. And you knew you were safe from hearing any gratuitous racist comments, because that's what you were having to avoid wherever you went throughout that period. At every dinner party there'd be some little thing, and you'd think, "Oh God, not here, as well." We were safe from that in the CP.'

It was not only at the local level that Labour disappointed. In 1977, the year after he replaced Harold Wilson as Prime Minister, Labour's James Callaghan formed a pact with the Liberals that moved the party sharply towards the middle ground – paving the way for the formation of the Social Democratic Party (SDP) in 1981. 'Jim Callaghan's government was pretty right-wing when it took over,' insists Wyatt. 'It was Jim Callaghan who instigated the short-shield, semi-militarised police force to deal with demonstrators. That wasn't the Conservatives, that was Jim Callaghan. And so I felt pushed more and more to the left.'

The final straw was the Iranian revolution of 1979. A watershed for both the USA and the USSR in terms of their relations with the developing world, Wyatt was particularly shocked to find foreign secretary David Owen, who later left Labour to co-found the SDP, supporting the Shah against the popular uprising (which at that stage has not been entirely taken over by Khomeini's Islamists). 'I thought, "What the fuck is that?"', remembers Wyatt, still aghast three decades later. '"That's not any kind of Labour that I know."'

What Robert saw as Labour compromises weren't even winning votes. Following the industrial disputes of the so-called winter of discontent, Thatcher's Conservatives would defeat Callaghan in the landmark election of May 1979. Robert, by that time, had settled on a more radical political solution: the Communist Party of Great Britain. Alfie, more inclined to anarchist approaches and by her own account 'not a joiner', didn't sign up straight away. Yet she was ideologically sympathetic – and, with CPGB meetings soon being held in their home, it would not be long before she, too, got her card.

The river that had its source in Robert's Fabian Society upbringing had meandered – via the LSE canteen, the Hendrix tour, Release, Alfie and the death of Mongezi Feza – to its mouth.

-»)«- -»)«- -»)«-

How could Robert Wyatt join a political party so closely affiliated with Soviet communism? While he was almost painfully empathic, the CPGB members of popular imagination were diehard Stalinists, denounced as 'Tankies' for presumed support of the Kremlin's foreign policy. There had been a mass exodus from the CPGB following Khrushchev's brutal stubbing out of the 1956 Hungarian Revolution, and another, twelve years later, when Brezhnev used tanks to silence the reformist voices of the Prague Spring. 'Ten years earlier, I would have thought it absurd that I would join the Communist Party,' Wyatt himself admits. 'I knew all about Hungary and Czechoslovakia. The great thing about being on the left in England is you're left in no doubt about every single possible thing that's gone wrong in your name. There's nothing you cannot know about what's wrong with Communism. The danger is that people here remain in blissful ignorance about what we in the *West* have done.'

One factor that influenced Robert was a radical change in the politics of his mother's second cousin. A Labour MP until 1970, Woodrow Wyatt had then swung dramatically across the political spectrum, embracing Margaret Thatcher and nailing his new colours to the mast in his 1977 book *What's Left of the Labour Party?*, lashing out at 'ignorant louts in hospital workers' unions' and 'ultra-left wing teachers who preach anarchy and the disruption of society'. The existence of such a high-profile relative left Robert wracked by guilt. 'He just loathed the "lower orders", he explains, 'and he was a creep. He just was everything that's loathsome to me. And I think the relevance of that may have been part of it, that it may have pushed me harder to reclaim the name a bit, politically.'

Equally influential was the shift in the whole political environment. Wyatt joined the CPGB just as Thatcher came to power, promising to reverse the socialist steps made by Labour in the aftermath of World War II. Dramatic change would not be immediate but it is clear in retrospect that this was the start of a new era. The Conservative Party would remain in power for a marathon eighteen years, while Ronald Reagan's victory two years later would usher in more than a decade of Republican rule in the US. 'I think that joining the Communist Party was wanting the conversation to remain open', Brian Eno has suggested, 'and deliberately being slightly provocative by choosing that particular way of doing it. It was so unfashionable to join the Communist Party. There was such an opposition to people showing compassion towards people at the bottom end of society – the people who actually made all the things that we eat and drive in and so on. And I really respect Robert for saying: "Well, I still care about them and I'm not afraid to say so."'

Robert's decision to join the CPGB, then, might have been another example of Alfred Jarry's concept of *antimony*: Pataphysical yin-yang. Just as he would sing the virtues of song to free-jazz fans whilst eulogising free jazz to lovers of pop, Robert was now attempting to counterpoise not just Woodrow but a broader drift to the right on both sides of the Atlantic. As Reagan and Thatcher ratcheted up the Cold War into something approaching an anti-communist crusade, Robert's instinct was to balance the scales. 'I decided to find out what it felt like to be "the enemy" of the time', Robert told the American website *Pitchfork*. 'People say communism is as bad as fascism, but while the rhetoric of fascism is horrible in the first place, the rhetoric of communism can be very attractive.'

'I think what the Right got wrong', he explains, 'was to think that the trouble was troublemakers called socialists – that there was no trouble, everything was perfectly all right until these perverts came along and said: "The world is unfair, we must change it!" Get rid of them, discredit

› Robert shows his colours after joining the CPGB.

them, and it will all be all right. No! They were right. It *is* unfair, and it hasn't been addressed. And, as Marx said, the oppressed and the exploited will continue to come to the surface as a worm comes to the surface of the soil when it rains.'

Viewed from the other side of the 2008 banking crisis and the Euro meltdown of 2011, Wyatt's desire for an alternative to capitalism might seem prescient. Yet the CPGB was not the only means of opposing the drift to the right. Chris Cutler recalls Marxism as 'the most plausible and successful analytical tool on offer' at the time, but adds that Henry Cow were sceptical of political parties – and that joining the CPGB, in the late 1970s, seemed 'quite perverse'. 'It was certainly a lost cause,' he explains. 'The Party, I mean, not the aspiration or the analysis. But it was a cause lost for a reason. By then, the CP, like the Labour Party – like the entire left, in fact – was either trying to deny its past or, in a Blairish way, dressing to the left while fighting tooth and nail for the Right. It was the same in France and, a little bit later, Italy. Suddenly socialism had become an embarrassment.'

'It's difficult, culturally,' Cutler continues, 'when an accepted language changes so completely, especially when it isn't changed *by* anyone. Suddenly analyses and verbal formulations that were once good currency hit the floor with a thud. Five years earlier, every third word would have been "bourgeois", its shorthand meaning understood and unquestioned. Now it sounded pathetic and hollow; counterfeit. The whole of the left found itself in a bewildering crisis of confidence... Given all that, joining the Party could be seen as eccentric. Or brave.'

Numerous Trotskyist splinter groups offered more fashionable options for the hard left. Yet they seemed, to Robert and Alfie, something of a cop-out next to the real-world Communist Party of Great Britain. Some Trots, says Alfie, were friends. 'But you were always put on the defensive because they in fact were supporting an *idea*, and we were trying to protect an existing system. We had all the gulags and horribleness and the deaths. We were personally responsible for all of those by continuing to support Marxism and for actually trying to stop all the wrong propaganda about the Soviet Union. They had no gory past. Their hero was killed with an ice-pick by one of Stalin's chaps. They were pure, innocent of everything.'

Wyatt liked the fact that the old-school communists, by contrast, were getting their hands dirty, particularly overseas; Oxfam and Survival International pamphlets, he says, inspired his CPGB membership as much as Marx and Engels. From an international perspective, the left was arguably in the ascendant: while America had been forced into a humiliating retreat from Vietnam in 1975, there were sixteen communist states by the end of the decade. Particularly in Asia and Africa, communism was strongly linked to anti-colonialism and the movement for national liberation.

South Africa was particularly important: the horrors experienced by Mongezi Feza and his fellow Blue Notes were ongoing. The Soweto Uprising of 1976 was followed by a massacre of almost 500 black South Africans, some as young as four years old; many shot by police, many in the back. Communist leader Joe Slovo was at the forefront of the ANC's armed wing, Umkhonto we Sizwe. Marxism 'was invaluable in the struggle against apartheid, which was one of the reasons I got involved', Wyatt later explained to the *Independent*. Castro's Cuba also played a role in Africa out of all proportion to its size, sending troops to Angola, the Congo, Guinea, Ethiopia, Mozambique and Benin.

Such a global perspective, easily forgotten in a historical account reduced to an epic fistfight between two superpowers, is crucial in explaining Robert's communism. Even so, he knew that his beliefs were awkward: 'I suppose I'm a Communist like Cliff Richard is a Christian,' he once joked to the *Morning Star*. 'People I'm with think, "Oh God, he's going to mention it again." It's just how I make sense of the world."

Wyatt's membership coincided with the USSR's invasion of Afghanistan, bringing to a sudden end the period of détente between the Soviet Union and the West and seen as proof of the Kremlin's aggression. Robert admits the invasion wobbled his faith. 'But then,' he said at the time, 'I look at all the people who've been anti-communist – Hitler, Mussolini, Franco, Pinochet, Nixon, Thatcher, Botha – and I think, well, communists must be doing something right.' From Wyatt's uncompromising perspective, the options were starkly binary.

It's hard to overstate the nostalgia of Wyatt's membership of the CPGB. Membership had peaked in the 1940s; by the time Robert joined, official British communism had for some time been dying on its feet. But, as Wyatt later explained, 'I've always been more interested in giving nice people and nice ideas a decent funeral than in being nursemaid to the latest new idea.' The Yesterday Man was perfectly happy amongst comrades old enough to have fought in the Spanish Civil War, whom he regarded as more dignified than a younger generation of testosterone-fuelled Trotskyists. 'I joined the Communist Party precisely at the point when it had obviously *had it*,' Robert concedes. 'In reality, the Communist Party of Great Britain was a sweet little party of broken dreams.'

–»)(«- –»)(«- –»)(«-

The problem with socialism, Oscar Wilde had it, was that it took up too many evenings. In the late 1970s, Nicaraguan solidarity events, with their generous supplies of Cuban rum, were as good as it got on the left. Robert even recalls a mixed economy versus state control drinking competition, in which the Communists drank Crimean wine, while the Labour Party wine came from Hungary. The Communists, he is adamant, emerged victorious. 'It was a walkover. A walkover! So fun was had by all.'

In 1981, Ken Livingstone – then still 'Red Ken' and, like Tony Benn, depicted by the tabloids as representing the 'loony left' – took charge of the Greater London Council. Robert and Alfie attended immigrants' dance and music nights at County Hall. Another regular haunt was the Royal Festival Hall, especially as the GLC kept prices low for wheelchair users. There were *Morning Star* fundraisers at Camden Town Hall and trips to see guest speakers at Conway Hall.

'Though people say it narrows you culturally,' says Wyatt, 'funnily enough communism opened the way. One of my best friends in the Party just liked Gilbert and Sullivan, didn't know anything about pop music. It was such a relief not to be on that cutting-edge treadmill.'

It wasn't only because he was now in his mid-thirties that Robert wanted to move away from the culture carousel, on which fads and fashions circled into eternity like unloved sushi. From a Marxist perspective, the use of revolutionary imagery by capitalist record companies, aiming simply to shift units, made rock music ring rather hollow. 'I was getting claustrophobia with a rock culture, and indeed an avant-garde culture generally, which had originally, as I understood it, been cheerleaders of the revolution. And then, when the revolution had

> Salon sessions – Robert and Flossie, Twickenham, mid-1970s.

been seen to fail, had become a kind of ersatz substitute for revolution. I started to get very irritated by the idea of people talking about certain kinds of rock being dangerous. And I thought, "You want danger? Look around, you know, there's some real stuff going on out there." *Street Fighting Man*, what's all that? For what? Danger to who?'

Robert was listening to foreign radio stations – Voice of the Islamic Republic of Tehran, Albania's Radio Tirana, Radio Vietnam, Radio Moscow – and corresponding with political prisoners around the world. The notion that a safety-pinned nose might be subversive seemed as absurd as a Rolling Stones song about the 1968 riots.

Stifled by the cultural climate, Robert hunkered down in Twickenham. Journalist Vivien Goldman, a friend of Brian Eno's, remembers a succession of Sunday afternoon 'salon sessions' in which Robert and Alfie received bulletins from the outside world: 'We just used to natter the afternoon away, listening to music and discussing the state of the world and the state of the industry. It's like T. S. Eliot, measuring out our life in coffee spoons. We had lengthy teas that went into dinners, doubtless fuelled by bottles of wine. We would play a lot of music and discuss it, and one would find Robert listening to Victor Jara and things like that. He was thirsty for music – shows like Charlie Gillett presenting world music, Alex Pascall's black music show, and Radio Moscow. Listening a lot to the radio, structuring his life to an extent, like the way people used to structure their life around *East Enders*.'

Casting a lengthening shadow over the good times, however, was a steadily deflating bank balance. Although Robert received mobility allowance to help with transport, it was twelve years after the accident before he and Alfie realised they were also eligible for attendance allowance, to cover personal care. Alfie would sell paintings, or do odd jobs – GLC surveys, the odd car boot sale – when she and Robert needed ready cash, but it was no long-term solution. And, despite her best efforts on the business side, royalty payments only trickled in. To this day, she says, Robert receives 'nothing whatsoever' for the first two Soft Machine albums.

Like Robert, Alfie is today philosophical on the subject: 'You could go crazy if you just thought: Where's my money?' she shrugs. 'At the moment we don't need it, so we're not going to burst our brains.' Back in the late 1970s, however, money was very tight indeed. And, since Wyatt's medical condition had stabilised, he too began to look for work. It wasn't just that they needed the money, says Alfie. His pride was at stake. 'What is very important in terms of the accident, is that he obviously feels diminished in his capacity to contribute,' she explains. 'Robert is terribly pleased that, through music, he's earned enough money for us. He's very proud of that – and if he didn't have that he'd feel utterly useless, I think. That's why it's important for him to keep doing stuff.'

Eventually, Robert did locate a job: painting chess pieces in a local factory. It was, he was apparently told, the only position available for someone in a wheelchair. 'But,' he laughs, 'Alfie said, "I'm not getting up early morning to drive you to the chess factory. This I will not do. I married a musician mainly because they're the only blokes I can think of who don't get up early in the morning. So sod that."'

Wyatt, it seemed, was unemployed and close to unemployable. But then Vivien Goldman suggested to her flatmate, Geoff Travis, that he might want to record Robert for his fledgling label. The retirement, it turned out, was a mere sabbatical.

14

FOREIGN ACCENTS

The Rough Trade singles

'The whole point about Rough Trade', explains label founder Geoff Travis, 'was that it was set up as a cooperative, and it was done on a socialist model. Everybody had the same wages and it wasn't meant to be the classic hierarchical situation. In our minds, we never thought: "We want to be like Richard Branson." It wasn't about making ourselves rich. It was more like a kibbutz, if you like.'

The archetypal indie label, Rough Trade really *was* the alternative, cottage industry that Virgin had resembled only in its early days. And its roster was enormously diverse: from the French punk of Metal Urbain to the oddball poems of Ivor Cutler, via the industrial strains of Cabaret Voltaire and the free jazz of James Blood Ulmer. The company had begun as a record shop in west London, around the corner from where Wyatt had lived in his Matching Mole days. By the time they made contact with Robert, they had grown into both a record label and a distributor, facilitating as well as epitomising the DIY ethos of punk.

Geoff Travis, who still regards The Soft Machine as one of the best groups of all time, was delighted to sign Robert (or, rather, Robert and Alfie: 'both of them are great artists, and I see them together') to the label, and suggested beginning with a single. Last time he had encountered the world of 45s, Wyatt had bolted – yet his new label didn't share Virgin's interest in commercial hits. 'A whole new kind of record company had been set up,' enthuses Robert. 'They didn't look down on musicians or up to musicians, they were just equal people. An egalitarian organisation:

it didn't seem possible before I met Geoff Travis. That was enormously important to us.'

Though Robert had listened to a lot of records since *Ruth Is Stranger Than Richard*, from calypso to Bulgarian folk to Soviet jazz, he hadn't composed a note of original music. The solution was a return to cover versions: 'Elvis Presley and Frank Sinatra', it dawned on him, 'never wrote a tune between them'. Rather than Neil Diamond and Chris Andrews, however, this time Robert would rework records that reflected both his panoramic musical interests and his increasingly robust political beliefs. Though some distance from *The End of an Ear*, or the John Cage numbers he had recorded for Brian Eno, these tunes were still avant-garde by Robert's own definition: searching for beauty in unexpected places.

'I look for the beautiful in people we are told to hate,' Wyatt explained to *Time Out*, 'whether it's the Russians or the Chinese or the Arabs. I look for the potential friend in the enemy. That's how I got into

> Geoff Travis on the counter of the Rough Trade shop, 1977.

what's now called world music. It's nothing worthy or moral, it's just a continuation of the avant-garde aesthetic. Looking for the beauty in what I'm told is ugly.' And, while *Little Red Record* had only flirted with Maoist imagery, the Rough Trade singles really were as red as rhubarb. Geoff Travis even suggested a politically sympathetic engineer in Adam 'Skipper' Kidron, whose family ran the radical publisher Pluto Press.

Wyatt broke his five-year silence in Spanish, with a song called *Arauco*. 'Latin languages are very easy to sing,' he explains, 'because they rhyme very easily. So it was another instrument I had at my disposal. Whereas, say, Brian Eno looks for new sounds in a new synthesiser, or a new electronic technique, I just look for new things I can do with my mouth, with my body, with my hands. It's not ideological. It's much more primitive.'

In fact, *Arauco* appealed ideologically as well as aesthetically. The song had been written by Violeta Parra, a Chilean folk singer and folklorist central to the left-wing *Nueva Canción* folk movement, and to the Latin American left. Parra herself had committed suicide in 1967 but her songs were part of the movement associated with Latin American revolution and especially with Chile under Salvador Allende, the first democratically elected Marxist president in Latin America. Allende's Chile, brought to a brutal end by Pinochet's US-backed coup of September 1973, had been a beacon for the international left in the 1970s, and Parra's lyrics remained resonant, listing indigenous chiefs who battled unsuccessfully against the Spanish, before suggesting that the Chilean people were now exploited by their fellow countrymen.

That exploitation of indigenous people was ongoing, Wyatt insisted in an interview with the *NME*, and the West was complicit: 'Pinochet is selling off their land to foreign big business, which means that most Indians are almost certain to be wiped out or just turned into slumland factory fodder, used up in the poorest jobs in the mines. If you say, "What's it got to do with us?" – well, we've got a government who're one of the main providers of finance for them to do this.'

The B-side to *Arauco* was also Latin American: the traditional Cuban song *Caimanera*, better known as *Guantanamera*. It's a tune that has often been diluted into easy listening. Yet Wyatt found a version by Castroist singer-songwriter Carlos Puebla, with lyrics that transformed the story of unrequited love into a post-revolution rebel anthem. On paper, *Caimanera* sounds like a protest song, but there are no exclamation marks in Wyatt's singing.

Robert sees himself as witness rather than activist – 'just putting a few bookmarks through history as I lived through it'. He has no more faith in the propaganda value of his own music than he does in that of hymns or national anthems – or, for that matter, love songs. 'I used to get questions like, "Do you think political art has any effect?"' he recalls with a chuckle. 'And my answer would be, if Stevie Wonder or anybody sings a love song, you don't judge it on whether it works, on "does he get the girl?" And so, when I sang *Caimanera*, which is about the insulting stain of American property on Cuba, I wouldn't like the song to be judged on whether or not the Americans have closed Guantanamo Bay.'

-»)《«- -»)《«- -»)《«-

At the end of the year, Rough Trade released Robert's next single: a version of *At Last I Am Free* by Chic. It was a surprising choice from a man now seen to represent left-wing integrity. What could he have in common with a group associated with disco hedonism and New York clubs like Studio 54?

Robert, however, defends their right to cashmere and white satin: 'When I was a teenager in the 50s,' he explains, 'black music was the template. The new generation tended to see black music as just slick empty disco stuff by men in suits, and therefore of no revolutionary value. My point was: it's a matter of sustaining respect for black American culture, wherever they take it. If you're a rich white kid, your idea of rebelling is to grow your hair long and to take drugs: two fingers to the establishment. You want to drop out. But this is music by people who haven't yet been allowed *in*.'

Although dismissed by many as lightweight escapism, disco was arguably more progressive than punk both racially and sexually. And, musically, guitarist Nile Rodgers and bassist Bernard Edwards represented the very apex of the genre, writing and producing with Sister Sledge, Diana Ross, David Bowie and Mick Jagger, as well as performing as Chic. *At Last I Am Free* was,

ROUGH TRADE

ROBERT WYATT

AT LAST I AM FREE
(Edwards, Rodgers)
Chic Music Inc/Warner Bros. Music Ltd
℗ 1980 Rough Trade
RT 052A

on one level, simply a great pop tune. But the apparently feel-good lyrics of Chic hits like *Le Freak*, *Dance Dance Dance (Yowsah Yowsah Yowsah)* and *Good Times* were in fact deeply ironic. And, while the verses of *At Last I Am Free* are those of a love song, Wyatt correctly supposed the chorus to have been written against the backdrop of the African-American civil rights movement: Rodgers had written the lines back when he was a Black Panther. In Chic's hands, the epic soul ballad had been pained but ultimately uplifting. Robert follows the phrasing of the original almost exactly, yet his version is forlorn rather than triumphant, as well as thoroughly English: the same words in a different font. If Virgin thought *Yesterday Man* was too lugubrious, it's a good thing they weren't asked to release *At Last I Am Free*.

Like *At Last I Am Free*, the track Robert chose as a B-side had originally been sung by a woman: he was, he later joked, still waiting for puberty. Although written by Abel Meeropol, a Jewish, communist schoolteacher from the Bronx, *Strange Fruit* was daunting because it was so strongly associated with Billie Holiday. As a white Englishman, Wyatt also hesitated before tackling a song about lynching in the American South: 'It's a bit inappropriate,' he admitted at the time, 'like asking a Jew to sing from the Koran.' Yet Wyatt's *Strange Fruit* is entirely convincing. Just as he found his own meaning in *At Last I Am Free*, Robert reimagined the context for *Strange Fruit*, shifting the setting 50 years and 9,000 miles. The title had originally referred to African Americans, hung from poplar trees in 1930s Indiana following a lynching. But Robert realised that the line could refer, just as chillingly, to apartheid South Africa. He dedicated the track to Winnie Mandela.

Stalin Wasn't Stallin', Wyatt's finger-clicking follow-up of February 1981, was both more upbeat and more overtly political. The song had been recorded during the Second World War by Virginia-based vocal group The Golden Gate Jubilee Quartet. With its polyphonic vocals, Wyatt's version retained traces of barbershop and gospel, as well as the original's infectiously jaunty feel. The lyrics, cheekily and overtly propagandistic, celebrated Nazi Germany's defeat on the eastern front by the 'Russian Bear': 'Then that bear smacked the Führer, with a mighty armoured paw / And Adolf broke all records running backwards to Krakow...'

Denounced as a Stalinist for his membership of the CPGB, Wyatt had come back with a tune praising Stalin – but one originally released by an *American* group. Demonstrating precisely the mischievous sense of humour that Tankies were supposed to lack, this was the epitome of the Pataphysical concept of *clinamen*: the slight swerve that creates an

> The cover of *Stalin Wasn't Stallin'* showed piles of German helmets – not a 45 cut for chart success, despite a catchy American tune.

entirely new meaning. It was also an uncomfortable reminder that, just a couple of decades earlier, the figurehead of what Reagan called 'the evil empire' had been good ol' Uncle Joe, the West's ally against Hitler.

The B-side to *Stalin Wasn't Stallin'* identified just as strongly with the communist old guard. Wyatt didn't appear at all on *Stalingrad*. Instead, the Barbadian socialist writer Peter Blackman paid solemn, unaccompanied tribute to those who lost their lives in that infamous battle: the Third Reich's first European defeat and quite possibly the battle that changed the course of the entire war.

Robert met Peter Blackman through his friend Chris Searle: for a period perhaps the most famous teacher in England as a standard-bearer for the idea that schools should encourage children to challenge established values. He was also a poet and author, and has for many years been the jazz critic for the socialist *Morning Star* newspaper. He first met Robert and Alfie in the late 1970s, as fellow members of an organisation called Art Against Racism and Fascism. Alfie, recalls Searle, designed the logo: 'It's very powerful. I was very impressed by that. She's a wonderful woman. Whenever I think of Robert, I think of Alfie, because I don't think I've ever seen one without the other.'

'I knew something of Robert's history, in the Soft Machine years,' continues Searle. 'I hadn't realised he was still making records. But he had this unique and extraordinary idea of backing up his own songs with very vibrant pieces of music of an internationalist nature, which was terrific. And if you look at the covers, they were pictorial suggestions of

> Saturday mornings in Twickenham – Robert selling the *Morning Star* with local Communist Party delegate Digby Jacks.

the music and the flipside. I remember the *Stalingrad* one. It was a photo taken just after the battle of Stalingrad, when all the Nazi helmets had been piled up, to be disposed of. It was a very dramatic picture.'

It is hardly surprising that some, such as the American critic Greil Marcus, took *Stalin Wasn't Stallin'* and its B-side at face value as a Stalinist rallying cry. Even Brian Eno describes Robert as the last person he knew who would still make pro-Stalin comments. 'I kind of admired it, in the face of the ever-growing mountain of evidence to the contrary,' chuckles Eno. 'I thought: "Well, at least he isn't swayed by fashion."'

But Eno also points out that Wyatt is anything but predictable: 'A lot of people, when you meet them, after a couple of sentences you know pretty much what they're going to think about everything else. They've bought *that* package rather than *that* one.' Robert, says Brian, is by contrast one of the few people with the stamina and stubbornness to think things out for himself.

Wyatt was a member of the Communist Party of Great Britain, affiliated to the traditional Soviet model, and he continues to wish that model had proved a success: 'I still think it was the noblest experiment in human history, the Soviet thing,' he told *The Wire*'s Biba Kopf in 1997, 'and its failure is nothing to be pleased about.' Yet Chris Searle suggests that it is a mistake to assume that to be a communist during the period was necessarily to be a Stalinist; in fact, he recalls a strong antipathy towards Stalinism within the CPGB and 'a strong libertarian vein too, particularly among those involved in different streams of culture'.

Stalin Wasn't Stallin' was a straw, poked into an overseas air pocket by someone who describes himself as asphyxiating in Western rock culture. The Soviet interest was far from exclusive. Robert also gulped air from other socialist countries, covering the Chilean track *Arauco* and Cuba's *Caimanera*. Forthcoming tracks *Chairman Mao* and *Amber and the Amberines*, meanwhile, looked to China and Grenada respectively.

Wyatt's next single, *Trade Union*, was equally political – an overt declaration of support for immigrant labour, at a time when unions were under attack from the Tories. As with *Stalingrad*, Robert didn't actually appear on the track; instead, the song was written and performed by the Bangladeshi group Dishari. 'What characterised Robert was a real internationalism,' says Chris Searle, who had introduced Wyatt to the group. 'He was very, very interested in all forms of art and music and poetry that had an internationalist philosophy and approach. He hated any form of chauvinism or racism or homophobia, and the internationalism was very much a part of that. His music at the time reflected that.'

Robert liked Dishari's music, rooted in the Bengali folk tradition, and was sympathetic to the song's message: a call for Bangladeshis to join trade unions. But there was also a practical reason for working with them. While he doesn't have much faith in the power of music itself to achieve political change, Robert does believe it can effect change on a granular level. 'There was this bunch of Bengali trade unionists who were being kicked out of Bangladesh', he recalls, 'and wanted asylum in England. The Home Office wanted to send them back. And I said, "I know they make music, at their political meetings they get up and sing songs. So if we recorded them then we could say to the Home Office that they're working here. They're musicians, they're not just asylum seekers."' It worked, too. The group's leader, Abdus Salique, went on to become a successful East End restaurateur and chairman of Brick Lane Traders' Association. 'That was great,' says Wyatt. 'It's not all failure, not at grassroots level. You're fighting little battles. Real activism tends to be around single issues.'

On the surface, *Trade Union* sounds nothing like a Robert Wyatt song. But there was something in the droning accompaniment that sounded oddly like Ivor Cutler, and which Wyatt emphasised through his use of harmonium – a Cutler trademark. So, for the flipside, Robert sang *Grass* from the Scotsman's *Velvet Donkey* album, while members of Dishari backed him on shenhai and tabla. The theme of grass, and grassroots union membership, was a further link.

Cutler's original had been both childlike and casually threatening: 'Do not mind if I thump you when I'm talking to you / I've something important to say.' Wyatt interpreted the lyrics as poking fun at those comrades on the hard left who believed that the ends always justified the means; that one couldn't make an omelette without breaking a few eggs. That he didn't go in for such pitiless platitudes himself is further evidence that Wyatt was no off-the-shelf Stalinist: his politics were always expressed on a deeply human level.

The interest in grassroots politics, the search for common humanity beneath the 'great man' theory of history, helps to explain why Soviet leaders didn't put him off: 'What people's lives mainly consist of is having families, girlfriends, trying to do a job, going to school, having fun, going to the market, having a dance on a Saturday night,' he later explained to Ryan Dombal of *Pitchfork*. 'And all these things were in fact going on in the Soviet Union, and China, and everywhere else. I mean, if the only thing you knew about the United States was that it bombed twenty-two different countries since the end of the Second World War, you'd think, "Wow, that's a terrible country." But those of us who know and love the United States know there's far more to it than that, and that you don't all just go around bombing people. Well, you're usually bombing *somebody*, but it's not all of you doing that.'

–»)(«- –»)(«- –»)(«-

From tunes first sung by Chic and Billie Holiday to Stalinist gospel and Bengali folk song, Wyatt's first batch of Rough Trade releases avoided every sort of pigeonhole. Yet the four singles were deemed to have enough in common to work as an LP. *Nothing Can Stop Us* was released in March 1982. And, like *Stalin Wasn't Stallin'*, the title was cheekily political. As Robert's scrawled sleevenotes pointed out, the phrase was actually lifted from *America Conquers Britain* by Ludwell Denny, an American journalist on the opposite side of the political spectrum.

Never had Wyatt recorded such a song-based collection and, to that extent, *Nothing Can Stop Us* encapsulates his love of pop. But this was a pop lover who also listened to international folk music as well as to an awful lot of jazz.

As well as Dishari, *Nothing Can Stop Us* featured the South African bassist Ernest Mothle, and Barbados-born trumpeter Harry Beckett. Wyatt's old mate Bill MacCormick played bass on *Arauco*. Yet there were fewer guests on these singles than on *Rock Bottom* or *Ruth Is Stranger Than Richard*: Robert contributed vocals and keyboards himself and even played the drum parts on hand percussion. This DIY approach lent *Nothing Can Stop Us* a bald, almost demo-like quality: jazz filtered through punk. As Wyatt acknowledged in his liner notes: 'You may notice some technical inadequacies in some of my performances – a hesitant beat here, a dodgy note there – these are of course entirely deliberate and reproduced as evidence of my almost painful sincerity.'

The impression was that Wyatt was no longer rubbing out his mistakes. In fact, the records are deliberately, *meticulously* scruffy – the art was in not making them sound clinical. 'You don't tidy up all the rough edges on a Cézanne,' as Robert chuckles; 'you wouldn't have anything left. I do leave the brush strokes, as it were.'

In addition to the four Rough Trade singles, *Nothing Can Stop Us* featured two new songs. Robert's version of socialist anthem *The Red Flag* reinforced his allegiance to the old left. Wyatt's version could have been recorded in a garden shed but, stripped of its grandeur, the anthem became all the more affecting. Like *Arauco*, it was, in Wyatt's hands, a song of broken dreams. The original idea had been to release *The Red*

› At last, an album of pop songs. Alfie's cover art for *Nothing Can Stop Us*.

Flag as a single, backed by socialist anthem *The Internationale*: working men of all countries, unite! Geoff Travis, however, was uncomfortable with the idea, apparently for artistic, rather than political, reasons.

The other new tune on *Nothing Can Stop Us* was the opener, *Born Again Cretin*: the only tune on the record written by Wyatt – and his first composition for five years. Recorded in a Twickenham studio run by jazz bassist Peter Ind, who also played on the track, it is surely one of the finest pieces of music Wyatt ever set to tape. The song is unusually linear in construction. The first half was apparently based on Ornette Coleman's *Peace*, but Wyatt sounds more like a restrained, downcast Bobby McFerrin: scatted brass over slow-motion, doo-wop backing vocals. Only after almost a minute and a half does he come in with the main vocal line, which continues straight through to the end. It's all over in three minutes: jazz squeezed into pop form, although never even stopping for a chorus.

So inviting are the slinky half-time beat and muddy mouth vocals that it's easy, at first, to miss the anger of the lyrics. Yet *Born Again Cretin* is a scathing attack on armchair liberals. Still furious that the West wasn't doing more to overthrow the system that had forced Mongezi Feza and his fellow Blue Notes into exile, Robert's tongue almost burst through his cheek as he sang:

> *Let Mandela rot in prison*
> *Someone should tell him how lucky he is*
> *Read him George Orwell, explain about Naipaul*
> *Because he must realise how he needs us*
> *What with our culture, and our charm, and our brains*

Liberals, mocked Wyatt, should be embarrassed by V. S. Naipaul. Born in Trinidad of Indian descent, the novelist is infamous for the contempt he shows for the developing world many expect him to represent. George Orwell was chosen as Naipaul's antithesis: the bedside reading of the stereotypical liberal.

'Born Again Cretin', says Wyatt, 'was about the fact that I knew a lot of people who had been on the left who read Solzhenitsyn and then thought: "Oh fuck, got that wrong." I wasn't having that, really. They were abandoning the really important struggles of the day, like the anti-apartheid movement, simply because it was supported by communists and therefore the left. I like books on etymology and I was amused by the fact that "cretin" is actually derived from "Christian". And I was fed up with this, "I'm just going to be religious now, I'm not going to get involved in sordid affairs of the world, there's no point." Well, it's all right for you, mate. If Mandela said that, we'd be stuffed, wouldn't we?'

Born Again Cretin typified a new quiet anger from Wyatt. Like the other songs he had covered on the Rough Trade singles, it was more consistently and convincingly political than anything he had previously released. Robert's vision had been focused by his membership of the CPGB, but it also helped that his label were at least broadly sympathetic.

You could make a strong case for *Nothing Can Stop Us* as a classic Wyatt album, the equal of any in his career. The music had all the economy of *O Caroline*, but the lyrics had moved from the painfully intimate to global perspectives. And, while *O Caroline* was an anomaly on *Matching Mole*, *Nothing Can Stop Us* was held together by the consistency of intent: a collection of folk tunes old and new.

For the front cover, Alfie contributed a pen and ink drawing of a car bonnet. In place of the usual Rolls-Royce logo, the woman with outstretched wings, she depicted a factory worker with one arm raised in revolutionary salute. But *Nothing Can Stop Us* was, to a large extent, a series of *failed* revolutionary anthems, its prevailing mood that of dignity in defeat. Rather than the Trotskyist polemic of the young left, Wyatt's was the sadder, older perspective of a man who didn't believe he had history on his side – but had signed up to the cause anyway.

'We have a strange curse,' Robert reflects, 'which is having won, within living memory, all the wars. Ever since the last colonial wars, where we beat off all others, eventually – French, Dutch, Spanish – and the English language started to reign supreme. Then we fought a couple of world wars, in which it is very easy to see us as being on the right side. I don't think anybody sensible would argue with that. But victors don't really examine themselves, whereas defeated people do. There's a sort of grace in defeat, which we've never achieved, and I would like us to be in that state of grace and modesty about our role in world history.'

➼❰‐ ‐➼❰‐ ‐➼❰‐

It was not only *Nothing Can Stop Us* that glowed with Wyatt's political convictions. The same ideology, again far from the steely eyed Stalinist stereotype, was evident in his soundtrack for *The Animals Film*, a 1982 documentary about the abuse of animals. Robert got the job via Julie Christie, the film's narrator, who suggested him to directors Victor Schonfeld and Myriam Alaux.

'Victor Schonfeld tried to get Talking Heads to do it,' Robert recalls, 'but they charged him five hudnred pounds just to use one song for the opening credits. And it was a budget film. Julie said, "I've got a friend who would do it for less than that, I think; why don't you ask him to do it?" And I did all the rest of the music for a hundred pounds. So Talking Heads got five hundred quid for the title sequence, and I got a hundred for the rest of the film. But I was very happy to do it.'

Abstract and sometimes abrasive, Wyatt's soundtrack was close to industrial music: more Throbbing Gristle or Cabaret Voltaire than Violeta Parra. The bleak, brutal sound suited the shocking images. Among the film's more stomach-churning scenes are the guillotining of chickens' beaks and a live dog on a laboratory slab with all its internal organs exposed. 'It was a gruelling thing to do,' recalls Wyatt. 'It's very hard to do music for a scene that's too unbearable to watch.'

Linking with his early interest in FREGG, a 'tiny, totally dotty organisation, full of Joyce Grenfell-type people' that campaigned for free range eggs, *The Animals Film* resonated with Wyatt's broader politics. As well as the abuse of animals, Schonfeld and Alaux addressed the underlying corporate greed that allowed and even encouraged such abuse. The film, Robert told the *Morning Star*, put 'a bit of political muscle into what previously seemed like the wishy-washy liberal pre-occupations of vegetarianism'. It was a radical agenda at the time, though the ideas are now almost mainstream.

Another chance to stretch out beyond the compact song structures of *Nothing Can Stop*

Narrated by *Julie Christie*
Music by *Robert Wyatt* and
David Byrne/Talking Heads

a film by Victor Schonfeld and Myriam Alaux

THE ANIMALS FILM

Us arrived when Robert and Alfie travelled to Rome at the invitation of the Italian public radio station RAI. The session would eventually appear on CD as *Radio Experiment Rome, February 1981*, but at the time there seemed no prospect of the tracks being heard outside Italy. The pressure was off, particularly as Robert was invited to record fragments and sketches, rather than finished songs.

Where nine of the ten tracks on *Nothing Can Stop Us* had been covers, the RAI sessions found him teeming with ideas in the same playfully experimental mood that had characterised *The End of an Ear*. Its two highlights were *Billie's Bounce*, in which Robert showed he really *could* sing Charlie Parker solos, even if he sounded like a man on helium, and *Opium War*, which married a staid Western report on the nineteenth-century Anglo-Chinese conflict with a Maoist analysis. The latter track has Robert manipulating the tape speed, evoking the medium of radio itself – and, specifically, the shortwave broadcasts from communist nations that made up a significant part of his listening during the period. 'I was invited to go for a week just to record the actual process of my working,' Wyatt later recalled. 'I deliberately went in there and improvised what I was doing, as well as how I did it. The point wasn't to have a finished result that could be listened to, the point was to see a process. It's only in retrospect that I can see that bits of some of them have some kind of coherence.'

There were collaborations, too. Signing to Rough Trade put Wyatt alongside such post-punk beacons as The Raincoats, Young Marble Giants, The Pop Group and The Fall. It was strange company for a musician associated with progressive jazz rock, yet the label didn't share punk's insistence on 1976 as musical year zero. Robert, in any case, had never been guilty of the aloofness that characterised prog at its worst. He had even pre-empted punk's DIY spirit back on The Soft Machine's *Thank You Pierrot Lunaire*: 'I still can't see why people listen instead of doing it themselves.'

He hadn't known it, tucked away in Twickenham, but Wyatt was in tune with the times – if not with punk, then certainly with post-punk, the arguably more creative and compelling era for which punk cleared the decks. Although initially uncomfortable with punk's efforts to appear edgy, Wyatt by this stage recognised an affinity with a younger generation of musicians: 'While my contemporaries in rock were getting more polished,' he explains, 'the punks were much more like us aspiring beatnik kids in our little cellars and clubs, who didn't give a fuck about fame or the public and all that. I liked what they were doing. I even thought of reworking The Fall's *Totally Wired* – as *Totally Wyatt.*'

The Rough Trade set-up was highly sociable and inherently collaborative: 'I don't know about brown rice,' says Scritti Politti's Green Gartside, of the label's worthy image, 'but there was lots of Red Stripe.' Slowly, Robert became less cut off from his contemporaries, opening himself up to a golden age of British pop. Whereas once he had been interested only in watching left-wing MPs like Dennis Skinner, he now went to see bands such as The Specials and The Clash. 'I felt like a teddy bear mascot at a football match,' Wyatt has recalled. 'It was a great role... I actually became more interested because it existed side-by-side with reggae. It really climaxed in the Two-Tone era, when people began digging up the old ska records. I loved Two-Tone. That was just about the last era of pop/rock music that I felt totally at one with. Jerry Dammers and The Beat and all those people – that whole environment really was like a breath of fresh air.

-»》《«- -»》《«- -»》《«-

Having got back into the studio with Rough Trade, Robert embarked on a series of collaborations with associated post-punk musicians. In the summer of 1980 he went into the studio with with his friend Vivien Goldman, who, as well as writing about music, had sung with dub producer Adrian Sherwood and The Flying Lizards, and asked Robert to play percussion on her single *Laundrette*.

Although he could no longer operate kick-drum and hi-hat pedals, Robert was more than capable of laying down drum parts with his hands alone and contributed a sparse percussion track. 'Robert had this whole vision,' recalls Goldman. 'When I heard it, I was like: "Oh, is that it?" And he said: "That's it, it doesn't need any more." And I listened to it and I said, "You know, you're right." It's very, very subtle and just really does the job in an economic way. Very unexpected, very organic. Obviously it's a big part of why that is a much-loved tune that keeps getting reissued.' A reggae fan, Wyatt liked Goldman's combination of Jamaican roots music and English post-punk, a marriage pioneered by Keith Levene and John Lydon of Public Image Ltd, both of whom appeared on the record, along with jazz improviser Steve Beresford. Lydon himself co-produced. 'A man of refreshingly few words in this role,' remembers Robert. 'In fact, I seem to remember: "Just make a fucking noise".'

The Raincoats were in a similar vein, a then all-female act signed to Rough Trade: a startlingly original mix of intuitive, mainly untrained musicians. The Slits' Palmolive had drummed on their first album but, when she left, the band brought in guests for their second, *Odyshape*. Robert was one of them. Vocalist and guitarist Ana da Silva recalls him doing wheelies around the studio. 'People think Robert is very serious,' she says, 'because he has such a beautiful voice, and he's an angel, really, as a person. But he really has a sense of humour as well.'

So warm was their relationship that Wyatt agreed to join the band onstage at London's Albany Theatre – his first live appearance since the ill-fated Rome gig with Henry Cow. The gig itself was not easy. 'I think he has an involuntary shake when he gets very nervous,' says Raincoats co-founder Gina Birch, 'and he was shaking like mad. But he did it, and that was amazing.' Wyatt only sang *Born Again Cretin*, but Rough Trade boss Geoff Travis recalls it as an extraordinary night. 'He took the roof off the venue. It was absolutely astonishing.'

Further guest sessions included a vocal, credited as Robert Ellidge, on *Jelly Babies* on the *Popular Classical* EP by Epic Soundtracks, formerly of Swell Maps, and piano and backing vocals for *Summer into Winter*, an EP of lustrous folk-pop by Ben Watt. 'He seemed to sing in a voice that I was trying to find myself,' says Watt, soon to be known as one half of Everything But The Girl but at that point signed to Cherry Red as a solo artist. 'There was a real movement at the time to avoid American FM radio clichés. Singing in English accents, austerity, experimentalism were all key ingredients in the underground zeitgeist at the time and Robert's music fitted in perfectly.'

Jelly Babies and *Summer into Winter* drew on Wyatt's talents as both pianist and singer, as did his most significant guest role of the early 1980s, with fellow Rough Trade artists Scritti Politti. Green Gartside, Scritti's sole constant member, had by his own admission been 'very, very much in love with Robert' since hearing *Little Red Record* as a teenager. Wyatt influenced Gartside's early vocal style and even the band name itself: as well as a reference to the *scritti politici* (or political writings) of the Italian Communist Antonio Gramsci, the name is a deliberate is subtle allusion to the 'not nit not' lyrics on *Rock Bottom*. Green had even written Robert a fan letter, care of John Peel, upon hearing of the fall. 'It was mainly about how brilliant a drummer I thought he was,' he recalls. 'And that all my friends thought Billy Cobham was a superior drummer and that I thought they were idiots and that Robert was by far the better.' When he mentioned this on a visit to Twickenham, having befriended his hero seven or eight years later, Green found to his delight that Robert and Alfie had not only received the letter but still had it in their flat.

By the time Green met Robert, Scritti Politti were an act in transition. In their early squat-land incarnation, the band had deliberately avoiding conventional musical structures, preferring an approach they called 'messthetics'. Yet they had recently changed direction, deciding that the best way to overthrow the cultural hegemony of the ruling class was in fact to make music aimed squarely at the charts. Morphing into a shiny electro-pop artist, Gartside would, by the middle of the decade, have succeeded in reaching the top ten.

Songs to Remember represented an interim phase: pop as a Trojan horse through which Derrida or Nietzsche could be smuggled into the mainstream. Wyatt played keyboards on several numbers, the standout track being the single *The 'Sweetest Girl'*. Although it had the romantic, reggae feel of lovers' rock, the song also had an emotionally detached quality, reflected in the inverted commas of the title: terms and conditions apply. Gartside recalls that the original idea had been for reggae star Gregory Isaacs to sing the vocal, over a backing track by German robotic pop act Kraftwerk. When that brilliantly unlikely collaboration fell through, he sang it himself. Wyatt provided accompaniment on piano and his trusty Riviera organ, bringing with it something of the timbre of *Rock Bottom*.

'Green was interested in how you can do chord changes on organ in a way that didn't arise so easily on a guitar,' says Robert, 'which is why,

> Scritti Politti, with Green centre, in their early Rough Trade days.

I think, he asked me to have a go on *The 'Sweetest Girl'*. I replaced the guitar with my organ part. Apparently it shocked a lot of people at Rough Trade because it didn't sound like scratchy indie guitars. And apparently I was responsible for leading Rough Trade on a more commercial path, which is very funny. I just couldn't play guitar.'

Green says it was thrilling to have Wyatt in the studio, not least because he turned up with Julie Christie. The session, however, didn't go entirely smoothly, Robert 'shaky' from being carried down a flight of stairs to the studio. He was embarrassed, too, by his lack of virtuosity when Green, enthused by his carefully prepared keyboard parts for *The 'Sweetest Girl'* asked him to contribute spontaneously to other tracks.

Geoff Travis acknowledges that Robert and Green had an intense but volatile relationship, characterised by political disagreements (Green was a fervent Eurocommunist) as well as mutual respect. Yet Travis regards *The 'Sweetest Girl'*, marrying Gartside's songwriting talents to Wyatt's peculiar brand of melancholia, as one of the best things Rough Trade has ever released.

15

DIVING FOR DEAR LIFE

Shipbuilding and *Work in Progress*

'**Shipbuilding just arrived on my mat**', Robert has recalled, 'in the form of a cassette, with a note from Geoff Travis of Rough Trade saying: "Elvis Costello and Clive Langer have asked if you'd sing this." So I stuck it on and sang along with it and I said I would. I was very honoured that such illustrious composers should ask me to sing for them, but my thoughts were technical – can I do this and just try to do what they imagine I could do?'

Already flattered that acts like Scritti Politti and The Raincoats wanted to work with him, Robert was amazed to be asked to collaborate with commercial heavyweights like Costello and Langer. Costello had already proved himself one of New Wave's most sophisticated, as well as most successful songwriters, with hits such as *Oliver's Army*. But, though Costello often gets solo credit for *Shipbuilding*, he in fact wrote only the lyrics. The music was by Clive Langer, whose work with acts such as Madness and Dexy's Midnight Runners made him one of the most acclaimed producers of the era.

Langer had been a Wyatt fan since The Soft Machine, and had been particularly struck by Robert's recent version of *Strange Fruit*. Yet the producer himself, as he happily admits, was no jazz musician. 'I listen to jazz, but fuck knows how you do it,' he laughs. 'So *Shipbuilding* is an odd song in that sense: pop people think it's jazz, and jazz people think it's pop.'

Langer recorded a demo of the song in Nick Lowe's home studio. Mark 'Bedders' Bedford, from Madness, played double bass; on drums was Martin Hughes, from Clive Langer and the Boxes. The producer attempted a vocal himself, and also recorded a take by Steve Allen, from another Langer band, Deaf School. But nothing seemed to work. Apart from anything else, Langer concedes, the lyrics he had written were 'ridiculously banal'. Then, at a party at Nick Lowe's house, Langer bumped into Elvis Costello, and took him outside to hear the demo on his car stereo. Costello agreed to write lyrics. The next the producer heard from Costello was a phone call from Australia, where the singer-songwriter was on tour. 'He said, "I've written the best lyrics I've ever written",' Langer recalls. 'And I said, "Well, it's the best tune I've ever written."' That, says the producer, remains the case even thirty years on.

According to Langer, Costello deliberately wrote *Shipbuilding*'s lyrics in a colloquial, Wyattesque style: 'A new winter coat and shoes for the wife / and a bicycle on the boy's birthday'. Clive Langer had also written his melody and chord sequence with Wyatt's *Strange Fruit* as the main reference point. But, says the producer, it was 'a dream come true' when Robert actually agreed to sing it.

It helped, perhaps, that Costello had picked a theme to which Wyatt was likely to be sympathetic. The song was, at least in part, about the Falklands War, which had broken out in April 1982. In particular, Costello was influenced by the jingoistic media response both in Australia and the UK – where the *Sun* newspaper notoriously responded to the sinking of Argentinian cruiser the Belgrano, which caused the loss of over 300 lives, with the headline 'Gotcha'. 'It was already pretty horrifying to see the glee with which the *Sun* and such papers marked things off in the conflict,' Costello has explained. 'Almost as though we were watching a football tournament. You obviously want the guys that are wearing your uniform to come home safely and prevail – I understand that – but there was no debate, and anybody that said otherwise was characterised as some kind of wet or traitor.'

The power of the song comes from the fact that it looks at the impact of war not on the front line but, instead, on the home front. Largely fought at sea, the Falklands conflict helped revitalise the shipbuilding industry in the north of England. Yet the extra income came at a ghastly

> The *Shipbuilding* single – with its cover illustration from Stanley Spencer's *Shipbuilding on the Clyde*. There were four covers, each with different details.

price. A parent whose son sailed to the south Atlantic, possibly in one of the very ships his father built, might receive a picture postcard – but just as likely was a telegram 'notifying the next of kin'.

'It wasn't that hard to imagine there being a need to both provide the means to get people to the conflict and the people to actually take part in the conflict,' Costello has explained. 'And in my understanding of history, British history particularly, they nearly always get a working class boy to do the killing.'

'All credit to Costello for pinning that down so eloquently,' nods Wyatt. 'My take on that certainly is very similar. It's funny that the upper classes don't despise the working classes all the time. They do when they're working. But when they put on a uniform, suddenly they're "our boys". All the old Tories would get very dewy-eyed about the working classes when it's "our Tommy".

The Falklands War lasted just seventy-four days – but long enough to give Thatcher the chance to play Churchill, and to ensure that she would be re-elected in 1983 with a stronger majority. Music, Robert insists, is the *result* of politics, rather than the cause.

Yet *Shipbuilding* is timeless as well as topical, since the lyrics never mention the Falklands directly: Costello goes no closer than a line about being taken 'to task', an oblique reference to the naval Task Force. The lyrics are about the effect of the Falklands War on northern shipyards, but also about the general decline of manufacturing under Thatcher, and the hunger for cannon fodder inherent in the whole military-industrial complex. As a piece of music, too, *Shipbuilding* was a triumph, and it is precisely Robert's resignation, his lack of faith in the revolutionary power of pop, that gives the track its poignancy and power. His delivery is neutral, almost deadpan, but the confusion, desperation and suppressed rage seep through.

Clive Langer asked Steve Nieve, from Elvis Costello's band, The Attractions, to replace his own rough piano part for the final version of *Shipbuilding*, but elected to leave the drum and creaking double-bass parts from the demo. The playing was rough around the edges, but had an emotional impact that might have eluded the slickest of session players. That jazz trio skeleton was fleshed out only by organ and Costello's restrained backing vocals. Muddy mouth hi-hat impressions from Wyatt, meanwhile, subtly but effectively lifted key sections by hinting at double time.

The hollow, unkempt arrangement left all the more room for Wyatt's voice. 'Robert is just completely naked,' says Geoff Travis, who released the single on his Rough Trade label, 'but without being self-indulgent. It's not primal screaming. It's just wonderful.' Costello admitted that he got choked up listening to Robert in the studio, and Langer too burst into tears when listening to the track after the final mixing session. 'I didn't want to go home or anything, I just stayed up, playing it and playing it,' he recalls. 'I got in at about four in the morning and woke my wife up and played it to her. It was just very special.'

Shipbuilding was released in August 1982, two months after Britain won the Falklands War. Unusually, Alfie didn't design the cover herself. Instead, she suggested using an image of the Glasgow shipyards by the neo-Romantic artist Stanley Spencer, part of the *Shipbuilding on the Clyde* series commissioned during World War II.

Though it failed to chart on its initial release, listeners to John Peel's show voted *Shipbuilding* the second best song of 1982, just behind *Temptation* by New Order, while the *NME* named it among their top three tracks of the year. Buoyed by such acclaim, Rough Trade re-released the single the following year, just as Thatcher was sweeping to a second term in government. This time it made the Top 40.

Dressed in his revolutionary uniform of beard, beret and khaki shirt, Wyatt performed the track on BBC2's *The Old Grey Whistle Test*. 'Here's another piece of completely escapist light entertainment,' he muttered, by way of introduction. The self-deprecation was an attempt to pre-empt and diffuse charges of worthiness. But Robert is also painfully eager to deflect praise for *Shipbuilding*, widely regarded as a pinnacle of political pop, onto Langer and Costello. It wasn't that he didn't like the song, Wyatt insists, but simply that it wasn't his to own. Overall, he found the *Shipbuilding* experience 'lovely'.

The only part of the experience that he found less agreeable was the promotional video: footage of Wyatt in his beret, wheeling past the hulk of a ship, intercut with dry-ice shots of a jazz club. Though relatively restrained for the New Romantic era, Robert regards the video as 'silly' and 'neutered'. Perhaps it was simply a case of two worlds colliding. Dave Robinson had co-founded punk and New Wave label Stiff Records, and was used to working with acts like Elvis Costello, Ian Dury and Madness. In the new era of MTV, Robinson would have regarded a video as a natural part of any promotional plan.

Uneasy as he might have been with the video, however, there's no doubt *Shipbuilding* provided a tremendous boost to Wyatt's profile. As much a cornerstone of his career as *Moon in June*, *O Caroline* and *Sea Song*, and a chart hit to boot, the song introduced Wyatt to a whole new generation. The income may have been indirect, but it must, over the years, have paid for the video several times over. Sam Ellidge remembers a moment, in his late teens, when he was sitting in a pub with some new friends and mentioned his dad was a musician called Robert Wyatt. 'And they went: "You are joking! We are not worthy, we are not worthy!" And I was thinking, "How on earth have they even heard of him?" Because I was used to most people going, "Who?"'

⟶⟶ ⟶⟶ ⟶⟶

Shipbuilding was just the most prominent of a number of collaborations in the early 1980s, not all with artists associated with Rough Trade. Robert

❯ Anton Corbijn's *NME* photo of Robert wheeling along the Thames at Twickenham, around the time of *Shipbuilding*.

contributed the loop-based *Rangers in the Night* to Morgan Fisher's *Miniatures* LP – an album of one-minute songs – and played drums on *Sanity Stomp* by Kevin Coyne, the blues-rock singer-songwriter with whom he had worked on Michael Mantler's *Silence*.

In the autumn of 1983, Wyatt went into the studio with the jazz-dance act Working Week, founded by guitarist Simon Booth with saxophonist Larry Stabbins, also of various Keith Tippett projects, including Centipede. On trombone was Lancashire's Annie Whitehead who, like Stabbins, had worked with some of Robert's favourite South African jazz musicians. She would become one of Wyatt's most important collaborators and a close friend. The song Booth had for Robert was a bilingual English/Spanish number called *Venceremos (We Will Win)*, a tribute to Chile's Unidad Popular movement. A version of the song, with lyrics by Victor Jara, had been Salvador Allende's campaign theme. It had even been sung by a defiant Jara, imprisoned following Pinochet's coup, before the prison guards took him away to be shot.

Working Week's 12-inch version of *Venceremos* would become something of a dancefloor anthem, helping to usher in the so-called British jazz revival, based around London clubs like the Wag and the Electric Ballroom. But the 7-inch 'bossa version' needed poignancy too, and Wyatt's backing vocal, echoing the lead line by Everything But The Girl's Tracey Thorn, helped to bring out the pathos that the song's chilling backstory demanded.

Wyatt also worked with Jerry Dammers on *The Wind of Change* – a record to raise awareness and funds for SWAPO, the Namibian resistance movement, then fighting South African occupation. As founder of The Specials and the 2 Tone label, Dammers had done more than anyone in the UK to show that political tunes did not have to be downbeat. With 1981's *Ghost Town*, The Specials had even taken the theme of urban decay to the top of the charts. Dammers' political vision was implicit in the multiracial make-up of many acts on Two-Tone, and reflected in the label's checkered black and white branding. Musically as well as politically, he insists, Robert felt more in common with the 2 Tone acts than with his own generation on the left. It's not so surprising, for Dammers was himself a jazz fan. He even owns up to being a fan of Robert's early work: 'I was into The Soft Machine. I think we're allowed to talk about that now, are we? The punk-prog war, is it finally over?'

After The Specials folded in 1981, Dammers had continued to demonstrate his rare gift for political pop that was artistically, and often commercially, successful. *Starvation* raised money for Ethiopian famine victims, while *Free Nelson Mandela*, produced by Elvis Costello, became a top ten hit for Dammers' new band, the Special AKA. Having also championed causes such as Rock Against Racism and Artists Against Apartheid, he was a natural choice to arrange and produce *The Wind of Change*, at the request of SWAPO.

The Wind of Change featured African musicians, including Ernest Mothle, the bassist who had played on *At Last I Am Free* and *Strange Fruit*, as well as Annie Whitehead of Working Week on trombone. Politically, Whitehead says, the track seemed to follow naturally from *Venceremos*. But she also points out that Robert was chosen not only for his political beliefs but also for his inimitable voice. 'I always joke

> The SWAPO singers. Jerry Dammers is standing, third from left. Annie Whitehead stands behind Robert.

with Robert that one of the reasons he's got such a long heritage is that he sang like an old man from day one,' agrees Jerry Dammers. 'But also, he sang like a choirboy: that weird thing of being an ageless voice. I can remember that voice from the 1960s, listening to John Peel and suddenly you heard songs like O Caroline. It was just an amazing voice that came out of the radio and stood out as something very different.'

'For me personally,' Dammers continues, of recording The Wind of Change, 'the biggest shock was actually recording it. Punk opened the door for a lot of people who didn't have the traditional singing skills, so recording vocals for me, up to that point, had always been really stressful. How out of tune is acceptable, you know? We always used to have to do loads of takes to get it right. But Robert just sang it. I nearly fell of my chair. I thought: "Well, what do I do now?" It was just brilliant. He is a fantastic musician.'

Written by Namibia's Jackson Kaujeua, the song was performed by Wyatt with the backing of the SWAPO Singers of the South West African People's Organisation. It aimed to remind the world, finally waking up to the horrors of apartheid South Africa, that life wasn't much better in neighbouring Namibia, where stories of the brutality of the Koevoet counter-insurgency force were legion.

Like Venceremos (We Will Win), the upbeat, ska-tinged The Wind of Change did not immediately convey the song's grisly inspiration. But the video was filmed outside South Africa House – 'Who would dream of doing such a directly political statement in a video nowadays?' sighs Dammers – and both he and Robert refused to pull punches in interviews. 'If you want to know how I view South Africa,' Dammers told one journalist at the time, 'I think of it as Nazism in practice.' They were also outspoken regarding the culpability of the UK government, arguing that their willingness to take a stand in Namibia was compromised by their interest in the country's uranium.

Despite the prodigious talents of Jerry Dammers, The Wind of Change, credited to Robert Wyatt and the SWAPO Singers, didn't make it past number eighty-six in the charts – rather short of the high bar set by Free Nelson Mandela. Yet Dammers remains upbeat. 'I still love that tune,' he enthuses, 'it's great. And it's Robert's voice as well. It's quite funny: I never thought he'd sing a quote from Harold Macmillan. But the whole point of writing a song, as opposed to making a political speech or writing a book, is that you're supposed to put the feeling, the emotion, into it. Robert's good at getting the emotional side of the struggle, as it was called. You have to sing it with some genuine feeling, and that has to be reflected in the song as well, to be convincing. That's what's very difficult. And if you don't really believe it, you're not going to convince anybody.'

-»)«- -»)«- -»)«-

Wyatt had remained reasonably busy with guest appearances since signing to Rough Trade – and, in Jerry Dammers and Elvis Costello, he was working with two of the finest political writers of the era. Yet, by his own admission prone to work avoidance, he was being gently hassled by Geoff Travis for a release under his own name.

However difficult he had found working in an ensemble, Robert struggled to motivate himself as a solo artist: 'The one good thing about a group', he explains, 'is that it's got a momentum of its own. So if any one particular person in it is losing it, the others will keep the thing going. Having to kickstart your own thing every time is the hardest bit.' (Wyatt has also joked that his slow work rate qualifies him as the ultimate minimalist: 'I am a real minimalist, because I don't do very much. I know some minimalists who call themselves minimalist but they do loads of minimalism. That is cheating.')

It is worth remembering that Robert had spent his first decade in music as a drummer, usually contributing lyrics and arrangements rather than original melodies. The long gaps between records were also due to Wyatt's perfectionism: it takes a lot of effort to make music sound effortless, and he tinkers almost obsessively. In a postcard to Hugh Hopper, sent around this time, Robert suggests that his physical condition, too, might have contributed to his creative inertia: 'What saps my concentration is partly physical boredom I think: just sort of sitting here watching the seasons through the holes in the walls.'

And then there was the intrusion of what Robert calls 'real life'. No artist, perhaps, can afford a sense of perspective, and music seemed particularly unimportant when set against what was happening abroad. Robert and Alfie joined vigils outside embassies, for instance, for Solomon Mahlangu, an ANC member executed by hanging in 1979. In 1983, when President Reagan sent American troops into the tiny Caribbean island of Grenada, Robert and Alfie went straight to the American Embassy to protest. They took with them Alfie's mum – and their pregnant dog.

'We were the only people there for about two hours,' says Alfie. 'I had a placard saying "US scum out of Grenada", or something, which

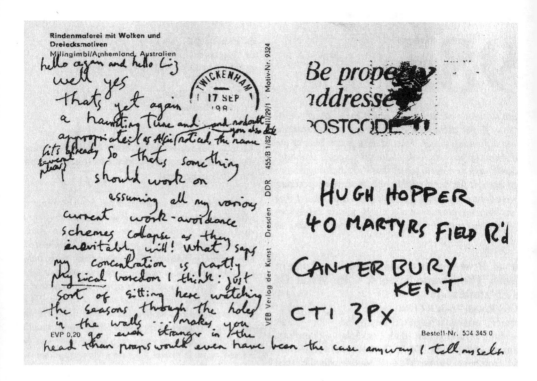

I quickly painted. We drove up to Grosvenor Square, and stood there. Various people looked out the window. Then somebody came over and said, "Who are you, what organisation?" And my mum said, "Old Aged Pensioners." And then eventually the Grenada support group turned up with Chris Searle, who's an important person in the Communist story. And he said to Robert, "You've got to write a song about this.'"

Amber and the Amberines, which borrowed a melody from Hugh Hopper, was Robert's response. The title of the song came from a provocative military exercise carried out by the US in advance of their invasion, its name an obvious and menacing allusion to Grenada and its sister islands the Grenadines. 'I knew that as soon as any opening or division opened up within the revolution, the US would be in like a shot,' says Searle, who had worked in Grenada as a teacher-trainer and developed a close friendship with Maurice Bishop, the Marxist-Leninist prime minister who was executed just before the US invasion during a bout of infighting. 'They were just waiting for a pretext to invade, and had been for three or four years.'

'*Amber and the Amberines*', explains Searle, 'was the Americans' name for the invasion rehearsal which took place on Vieques, which is the small island off Puerto Rico where the US rehearse all their sea-borne invasions. It was highly publicised so as to frighten any progressive movement in the Caribbean. It was called *Amber and the Amberines*, and of course the official name of the state of Grenada is Grenada and the Grenadines. It was an obvious incitement to invasion – an open dress rehearsal to frighten any progressive movement in the Caribbean.

'At that time, of course, you didn't just have Grenada, you had Nicaragua and, of course, Cuba and Suriname. And there were progressive movements breaking out on some of the smaller islands, too. So the US, particularly Reagan, were in dire fear of any more Grenadas. Grenada was called by Bishop "a big revolution in a small country", and of course it was. And had an effect out of all comparison with the size of the country.'

Originally recorded in late 1983 for *NME's Department of Enjoyment* cassette (alongside The Smiths, Cocteau Twins and Billy Bragg), *Amber and the Amberines* had a home-made feel. Its arrangement was scrawny, Wyatt's keyboard breathy but battered: a Mellotron for the Thatcher age. Its lyrics paid tribute not to the Marxist leaders but to 'friends like Chris, working in the classrooms, London to Mozambique, nursing wounds of empire'. The song also praised the Cuban construction workers who helped Maurice Bishop's New Jewel Movement and the grassroots membership of the organisation. The chorus was a plea for solidarity: 'Everyone needs to feel at home / Nobody wins who fights alone.'

Amber and the Amberines provided a renewed impetus and direction for Robert, spurring him to compose more of his own material, which would surface the following year on *Old Rottenhat*. Meantime, it became the cornerstone of *Work in Progress*, an EP of 'secular hymns' released the following August. The other three songs on the EP were politically driven covers, each associated with a different part of the world: radial lines connecting Twickenham not only to Grenada but also to South Africa, Cuba and Chile.

Te Recuerdo Amanda was a composition by Victor Jara, the Chilean composer of *Venceremos* and perhaps the ultimate Latin American revolutionary singer; his songs were judged so dangerous that he had been killed in Pinochet's CIA-backed military junta. To the uninitiated, however, Jara sounds as if he is singing straightforward love songs. 'People here hadn't realised it,' says Wyatt, 'but they'd settled into patterns. For example, if you were angry, you did songs where you shouted and played fast. And if you were in love, you did songs slow and quiet. I was very struck by punk, which I admired enormously, but I was also listening to

rebel music by people who really had their
lives on the line. In jungles in South America, in hiding,
these were people who were facing bullets and torture every day of their
lives – and they were singing gentle Latin American ballads.'

Pablo Milanés, the Cuban songwriter who composed *Yolanda*, the
other Spanish tune on the EP, had a delivery even smoother than Victor
Jara. A crucial figure in the *Nueva Trova* movement of the 1960s, a
Cuban parallel to Latin America's *Nueva Canción*, Milanés was seen by
many as Castro's minstrel. Though *Yolanda* was a love song, Wyatt saw
its sense of longing as political too. He would dedicate his version to the
Cuban construction workers killed in Grenada.

Completing the EP was *Biko*, a Peter Gabriel song paying tribute
to the South African activist. Described by Wyatt as the Malcolm X
to Mandela's Martin Luther King, Steve Biko's death in police custody
had been shocking even by the grim standards of the apartheid regime;
almost as chilling was the announcement by Jimmy Kruger, South
Africa's Minister of Justice and Police, that Biko's death 'leaves me cold'.

Still furious at the death of Mongezi Feza, Wyatt's version has an
undertow of anger but resists the temptation to emote *at* the listener.
He instead comes across like an English Victor Jara, apparently tranquil
even as he delivers the most defiant lines: 'You can blow out a candle /
But you can't blow out a fire / Once the flames begin to catch / The wind
will blow it higher.'

Work in Progress, a short story of a record, was released in August
1984. Despite their sketched, demo-like quality, the four tracks were not

really inchoate. Wyatt was developing the defeated, DIY sound he had first explored on his Rough Trade singles: a sound he later described as 'punk on valium'. The arrangements were deliberately desolate, featuring only vocals, drums, keyboards and slithering, slippery Wasp synth bass lines. The same palette and the same tone, crumpled but with a glance of light just cutting into the frame, would feature on Wyatt's next full album. And, for the first time since *Rock Bottom*, all ten tunes would be originals.

16

THE AGE OF SELF

Old Rottenhat: English as a foreign language

'**The very first time that I met Robert Wyatt and his wife,** at a Cuba Solidarity benefit in 1984, I approached the wheelchair-bound figure to ask if he was, indeed, Robert Wyatt,' wrote *Morning Star* journalist David Granville in 1990. '"Well, I used to be," he replied.'

With no studio album since 1975's *Ruth Is Stranger Than Richard*, Wyatt was so far into another sabbatical that he had apparently reverted in his mind to the surname Ellidge. Whatever he joked to Granville, however, Robert had hardly stopped making music. The decade since *Ruth* had seen collaborations like *Shipbuilding* and *The 'Sweetest Girl'*, as well as the Rough Trade singles collected on *Nothing Can Stop Us* and the *Work in Progress* EP. But Robert had contributed only one of his own compositions to *Nothing Can Stop Us*, while *Work in Progress* featured only one original – and even that was co-written with Hugh Hopper.

Old Rottenhat, released in November 1985 behind a sandy, minimalist cover from Alfie, marked the return of Wyatt the writer. It was also a solo album in the strictest sense: he wrote every song and, aside from a four-second cameo from Alfie, played every note. '*Rock Bottom* and *Ruth Is Stranger Than Richard* were both, in a way, recreating a group in the studio,' explains Wyatt. 'But I gradually withdrew from groups. Life on the road gradually receded from my mind and I started to work more like a writer or a painter would work, just on their own, doing

> Robert, at the time of the miners' strike, fronting an array of political posters.

their thing. Music ceased to be a social activity in the sense that it had been before.'

If you're listening to Violeta Parra and Radio Moscow, Robert points out, you're not likely to pick up many potential collaborators. He was also reluctant to ask anyone to play on his records because he couldn't afford Musicians' Union rates yet refused to offer less. Then there was an element of what Robert calls 'paraplegic vanity' in wanting to prove he could be creatively self-sufficient.

'Robert always said, I think it was semi-joking, that it was part of the Paraplegic Liberation Front,' recalls Geoff Travis. 'To do everything yourself, to prove you didn't have to rely on anyone else. But it's also a fear of coming into contact with other people. Fear in terms of being depressed and also the difficulty of being able to translate your ideas sufficiently well to another musician, so that they play what you want them to play. I don't think he had any problems when it came down to it – but we're not inside his head.'

'Old Rottenhat' was an insult, shouted at someone wearing fancy clothes: 'Someone who has dressed up posh', says Wyatt, 'even if, perhaps, they're not.' With his beret and Free Nelson Mandela T-shirt, it was hardly a charge that could have been levelled at Robert, yet he identified with the sense of a man out of place. 'I was becoming more and more alarmed at the gradual return to a kind of right-wing politics,' he recalls, 'which those of us born at the end of the Second World War thought had gone for ever. And so there's that kind of – not anger, but just sadness, because I'm not revolutionary by inclination.'

That *Old Rottenhat* is the least playful record of Wyatt's career is no coincidence. Twiddling the radio dial, he had stumbled upon Voice of America or Radio Free Europe – 'one of those Western propaganda programmes' – and, to his horror, heard one of his old songs. Determined that such an insult would not be repeated, Robert set out to make 'un-misusable music': songs that could not possibly be appropriated by his political opponents. Robert, as usual, was correcting an imbalance: 'Anybody who is in rock has to be interested in politics,' he explained to Jack Barron of *Sounds*; 'you really haven't got the choice. I get impatient with people who tell you to leave politics out of it. You wake up every morning and you get politics shoved down your face of the right-wing kind, the BBC and Fleet Street and everything else. And if you've got any pride at all you've got to resist it and work out your own vision of what's going on.'

Old Rottenhat was an attempt to right the scales: an attempt to show that not every inhuman action of the twentieth century was perpetrated by communists. Wyatt dedicated the album to Michael Bettaney, an MI5 officer jailed the previous year for passing official secrets to the Soviet Union. Robert sympathised with Bettaney as an innocent burned by realpolitik, but also wanted to make a broader point about freedom of speech: 'I don't remember the declaration of war against the Soviet Union; last I knew they were our allies in the Second World War. So how come suddenly talking to the Russians about what your government's doing – we tell the Americans, we tell Mossad, we tell every bloody bastard – how come that's suddenly an imprisonable offence? I thought, "That is not freedom of speech". It's totally reasonable, just as it was, later, for Mordechai Vanunu to tell the world about Israel's nuclear weapons. You boast about being a free and open society where you don't hide your problems. And somebody actually says the truth about something and you bang him in the nick and call him a traitor.'

If the Cold War provided the international dimension of *Old Rottenhat*, its domestic backdrop was the miners' strike: the most prolonged and violent of Britain's industrial disputes, and the culmination of Thatcher's fight against the unions. Chris Cutler compares it to Norse mythology's Doom of the Gods: 'That strike was the Ragnarök of old Britain,' says the drummer, 'and it was a long and expensive affair. After many months the miners were in serious need of money. It was clear that they were the last redoubt against the Thatcherite no-such-thing-as-society revolution, so it seemed essential to support them – especially in the face of the shameful spinelessness of the Labour Party and the TUC.'

Wyatt did his bit, collecting money for the miners on the street and recording two tracks for Cutler's fundraising EP, *The Last Nightingale*, featuring artwork by Gonzo cartoonist Ralph Steadman. He also released a track, *The Age of Self*, to raise money for the Miners' Hardship Fund, which the *NME* made their single of the week.

> Robert's vinyl contribution for the striking miners.

To an extent, Robert holds Russian dissidents such as Aleksandr Solzhenitsyn and the nuclear physicist Andrei Sakharov responsible for the ideological ascendance of Thatcherism in the UK. 'Part of Thatcher's success', he explains, 'was to do with the demonising of socialism, which was suddenly illustrated by this godsend to the right wing: the great dissident movement in the communist countries. It was a dream script for Tories. It was the moral high ground given to them by the Russian dissidents that enabled her to crush the miners with such ferocity and to demonise Arthur Scargill and so on. This is not perverse, but I thought, "This is exactly the point to remember that there was a *reason* for socialism, and it hasn't been addressed."'

As much as he felt alienated by the rise of Thatcher and the right, Wyatt was a misfit – an Old Rottenhat – because he didn't see eye-to-eye even with the majority of his supposed comrades on the left. Where Communist Party membership had doubled during the famous General Strike of 1926, the Party actually *lost* members in the coalfields when the miners, under Arthur Scargill, went on strike sixty years later.

The 1983 manifesto of Labour leader Michael Foot had taken mainstream politics about as far to the left as it could go – and was famously dismissed as the longest suicide note in history. Foot's successor, Neil Kinnock, began to distance the party from its traditional support base in unions – including Scargill's National Union of Mineworkers. This came too late for the so-called 'gang of four', right-leaning Labour politicians who had already left Labour to set up the centrist Social Democratic Party (and later formed an alliance with the Liberal Party that was a precursor to today's Liberal Democrats).

Wyatt was no fan of the move, feeling betrayed in particular by SDP leader David Owen. 'It gets on people's nerves sometimes', Robert laughs, 'but I will take a pretty tune and the lyrics will be a damning indictment of the SDP, which completely spoils what would have been a good song.' *Alliance*, taking its name from the SDP–Liberal pact, made for a particularly bleak opening to *Old Rottenhat*. On lines like 'You say you're self-sufficient but you don't dig your own coal', Wyatt sounds as heartbroken as he had on *O Caroline*. Rather than a failed love affair, however, the song laments a friendship lost to the SDP–Liberal Alliance.

'I've got a couple of friends who, over the years, drifted towards the Alliance', Wyatt told the *NME*'s Sean O'Hagan, 'and what was nightmarish for me during 1984 was that the official opposition – as well as the usual right-wingers who want to smash the unions good and proper – were all so busy evading the issues. That song is about being painted into a corner called *extremism*; you're pushed into a position because of the sheer unreasonableness of mainstream alternatives.'

As Labour moved towards the political centre, it left in its wake a fragmented hard left. The divide between CPGB and Trotskyists was nothing new, but a more damaging split was emerging within the CPGB itself. 'There was this magazine called *Marxism Today*,' says Alfie, 'which got taken over by various people who more or less wanted to form New Labour within the Communist Party. Which is fine, but do it somewhere else. Don't take away the assets of these old people, don't steal the buildings – which they did, took over the actual headquarters. They pinched the magazine and they wanted a newspaper. In fact they never got the newspaper. That's the one thing they didn't get.'

The newspaper was the *Morning Star*, which remained in the hands of the traditional CPGB members, broadly loyal to Soviet communism and the trade unions. On the other side was an increasingly powerful revisionist movement. In Spain and Italy, so-called Eurocommunists had broken from the Soviet Union and were attempting to combine socialism with their own democratic values. *Marxism Today* – the party's theoretical journal, reinvented as a glossy magazine – represented a similar Eurocommunist shift in the UK, a modernising impulse that would lead, ultimately, to New Labour.

The Age of Self, the central track on *Old Rottenhat*, explored this split within the left: 'They say the working class is dead, we're all consumers now / They said that we have moved ahead, we're all just people now.' It was a summary reference to *Forward March of Labour Halted?*, an influential and controversial article by historian and fellow jazz fan Eric Hobsbawm that had appeared in *Marxism Today*. Given the perceived decline of the industrial working class that had traditionally formed the bedrock of Labour support there was a widespread belief that Labour was a party in terminal decline. Yet, by arguing that the left needed to be pragmatic in order to survive, *Marxism Today* seemed to Robert to be abandoning the class struggle in favour of cultural studies. 'What shocked me,' says Wyatt, 'was that they were talking about *England*. I was very aware of terrible and desperate battles for workers from Columbia to the Philippines, but *Forward March of Labour Halted?* was actually very parochial. And the one thing that's meant to make communism different from all the other parties is that it *isn't* parochial.'

Wyatt's own horizons on *Old Rottenhat*, by contrast, were global. Rio Tinto, mentioned on *The Age of Self*, was a mining giant, stained by its associations with apartheid South Africa. *The British Road* mocked the unctuous belief that British imperialists played fair: 'The foreigners are at it again / When will they learn to fight like our men?'

In musical terms, *Old Rottenhat* struck a rare balance between consistency and evolution. The record saw a return to the carpet-like drones of Wyatt's short film soundtrack, *Solar Flares Burn for You*. Since Robert took into the studio only a small keyboard, a pair of timbales and a bag of hand percussion, that carpet was thin and threadbare. Though the arrangements are stark, however, the songs themselves are as complex as they are catchy. *Gharbzadegi*, which took its title from an Iranian term meaning 'West-mania', featured an ascending scale played on the studio's 'self-prepared, organic John Cage piano'. Nimbly snaking back on itself, the line seemed to rise higher and higher for three full minutes without ever reaching the top of the keyboard.

Live music is a blunt tool at the best of times, and the decision not to perform gave Wyatt a vastly greater degree of creative control. Robert recorded music for *Old Rottenhat* that he could never recreate live (he insists that he can't play the piano with both hands simultaneously, for instance, let alone sing along, too). However, the reviewers – supporters and detractors alike – tended to neglect the musical component of *Old Rottenhat*, instead concentrating on its lyrics. 'Not since the golden days of Sixties protest pop has there been a politically motivated singer and songwriter of such striking originally and eloquent conviction as Robert Wyatt,' wrote David Fricke of *Rolling Stone*, when the album was released in the US. In the opposite corner, Robert Christgau, self-proclaimed dean of rock critics, got really quite cross: 'Set your political statements to unprepossessingly hypnotic music and you'd better be sure your politics are spot on – astute, clear, epigrammatic, correct. Don't deploy a slur like "Aryan" anachronistically or attribute a phrase of Harold Rosenberg's to Noam Chomsky. Don't insult the genocide in East Timor with minimalist obscurantism. Don't preach to the converted until you've made more converts.'

With its unavoidable Nazi connotations, Wyatt's line – on *The United States of Amnesia* – about the US attempting to build its own 'Aryan empire', having 'killed all those redskins', was certainly startling. And he would make the same allusion on his next album: the track *Left on Man* featured the line 'Pentagon über alles'. Robert, talking about the album today, is unrepentant. 'When everyone talks about genocide and those killings, I remind people that Europeans – really led by English-speaking people in the north and the Spanish

> Alfie's minimalist, Miró-like *Old Rottenhat* cover.

and Portuguese in the south – actually obliterated the entire people of the American continent. If we're talking about ethnic cleansing, this is fairly heavyweight stuff. So you can't say the first ever awful thing was fascism or communism.'

Christgau is right that the description of intellectuals as 'a herd of independent minds' originated with the American art critic Harold Rosenberg. Yet Chomsky, to whom Wyatt attributes the phrase on *Alliance*, uses it too. And Robert certainly wasn't insulting East Timor on the track of that name, though his references might have required unpacking. According to Chomsky, perhaps 200,000 East Timorese had died during the Indonesian occupation of the country now known as Timor-Lest: the worst slaughter, relative to population, since the Holocaust. And yet all Wyatt sings is: 'East Timor, East Timor, who's your fancy friend, Indonesia?' 'It's reduced to ciphers,' explains Robert. 'If I was trying to change the world, or thought I could, that is not what I would do. But if somebody did look up East Timor and Indonesia, if they wanted to follow it up, they could actually find all this stuff out. There's just enough, the bare minimum there.'

Christgau's anger seemed to suggest that Wyatt had at least succeeded in making the record unmisusable – and, in describing America as an 'Aryan empire', he certainly wasn't courting daytime radio plays. But Robert now admits that it is not possible to control the fate of a song once it has been released.

In a sense, however, the fact that those who do not share the viewpoint expressed in the lyrics can still warm to the music is testament to Wyatt's skill as a songwriter and arranger. Robert's failure to make *Old Rottenhat* unmisusable also allowed him to include non-political material such as *P.L.A.* – an acronym usually associated with China's People's Liberation Army, but in this context standing for 'poor little Alfie'. On paper, it's a curiously personal end to an otherwise highly political record, yet the track doesn't feel out of place. And when we hear a brief snippet of *The Internationale*, towards the end of the album, it's played on a plinky-plonky music box: a lefty lullaby.

Wyatt himself is protective of *Old Rottenhat*, in part because it has been relatively neglected. But he is also absolutely prepared to defend its politics. 'To the question, "Is there anything you think you got wrong, that is anachronistic about your political songs?",' he says, 'the answer is: "I wish." If people can say, "That obviously doesn't happen," that Rio Tinto Zinc no longer treat the Third World like slaves, whilst the liberal left here ponces on about the new man or whatever they're on about – if that ever changed, I'd be the happiest man. But, as far as I can see, it's still more or less the case.'

⇥⇤ ⇥⇤ ⇥⇤

Robert's next solo recording, early the following year, was another superbly political song – *Pigs… (In There)*, a semi-improvised monologue over sepulchral organ and gnawing Doppler bass, for an *Artists for Animals* compilation. It remains one of the odder tracks in the Wyatt canon, but it is also one of the most appealing. That song aside, though, it was mostly back to other people's records.

Notable among these was a track for *Darn It!*, an album based on poems by *Escalator Over the Hill* lyricist Paul Haines. *Curtsy* found him playing keyboards and percussion, as well as singing. Evan Parker, perhaps the finest British free-jazz saxophonist of his generation, joined on soprano sax midway through. 'The playing on Robert's track was a spontaneous invitation from Robert made in the studio,' recalls Parker, 'and was not planned in advance. But I think it represents my best surviving contribution to the project.'

Robert also went into the studio with the trumpeter Mike Mantler, appearing alongside Jack Bruce and Marianne Faithfull on the album *Many Have No Speech*. And he recorded with Chris Carter and Cosey Fanni Tutti, formerly of industrial pioneers Throbbing Gristle but now working together as both Chris & Cosey and CTI. His contribution, sandwiched between sound collage and dystopian disco, was the unreal, disembodied *Unmasked* (he would later revisit the track on his EP *A Short Break*).

There was a guest appearance, too, with Chris Cutler's group, News from Babel, named after the landmark book by George Steiner. On *Letters Home*, their superb second album, song form was extended with rare imagination and sensitivity. The vocal parts were challenging, says Cutler, but to Wyatt posed 'no trouble at all'. 'Robert's voice could be called limited', Cutler contends, 'in the sense that, I suspect, he can only sing that way. It's the voice he's been given. If you have a voice like Beyoncé, the sky's the limit, but you're also in the middle of the bell curve of voices, hundreds of which sound just like yours. So you're trapped in a continuum of sameness until listeners can hardly tell who's who any more. That's not a problem for "limited" voices, like Robert's, or Dagmar's, or Dylan's, or Blind Lemon Jefferson's.'

Cutler had also set up a label and distribution arm called Recommended Records, which produced the *ReR Quarterly*, a 'sound magazine' that combined words and vinyl. Robert contributed to a 1987 issue his most nakedly political track of the period, the droning, austere *Chairman Mao*. This found him setting lyrics to a melody by Charlie Haden, originally recorded by the bassist's Old and New Dreams quartet. Robert's words discussed Mao's haircut, as well as the Long March, the much-mythologised series of retreats in which the chief architect of the Chinese revolution first came to prominence.

Mao's haircut was, to Robert, emblematic of a broader paradox: 'For revolutionaries, the thing is not to be a colourful peasant, or different, but to be just as modern as the big modern powers. So you need an army, you need short hair, you need suits.' But the real subject of the song was the impact of nineteenth-century British imperialism on China: 'I'm simply trying to describe what happens to a country that has been regarded as backward, and has been fairly brutally colonised – people forget that

China has been, by us, and then later by others – what the world might look like from their point of view. What their challenge is. And how that doesn't match what even rebels here might wish they were like.'

–») ((– –») ((– –») ((–

Like the equally uncompromising *Old Rottenhat, Chairman Mao* and *Letters Home* were released in the mid-1980s – around Robert's fortieth birthday. What about the aphorism, sometimes, perhaps falsely, attributed to Winston Churchill, that if you're not a liberal when you're twenty-five, you have no heart, but if you're not a conservative by the time you're thirty-five, you have no brain? Robert simply chuckles. 'I think I may be not just retarded, but actually in reverse. I felt he could have been talking about me when Harold Wilson said of Tony Benn that he immatured with age. I thought, that's about what's happened to me, too. I've felt a sort of kinship with Tony Benn ever since.'

So remote did Wyatt feel from his own culture that he had at one stage thought of calling *Old Rottenhat* by an alternative title: *English as a Foreign Language.* His own neighbourhood, Lebanon Park, in particular, had changed dramatically since Robert and Alfie arrived in the mid-1970s. 'We lived in a very nice bit of Twickenham,' Alfie recalls. 'It wasn't a posh street, it just had big houses. Then suddenly the 1980s came and it became totally yuppified. People would come in and gut the houses. They'd have one house to themselves, two cars outside. There were kitchens in skips every other week. Neighbours would complain about our posters for anti-apartheid marches. The woman opposite said, "We haven't paid a huge amount of money to come and live here to have to look at those."'

Although international travel wasn't easy in a wheelchair, Robert and Alfie began making ever more frequent attempts to leave suburban Richmond for more sympathetic horizons. *Le trac* prevented Robert from performing, but he was happy to speak on political issues such as SWAPO at festivals in Italy, which had one of the largest communist parties in Western Europe. And Italian comrades in particular shared Robert's decidedly un-puritan take on socialism: the climate, the al fresco meals and the local wine were absolutely part of the appeal. Wyatt would later cite a couple of communist festivals in Italy, in the mid-1980s, as the happiest moments of his life.

Robert also visited East Berlin, reviewing the 1984 Rock for Peace festival for the *NME* ('careful people trying that bit harder', he concluded), and was invited to a political and musical festival in Finland by composer and trumpeter Henrik Otto Donner. Finland, too, was a country in which the Communist Party was a serious political force – and, says Robert, the trip had a deep impact on his subsequent thinking.

'Because of being in the Communist Party,' recalls Alfie, 'we went to Italy and were invited to things organised by the party. Italian communists controlled councils, and where they had councils they had the most wonderful festivals. Robert would be asked to say a little bit about SWAPO. So they would pay for us to go over to Italy, give us this lovely driver, feed us beautifully at this wonderful festival, which was nothing but restaurants. A wonderful councillor would come in, have a chat, then we'd go and have supper in his garden with a nightingale singing.'

> Robert speaking at a communist-run music festival in Reggio Emilia, Italy, 1986.

Most important of all, however, were the two winters Robert and Alfie spent in Spain: one in 1982–83, between the release and re-release of *Shipbuilding*, and another, four years later, in the wake of *Old Rottenhat*. On both occasions, they travelled for free, Robert having been asked over for work – on the second time for a forty-minute film, *The Voyage of Robert Wyatt*, for Catalan TV. And each time, Alfie requested open tickets, allowing them to stay on in exactly the same spot: Castelldefels, just south of Barcelona.

Primarily a tourist destination, Castelldefels was cheap off season and Robert and Alfie's room cost no more than their central heating bill back in London. The beach resort itself was almost deserted during winter months but, a mile or two inland, within a community of factory workers, Robert discovered what he calls an authentic folk culture. 'What I liked', he recalls, 'was that there was not a generational divide. There would be all the grannies sitting around the back, and the little old men. The younger ones would all come up and sing – there'd be one guitarist who would know all the flamenco songs. Earlier in the evening there'd be children's stuff, dancing and faffing about in their incredibly elaborate costumes, but also there'd be teenagers snaking about, eyeing each other up. All in the same space, all able to function at different dimensions in the same room.'

Although Castelldefels was in northern Spain, many of the workers were migrants from Andalusia, the heartland of flamenco – described by Robert as one of his most important sources of musical inspiration. 'The thing about flamenco', Robert explains, 'is it's got a lot of stuff that R'n'B had in the first place. It's got a lot of soul, a lot of rhythm. It can be raggedy, and a lot of people can do it. You almost felt the professionals had a hard time being as good as the amateurs, just as I imagine in the early days of blues. The local bloke who sat on his porch playing the blues is probably about as good as it gets.'

The area of Spain in which Robert and Alfie were staying was a working-class zone, known as the Red Belt. 'It had just become de-Franco-ised', explains Alfie. 'There was this wonderful feeling of a place which had just elected a socialist government. So we were somewhere good. And also, culturally, they know how to live in Spain, they know what life's for – siestas and days off.' Robert was also respected in Barcelona. In addition to the Catalan TV documentary, he recorded Spanish vocals (on a song called *Tu Traición*) with Barcelona group Claustrofobia, another quiet triumph that would have been at home on one of his own albums.

> Robert admiring the Catalan street art in Castelldefels, Spain, alongside a visiting Julie Christie.

There was plenty of partying, too. On the second visit in particular, Robert and Alfie hit the sangria and *fino quinta* hard – so much so that, on one occasion, Robert fell out of his wheelchair. It was a beguiling cocktail of socialism and sangria and, for a while, the move to Spain looked permanent. That he and Alfie did return to the UK, says Robert, was chiefly because Spain was yet to join the EU and he needed medical support from the NHS.

Back in England, however, Alfie was adamant that she didn't want to die in Twickenham. For one thing, she says, it felt like 'enemy territory'. Another issue was that constant visits from family, friends and occasionally fans were turning Lebanon Park into another Dalmore Road. Alfie was meant to be illustrating one of Ivor Cutler's wonderful *Herbert* books for children, but instead found herself forever playing host. Robert, too, was finding it difficult to work. 'Being paraplegic,'

> Alfie in Spain, at work illustrating a children's book by Ivor Cutler.

explains Alfie, 'you can't visit anybody in London, because everybody lives upstairs. So our house became a sort of drop-in centre. And how can you work when there are people dropping in the whole time, when people come and stay? So for a long time Robert did nothing. There was no way he *could* do anything, because he was never on his own.' In addition, the Twickenham flat was too small to have a dedicated music room. On the rare occasions on which Robert did try to write or record, noise complaints from neighbours soon put paid to his efforts.

Maybe the inability to make music caused his spirits to sink; maybe it was the other way round. Either way, Robert became submerged in the all-too-familiar sense that he was creatively burned out. His depression was only worsened by the steady drift to the right in the UK political landscape, not to mention the schism that was splitting the left. Emotionally, according to Alfie, he was on the verge. 'Robert has these periods every few years,' she sighs, 'where he has a little bit of a breakdown. He started crying a lot. And I thought: "We've got to change our life."'

'Robert tried counselling', says Alfie, 'but it was a disaster. And I probably would say that,' she laughs, 'because one of the things that she was trying to impress on Robert was that he was too dependent on me.' But Robert too disliked the counselling, particularly the attempt to shift blame onto his parents. 'There was this tennis racket on a cushion,' he recalls, 'and I knew that, after about three sessions, I was going to be expected to say, "That cushion is everybody who tells me what to do, and I'm going to beat them with the tennis racket." This woman was bonkers. She hated her parents and she wanted everyone else to blame their parents as well. So we got out of that.'

Instead, Alfie came up with an alternative solution: they would sell the Twickenham flat and move somewhere sufficiently large to have a dedicated music room, and where social life could be conducted on their own terms. It would mean leaving London for a part of the country in which they could buy an entire house for the price of their Lebanon Park flat. An estate agent suggested Lincolnshire. Alfie and her mum spent five days driving around the county, on England's east coast. Alfie couldn't picture life in Cleethorpes, Skegness, Grimsby. Then she stumbled upon Louth.

17

CP JEEBIES

Dondestan: Pataphysical postcards from Louth

That Robert and Alfie chose to leave the skips and scaffolding of Twickenham yuppiedom at the end of the 1980s is understandable. The surprise was that they moved to a market town described as 200 miles and three decades from London. As far north as Manchester or Sheffield but roughly south of Hull, Louth was an unexpected choice for a couple deeply immersed in international politics. That they were no longer at the heart of things, laughs Robert, really dawned on them when the first Gulf War broke out in 1991 – and there was no nearby embassy at which to protest. Friends and family, too, were puzzled, and even today Robert and Alfie still describe themselves as Londoners in exile.

Twenty-five years later, however, they still live in the same Georgian town house. There were adjustments when they moved in: the bathroom door had to be widened to accommodate a wheelchair, and a ramp installed so that Robert could reach the front door. But part of the appeal was that the house already had a ground-floor bathroom, with room for both a bedroom and a music room also on ground level. And though, to Robert, any building without a lift may as well be a bungalow, Alfie now had a studio on the first floor. In London, she says, only a millionaire could afford this much space.

Robert might have hated provincial Lydden as a teenager, but he happily immersed himself in Louth life. He was soon a regular in the town square, where a sausage sandwich and a 50p cup of tea from the burger van is his way of fighting off the cabin fever that threatens all who work from home. And from accountant to plumber to doctor, everything Robert needs is within wheeling distance. 'It's handy,' he explains. 'We live so near the middle of town. Alfie thought, "It's a good town for Robert because he can get around on his own here." There are some great places in London but it's expensive, and it's actually quite hard to wheel around. This works fine. It's very homely. It's easy to live here, you know.'

Crucially, Robert can also wheel to the post office to send his trademark postcards. 'He's always writing,' says Alfie. 'He gets quite a lot of letters from people and fans. And people all over the world have his mad postcards.' A CD inlay, torn-out newspaper advert, shred of cereal packet or even a napkin might be repurposed as a DIY postcard. Slapped with a stamp and entrusted to the Royal Mail, they are somehow particularly appealing in an age of texts and tweets, when the postman usually brings little but bills and junk mail.

'Whenever I got anything from Robert,' remembers Julie Christie, 'it was always written on the corner of a cornflakes packet. That would be the postcard: something torn off the corner of a cereal packet, or any old piece of card that probably appealed to him for what reason I know not.

> A typical Robert postcard – handy for choco-crispie recipes..

And the writing is very interesting, too. It's very stream of consciousness: it doesn't quite fit together. You get the sentiment behind it. It's usually a joke, you kind of get the joke, but it's not actually written like a whole proper person, it's as though it's been written by some child somewhere, except the joke is much more sophisticated than a child's.'

Louth would always have represented a new chapter for Robert and Alfie, very much distinct from the decade and a half in Twickenham. But what Robert calls a 'whole life change' was intensified by the fact that the move more or less coincided with his withdrawal from the Communist Party. 1989 was an epochal year: Tiananmen Square, the triumph of Solidarity in Poland, the execution of Romanian dictator Ceausescu, the fall of the Berlin Wall. Yet Wyatt is adamant that leaving the Party was not related to events in the world at large. In fact, he says, he didn't leave the Party: the Party, increasingly dominated by the younger revisionists, left him. The move to Louth was also significant: there were, laughs Alfie, only two *Morning Star* readers in the whole of Lincolnshire.

Wyatt insists that his beliefs have hardly changed even since the collapse of the Soviet Union in 1991, and the end of a Cold War as old as Robert himself. He admits that communism 'was more than a failure, it was a catastrophe. This is totally evident from Czechoslovakia, Poland, Romania and Russia, of course, and also in China.' Yet he continues to see Marxism as the best lens through which to view relations between the West and the developing world. 'I don't have the optimism that socialists are meant to have,' he explains. 'Never have had. I just think that they're the more right about how the world is run, and it kind of exposes the way the people who *do* run it talk about what they're doing, which I find utterly phoney.'

Also keeping Robert on the left is the fact that his gaze is global. Speaking to *Clash* magazine in 2008, Robert admitted that communism was a failure as a mass movement, its mistakes 'so obvious they are hardly worth pointing out.' But, he continues, 'I think that it has to be said that the Communist Party came about for a reason – that the capitalist system around the world just wouldn't do, and still won't as far as I am concerned. There are still trade unionists being killed all around the world, from Columbia to the Philippines, and people are still being forced to work for the big companies. I still think it's wrong, and it may be slightly old-fashioned of me but I still think it's completely out of order – so I still stay on the left, while that problem remains.'

The move to Louth also brought about a return to making music, on his own records, and with various collaborators. One such was a jazz big band, The Happy End, who took their name from a play by Bertolt Brecht, Kurt Weill and Elisabeth Hauptmann. *Turn Things Upside Down*, from the 1990 album of the same title, combined sinuous brass arrangements with defiant politics: 'We'll turn things upside down when the revolution comes', sings Robert, over massed, moody horns.

Another was with Ryuichi Sakamoto, best known for electronic pop trio Yellow Magic Orchestra and his soundtrack to the film *Merry Christmas, Mr Lawrence*. Sakamoto had been a Soft Machine fan and had fallen in love with Robert's rendition of *At Last I Am Free*. He asked Robert to contribute vocals on *We Love You*, a track originally recorded by The Rolling Stones. What he needed, explained the Japanese musician and producer, was 'a very unique, very special quality of vocal... the saddest voice in the world'. That is precisely what he got: over a bed of glossy global funk, Wyatt's blank voice transformed The Stones' hedonistic, pouting 1960s psychedelic anthem into a bittersweet disco lament. 'It fitted perfectly,' says Sakamoto. 'The sadness of that song and the sadness of his quality of voice. Probably, for regular people, being sad is not a good thing. But I think, in music, sadness is a strong element. Even if the key is major, sometimes we feel saddened. Robert's voice, certainly, makes me feel very sad – but that is not necessarily a bad thing. Maybe I mean more longing or nostalgic.'

Most importantly, Wyatt also started to work on original material. As usual, the process was incremental. But when he augmented his own compositions with lines written by Alfie back in Spain, Robert realised he had a whole new album.

-»» ««- -»» ««- -»» ««-

The record that took shape in Wyatt's Queen Street music room sounded boarded up, as uninhabited as off-season Castelldefels. Their room in the Spanish beach resort is depicted on the album's Hockneyesque front cover. Alfie included a poster for their favourite bar and the local communist newspaper; even Francis, the African trinket-seller, down on the beach.

The album title, *Dondestan*, was a pun on '¿Dónde están?', Spanish for 'where are they?'. 'And the answer to that question was,' grins Robert, 'just south of Barcelona.' But the -stan suffix was also a deliberate echo of the term used in Central Asia to denote country or place. By the end of 1991, the year of the album's release, the Soviet Union had splintered into fifteen countries – among them Uzbekistan, Tajikistan, Kazakhstan and

Turkmenistan. The left had splintered, too. As old guard communists squeezed out by the young guns of Eurocommunism, Robert and Alfie were on the edge of things.

Dondestan might sound unpolished, but it is the product of a perfectionist mind: Wyatt recorded ten draft versions on a four-track tape recorder before he even entered the studio. 'I worked on it a lot,' he told *Musician* magazine, 'because I wanted the end result to sound fairly spontaneous.' As on *Old Rottenhat*, he played everything on the album, including the most mournful melodica this side of Augustus Pablo. Textures were sparse, but that only left more room for the lyrics: 'One of Brian Eno's many, many, many wise sayings', says Robert, 'is: every object obscures another object. Conversely, the more you take away, the bigger the things that are left. And, indeed, I was really happy, when I stripped things down, with how strong the voice became, how much space it could take up. It's up to how you sing.'

Like *Old Rottenhat*, *Dondestan* addressed the split within the left, although Robert's treatment of the CPGB was now valedictory: 'After the party's over my friend,' runs *CP Jeebies*, 'there will be nothing you can put your finger on, just a parasol.' It is the morning after the night before – and 'party', of course, should really have an upper case 'P'. Wyatt then goes on to launch an oblique attack on wishy-washy, rainbow coalition socialism: less red than 'green and yellow pinky blue'. It is, he says, a song about 'my despair at what turned into New Labour taking over the left'. 'There's no such place as middle ground,' as he sang on another track, *Left on Man*, 'Left or Right of the equator.'

Yet the album is not only about where the left has gone wrong. *NIO* is an attack on the Conservative Party's obsession with selling off the family silver: 'Privatise / next / the airforce / then the police force / royal family / let them be / private at last.' The free market, Robert was suggesting, is an illusion: 'If you said to a Tory: let's privatise the army and the royal family, they'd be horrified,' he explained at the time. 'They'd say that they were too important to leave to free-market forces and you'd say: "Quite!" Well, we think that hospitals and schools are too important as well, and that's the point.'

Lisp Service employed a melody by Hugh Hopper. As well as acknowledging his own slight and inconsistent lisp, it became, in Robert's hands, a riposte to Billy Joel's hit *We Didn't Start the Fire*, essentially an apology for US foreign policy: 'Trouble isn't my middle name / Left in peace would make my day / You started the fire not me.' 'Suddenly we're all very Amnesty International,' Robert explains. 'We've won, we've

> Looking onto the beach at Castelldefels – Alfie's painting for *Dondestan*.

got stuff. And now we go round the world telling everybody: "You can't behave like that, that's not the way any more, it's old-fashioned." Well, we didn't say that when we were doing it. There's a fantastic amount, at the moment, of that sort of hypocrisy.'

The theme of the displaced and the dispossessed reaches its apogee on the album's title track: 'Palestine's a country', sings Wyatt over timbale and brisk, buoyant piano, 'or at least used to be'. Not for the first time, he seems at his jolliest when tackling the most depressing of subjects. 'I'm not very introspective,' says Robert, 'but I'm pretty easily and deeply depressed about things. I get very sad. And, in a way, I suppose the music is exorcising that. It's very hard to say that the blues is sad, for example. Obviously, some blues is sort of sad, but if it was *that sad*, you wouldn't listen to it, would you? People get a positive from it; otherwise, they wouldn't listen. So the word "sad" is inadequate for sad music; otherwise, nobody would listen to it. The fact is that the kind of melancholy induced by certain kinds of minor chords, and so on, can give pleasure. Conversely, the sturdy major chords of bafflingly dull sports programme theme music and Souza marches can be deeply depressing within seconds. So it's very hard to find words to fit the way in which music slithers about amongst the emotions.'

–»)《«– –»)《«– –»)《«–

So far, so *Old Rottenhat*. But *Dondestan* is a less relentlessly political record than its predecessor – and, although they are both billed as one-man-band albums, *Dondestan* is in fact very much a collaboration. Alfie had composed diary entries during their two stints in Spain, which she later distilled into poems. When a creatively blocked Robert turned to these pages for inspiration, Alfie – already wife, manager and album art designer – became co-lyricist, too. She would contribute lyrics to all Robert's subsequent albums.

Alfie's lyrics provide some of the record's highlights, as well as its breaks from overt politics: rather than attacking *Marxism Today* or Israeli foreign policy, she takes the listener to out-of-season Spain, picking out details with a painter's eye. 'I'm grateful to Alfie,' says Robert, 'because she does use specific imagery – pictures – from which you can deduce ideas. I tend to go straight in with the ideas and just use wordplay and puns. That's really what I do – a combination of applying Lewis Carroll and Edward Lear techniques to a rigorous Marxist overview.'

Instead of chiselling the words to fit a pre-written melody, the need to fit music to Alfie's words also obliged Robert to adopt a new approach to writing music. The fact that *Sight of the Wind* uses only two chords allows Wyatt to run some parts backwards, emulating the unsettled feel of shifting sands. The vocal might sound improvised, but it is in fact very much composed. And the 7/4 time signature, subtler and less showy than it might have been back in The Soft Machine, absolutely serves the song. Intimate and introvert, it is one of the tracks in his whole career of which Robert is most proud.

Also clearly inspired by the stay in Catalonia, *Costa*, another of Robert's favourites, begins with a sunset, the 'fierce orange of the egg-shaped fireball'. Yet Alfie's lyrics soon move to the 'scratched orange of the gas bottle / delivered for lack of pipeline'. The subject is a town, such as Castelldefels, that looks good only in summer, since tourists take precedence over residents. The point, subtle in the song itself, comes through more powerfully in the subtitle – *Memories of Under-Development*, borrowed from the 1968 film by Cuba's Tomas Gutiérrez Alea.

The other change since *Old Rottenhat* was that Wyatt was now free of the space restraints and noise complaints that had stymied his music-making back in Twickenham. In Louth, he finally had his own practice room, and installed a Yamaha baby grand. (It promptly fell through the rotten floorboards. The new floor was tiled in black and white to resemble a kitchen, as Robert points out, the heart of any decent house party.)

The music room also allowed Robert to leave his drums – or, at least, cymbals, timbales and cowbell – permanently set up. Commentators often note the influence of jazz on his playing, but the impact of Latin music has also been considerable. With its reliance on congas, bongos, güiro and timbales, Cuban music must have been particularly appealing to a drummer who could no longer use the bottom half of the kit. Ramón Farrán recalls that, even back in Mallorca, Wyatt had been fascinated by his timbales. In Matching Mole, Robert had achieved a similar sound by disengaging the snare on his snare drum. Now he had his own pair – although, as Robert himself is all too aware, he continued to teeter on the brink of absurdity: 'I remember when I was doing the drum solo on *Dondestan*,' says Robert. 'I was in the corner of this vast studio, hammering away, nearly knocking the timbales over, nearly falling out my wheelchair, and the engineer just had a fit of hysterics. He said, "That's the most ridiculous sight I've ever seen."'

In fact, Wyatt's drumming on the album is superb, from the timbale rolls of the title track to the deft brushwork of *Left on Man* and the jazzy ride cymbal of *NIO*. Though the bass drum went relatively unmissed, Robert's inability to use the hi-hat pedal, following the fall, proved more challenging. On *Shipbuilding*, as on *Sight of the Wind*, he had substituted vocal sounds, a gentle 'tch' hinting at double time. Robert now realised that, with the right flick of the wrist, he could get the same effect by using brushes – a tip he picked up from jazz greats such as Billy Higgins.

'If you ever watch Billy Higgins on film, the older he got, the less he compressed the hi-hat to make it snap – to the point where, in fact, the two hi-hat cymbals don't seem to be hitting each other at all. He just seems to press his foot down and they squash air.'

'When people think of drum technique,' he goes on, 'they think of people playing very, very fast, or clever little tricks. But these touches of pure class, craftsmanship, these are the elements of drumming I've

> Robert in Louth with Alfie, his co-lyricist for *Dondestan*, recorded in the nearby Chapel Studios in South Thoresby.

got interested in as a paraplegic, because they're not about the full kit. They're closing in on a much more close, intimate side of drumming.'

Jazz and Latin music influenced Robert's singing as well as his drumming. The vocal chant on *Left on Man* – 'simplify, reduce, oversimplify' – was inspired by the Afro-Cuban jazz group Irakere. *Shrinkrap*, meanwhile, reflected Robert's more recent interest in hip-hop – logical enough for someone who believed so passionately that singing should follow the rhythms of speech. Rather than straight rap, however, the humorous treatment of his counselling catastrophe is in fact closer to Ian Dury. Like flamenco and Latin jazz, the hip-hop influences were refracted, albeit in reverse: in went the multifarious, multicoloured experiences; out came their unified, assimilated expression.

-»)(«- -»)(«- -»)(«-

Dondestan was released in August 1991. 'Robert Wyatt's muse is back on-line,' wrote Ben Watson in *The Wire* magazine. 'His new release is as telling and sensual as anything he has produced over the last three decades.' And if not everyone regarded it as a career peak, many critics regarded *Dondestan* as Wyatt's best work since *Rock Bottom*. Certainly, there is a clear link between the two albums that goes beyond the fact that both prominently feature the Riviera organ. Both were written abroad, at least in part, and recorded outside London. Perhaps as a result, both are intimate, tightly coherent pieces of work: occasions, as Robert puts it, when he swims in his own river for a whole album.

Much of the coverage of *Dondestan*, however, had a Yesterday Man tinge. The *NME* sent a self-declared Trot to lock horns with this ageing 'Tankie'; *Time Out* called Wyatt 'popular music's best-loved unreconstructed socialist'; the *New Statesman* called him 'rock's last communist', asking, 'Is there anyone more out of time than Robert Wyatt?' As far as the mainstream was concerned, Robert remained firmly beneath the radar. There was also a sense that political pop music was out of favour, fans and critics alike ready for a change after the heyday of The Clash and Red Wedge, the group of musicians that had attempted to raise support for Labour in the run-up to the 1987 general election. That only makes Robert, usually painfully self-effacing about his output, more willing to speak up for *Dondestan*.

'It's a bit like having children,' he reflects. 'Me and Alfie don't have children together, and in a way our records are our children, especially since she's been doing my lyrics. And the ones that fare least well in the world tend to be the ones I feel most protective and poignant about. You know, they had their worth, too. Whereas some of the more robust records look after themselves, and I'm very relieved that they do.'

'Something like *Comicopera*', he goes on, 'is very robust, takes care of itself, don't need to worry about that. But, I worry about poor little *Dondestan*. It's maybe the runt of the pack, but in a way I feel so affectionate towards it, because it's all me in there, with very little help, stripped down, without the immense amount of help I got on the last three records. Just me. It's the nearest I get to that Adrian Mole-like bedsit person.'

Curiously, it was *Dondestan* that, a decade and a half after its initial release, gave rise to the verb 'to Wyatt': to choose deliberately obscure or challenging music on an Internet-powered pub jukebox, with the aim of annoying fellow customers. Brian Eno, Evan Parker or Merzbow were worth a go, according to a 2006 article in the *Guardian*, but *Dondestan* was 'the perfect way to disrupt a busy Friday night in a high street pub'. It's not a concept embraced by Alfie. 'This Wyatting thing made me very angry,' she explains. 'That Robert should be used as a means of clever-dicks asserting their superiority in pubs, when what you want to hear in a pub is *River Deep Mountain High*. I mean, if we were in a pub, that's what we want to hear. It's not his fault that some of his music is maybe difficult for people. He's not imposing it on anybody, and never would. It's so unlike Robert, because he's so appreciative of the strengths of pop music. So that, I think, is a real unfairness. The man who coined it, I should like to punch him on the nose.'

⟫⟪ ⟫⟪ ⟫⟪

Dondestan was followed unusually quickly: Robert released the EP *A Short Break* just over a year later, on the new independent label Voiceprint. For all their intentions, Rough Trade were in dire straits; they would struggle on a little longer before going under, but would not properly relaunch until the new millennium.

A Short Break was a charmingly DIY effort, recorded at home on a four-track recorder for a total cost of £15. On the front cover was a shot of Robert taken on his trip to Portugal as a young boy. As if still dreaming of that holiday four decades earlier, Robert's voice on the EP is distant, resembling someone learning a song more than a finished recording. The underlying structures, however, are highly sophisticated. *Ventiu Latir* is in 5/4 time, its slowly evolving piano loops reminiscent of Wyatt's 1975 Offenbach-inspired instrumental, *Five Black Notes and One White Note*. The EP is also informed by twentieth-century minimalism, with its emphasis on rhythm, hints of jazz and sense of beauty beneath an unpolished – even apparently unfinished – surface.

The end result is somewhere between home recording champion R Stevie Moore and the blind composer and street musician Moondog – but with Robert's unmistakably tremulous, transparent voice drifting over the top. Though no longer a member of the CPGB, Wyatt's output – even at its most gauzy – remained subtly political. The track titles are in Wolof, the language spoken in the Gambia and Senegal, and come from *Our Grandmothers' Drums*, Mark Hudson's award-winning book about a year in a remote Gambian village. (*Tubab*, the cascading, eddying opening track, takes its name from the term for 'a European, a rich person, anyone not of African origin', for instance.)

A Short Break is one of the releases of which Wyatt is most proud – particularly as it attracted less attention even than *Dondestan*. 'It means a

> Robert in his new music room at Louth, around the time of *Dondestan*.

lot to me, that little record. It's unique. I think it's a little rough diamond.' The only downside of the EP, says Robert, is that it used up some of the 'trance ideas' that could have been interludes and instrumental sections on his next full album. It would be another long wait.

In the meantime, there was a string of compilations. In 1993, Rough Trade issued *Mid-Eighties*, combining *Work in Progress* with *Old Rottenhat* and tracks such as *Pigs* and *Chairman Mao*. Then the following year Virgin put out *Going Back a Bit: A Little History of Robert Wyatt*, a two-CD set which for the first time pulled together material from The Soft Machine, Matching Mole and Robert's solo career from Virgin, while Rough Trade issued the lovingly compiled *Flotsam Jetsam*. This allowed Wyatt enthusiasts to discover some gorgeous obscurities, like *Slow Walkin' Talk*, the track Robert recorded with Hendrix on bass, alongside guest spots with Slapp Happy, Lol Coxhill, Gary Windo and the Catalan band Claustrofobia. The excavation was the work of Michael King, who in the same year published an extensive biographical chronology, *Wrong Movements: A Robert Wyatt History*.

There were, as ever, a few guest appearances. Ambient techno duo Ultramarine, who were signed to Geoff Travis's other label, Blanco Y Negro, invited Robert to contribute to *United Kingdoms*, an album of pastoral, penumbral electronica. Robert also joined Belgium's Jo Bogaert for another electronica project, Millennium, on the album *A Civilised Word*. There was 1996's *School of Understanding, to,* a 'sort-of-an-opera' project for an an older friend, Mike Mantler. Mantler was once again working with vocalists, and invited Robert to contribute along with John Greaves, the former Henry Cow bassist.

Wyatt also contributed to Greaves's own album, *Songs*. Although he had known Wyatt for many years, the bassist still expected his request to be turned down: 'Robert doesn't say no,' he laughs. 'He says, "Well, do I have to? There are lots of people who sing much better than me." And he gave me a list, he was very helpful: "Why don't you try Annette Peacock?" I said, 'Well, Robert, that's fine, but actually the person I want is you."'

Songs found Wyatt in jazz-tinged folk mode, covering two tracks from *Kew.Rhone*, the Wyatt-inspired album Greaves had released in 1977 with Peter Blegvad. In the title track, Robert finally got his chance to sing what is surely the longest grammatically correct palindrome in popular music: 'Peel's foe, not a set animal, laminates a tone of sleep.' It was Pataphysical through and through – and, where Lisa Herman had been a slightly remote, stalactite presence on the original album,

Robert brought *Kew.Rhone* and *Gegenstand* down to earth with his casual, conversational delivery. 'We had a very nice time up in the studio at South Thoresby,' recalls Greaves, 'a lovely little village which is just a church and a studio and pub. We didn't go much to church but we finished up the session nicely in the pub. I remember being locked in and then losing Robert on the darkened road. Coming out of there at midnight, he sped off into the darkness. Fortunately the young and lithe and fit sound engineer went rushing after him and saved him.'

Despite this activity in – and out of – the studio, Robert was not composing material of his own, and was suffering from the horribly familiar sense of running on empty. 'I knew there was more in there,' he says, 'but the technique for getting music out seemed to have burned out. It was a bit like, the engine's in good nick but the car's broken, it's

> Memories of Portugal – *A Short Break*.

rusty, the tyres have burst. So this engine is ready to go, but the car doesn't work. That kind of feeling, like a living death, really.' He was also frustrated with *Dondestan*, feeling he had neglected the mixing process, in part due to physical restraints: despite installing a ramp to help him access some parts of the studio, he still couldn't get to the mixing desk. 'I was depressed that I hadn't really had the budget to mix the album properly,' Robert recalls. 'It was OK, but it was sort of feeble. I looked back to the sort of racket I'd made in the days of Matching Mole, and I thought, "What happened? I've lost something." It was a period of grieving for what I had been and for what I would never be – a sort of double grieving.'

Compounding the problem was the fact that Robert had once again fallen out of his wheelchair, breaking both legs. He lost a year's working time: with his legs set straight out in front of him, he couldn't get to the piano keys. 'That's the thing about wheelchairs,' reflects Robert, typically sanguine. 'It's all right falling backwards: the ground hits the handles and not your head. But the dangerous thing is if you fall forward, because your feet tend to get tangled up in the footplates, and you crash either on your knees or your hands or both. It's a bit of a mess.'

Robert did eventually get into a local studio once his legs had healed, but found himself troubled by the expense. Rough Trade had imploded, and temporarily gone out of business, so he and Alfie were obliged to front the recording costs themselves. It was a considerable risk and especially daunting for someone who was already, in Alfie's words, 'a bundle of fear and worry'. After a few days, Robert lost his nerve and declared the recordings unusable. That, says Alfie, is when he really started to go downhill. 'And,' she goes on, 'for the next four years, he did nothing. His confidence went right down. He thought that was it, he was finished, his life was over. I mean, he didn't say that, but that was what was happening. He just went into this complete panic and he couldn't sleep for months.'

–»)(«– –»)(«– –»)(«–

The move to Louth, it transpired, had postponed rather than banished Robert's depression. Its cause was political as well as professional: the sudden collapse of the Soviet Union didn't mark the end of international communism, but it was a tremendous blow to the movement's geopolitical importance. At home, John Major's electoral success in 1992 marked a fourth successive victory for the Tories. 'The

> Robert flanked by Ian Cooper and Paul Hammond of Ultramarine. He sung on three tracks of their 1993 *United Kingdoms* album and appeared as King Arthur in the video of *Kingdom*.

right-wing triumphalism of the eighties got to me,' Robert told the *Guardian*. 'The propaganda war is designed to demoralise rather than kill, and it works.'

Alfie was used to these crisis points, which seemed to recur every few years. The depression of the mid-1990s, however, was the worst of Wyatt's life: now he really *had* hit rock bottom. 'It was hell,' he says. 'It was my *real* season in hell, much worse than anything beforehand.' And, he admits, it was no less hellish for Alfie: 'She said, "When you're young, having a depressed young man is all part of the romance. When you're older, they're just a fucking bore." And I can see that. I really couldn't help it, I just did collapse.'

Alfie is no softie when it comes to depression. Some sufferers, she suggests, 'have girlfriends who actually need them to be ill, so that they can be Florence Nightingale'. Robert, she insists, is not like that. 'So, when it happens, it's really *real*. It isn't because he's got to pull his socks up. It's not egotistical, it's not wallowing in thinking about himself all the time.' She does admit, though, that 'Robert feels guilt about things all the time. If there was a situation in which somebody had blame, he would blame himself even when he's got nothing to do with it whatsoever. It would be his fault.'

The anguish of severe depression is perhaps unimaginable to the unafflicted, but this was migraine-pitch melancholia: Alfie recalls Robert's acute 'fear of me leaving the house, fear that I wouldn't come back'. The sense of dread he had previously felt about appearing onstage now extended to almost every aspect of his life.

One symptom of what Robert now regards as a nervous breakdown was severe insomnia, including a two-month period during which he apparently didn't sleep at all. 'He aged about twenty years,' says Alfie, 'he just looked so haggard.' *Little Red Robin Hood*, a sketchy but evocative Italian documentary released in 1998, gives a sense of how bad things had become. The film features interviews with Elvis Costello, Brian Eno, Nick Mason and Andy Summers, as well as a dust-pale Robert.

'I don't want to be fossilised,' says Robert, looking like a Russian monk – albeit one with a melodica resting on his lap. 'I always had a problem with playing something that I'd already played, because I'm not a museum. So there has to be a new reason for me to do something. Not that the whole thing must be new, but there has to be something new to make it new again.'

Today, Robert is able to laugh about another photograph from the era, in which he is wrapped up in a duvet: 'I look like a sarcophagus of

Lenin'. But things, he admits, were going seriously wrong: 'I realised I was going mad, and it was very scary. It's a bit like when you have an accident, that slow thing of: *it's coming*. For example, if you're in a slide on ice, and there's a car ahead, and you suddenly think, "I don't know how to get away from this." Or if you're on your bike and it's going over, that immense amount of time before the drop. And I could see that I was sliding. I was just doing things that were completely wrong, saying things that were wrong. Alfie was getting upset, because this madman was the last thing she needed at this particular point in her trajectory.'

It is sometimes said that an artist's relationship with his manager is closer than his relationship with anyone except his wife – and Alfie, of course, was both. She did manage solo trips to Nicaragua (part of a cultural delegation that included Julie Christie and David Hare) and Tunisia, during which her mum Irena would pop round to keep Robert company. She even accompanied Christie to Canada for the filming of *Afterglow*, produced by Robert Altman, on which she helped on the dialogue. The move to Louth also gave Alfie her own studio. But these few international trips and a room of her own didn't offer much of a safety valve. However stoic, she could only be a shoulder to cry on for so long.

'I'd always avoided Robert going to doctors,' sighs Alfie, not one to gloss over difficulties. 'I'd always thought, "We can sort this out." And on the whole we have – I mean, not properly, because the drink was obviously part of that whole thing. But finally, I suddenly decided I couldn't bear being nursey any more. And I was so angry with him, because I'd done everything I could think of to make life better.'

'I mean, I felt so sorry for him,' she goes on, 'but I just couldn't bear it. He got so clingy. I couldn't leave the house without him fretting. I just couldn't deal with it. So I said, "Go to the doctor."'

–»)&– –»)&– –»)&–

Prescribed antidepressants, Robert played up to Alfie's fears that the pills might alter his personality. 'Hi, Alfie! How are you?' he chuckles at the memory, adopting an American accent and dementedly sunny countenance. 'Are you in a good place? I'm in a good place right now!'

Yet the Prozac, Wyatt believes, really did help: 'It was an artificial stimulus, which just lightened the load. But it also helped me do what is a Californian thing: *think positive*. Just to notice all the nice, good things that happen, and the not bad things that happen. "Yes, I was hit

> One of the bonuses of Virgin's *Going Back a Bit* was a glimpse of several of Alfie's paintings featuring Robert in dreamlike scenarios.

by that car, but no, it didn't kill me." And really trying to enjoy stuff, even retrospectively. Think, "I can't do that drumming *now*, but by the time I got to Matching Mole, I was really good for a couple of years."

Counselling, a failure last time the black dog had bitten, also proved successful this time – perhaps because this time there was no cushion to punch. 'I had this brilliant counselling,' says Wyatt. 'Free on the NHS, I point out to my American friends. He said, "What you've got to realise is, *things go wrong*. Not everything you do is going to be perfect. Some of it works out right and some of it goes wrong. Don't be frightened that you're a complete and utter failure because things go wrong. Of course things go wrong. Who the fuck do you think you are?"'

The advice might sound simple, says Wyatt, but it was a breakthrough moment. No-one listening to his superficially unkempt music, he laughs, would mark him down as a perfectionist, yet Robert is, in fact, his own harshest critic. Back in Soft Machine, he had been known to burst into tears if a gig went badly. 'If a recording had collapsed,' he admits, 'or I had a bit on a record that I couldn't change and didn't like, I just felt like I shouldn't have been born and then this would never have happened. I felt shame, utter shame.'

On the one hand, Robert is almost embarrassed at being a musician, troubled by the fundamental uselessness of art: 'Artists: who the fuck do we think we are?' Wyatt asked rhetorically in conversation with *The Wire*'s Tony Herrington in 2012. 'The definition of art is something you can't use. If it's completely useless, it's art.' On the other hand, the assiduous, syllable-by-syllable editing of his own vocal takes does not fit with the belief that music lacks value. This, after all, is the man who was reluctant to go to Venice with Alfie and Julie Christie because he was so obsessed with setting up a new band. And, if music was so worthless, why was Robert so concerned to make it unmisusable, or so terrified of live performance?

The counselling helped overcome this strange dualism: terror of being average, combined with a terror of being a snob. Having long been freighted with *künstlerschuld*, Wyatt began to lighten up in the mid-1990s. He had been suggesting for years that making music could never be as important as fighting for a socialist world, yet only now, perhaps, did Robert begin to believe in his heart what he knew in his head. The Prozac helped. So did the counselling. But the real breakthrough was returning to the studio. With a nod to his insomnia, and the Jewish humour of his friend Ronnie Scott, who died in December 1996, the new record would be called *Shleep*.

18

THE WINTER OF OUR DISCOTHEQUE

Shleep and the thaw after
a very long winter

Like Alice in Wonderland, says Wyatt, he disappeared down a wormhole in the mid-1990s. He resurfaced in Phil Manzanera's studio. Robert had not worked with the guitarist since *Diamond Head* in 1975, but they had stayed in touch thanks to mutual friends like Brian Eno and Bill MacCormick. Then on a 'long break' from Roxy Music, Manzanera offered Robert the use of his studio on uniquely generous terms. 'Phil just said, "Give me what you can afford,"' recalls Alfie, "it doesn't matter how long it takes".'

'I bumped into Robert at some do,' Manzanera remembers, 'and I said: "I'm surprised you haven't asked me to use the studio, because you're absolutely welcome." This is one of my heroes and I owe a lot to him, through that vicarious living, and the channelling down, through the MacCormicks, of music and what he was into. They hero-worshipped him, really, and that was passed onto me. So part of my inspiration, psychologically, as a musician, was to aspire to what he was into and his attitude to music. In my mind it was payback time, for that initial spark of inspiration.'

Wyatt eventually entered Manzanera's Surrey studio in the autumn of 1996. The guitarist would, from now on, be a cornerstone of Wyatt's working life: every subsequent album would be recorded in his studio, and Robert, in turn, would contribute to several further Manzanera solo releases. For the first time since *Ruth Is Stranger Than Richard*, *Shleep* was a band album. It had in part been fear of embarrassment that put Wyatt off collaborating, but he felt much more comfortable asking musicians to drop into a studio close to London than obliging them to travel all the way to Lincolnshire. Installed in Gallery Studios, Robert brought in guests on the same song-by-song basis he had employed on *Rock Bottom*. Manzanera contributed a soaring guitar solo to *Alien*, over a Latin bassline by Columbia's Chucho Merchan. Belgian guitarist Philip Catherine contributed rippling broken chords to *Maryan*, a track based on his composition *Nairam*. And, with engineer Jamie Johnson doing his best Bo Diddley impression on *Heaps of Sheeps*, this was Wyatt's most guitar-orientated album.

The most surprising guest, playing guitar on two numbers, was Paul Weller, whose involvement came about through sheer serendipity. 'I was doing some demos in Phil's studio,' Weller recalls, 'and Robert was in a week later. And I got a message through Phil and Jamie that he was going to do a cover of an old Style Council song, *The Whole Point of No Return*. And I half-jokingly said, "Well if he wants any guitar work or anything, give us a shout." Which he did.'

Though best known as the punk-era mod of The Jam, Weller had embraced jazz back in the 1980s with his subsequent band, The Style Council. Like Robert, Weller was also a huge fan of American soul music. And, though he had stepped back from politics since his days with Red Wedge, an ideological affinity remained. The collaboration might not have worked, notes Weller drily, if Wyatt had voted Conservative.

'I just love working with him,' enthuses Weller, who names Robert his favourite ever collaborator. 'And it wasn't what I thought it was going to be. Because he was coming from that jazz angle, I thought it might be technical playing, which I can't fucking do anyway. But it wasn't like that. He liked all the burps and noises and all that sort of thing, and I really liked that.'

Weller was bowled over by one track in particular: '*Free Will and Testament*', he recalls, 'just floored me. I just thought it was a fucking amazing song.' The lyrics of *Free Will and Testament* emerged from the depths of despair. During one take, Robert actually burst into tears. Weller, who contributed restrained slide guitar, recognises the sense of

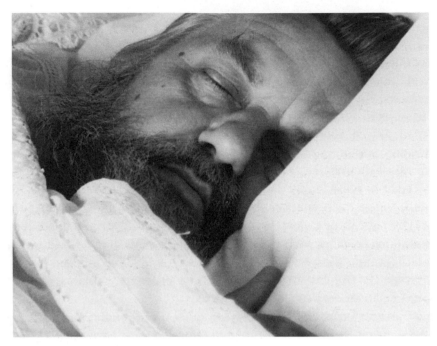

> Promotional photo for *Shleep*.

catharsis: 'You get your fucking balls out on the table and that kind of changes things. It changes your perception, as well. Just lay it down in front of the world and sometimes the world comes back smiling. That's a strange effect in music.'

The song explores the limits of free will, the get-out-of-jail-free card played by religious apologists struggling to explain how an omnipotent god could also be a benevolent one. It is also about wishing for oblivion – not quite for suicide, but rather never to have existed at all: 'Had I been free, I could have chosen not to be me.' *Free Will and Testament* also explored the fear that he had 'torpedoed' Alfie's life. 'Alfie had looked after me, brought me here,' sighs Robert. 'She'd done so much ever since I'd been disabled, and before, to set me up. She's always the one who takes the initiative, getting me a wheelchair, getting the ramp built at home, get things right for Robert, get a music room for him, get a piano for him, a tape recorder. She would even get my clothes and everything done for me. And I still collapsed.' Also underpinning *Free Will and Testament* were splits from decades gone by – from The Soft Machine, even from Pam. 'All I've done to people is just fuck them up,' Wyatt explains, with typical self-flagellation. 'That was what that song was about.'

Was a Friend, another album high point, recalled a dream of awkward semi-reconciliation: 'I almost forgot where we buried the hatchet / "Bin a long time no see," (pidgin English / native to none).' The song, surely, was about Hugh Hopper, who had composed the music. Wyatt, who wrote the lyrics, will neither confirm nor deny the suggestion, although *Was a Friend* did roughly coincide with a period of at least partial *Glasnost* in Robert's attitude to his former bandmates. 'Old wounds are healing', as the song has it. 'Faded scars are painless, just an itch.'

Although Robert had used melodies by Hugh on earlier releases such as *Work in Progress* and *Dondestan*, it had been some time since the old friends had met face-to-face. Yet even if the reconciliation described in *Was a Friend* turns out to have been imaginary, Robert and Hugh did eventually meet up during the period and there would be several other collaborations before the bassist's death from leukaemia in 2009.

-»)《«- -»)《«- -»)《«-

According to Paul Weller, Robert didn't seem particularly depressed during the recordings, but he adds: 'We were both fucking pissed, as well, so it's hard to honestly say. We got through quite a few bottles of wine on that session. So it was quite jolly.'

He might have hidden it in public but, by his own admission, Wyatt *was* depressed when he began to record *Shleep*. It was the studio experience itself that restored him: both the music itself and the return to making music as a social act. The atmosphere during the sessions, says Manzanera, was 'very convivial, easy-going'. In terms of recovering from depression, Robert says getting drunk with Weller was 'fantastic... better than Prozac'.

'I've no idea what his drinking was like at that point,' says engineer Jamie Johnson, 'but you could tell there was an issue. And after a few days, when Alfie came back to pick him up, you could tell there was a kind of: "Phew, he's happy, things are going well." You could feel there had been a tension, and that tension was dissipating.'

After a period during which, Alfie says, he looked about ninety-five years old, Robert finally conquered his insomnia. Alfie's album cover depicts him with eyes gently closed, clad in pyjamas, cuddling a dove in flight. It was, says Wyatt, the thaw after a very long winter.

Thanks to Manzanera's generosity, Wyatt could be as meticulous as he liked when recording *Shleep*. No longer would he have to choose between time in the studio or time mixing, as on *Dondestan*; gone, too, was the anxious clock-watching that had stymied the aborted follow-up. But Robert also carried into the studio something gleaned from his counselling: 'I went into work preparing for the inevitability of mistakes,' he recalls, 'and determined not to withdraw into my shell. Just think: "That was a mistake. Oh dear, how sad, never mind."'

While *Free Will and Testament* and *Was a Friend* emerged from the depths of despair, other tunes on *Shleep* were effervescent. Opener *Heaps of Sheeps* is as light as an empty eggbox, Wyatt and Brian Eno reprising the high-pitched backing vocals of 1974's *Put a Straw Under Baby*. Another upbeat moment was the drunkenly exuberant *Blues in Bob Minor*: a tongue-tying tribute to Dylan's *Subterranean Homesick Blues*. 'Alfie was away for a weekend,' Robert recalls of writing the song, 'and I spent the entire weekend – apart from, I suppose, a bit of breakfast – on brandy, in the backyard, in sunny weather, writing *Blues in Bob Minor*. It was pouring out of me. And I suddenly thought: "In this state, I could do hundreds of blinding lyrics." Suddenly I'd found a tap to turn on.' But although the track marked the start of an increasing reliance on booze as a creative crutch, the words, at this stage, were still edited in sobriety.

Where previous engineers hadn't always been keen on Robert's scuffed edges approach, Phil's studio engineer, Jamie Johnson, happily embraced Robert's newfound willingness to take risks. 'One of the troubles for engineers', says Robert, 'is that they have their own CVs. They are very conscious in their world of being heard by other engineers, and they don't want to be associated with records with bad sound. I often *want* what they would think of as a bad sound. And Jamie didn't give a toss. I would bring him tapes made at home, with traffic going by, recorded in my front room with hiss on.'

'The kind of music I love to listen to, old Bob Marley recordings, say, some of them sound terrible,' Johnson explains. 'But I love them. I'm not *trying* to make things sound terrible, but it's just part of the character. I think when you iron off the edges, it does take people further away. There was something wrong on *Shleep*, I can't remember what song it was, but something didn't sound right, maybe on one of the drums. And Robert just said, "Oh, I'll make a noise or something to cover it up." And he just got a microphone and went "phhh" at the point where there was a mistake. It was a weird sound, it sounded amazing, and it covered up the mistake. Great. He does that quite a lot.'

Crucially for Robert, whom Alfie describes as 'technologically illiterate', Jamie Johnson could also take care of post-production nips

shleep robert wyatt

> Alfie's cover for *Shleep* – Robert takes to the air.

and tucks: not necessarily cleaning up mistakes, says Manzanera, but exploring new possibilities. 'Robert might say: "What would happen if you took that bit and put it back there, and you put it backwards, and put that other bit under there? In other words, your creative palette is increased enormously. And someone with imagination, who wants to go down a particular road, can achieve that with somebody like Jamie. He is the perfect engineer for a musician who wants to try out a few things.'

Some of Robert's gnomic messages for Jamie still sit on the mixing desk in Phil Manzanera's studio. The messages, written on the back of a Toblerone wrapper and folded up like a paper fortune teller, read like Eno's Oblique Strategies: 'Not now, don't even think about it', 'Hang about', 'OK what?'

Phil and Jamie were not the only extra characters in the studio. As well as a return to the playful spirit of earlier tracks like *Soup Song*, another aspect of the thaw was a return to jazz. Side projects aside, Wyatt had avoided working with jazz musicians since the 1970s. 'After Soft Machine, I'd sort of been scared of them,' he admits, 'because my memory of jazz musicians was that I was just too primitive for them.' The second half of *Shleep* saw him creeping back.

'There seemed to be a new zeitgeist or a new generation,' he continues. 'People like Annie Whitehead, a very skilled musician. But her favourite music was reggae and South African music. She was very happy working

> A light-bulb moment: Robert cracks the *Shleep* running order.

with people who didn't have the slick savvy of session musicians, but who had their own voices and their own way of doing things.'

'He just rang up out of the blue,' recalls Annie, 'and said, "You probably don't want to do it, but..." The usual. "Only come down if it suits you, I don't want to put you out. Is next Sunday OK? Are you sure?" I said, "Yeah, yeah, yeah, yeah, I'll come down." I was really looking forward to seeing him.'

Robert had worked with Annie over a decade previously, on *Venceremos* by Working Week and *The Wind of Change*, produced by Jerry Dammers. Impressed by the sensitivity and musicality of her playing, he came to regard Annie's trombone as the vocal foil he had previously found in the trumpet playing of Mongezi Feza. So fundamental would Annie become as a collaborator, says Robert, that he would now be superstitious about making an album without her.

The trombonist, in turn, provides a useful musician's perspective on Wyatt's music. 'You talk to Robert and he goes, "Oh, my silly old songs," but he is just so clever, musically. I don't mean clever without heart. He's just got a musical intelligence. He ends up sounding like it's just happened, but it really, really hasn't. When you really get inside his music, it's very, very well put together. Because he's a drummer, he plays around with time a lot. Sometimes it is very subtle, but it's still there and it's easy to miss. And it's easy to think, "Oh yeah, I know that bit." But actually, if you really listen to it, the way it's placed across the beat is very particular.'

On one *Shleep* track, *September the Ninth*, Annie Whitehead was joined by saxophonist Evan Parker for four minutes of weighty, Mingus-inspired scene-setting before Wyatt's vocal glides in. Alfie's lyrics for the song had been written at Humberston Fitties, the salt marsh formed where the Humber estuary meets the North Sea. She and Robert had recently bought what Alfie calls a 'dacha' there; non-Russophiles might prefer the term 'holiday chalet'. The 'dacha' was made of wood and lacked electricity, yet it provided exactly the bolthole that Robert and Alfie needed. And Humberston Fitties, half an hour from Louth by car, was rather closer than Castelldefels.

The rugged sand dunes and marram grass on the banks of the Humber made for a galvanising backdrop. In days gone by, both composer Ralph Vaughan Williams and the poet Philip Larkin had sought inspiration at Spurn Point, the 'beach of shapes and shingle' on the opposite side of the estuary. Wildlife at the Fitties, meanwhile, inspired some of Alfie's finest lyrics, including the 'woman wishing for wings' on *September the Ninth*.

> Alfie's self-portrait at the Fitties, with swallows. One of the illustrations used on the *Shleep* CD booklet.

'Robert woke me up at about seven one morning,' recalls Alfie, of the incident that inspired the song, 'and said: "Come and look, come and look." The back of our field had lots of wire fences, and every inch was covered in swallows. And for a couple of hours they twittered around and spoke to each other. They were all gathering for their goodbye. It was absolute magic. Eventually they all rose up into the sky, just like little bits of pepper, and, suddenly, they were gone. It was the most fantastic experience.'

Evan Parker also played on *The Duchess* – named after a character in *Alice's Adventures in Wonderland*. Like *Sea Song*, *Alifib* and *P.L.A.*, the song is about Alfie, in all her paradoxical glory: 'Oh my wife is old and young / So sweet with her poison tongue.' It comes across as childishly simple: at one point, Wyatt even scrapes out *The Grand Old Duke of York* on the violin. His songs, Robert later suggested, were 'basically slightly out-of-tune nursery rhymes'. The music underneath, however, is intricate: these were the nursery rhymes of a man able to cross the *Grand Old Duke of York* with Duke Ellington. While the piano holds down a lopsided 5/4, Brian Eno bubbles away on synthesiser and Evan Parker wanders around in the background on soprano sax.

Does Parker see Wyatt as a jazz musician? 'The term "jazz" doesn't mean that much to me,' he replies. 'There are "jazz" musicians who are my heroes and there are "jazz" musicians who are an embarrassment to the human race. At best it indicates an attitude towards music-making that emphasises spontaneity and social interaction, both between the players and the audience.' Jamie Johnson also reflects on this: 'Robert's style of music is jazz-influenced,' he says. 'There are beautiful scales and weird notes working together. He loves getting two notes that shouldn't fit together to fit together somehow.' But, he adds, there is another side to Robert, one that loves Paul Weller for his 'attitude and ballsiness and rock'n'roll energy'.

After two decades as a solo musician, Robert *was* rediscovering a camaraderie that had largely disappeared with his ability to play a full drumkit. *Shleep* marked the beginning of what Wyatt calls his imaginary band: imaginary because, since they record separately and never perform onstage, many of the musicians have never actually met. 'Over the last few years,' he muses, 'there's a loose gang of friends and musicians I can turn to, who are fantastically sympathetic and helpful and want to help me get my songs right – or better than they might otherwise have been. I've become much more of a social musician again.'

The appearance of such a disparate range of musicians on a single album, however, is unique. What other artist would comfortably find room on the same record for Paul Weller, Brian Eno and Evan Parker?

–»)(«– –»)(«– –»)(«–

When Wyatt left Phil Manzanera's studio, he still didn't know who would release the recordings. With no label backing, Robert and Alfie had fronted the recording costs themselves – quite a gamble even if the guitarist wasn't asking for the money up front.

'Basically, we start from a premise that it's not going to cost them anything,' Manzanera explains. 'And then, if they get any money from anywhere, Alfie then says: "Look, take this." And I say: "No, no, no," and they say: "Yes, yes, yes." There's never a question of talking about money first and then they come here and record. It's always: come and do whatever you like, don't worry about it.'

Rough Trade was not yet up and running again, but Geoff Travis, then working as a manager with acts such as Pulp, suggested that they approach Andy Childs. Formerly general manager at Rough Trade, he was now general manager at Rykodisc. 'I was in the office one day,' recalls Childs, 'and the girl from reception put a tape on my desk and said, "Someone's just dropped this off." It was a cassette with three tracks on. I said, "Who?" And she said, "Some lady called Alfie. I went back, played the tape – and it was three tracks from *Shleep*. Fantastic. They were great. I played them to people in the office and everyone got *really* excited. And I thought: "Well, we can't turn this down – it's perfect!"'

Thanked in the *Shleep* liner notes as 'the good shepherd', Geoff Travis came with Alfie to negotiate the deal with Ryko. They presented the new label with a shrewd list of demands: albums would be merely licensed for a certain period, rather than signed over in perpetuity; Robert would share profits and expenses with the label on a 50:50 basis; records had to remain available, not go out of print; and Robert would be free to leave if the label went bust.

According to Geoff Travis, not all labels would have accepted such terms. But in return, Robert and Alfie were asking for no advance beyond what they owed Manzanera for the studio time. To Childs, who had followed Wyatt's career ever since he saw The Soft Machine at the Proms, signing Robert was 'a no-brainer'. That the new album was, as Childs puts it, 'as near a pop record as Robert is going to make' made it easier to convince his superiors. The deal was inked – although, due to a technicality, Robert signed not with Ryko but with Hannibal, a sibling label run by Joe Boyd, who three decades earlier had booked The Soft Machine to play his UFO club night.

One side effect of leaving such long gaps between albums is that almost every Wyatt album feels like a comeback. But *Shleep*, released in the autumn of 1997, really did bring Robert back to public consciousness after the relative obscurity of *Old Rottenhat* and *Dondestan*. 'Everyone who interviewed Robert found him in great shape,' remembers Andy Childs. 'He did a lot of press for it. He worked really hard, he didn't turn anybody down – except anybody writing for the politically hostile press. I think he enjoyed doing it and it made him realise just how loved and respected he actually was. I think perhaps his self-belief had taken a battering. And *Shleep* made him realise how much he was held in such high esteem by everyone. That was important.'

The *Independent* named *Shleep* album of the year, while *The Wire* put Wyatt on their front cover. It was a remarkable achievement for a man in his early fifties – and who had just become a grandfather. (Today, he has two granddaughters by Sam – Caitlin and Rebecca.)

Some critics pointed out that *Shleep* was a less political record: was it a coincidence that Robert's two most overtly left-wing albums, *Old Rottenhat* and *Dondestan*, had been made alone? In fact, there were still lines like 'Don't let the gringos grind you down' on *Blues in Bob Minor*. Yet Wyatt had given up his quest to make 'unmisusable music'. He stepped back from the barricades, he says, following the fall of apartheid in South Africa.

Shleep was a warmer record than *Dondestan* and, boosted by the clout of Ryko/Hannibal, far outsold its predecessor. Although Rough Trade had been honest to the bone, money from the new label also tended to arrive more promptly. And Alfie – who didn't relish the number-crunching side of the manager's role – now felt confident in leaving many of the business decisions to Andy Childs.

It was, she says, a dream record company, and Childs joins Phil Manzanera and Geoff Travis in her pantheon of heroes: 'He made it possible to earn in such a way that ever since then we've been able to have money,' she explains. 'We're not going to be starving old people.' The respect is reciprocal: Childs says he is more proud of his work with Robert and Alfie than of anything in his career, in part because of their appeal as human beings and in part because of the distinctiveness of the music: 'Robert doesn't sound like anybody else, and no-one else sounds like Robert.'

–»)(«– –»)(«– –»)(«–

The momentum continued to build after *Shleep*, particularly in Italy and France. Annie Whitehead remembers Robert saying it was Italy – the country so loved by his father, George – that had kept him going, both emotionally and financially, during the Rough Trade years. And in the mid-1990s it was clear to see. Michael King's *Wrong Movements: A Robert Wyatt History* was issued in an Italian edition and a group of Italian artists released *The Different You: Robert Wyatt e Noi*, their reinterpretations of Wyatt tracks. Robert himself sang *Del Mondo* with the band CSI, which later appeared on *Comicopera*, while they, in turn, reworked *Chairman Mao*.

Other Italian projects followed. Singer-songwriter Cristina Donà, who contributed to *The Different You*, also invited Robert to sing and play cornet on her understatedly majestic track *Goccia*. The 2002 book *Postcards from Italy*, meanwhile, combined Wyatt interviews in English

MW
pour Robert Wyatt

the different y...
Robert Wyatt e...

> Europe looks to Robert Wyatt as a songwriter – anthologies from France and Italy featuring the likes of Pascal Comelade and Cristina Donà.

and Italian with a CD of three wonderfully out-there variations of *The Duchess* by cellist and electronic musician Walter Prati.

France was another key territory. A Gallic counterpart to *The Different You* arrived in the form of the compilation *MW pour Robert Wyatt*, featuring cover versions of his tunes by various French acts – and a front photograph depicting Robert and Alfie amongst the wild grass of the Fitties. There was a book project too, with Jean-Michel Marchetti, who published lyrics by Robert and Alfie with translations and pictures, culminating in the *Anthologie du Projet MW* book of 2009.

Among those who contributed to the *MW pour Robert Wyatt* compilation was French Catalan musician Pascal Comelade, best known for toy instrument 'pocket symphonies'. Robert went on to appear on the title track of Comelade's 2000 EP *September Song*: a Kurt Weill number, previously sung by Frank Sinatra, Billy Eckstine and Nat 'King' Cole.

As a teenager, Robert's jazz heroes had been at the forefront of the late 1950s avant-garde. But, as he moved into the 'September' of his life, his favourite jazz era slipped backwards in time like Lewis Carroll's White Queen. Today, visitors to Queen Street are most likely to find Wyatt blasting out the music of earlier eras: bebop, Dixieland, and even crooners singing standards. 'I do now like the standard, great, famous singers of popular song,' he explains, 'particularly Nat "King" Cole and so on. But in the old days, as a jazz fan, I didn't get that stuff. It seemed to me very un-hip. It didn't sound *other* enough to me. It didn't sound like jazz's *other*.'

Continuing the avian theme of *Shleep*, Robert contributed – alongside Nick Cave and French composer Bruno Coulais – to the soundtrack of the award-winning French documentary *Winged Migration*, a film that followed the migration of birds across all seven continents, from the Arctic to the Amazon via Paris and New York. Bruno Coulais, who wrote the music, describes Wyatt on the accompanying documentary as 'a living legend'. Robert also collaborated with a Japanese duo, Tomoyasu Hayakawa and Tomoko Noro, who adapted a song called *Brian the Fox*, which later surfaced on *Cuckooland*. The pair also opened a restaurant in his honour, naming it, at Robert's suggestion, 'Happy Mouth'.

In Britain, too, Robert's reputation was being revived. Hard as it is to envisage in the era of Spotify, many Wyatt releases were by this stage difficult to obtain. But in 1998, all his solo albums, with the exception of *The End of an Ear*, were reissued by Ryko/Hannibal. 'Suddenly,' he says, 'I had a back catalogue.' Most importantly, the various miscellaneous releases from this back catalogue were corralled into five, carefully sequenced EPs, issued as a box set. Singles such as *Shipbuilding* and *I'm a Believer* now rubbed shoulders with glorious oddities such as *Pigs…* (*In There*). The box set was Alfie's idea. 'They were going to do simply a compilation,' she recalls. 'But Virgin did a compilation once, and you couldn't listen to it. There was a bit of this, bit of that, it was all on one thing and it was unwieldy. I persuaded Andy to spend a lot of money on separating them, and making a thing that was special, so that the tracks didn't kill each other.'

Alfie also designed the artwork for the box set, drawing on her art school training in graphics and typography. It is, she says, her favourite artwork package she has designed for Robert. 'I did the *EPs* at the Fitties,' she recalls. 'I didn't have all my paints. And I'd been upset because, with oil paints, the colours never come out right. And the exact colour to me is really important, how it zizzles with another colour. I thought: "If I use coloured paper, they're much more likely to get the colours right." So I started to cut and paste, which I've been doing more or less ever since.'

The *EPs* box set is a good example of Alfie's approach to management: rooted in a deep affinity for the music and lyrics, some of which, of course, she had actually written. She would have been more than

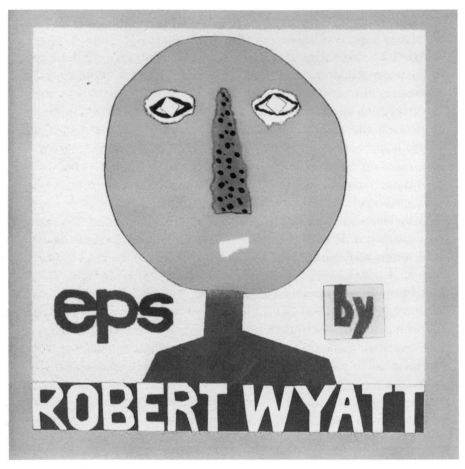

> Part of Alfie's collage artwork for *EPs* – zizzling colours sadly not depicted.

content, she explains, to continue as a dreamer herself. 'If I could be doing artwork and lyrics all day,' she laughs, 'I'd be happy as a sandboy.'

Alfie's contribution to the records that bear her husband's name is woefully underappreciated: even in her presence, journalists routinely ask Robert about lyrics that were in fact written by Alfie. As an artist in her own right, Alfie's output has been confined to occasional painting exhibitions and magazine illustrations, a couple of children's books with Ivor Cutler, and album covers for a handful of acts – Fred Frith, Annette Peacock, Welsh psych folk group Gorky's Zygotic Mynci, the French band Klimperei. The re-release of all Robert's albums offered a chance to reappraise the album covers as an unusually coherent body of work: for a musician to work with the same art designer over what is now four decades is almost unprecedented. Like Robert's music, Alfie's covers combined diversity with consistency, the two artforms evolving absolutely in parallel from one release to the next.

Alfie is as self-effacing as her husband on the subject: 'I don't think any of them are wonderful, but I think they work.' Robert is able to be more expansive: 'The variety of skill and pertinence and hipness of her covers is a great thing to see in a row,' he says. 'It's really dazzling, when you go from one to the other. It's all the same person, *for* the same person. And it's really great when someone says, "I only know about you because I saw the record cover for *Ruth Is Stranger Than Richard*, and I liked the painting so I bought the record." That's terrific when it happens, it really is. It just sort of completes the picture.'

Ryko/Hannibal also released a recording of Robert's one proper solo performance: at Drury Lane back in 1974. More unusually, the reissue programme allowed Robert to scratch an itch that had been bothering him for the best part of a decade. Never happy with the final mix of *Dondestan*, he now remixed the album and changed the track order. The result was *Dondestan Revisited* – a kind of director's cut. 'It's still the same old whine,' noted Robert in the liner notes, 'with a little more bottle.'

Shleep itself marked the start of a new trio of records, distinct from the more solitary, more overtly political Rough Trade releases. It also marked a new appreciation of Wyatt at home. 'I'd always have been perfectly all right without putting out any records in England at all, and I still would,' says Robert. 'But since Ryko, and Joe Boyd's Hannibal Records, enough people buy my records here that I feel much more at home, as opposed to always having to mentally be somewhere else.'

To make England fully take notice of this supposedly quintessentially English musician, however, would require an Anglophile American: a man named Glenn Max.

19

SPEECHLESS

A moment in heaven
on London's South Bank

'**I love Robert's music, I love his voice, I love his whole approach,**' says Glenn Max, an energetic New Yorker with a hairstyle midway between Frank Zappa and a Civil War cavalier. 'He is one of the few experimentalists that's so interesting and so light. It's serious enough but whimsical enough. It's tragic but it never becomes humourless – or when it's humourless, it's *appropriately* humourless. Robert Wyatt, to me, is just an unparalleled artist.'

As creative director of New York's Knitting Factory, Glenn Max had already programmed a tribute to Wyatt which featured the likes of Hugh Hopper and Daevid Allen. When he moved to England in 2000, to take up a new position as producer of contemporary music at London's Southbank Centre, one of his first tasks was to find a guest curator for the following year's Meltdown festival. Unable to resist the chance to repeat the New York event on a far larger scale, he soon phoned Robert.

The curator slot was prestigious: the Southbank is one of the largest arts centres in the world, and Meltdown was well on its way to becoming the most prominent fixture in their annual calendar. Although it had begun primarily as a festival of contemporary classical music, previous curators included Scott Walker, Nick Cave, John Peel and Elvis Costello. Yet, although he had loved the Southbank Centre since he was a child, Wyatt initially declined Glenn Max's invitation. Most of his favourite musicians were dead, he explained – and working with those still alive would create too much potential for embarrassment: 'I just couldn't think of anybody,' he sighs. 'And the other thing that worried me, I thought, "Supposing I get people to come and then nobody likes them or they get bad reviews? How awful would that be?"'

Thankfully, Alfie and Glenn Max were able to change Robert's mind and, a decade later, the filament inside Max still glows: 'Robert is just effusive with kindness and patience and a natural empathy and humour. You just *adore* this guy. And Alfie, too. Alfie can be quite intimidating when you first meet her. Then, as soon as you break through that, she's just so open and so smart and so compassionate.'

In booking Wyatt, Glenn Max was taking a considerable risk. From today's perspective, Robert was a natural fit for Meltdown. Despite the success of *Shleep*, however, Robert was an unlikely candidate for the job in 2001. Even with his background at the Knitting Factory, then one of New York's leading avant-garde venues, Glenn Max admits to having been daunted by the prospect of promoting the artists he expected Wyatt to choose. When Morrissey curated the festival, he had got The New York Dolls to re-form, while Elvis Costello had played host to Jeff Buckley's last ever UK show. What would Robert go for? Three weeks of Stalinist free jazz?

As it turned out, Glenn Max needn't have worried. As well as soul singer Macy Gray and Wyclef Jean of The Fugees, Robert talked of booking the 1990s R&B girl group Eternal and even Hear'Say, a shamelessly manufactured reality TV act then enjoying their fifteen seconds of fame. Although none of these choices would make the final cut, the breadth of vision was startling. Wyatt did, however, consider a 'Political Correctness Gone Mad' festival, in which he would have banned all English-speaking white male performers. He also wondered about turning the whole event into a stand against the then Shadow Home Secretary, expressing his intention to gather 'every single economic migrant and bogus asylum seeker who could sing or play a musical instrument and let them completely take over the Southbank. And call the whole thing the Ann Widdecombe Special.'

In the event, although some of the final programme did have a political edge, any message was often implicit. Senegal's Baaba Maal, for instance, had spoken for the United Nations on AIDS and HIV, and campaigned against female genital mutilation, yet his closing concert was celebratory. Wyatt recalls it as 'unfollowably gobsmacking – so it's just as well he was the last act'.

> Posters for the 2001 Robert Wyatt's Meltdown concerts.

Bebop pioneer Max Roach was another politically resonant choice. Back in 1960, the drummer had protested against what he considered racist booking practices at the Newport Jazz Festival by organising a rival 'rebel festival' just down the street; the following year, he picketed a Miles Davis concert in protest against the involvement of the allegedly colonial Africa Research Foundation. Roach, who had played with Charlie Parker when still a teenager, was in his seventies by the time of Meltdown. 'That was virtually one of the last gigs he did,' sighs Robert, who still has a framed poster advertising the show on his wall in Louth, 'and he was obviously really struggling. Once he sat at the drumkit he was all right – but even then, he was struggling. The poignancy of that, for me, cannot be overestimated.'

Only one or two events were more overtly political. Partially inspired by *Trade Union*, the track recorded by Dishari back in Rough Trade days, Robert staged a Refugee Arts Festival, with the help of the *Red Pepper* columnist and campaigner Amanda Sebestyen. 'I remembered this thing we'd done with the Bangladeshis on Rough Trade,' says Wyatt. 'And I said, "Who do you know? Can you get together any of these people playing instruments?" And we did and it was fantastic. We had

Somalians, we had a Kazakh lot, we had all kinds of things. But it wasn't just worthy, it was a really rocking gig.'

Another event, Arab-Israeli Connections, brought together Palestinian singer Amal Murkus with the Israeli pop star Eviatar Banai. 'Amal Murkus came on first,' Wyatt remembers, 'with a pianist and an oud player. Most of the audience had come because of the advert in the *Jewish Chronicle* for Eviatar Banai. And, because they hadn't mentioned her, because she's not Jewish therefore she doesn't exist, they just thought she was this Israeli pop singer. So all these London Jews turn up, hundreds of them, and they all sat through. But they were really impressed because she's a really classy act – not rock'n'roll, it's kind of folk-based. Stunning stuff. And I don't think any of those people could go on and think: "These people are just animals." Never. They couldn't do it. It was such a hip, dignified, witty performance.'

Looking beyond music, Wyatt also found space for Mark Thomas, an anarchist comedian who combines the campaigning zeal of John Pilger with the wit of Lenny Bruce. 'I amazed Mark Thomas's anarchist, deeply anti-Stalinist friends', Robert recalls, 'by inviting him to do an afternoon of whatever he wanted to do – even if it meant slagging off the Communist Party.' The agit-com went on for two hours.

'Mark Thomas, he won't stop,' laughs Robert. 'All the way, preparing for it, you think, "Why are you talking? You should be saving this up." But that's how he does it. He gets his gang of anarchists together, they're all arguing away. Then he goes onstage, carries on without them, deals with hecklers. Then afterwards, "Do you want to come back? We carry on now the show's over." And they do. Everybody in the audience sits around and talks about what he's been talking about.'

⋯ ⋯ ⋯

Once he was over his initial reluctance, the curator slot suited Robert down to the ground. 'I loved it once I got into it,' he nods. 'The staff at the Festival Hall – Jane, Ed, Beverley and the rest – were fantastic. And you could wheel about in there, see free things, drift about, fantastic bookshop, and smoke and drink and see friends. It was a great place. Although I don't believe in God and the Devil, I do believe in heaven and hell, because I've visited both. That was a moment in heaven.'

Robert and Alfie stayed in a flat overlooking the Royal Festival Hall, with a view of the Thames and the London Eye. And they went to every single show. 'Apparently, no-one else had ever done that,' chuckles Robert. 'But me and Alfie were always the first two people at any party and the last to leave, when I would go round and drain everybody else's drinks. We felt like the Pearly King and Queen, Lord and Lady Muck for a month.'

'They were definitely partying,' grins Glenn Max. 'They were great. Meltdown is a party, an opportunity to put yourself in a more social mode than you would otherwise. I know, for Patti Smith, in some weird way it was a bit of a coming out party. I think for Robert and Alfie it was a bit of a coming out party, too. It was an opportunity for them to be in London, to see old friends.'

Meltdown was a chance, too, for this most generous of musicians to publicly endorse old collaborators. Robert found space, for instance, for former Rough Trade labelmates The Raincoats. 'We'd bumped into him once or twice over the years,' says Gina Birch. 'His beard had grown and he had this elder statesman thing going on. At Meltdown, he was sitting right in front of me as I was singing, and I remember feeling: "Wow, here I am on this stage and there's *Robert* sitting there." It's a weird place to play, it's a bit sterile. You're very aware of the audience in these rows. But I felt very honoured. It was great that somebody like Robert chose us for his Meltdown.'

'Robert and Alfie were there,' remembers her bandmate Ana da Silva. 'So was Julie Christie. I thought she was there because she was a really good friend of Robert's. I said, "Oh, have you seen many gigs?" She said, "No, no, I just phoned Robert because I knew you were playing." So we were very chuffed with that. Because when we released *Odyshape* – I can't remember if it was *Odyshape* or the first album – Julie Christie's secretary apparently came in and bought three copies.'

Jazz pianist and composer Keith Tippett performed, as did minimalist composer Terry Riley. Cristina Donà appeared on the same bill as Norway's Anja Garbarek, Robert having just sung on the *Smiling and Waving* album by Garbarek, the daughter of torch-in-the-tundra saxophonist Jan. Another offbeat triumph was Ivor Cutler, who supported Elvis Costello. 'Ivor was very ill by that time,' recalls Robert. 'He was frail, he was shaking, and getting forgetful. And Glenn said, "Will he be all right? This is a rock'n'roll audience; how's he going to be?" I said, "You don't know England. Ivor's all right. It'll be OK." And he went on and he was fantastic. Some people said Ivor was the best thing. Because he's very funny with his little harmonium, reading out his little poems and so on. He's unique. And people loved it. "We love

> The Royal Festival Hall foyer during Meltdown: Robert, Ivor Cutler, Alfie and Mark Thomas.

you, Ivor!" they shouted at the end. "Oh," he said, "I don't think you know me well enough to say that.'"

Fred Frith performed with Massacre, alongside Bill Laswell – the man who had once covered *Memories* with a then unknown Whitney Houston. But this performance, featuring drummer Charles Hayward, formerly of Quiet Sun and This Heat, was at the opposite end of the scale from The Wilde Flowers: a lacerating mix of dub, funk, jazz and heavy metal, later released as *Melt Down*.

Naturally for a Marxist, Robert was also attuned to the economics of his Meltdown programme. The artists he selected were not all guaranteed to put bums on seats, but he was determined that, overall, the festival would not lose money. 'Those things often go into the red,' he explains, 'but I didn't want to do that. I wanted it to *make* money, because it's public money. I was very glad to have some things that were surefire concert-hall fillers.' One such was Elvis Costello. 'He did a bunch of songs in a small group with Steve Nieve,' remembers Wyatt. 'Then he brought the Brodsky Quartet on, and did a whole bunch of stuff with a string quartet. That could have been the concert. But everything was suddenly moved offstage and on came The Attractions with a drumkit. And suddenly, after about an hour and a half, a rock'n'roll Attractions set. What a lovely man. Unceremoniously magnificent.'

David Gilmour agreed to perform, too, despite the fact that he didn't even have a band available when he got the call. It was the first London show the Pink Floyd singer and guitarist had played in a decade, and helped bring about his resurgence as a solo artist. 'I phoned him up', Robert recalls, 'and said, "Could you do this?" He said no. Then he phoned back, and said, "I could do it if I could bring a cellist." I said, "Yeah, you can bring a cellist." Then, about a week later, he said, "I could do it if I could have a little choral group." I said, "Yeah, you could have a little choral group." And he came along and did this very straight set, very un-Floyd in a way, but with all the background and authority that he has. Beautifully simple. Simply beautiful.'

While he was keen to feature former collaborators, Wyatt chose other artists simply as a fan – from Ray Gelato's Giants, a jump-band in 1940s tradition, to Andrew Cyrille, the avant-garde drummer best known for his work with Cecil Taylor but who had also played in Charlie Haden's Liberation Music Orchestra and on the Greaves/Blegvad album *Kew. Rhone*. Avant-garde art collective The Residents played too, anonymous behind their trademark eyeball masks. Similarly Pataphysical in spirit were psychedelic Welsh act Gorky's Zygotic Mynci, who had covered *Why Are We Sleeping?* and *O Caroline*.

Tricky, Bristolian purveyor of sultry, skunk-fuelled sprechgesang, was Alfie's choice. Back on form after a lost half-decade, his show rescued triphop from its growing reputation as dinner party muzak. 'Tricky was stunning,' says Robert. 'And I was old enough to know that what he was doing was almost like Pink Floyd via a drum'n'bass band. Very early Floyd, when it was a mad, swirling, stormy thing, but with this incredible rhythmic pulse. And him standing in the corner, shivering and strange, and amazing girl singers. That was a fantastic show.'

–»)《«– –»)《«– –»)《«–

Talking his curator out of the Ann Widdecombe Special was only the initial hurdle facing Glenn Max. Fans were going to expect to see Robert's old bandmates on the bill, yet it was hard to picture him shoulder to shoulder with Mike Ratledge and Elton Dean, sharing a microphone for a singalong finale of *We Did It Again*.

> Robert in the wings at David Gilmour's Meltdown concert, singing the opening verse of *Comfortably Numb*.

'Meltdown directors – I'd say, without fail – do not want to re-hash the past,' sighs Max. 'Patti Smith does not want to create CBGBs at Meltdown. Massive Attack do not want to create The Wild Bunch. You can't help but think of these ideas: "Let's do a Wild Bunch night, guys!" No. Because it's politics, because it's old, because they want to be seen as contemporary, not resting on their laurels, because of the mythology of what that was. Robert Wyatt is not going to want to do Soft Machine.'

Not performing with the musicians from the so-called Canterbury Scene was fair enough. But part of the Meltdown curator's job is to play live, sometimes several times, and Robert didn't want to go onstage *at all*. It could have seemed churlish: if the chance to put on concerts by his favourite musicians in the world wasn't enough, Meltdown would raise his profile significantly. He would even get paid for his troubles. Could he not manage a one-hour set in return?

Since the Henry Cow dates of the 1970s, Robert has had something approaching a phobia of playing live: a sense of trepidation that borders on dread. 'You just get such an immediate sense from Robert, when you bring up playing live, how absolutely terrified he is,' recalls Max. 'You can see it in his eyes if you discuss it face-to-face with him. It became a condition for agreeing to the festival. As long as he didn't have to perform, he could do it. So I had to say yes. And once I'd agreed to that, I couldn't push it. I couldn't really even bring it up.'

Yet, although Wyatt absolutely refused to perform as a headline act, David Gilmour did coax Robert into his first public performance since The Raincoats in 1981, singing the opening verse of Floyd favourite *Comfortably Numb*, originally sung by Roger Waters. 'Robert's got one of the great voices,' says Gilmour. 'That slot, singing *Comfortably Numb*, it's Roger's slot; he's no longer around in my sphere – and it's always nice to get someone to do that. Robert was around, and I love his voice. So why *wouldn't* I ask him? I think he said no initially, that he didn't ever do that. But I bullied him a bit and eventually he got up there and did a little bit. Which was great. He was happy afterwards that I'd forced him.'

Even with Gilmour's 'bullying', however, Wyatt didn't quite make it onto the stage. 'Robert sung from *in front of* the stage,' recalls Glenn Max. 'He didn't want all the shenanigans, too much fuss around him, so he sang from the floor. And of course he sounded beautiful, but with this terrified look in his eye. He came offstage and he was shaking, he was almost in a state of panic.'

Aware that the Gilmour guest slot would not entirely satisfy fans, Glenn Max conceived of a way for Wyatt's own compositions to be performed – as well as to coax Robert into a second ghostly guest appearance. Soupsongs, dedicated to performing the music of Robert Wyatt, had been conceived for another festival. As well as trombonist Annie Whitehead and members of her regular band, the group has at various times included Barbados-born trumpeter Harry Beckett, who had played on Robert's *Caimanera*, Larry Stabbins of Centipede, Phil Manzanera, saxophonists Brian Hopper, George Khan and Gong's Didier Malherbe, and vocalist Julie Tippetts, who had performed alongside Robert at Drury Lane in 1974.

Glenn Max's suggestion was that Soupsongs perform at Meltdown, but with an extended list of guest vocalists. It was hard to find singers who could sing Robert's work, he recalls, but the eventual line-up saw Tippetts joined by vocalists including Elvis Costello and Karen Mantler, the daughter of Mike Mantler and Carla Bley. Soul singer Carleen Anderson, of Young Disciples and Brand New Heavies, sang *Strange Fruit* – according to Alfie, the best version of the song she has ever heard.

The musicians were first-rate, and fans were delighted to see Robert's music played live. They even got a glimpse – though nothing more – of the man himself. 'At the Soupsongs performance,' remembers Glenn Max, 'Robert had agreed with Alfie to close the show: to sing in the dark from the ceremonial box, which is the big box where the Queen sits if she ever visits. They were just going to do this a capella. And when the time came, he literally was crouching down so you couldn't see him, he was so nervous. He didn't want to even be onstage, he didn't want to be introduced. We were all looking up at the box, but you could only see the top of their backs, bent over.'

Tantalisingly, Glenn Max recalls that *le trac* evaporated with the last audience member: backstage, late at night, Robert would sit at the piano and sing. 'I remember he and Alfie were doing something at the piano,' says Max. 'And the three or four people in the room would be looking at each other like: "Oh shit. We're getting a little Robert Wyatt performance here."' How did he sound? 'He sounded like Robert Wyatt,' grins Max. 'He sounded fucking great.'

> Robert with essential collaborator and Soupsongs director Annie Whitehead.

Even if he couldn't physically face his audience, however, Soupsongs did allow Robert to witness his fanbase firsthand. And to hear this music finally played live, says Annie Whitehead, was an emotional experience, for Alfie as well as for Robert. In professional terms, meanwhile, Meltdown gave a hefty boost to a profile already bolstered by *Shleep* – so much so that Glenn Max joins Rough Trade boss Geoff Travis, Roxy Music guitarist Phil Manzanera and Rykodisc's Andy Childs in Alfie's roll of heroes.

'I don't follow the media stuff', says Robert, 'but I noticed a sense of "in from the cold". I'd never had any *authority* before, if I can use that word. I did what I did – this nutter who does stuff – but the idea of giving me any responsibility like that, I don't think would have occurred to anybody in England. And I don't think I could have done it, actually, without Glenn.'

The Southbank Centre paid enduring tribute to Wyatt's Meltdown: a lifesize, black and white stencil drawing of Robert by graffiti artist Stewy appeared next to the stage entrance in 2011. Robert, too, has his Meltdown memento: a framed disc of Royal Festival Hall carpet adorns his wall in Louth.

20

HOPE CAN STILL FEEL PRETTY GOOD

Cuckooland: ditties from the Fitties

It was while driving back from Phil Manzanera's studio that Alfie came up with a title for Robert's next album – one that would build on the momentum of Meltdown and win even more plaudits than *Shleep*. 'It means just somewhere where everything's mad,' Robert explains, 'an *Alice in Wonderland* place. If someone's in cloud cuckoo land, it means they're nuts, away with the fairies.'

Cuckooland is the sound of a man idly looking for shapes in the clouds, but the title also had a less nebulous inspiration: one of the album's key tracks was *Cuckoo Madame*. Some critics heard lines about the 'solitary madam', 'the witch of Salem', and assumed that the song was about Margaret Thatcher. No, laughs Robert. It's about a cuckoo. ('I couldn't bear to do a song with Thatcher in it,' says Alfie, who had written the lyrics. 'Her face would be creeping into my head all the time.')

The song did, in fact, have an allegorical aspect, but the reference was to Humberston Fitties, where Robert and Alfie had their 'dacha' and had been involved in a protracted and painful planning dispute. 'Early in the season,' Alfie recalls, 'I was there on my own for a couple of weeks and a cuckoo would come every day and sit on the wire fencing. I knew the nest it was after, because there were some meadow pipits and

I saw it eating caterpillars. I started thinking about its life – and then that got muddled up with the perception of me by a lot of those people. The cuckoo as this alien bird, landing and being hated: *you're too bloody lonely for the likes of us.'*

Robert regards *Cuckoo Madame* as one of Alfie's most brilliant lyrics. It was also one of the hardest to set to music, but it pushed him into a new approach to melody and harmony, borrowing from two of England's finest twentieth-century composers. 'Writing *Cuckoo Madame*,' he explains, 'turned out to be the nearest I'd ever got to the stuff I'd tried to learn as a child from people like Benjamin Britten and Vaughan Williams. They were modern but in a different way. People associate the term with dramatic dissonance, but to me the thing that they brought to the surface – and which was innovative – was their using the archaic scales of folk music that weren't either major or minor.'

Cuckooland as a whole was a deeply English record, informed by the Lincolnshire coast – just as Vaughan Williams had been inspired by Spurn Point, slightly to the north, and Britten's compositions reflected the wind and waves of Suffolk. Alongside more demotic artists such as Dionne Warwick, Wyatt cites Britten's partner Peter Pears, known for his high-pitched and decidedly English voice, as an influence on his own singing. David Bedford, who worked with Pears, recalled that Robert's impression of the tenor was spot on.

One theme that emerged on *Cuckooland*, as the album took shape over 2002 and 2003, was that of looking for reassurance, sometimes in irrational places. One mooted title had been *Touching Wood* – dropped, as music was now increasingly being consumed online, for its pornographic connotations. In its intended sense, however, the phrase was apt, casting Wyatt as shipwreck survivor, clutching at passing driftwood for those moments when reason alone couldn't quite keep him afloat. There may, too, be an elegiac aspect to the album, which was the first that Robert had recorded since the death of his mother, Honor, in 1998.

–»)〈«– –»)〈«– –»)〈«–

Where *Shleep* had begun with 'girly choruses' sung with Brian Eno, the first words of *Cuckooland* were more reflective: 'Faith may not be such a bad thing' began *Just a Bit;* 'hope can still feel pretty good'. The track is dedicated to Richard Dawkins, the evolutionary biologist whose campaign against religious fundamentalism has earned him the

> The Wyatt 'dacha' at the Humberstone Fitties, inspiration for *Cuckooland*.

nickname 'Darwin's Rottweiler'. Maybe he deserves the sobriquet when confronting wilfully ignorant creationists (or, to use his term, history-deniers) in books such as *The God Delusion*. But Robert's point was that, contrary to what critics claim, Dawkins *does* retain a sense of wonder, in no way incompatible with scientific rigour.

'Mysteries don't lose their poetry because they are solved,' Dawkins has written. 'Quite the contrary. The solution often turns out more beautiful than the puzzle, and anyway the solution uncovers deeper mystery.' The professor was moved to tears upon visiting the Hadron Collider, and is capable of talking of scientific experiments as 'almost too wonderful to bear'.

Wyatt, the secular Christian, entirely understands the religious impulse, but has little time for the metaphysics at the core of religious belief. 'I don't think the word "belief" means anything,' he explains. 'It's a hovering, wobbly, jelly phrase meaning something like: "I've decided to think something's true because I wish it were true." "Why do you think it's true?" "Because I really, really wish it was." It just wobbles. If you try and hold it, it melts like a jellyfish in the sun.'

'I'm interested in behaviour, really,' he goes on. 'Guides to behaviour. And also the stories and metaphors and fables and bits of skewed history that people assemble as guidelines as to how to behave. And how to live with turbulent and unpredictable reality around them, I think that's very interesting. I like what Robert Graves said about mythology: it's not a question of any myth being true, but the study of mythology tells you about the collective zeitgeist of the people you're writing about.'

In *Just a Bit*, Robert concedes that we all need 'totem poles and icons' with which to 'camouflage the daily grind', whether we think of them as religious or – like touching wood – merely superstitious. Robert's own icons were not all jazz musicians. Originally released by Buddy Holly, *Raining in My Heart* had been composed by Felice and Boudleaux Bryant, a husband-and-wife team best known for writing for the Everly Brothers. Wistfully, Wyatt's created an imaginary backstory that pushed the song back in time much further than his own adolescence. 'Instead of doing a more modern version,' he explains, 'which is what you'd assume you'd do with a 1950s pop song, I tried to imagine that the Bryants themselves had heard it as a late nineteenth-century Victorian parlour song. I just sort of reversed the process.'

Cuckooland was soaked in nostalgia, and not only for rock'n'roll and parlour music. *Old Europe* found Robert taking refuge in post-war Paris. Jazz had been played on the Left Bank since the 1920s, and flourished in particular after World War II. As well as Miles Davis and Juliette Greco, whose love affair was played out in the city, the song references Parisian jazz haunts Le Chat Qui Pêche and Club St Germain – the latter simply by its address, Rue St Benoît. The tune was dedicated to Mike Zwerin, who had played briefly with Miles before writing about The Soft Machine for *Downbeat* magazine back in the 1960s and went on to live in Paris.

Jazz was a more obvious influence on *Cuckooland* than on any of Wyatt's other solo releases: it's there in the trombone solo on *Lullaby for Hamza*, the walking double bass on *Trickle Down*, the clarinet on a version of bossa classic *Insensatez*, the trumpet on *Beware*. Robert played this last part, like the lyrical solo on *Old Europe*, himself, after Alfie picked up the instrument at a car-boot sale. Paul Weller calls Wyatt 'the English Chet Baker', and he could now replicate the papery sound of jazz's leading doomed romantic on trumpet as well as vocals. Those lessons, back in Wellington House days, hadn't been wasted after all.

'That physical, hands-on feel of playing a trumpet is one of the greatest physical pleasures I've had from doing music since drumming,' enthuses Robert, 'because writing songs is of course rather abstract – as is keyboard playing, really.' Trumpet and cornet also brought about a new way of writing, using existing jazz records as a point of departure – a process Robert calls 'karaoke trumpet'.

'Improvisation – that's the joy of jazz, really – is just infinite variety of notes in a fixed set of circumstances. So you are composing: the moment you depart from the given notes of a tune, you are starting to compose. So it's just carrying on that. And then eventually you can sort of let the undercarriage, the chassis, the chord sequence, go, and just carry on with the tune. That's the main way I think I seem to work: humming along with tunes until they're unrecognisabe. There's still a scandalous amount of plagiarism goes on,' he laughs, 'but I'm not going to tell anybody what it is in case I get done.'

–»)《«- –»)《«- –»)《«-

Though *Cuckooland* as a whole was as beguiling as a daydream, several of the tracks were inspired by real world events – domestic as well as international. References, as usual, were reduced to ciphers, but decoding was made easier by unusually informative sleevenotes.

Forest sounds innocuous enough on first listen: a gentle ballad about a gypsy girl singing in the moonlight. But the lyrics then move onto the white cliffs of Dover – and we're a long way from Vera Lynn. Instead, what unfolds, still over a gentle 6/8 ride cymbal pattern, is a story of Romany gypsies and fellow asylum seekers, whose arrival in the Kent port was then inspiring moral outrage on tabloid front pages. Eventually, the lyrics take in Lety and Auschwitz – although the words are sung so softly, against a counter-melody, that they are much less startling than they seem on the page. Lety, as the liner notes explain, was an extermination camp for gypsies during the Second World War; Auschwitz, although most closely associated with the genocide of Jews, served a similar function. Between 1941 and 1944, some 23,000 European Roma were transported to the death camp, of whom only 2,000 survived. The track is dedicated to Sinti and Roma civil rights activist Romani Rose.

On *Foreign Accents*, the ciphers again come with explanatory notes. Robert's lyrics are minimal yet reference Mordechai Vanunu, the Israeli scientist who, for blowing the whistle on Israel's secret nuclear weapons, was then serving an eighteen-year sentence for treason, and Iranian prime minister Mohammad Mossadegh, removed in 1953 in a coup backed by British and American agents, for the crime of nationalising Iranian oil. *Foreign Accents* also references Hiroshima and Nagasaki, Wyatt adding his own spin by describing the effect of the atomic bombings, in the sleevenotes, as 'Mass Destruction'. He doesn't go into detail: the syllables simply loop, again and again, over staccato stabs. But it was a charged term in an era when the US and the UK were using the alleged – and, as has now been shown, largely fabricated – existence of Weapons of Mass Destruction to justify the forthcoming invasion of Iraq.

That there is more politics on *Cuckooland* than there had been on *Shleep* is unsurprising, given that Bush and Blair, having already sent troops into Afghanistan, were by now clearly preparing to invade Iraq. Robert and Alfie happened to be at the Fitties on 9/11, and watched on a portable TV as the Twin Towers fell. Living in Lincolnshire, a county synonymous with the Royal Air Force since the Dam Busters raids of World War II, made the ensuing 'War on Terror' particularly hard to avoid: 'This is bomber country,' as Robert later pointed out. 'They practise here. For us it's not just an abstract issue.'

As Hollywood's default villain morphed from Russian into Arab, there was a parallel shift in those to whose plight Wyatt chose to call attention. 'Chomsky anticipated,' explains Robert, 'that at the end of the Cold War we were going to need new enemies, and it would be the Arabs. He got that right. But in fact the paradox is that Britain and America spent so much of their military aid on Afghanistan, against the Soviet Union. The Mujahideen were very romanticised, as defenders of religion and tradition against this brutal, secular invasion. That was the whole shtick at that time, and it worked. Then you have these fantastically well-tooled-up Muslims, who'd found global solidarity, who think, "Right, here we are, now *you* fuck off, too." So suddenly they're evil fundamentalists.'

The build-up to the Iraq War, which broke out the day *Cuckooland* was finished, overshadowed the whole writing and recording process. Most obviously, *Lullaby for Hamza* is about an Iraqi woman whose son, Hamza, was born in Baghdad just as the first bombs fell in the Gulf War of 1991. He had spent the first forty days of his life in an underground shelter. As a girl, Alfie later explained, she had had nightmares about World War II. 'I thought about these children in Iraq having the same nightmares,' she went on. 'I have no children of my own, so the Iraqi children seemed the perfect people to have a lullaby for.'

Closing number *La Ahada Yalam* was again only subtly political. The version that closes *Cuckooland* is instrumental, all breathy clarinet over acoustic guitar and double bass. But it had originally been sung, in Arabic, by Amal Murkus, one of the artists Wyatt had booked for Meltdown, and a translation of the lyrics appears in the sleevenotes:

No-one knows / whose turn it will be tomorrow
The skies above the refugee camp are grey.
Dreams hastily scrawled on the walls.

-»)) ((«-   -»)) ((«-   -»)) ((«-

Like *Shleep*, *Cuckooland* was recorded with Phil Manzanera, although he had now moved from Surrey to West London. Designed with Robert and Alfie in mind, the new studio included a wheelchair-accessible loo, ramps, even a place in which Robert and Alfie could sleep. 'Occasionally we meet for dinner on our dining table,' says Manzanera, who lives next door, 'but they can have their own world.' The only issue is that Manzanera's studio is on the third floor – so, as the guitarist puts it, 'once Robert's up here, he's stuck up here'. Wyatt is carried up the stairs when he arrives, by two Romanians who work on the ground floor, and carried down again only when he is ready to head back to Louth.

Cuckooland was very much a post-Meltdown record, and not only because of the Amal Murkus number. Jennifer Maidman from the Soupsongs band played accordion and acoustic guitar. David Gilmour appeared, too, contributing to *Forest* the blues guitar licks otherwise absent from Wyatt's oeuvre, as well as a swooping, string-like harmonies. Most significantly, Karen Mantler appeared on four songs, building on Robert's lengthy musical relationship with her parents, Mike Mantler and Carla Bley.

'I'd met her a few times as a teenager,' recalls Wyatt, 'and was very impressed to meet a teenage girl who understood her mother's assertion that most jazz had already been done in the late 1920s because Duke Ellington had done *East St Louis Toodle-oo*. To find a teenage girl who knew exactly what that was all about was a wonderful thing. And I love the way she sings and her take on things. Over the years Karen's been

353

making these solo records, which she used to send to me, mostly about her cat, Arnold. They're incredibly doomy little songs, but really nice harmonically. And closer to my idiom, in a way, than what her parents do.'

Karen had grown up immersed in the jazz avant-garde: she had actually featured, aged four, on her mother's epic *Escalator Over the Hill* album. Yet she also had a love of short tunes and strong melodies – and, crucially, she shared Robert's sense of humour. Of the three Mantler tracks Wyatt covered on his new album, two – *Mister E* and *Life Is Sheep* – had pun-based titles.

Karen spent a week in Phil Manzanera's studio, recording vocals, harmonica and some keyboard parts. Simple generosity was one reason for Wyatt's invitation: she had just been dropped by her label. But there was also the fact that smoking had robbed Robert of half an octave at the top of his vocal range – and Karen could hit the notes that he himself could no longer reach. Their voices were similar too, Karen sharing Robert's ability to pick out even the most demanding melodies, as well as a deadpan and apparently offhand delivery.

'It might have something to do with the fact that I listened to him from a very early age,' she nods. 'My parents encouraged me to be a singer who didn't have a lot of vibrato and who hit the notes right on the head. I suppose that's what they liked about Robert, too.'

Where Karen's originals had been understated, as stripped down as *Old Rottenhat* or *Dondestan*, the tunes in Robert's hands became lacquered and lush. Much of the change in palette is down to the 'tron': a sort of human synthesiser, and the ultimate expression of his voice-as-

> Karen Mantler with her cat, Arnold.

instrument muddy mouth technique. 'Robert said, "I'm going to sample you singing every note in an octave," Karen remembers. '"My engineer can make it so that that's now the synth sound, and I can play your voice as I want." He said, "I think everybody should have their own tron." So there was an Alfie-o-tron, and the engineer had one. And then, on the later record, Brian Eno had an Enotron. I thought it was a great way to combine old-fashioned mellotron with the new digital age.'

As well as her own three compositions, Karen appeared on *Insensatez*, an after-the-affair ballad by Brazil's Antônio Carlos Jobim. Robert, again, was looking for beauty where it was least expected. Bossa can be dismissed as elevator music by those who don't look beyond *Girl from Ipanema*, but it is in fact a supple and sophisticated blend of *samba-canção* and jazz – and, back in the late 1950s and early 1960s, it was the radical soundtrack to a newly emergent Brazil.

Though Meltdown was an important influence on *Cuckooland*, one of the album's most prominent guests had not played at the festival. Instead, Gilad Atzmon had been introduced to Robert by his old friend Chris Searle. 'I was a great admirer of Gilad's music,' explains the *Morning Star* jazz critic, 'and of his political commitment towards the Palestinians. And obviously Robert was, too. I think they're kindred spirits. Both with a very beautiful conception of music and ordinary people and political struggle.' Gilad's approach to jazz as a music of resistance, suggests Searle, is reminiscent of South African exiles such as The Blue Notes. Rather than South African township music, however, his sound draws on the folk music of Eastern Europe, North Africa and the Middle East. On *Cuckooland*, he played flute and clarinet on the Arabic *La Ahada Yalam* and the Jobim bossa nova, as well as soprano, alto and tenor saxophones on more obviously jazz-indebted tracks such as *Old Europe*.

Born in Israel but resident in the UK, Atzmon is a prolific writer of online polemic as well as the author of several books. He is, says Wyatt, 'the most radical pro-Palestinian I know'. For Robert, who still refers to Israel as 'occupied Palestine', the reed player's politics only added to the appeal. Like Henry Cow, Jerry Dammers and Charlie Haden, Atzmon represented a meeting of the crosshairs: the thin black perpendicular lines of politics and music.

Keen to feature the saxophonist on his next album, Wyatt went to see him perform in nearby Cleethorpes. When the gig finished, however, Robert lost his nerve – and Alfie had to approach Gilad in her husband's place. 'Alfie came to me,' recalls Gilad. 'She told me, "My husband is very shy. He really wants to come and talk to you. Is it OK with you?" I was just signing CDs. I said, "Yeah, for sure." He came in the wheelchair, and he said, "I'm an amateur musician, but I really like you and I would like you to record on my music." I was new to British modesty, because it doesn't exist in Jewish culture at all. And I told him, "Listen, man, for sure."'

It's hard to imagine any other musician who had just curated Meltdown claiming to be an amateur: evidence again of Robert's sometimes breathtaking diffidence. The gregarious Gilad, a true force of nature, represents the opposite personality extreme. In a typical performance with his band, he might refer to the Chilcot Inquiry into the UK's role in the Iraq War, describe Louis Armstrong as his favourite Palestinian composer, and dedicate a tune to 'the biggest assholes on the planet', shouting out the names of politicians in the snatched breaths between saxophone phrases. 'He is', chuckles Wyatt, 'a unique character. There is *nobody* like Gilad.'

'The first time I spoke to Gilad on the phone', Robert goes on, laughing at the memory, 'he said, "You know, Robert, I warn you, working with me is trouble." And I said, "I'm always in trouble, too. You get called a self-hating Jew, I get called a Stalinist. We're both used to this."' The two would work together regularly over the next decade, with Gilad's bassist Yaron Stavi soon another addition to Wyatt's imaginary band.

Like the band assembled for *Rock Bottom* and *Ruth Is Stranger Than Richard*, the *Cuckooland* musicians were a diverse bunch, fittingly for an album that combined pop with jazz, folk, bossa nova, Arabic music and even traces of the English classical tradition. It was one way to win the war against musical cliché: Robert later suggested he was 'a kind of folk musician representing an unknown tribe, of which there may be no other members'. With its sixteen tracks clocking in at just over seventy-five minutes, *Cuckooland* – released in October 2003 – was by some distance Wyatt's longest record. Through worrying that he didn't have enough songs, he laughs, he had ended up with too many: essentially a double album. Robert's solution was to split the record in half. Not doing much to counter the notion that he was quintessentially English, he even built in a thirty-second tea-break: 'A suitable place for those with tired ears to pause and resume listening later'.

The arrangements were richer and more complex than Robert had attempted in recent years. *Cuckoo Madame*, as Robert says, borrowed Benjamin Britten's almost bluesy habit of wavering between major and minor keys. But the track also featured a slowly swinging ride cymbal, taken straight from jazz. What might in Britten have been vocal or string

> Gilad Atzmon – Robert's troublemaking new collaborator.

parts, meanwhile, were here arranged for 'Karenotron': the sampled voice of Karen Mantler. 'There's a thing I can see now,' Wyatt explains, 'from *Rock Bottom* straight through to something like *Cuckooland*. On *Trickle Down*, what I'm singing is like an old English folk song: you could almost see it done by Fairport Convention. But in fact I got Yaron doing a jazz walking bass line all the way through it. And Brian Eno brought a Kaoss Pad, and I used that, joining in with my own cymbals. Just because I'm using the simple song element doesn't mean to say I have to use the sort of backing you'd associate with that. It's very simple, but it's just a freedom I feel allowed.'

With the help of engineer Jamie Johnson, Wyatt was finally nailing that elusive goal of upside-down – or, perhaps, back-to-front – jazz-rock. 'I was able to do jazz, but backwards,' explains Robert. 'Jazz normally starts out from a fixed point and then goes into improvisation. Whereas I would take lots of notes and solos, whether it was Gilad or bass notes of Yaron's or David Gilmour's guitar parts, and edit them

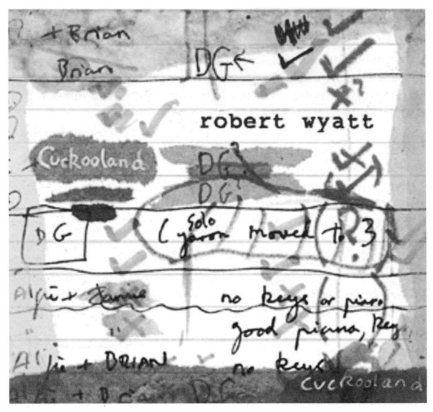

> Robert's notes for *Cuckooland* transformed into cover art.

and edit them and edit them, almost note by note. Jamie was amazingly skilful. I'd say, "After the eighth bar, there's a B-flat; we don't need that." And he'd go there and nip it. It was that precise. And I'd seldom worked with anybody who actually knew what I meant and could do it.'

More than anything, however, it is Robert's vocals that define the album. His singing, on *Old Europe*, for instance, is often double-tracked, like a double-exposed photograph – just as it had been back on the first Soft Machine album. Though Wyatt dismissed his voice as a wino's mutter, *Cuckooland* is in fact the work of a singer who knows himself utterly: the lost notes at the top of his range were more than made up for in maturity. When Robert sings, on *Just a Bit*, that touching wood is 'just a bit maaaaaaad', it is no accident that his voice breaks affectingly, and not a little madly, halfway through that extended final word.

At the same time, Alfie's artwork, based on Robert's working notes, suggests an enduring childlike aspect. Bordered in green and yellow, the cover takes as its starting point his scribbled jottings, a multicoloured riot of note names, arrows, ticks, crosses and question marks. Inside, we are treated to more detailed documentation of an autodidact's musical shorthand. Handwritten notes in red crayon and blue biro include 'add bass guitar back in', 'reduce/trim/edit(?)' and 'chorus words – too many'. Once again, the notes show that, for all its apparent scruffiness and spontaneity, Wyatt's music was meticulously precise.

'*Cuckooland* feels unfinished and maybe unfinishable,' said New York's *Village Voice*. 'It's got some of Wyatt's most nuanced singing, and oodles of casual charm; the amateur trumpet playing is right on.' (They weren't so keen, however, on the production: 'some of the most god-awful synthesiser presets ever'.)

The reception in the UK was more positive. *The Wire* magazine made it their record of the year. Some critics regarded the album as a career pinnacle, not something that would have been said, in 2003, of many of Wyatt's baby-boomer contemporaries. Alfie, too, believes it could be Robert's most coherent and mature record. 'It's a journey, a fantastic journey, which is totally satisfying to me. I haven't got any quibbles about it. I think that's terribly difficult to achieve.'

–»»««– –»»««– –»»««–

Cuckooland was shortlisted for the 2004 Mercury Music Prize, the most prestigious music award in the UK. Set up by Simon Frith, music journalist, sociologist and brother of former Henry Cow guitarist Fred, the award aims to identify the finest UK album of the year, in any genre. Wyatt, pushing sixty, found himself shortlisted alongside singer Amy Winehouse and acts even further within the pop mainstream: Joss Stone, Snow Patrol, Keane.

Although understandably unwilling to shed light on the secret workings of the Mercury panel, Simon Frith does remember that judges less familiar with Wyatt's back catalogue tended to be, if anything, even *more* in favour of his nomination. The appeal of *Cuckooland*, he remembers, lay in its 'absolute clarity of sensibility – and it was also an utterly charming album'. Ryko's Andy Childs says that, although hugely gratifying, he didn't find the nomination surprising: 'I knew it was such a fantastic record and I knew Robert's standing was at such a level that you couldn't ignore it. I don't think anyone could ignore the fact that *Shleep* wasn't a one-off. He'd come back and made an even better record.'

Childs also recalls the award ceremony with warmth: 'It was a great evening, because everybody wanted to talk to Robert. Amy Winehouse, all these people – they all wanted to meet Robert. One by one they came to his table and paid homage, because he is such a respected figure and all those people know of him.'

In the end, the prize went to Glaswegian indie rock act Franz Ferdinand. But winning the Mercury, infamously, can be a curse: it is those on the shortlist that arguably benefit most. Coming after Meltdown, as well as the critical acclaim afforded both *Shleep* and *Cuckooland*, the nomination was another step in establishing Robert's now regularly mooted status as a national treasure.

And the momentum continued to build. Robert recorded a track for the Radio 3 poetry show *The Verb*, on which the secular Christian pondered how the Ten Commandments might be dusted off for the modern age. More cheekily biblical was his spoken word contribution to *Musik/Re-Arranging the 20th Century* by Gilad Atzmon's Orient House Ensemble: 'In the beginning was the Bird, and the Bird was bop.'

Wyatt also appeared, alongside Danish singer-songwriter Susi Hyldgaard, on *Hide and Seek*, Mike Mantler's 2001 'suite of songs and interludes' based on a short play by the American novelist and essayist Paul Auster. There was another album with John Greaves, too. 'I opportunistically went to grab him,' says Greaves, of Robert's contribution to 2004's *Chansons*, 'because I heard he was in Paris, and he was staying in a hotel about a hundred metres away from the studio I record in. Alfie said, "You can only have him for half an hour, don't get drunk." So we obviously ordered lots of wine.'

Robert even got a call from Björk, then working on the all-vocal *Medulla*, her own 'muddy mouth' album, which also featured an Inuit throat singer, human beatboxers and Mike Patton of Faith No More and Mr Bungle. 'Robert has got an incredible range in his voice,' Björk explains. 'It's similar to Thom Yorke, that tenor. Really high, gentle notes. Really sensitive. I was trying to find somebody with a voice that sounded very individual, that was a character. You know what it's like: you have your rock singers, soul singers. Robert is not really like that. He has maybe a little bit of folk in it, somehow. I was really trying to avoid genres, of course. But if there was one genre with *Medulla*, I think folk was something I was trying to tap into.'

Although Wyatt normally protests his ignorance of contemporary culture, he was familiar with Björk's output, and describes himself as 'starstruck' when she came to see him in Louth. It's not a term he uses about Hendrix or Eno or Weller or Gilmour or Costello. So nervous did he feel, in fact, that he ended up asking her to leave the house during

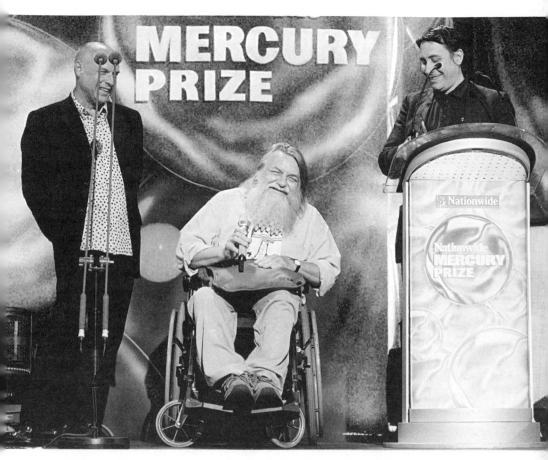

> Robert collects his Mercury gong from Brian Eno and Jools Holland.

his takes, which were recorded with producer and engineer Valgeir Sigurðsson. 'I threw everything at it,' Wyatt recalls. 'I double-tracked, I did harmonies, I did two octaves. Then, when she came back, I said: "In case any of those notes aren't any use, I'll sing you some notes." So I did an octave or two, just note by note.'

Björk was allowed to return to the house when the session was complete. Joined by various friends, she then spent the evening with Robert and Alfie, listening to Sun Ra and John Cage records. Robert had a ball – 'She was everything that you might hope she would be: she was funny, she was witty, she was amazing to look at' – and so did Björk. 'It really felt like you were visiting another little world,' she recalls. 'And it was really very charming. They've got a little two-people galaxy that functions, and has its dark sides and its harmonious sides. And they're not trying to hide, either. They were very blunt and honest, both of them.' Two tracks from the session ended up on *Medulla*, both as immersive as memory foam. *Oceania* featured the 'Wyattatron': Robert's voice reinvented as human synth. It is, says Valgeir Sigurðsson, 'a beautiful instrument' – and so imbued with personality that recording Robert for his sample library, he recalls, felt like taking photos of an indigenous tribesman.

Two more compilations emerged, too: *Solar Flares Burn for You*, an assembly of unreleased tracks, and the unashamedly titled *His Greatest Misses*. Doing the most to boost Wyatt's profile, however, was BBC4's *Free Will and Testament: The Robert Wyatt Story*, a full-length documentary on the self-confessed woolgatherer. 'As far as I'm concerned,' runs Robert's introductory voiceover, 'I'm dreaming all the time. The only difference is that I come up for daylight and other people the way a whale has to come up for air.' Directed by Mark Kidel, *Free Will and Testament* was an impressive film, celebrating Robert's fifty-year career while allowing its subject to remain entirely honest and self-effacing. Sam Ellidge says he learned more about his dad from the documentary than from a lifetime of conversation. 'I go on the internet and I do searches. I mean, why should you find out about your dad by the internet? I love him to bits, but he drives me absolutely nuts.'

Best of all, *Free Will and Testament* found Robert performing, albeit without a live audience. He runs through key works from *Sea Song* to *Free Will and Testament*, with a band that includes Annie Whitehead, Paul Weller and keyboard player Janette Mason. Robert looks surprisingly relaxed during these filmed performances. Cigarette in hand, peering at the lyrics through reading specs, he clicks his fingers and even manages the occasional smile.

The musicians, many now firm friends, were equally enthusiastic. 'I loved it,' Paul Weller recalls. 'The sound wasn't great, but aside from that, everything was great. And it was great to actually see Robert performing. I remember at the time, probably because I was pissed as well, I kept bugging him about live shows.' Like all Wyattophiles, Weller still dreams of an actual headline gig, although he is reconciled to the fact that it will probably never happen.

In August 2004, however, Björk performed the track *Oceania* – replete with Robert's sampled vocals – at the opening ceremony for the Athens Olympic Games. 'It is,' laughs the stage-fright victim, 'the only time I've sung to millions all around the world.'

21

THAT LOOK IN YOUR EYES

Comicopera and getting on the wagon

Mojo magazine's 2005 award ceremony, held at Porchester Hall in central London, saw prizes going to Paul Weller, Steve Earle, Jeff Beck, Dr John, Gang of Four, Roy Harper and The Fall. The most prestigious award, 'the ultimate accolade that celebrates a unique contribution as we know it', was the Lifetime Achievement Award. The presenter was David Gilmour. The winner was Robert Wyatt.

In the wake of *Shleep* and *Cuckooland*, Meltdown and the 2004 Mercury nomination, Wyatt was enjoying an Indian summer. When David Gilmour recorded *On an Island*, his first solo album in twenty-two years, Robert was a natural guest to play cornet on the dozy, delicate *Then I Close My Eyes*. And, although their brief Southbank Centre performance had left him literally trembling with fear, Gilmour somehow managed to persuade Wyatt to go onstage at the Royal Albert Hall in 2006. 'He has one of those voices which just tear at your soul,' says Gilmour. 'There's the old cliché about singing the phone book, but he really does have a voice which endears itself to you and tugs at the heartstrings. But he's also a very, very accomplished musician. He still

> Back at the Royal Albert Hall: David Gilmour – just about the only man who can get Robert onstage – salutes his cornet solo on *Then I Close My Eyes*.

does drumming things, in the way that he can do it. And he has always had a very original take on everything that goes on in life – lyrically and in all his thought processes. He doesn't come at things from the usual angle.'

Having wheeled onto the stage, Robert sat, fag in mouth, for five minutes without playing a note. But, when the time came, his distilled, deeply lyrical cornet solo curled like smoke above Gilmour's gently looping guitar part. The DVD *Remember That Night* captures the guitarist's broad, and possibly relieved, smile as Robert takes off.

Wyatt remembers the show with warmth, particularly as it also featured the Floyd's drummer Nick Mason and keyboard player Rick Wright – who would die of cancer in 2008. 'It was very nice onstage with Rick,' recalls Robert of the man who had so influenced his organ playing on *Rock Bottom*. 'I didn't know that was more or less the last time we'd see him. It was very sad, because he was working on a solo LP, and in fact I was plucking up courage to ask if I could sing on it. That didn't happen, of course. But I was so glad I got that moment with him onstage.'

The guest outings nonetheless continued to stack up. Wyatt joined his old friend Brian Hopper on 2005's *If Ever I Am*, while Steve Nieve, who had played piano on *Shipbuilding*, invited him to contribute to the album version of *Welcome to the Voice*, a modern opera on the theme of class conflict. 'Post-classical' composer Max Richter persuaded Robert to read passages by Japanese author Haruki Murakami on his 2006 album *Songs from Before*. And then Robert teamed up again with Brian Eno to record a track for *Plague Songs*, linked to a contemporary version of the Book of Exodus being staged in Margate, Kent – not too far from Robert's adolescent home. The artists, who included Scott Walker and Laurie Anderson, were each asked to contribute a piece based on one of the biblical plagues. 'That was really good,' Wyatt told *Pitchfork*, about working with Eno on their track, *Flies*. 'He said to me, "Robert, can you do me some flies?" So I said, right, great! So I imagined I was a fly – I method-acted my way into being a swarm of flies. And then we found out the tempo of *Superfly* by Curtis Mayfield, so that was obviously going to be the bpm. And I thought I'd do it in the key of F for Fly. But it's basically atonal. And then Brian put a song around it. It was a very specific request!'

The Mojo award, which sits unobtrusively on Wyatt's mantelpiece, alongside a small trophy celebrating his Mercury nomination, could have meant that Robert's best work was behind him; even that his back catalogue was complete. But, perhaps because he hadn't made a rock star's fortune, or perhaps because, still plagued by self-doubt, he wasn't fully happy with anything in his back catalogue, Robert was also working towards a new album of his own – albeit at his usual slow pace.

–»)》«– –»)》«– –»)》«–

As a title, *Comicopera* – the next Robert Wyatt album – was open to multiple interpretations. Most obviously, it referred to the light, often comical operas by the likes of Jacques Offenbach or Gilbert and Sullivan, to whom Robert had been introduced as a child by his half-brother Julian. But the album title, typically, was a pun: it could be a Commie cornucopia or, for those who spoke Spanish, something like a 'funny pear' as well. The 'comic strip' aspect, meanwhile, was brought out in Alfie's front cover image, which was divided into four boxes, each with its own abstract speech bubble.

One of Wyatt's more masochistic habits is to compare his albums to the output of Charles Mingus, truly a Duke Ellington for the Civil

Rights era. On *Comicopera*, Robert set out to capture some of the bassist's grit and growl. Compared to the polish of *Cuckooland*, it felt like unvarnished wood. 'Usually what happens', he explains, 'is that on every record I get something right that I hadn't got right before, and only retrospectively I realise I'd missed something else. So on *Cuckooland*, I got the lightness, music-made-in-a-floating-cloud feel that I wanted. But then, the Mingus test. I just thought: "Where's the blood? Where's the bone-crunching rawness?" So, in response to *Cuckooland*, I thought: "Get more physical again, more biting sound of the instruments, more drama in the light and shade." *Cuckooland* was about an almost gaseous fluidity. *Comicopera* was much more about solid objects, chunks of sound, and to hell with continuity.'

The record features Karenotron, Enotron and Monicatron: the voices of Karen Mantler, Brian Eno and Brazilian singer Monica Vasconcelos, each sampled and turned into a highly personalised keyboard sound. Yet *Comicopera* draws more heavily on live instruments. Joining Annie Whitehead and Gilad Atzmon were musicians from beyond jazz: Brian Eno, Phil Manzanera, Paul Weller, even former Matching Mole member Dave Sinclair, a favour Robert would repay by appearing on the keyboard player's 2011 album, *Stream*.

Where *Cuckooland* had been split in half, *Comicopera* came divided neatly into thirds. The first segment, subtitled *Lost in Noise*, opens with Anja Garbarek's ethereal *Stay Tuned*, featuring a theremin-like soprano from vocalist and composer Seaming To. The opening section of the record is dominated by *Just As You Are* – an unusually straightforward number, of the sort Wyatt would normally attempt only if borrowed from another writer. In fact he co-wrote the track with Alfie, and regards it as something of a breakthrough: 'I was very affected by people like Johnny Cash, and the completely uncryptic, unhidden, completely straight song about life that anybody might be able to understand. That very straight, uncomplicated honesty that you get in the best country music, which I'd never listened to before at all.'

Country music was not the typical home of a Marxist jazz fan. Brian Eno, however, sees much of Wyatt's output as falling within the genre: 'He writes about things that you could think about as a grown-up', Eno explains. 'Whereas – I'm not putting pop music down when I say this – but it's mostly about the kind of things that you think about as an adolescent. Flirting and sex and dancing and that kind of thing. It mostly belongs to your adolescent and student years. Pop records don't tend to be about mortgages and who's going to look after the children if we separate, which are the kind of things that country records are about.'

'Robert's stuff has always been quite grown-up in that respect,' continues Eno. 'Even the closeness of his relationship with Alfie: when he sings about that on the records, he doesn't sing about it as a teenager. It's as a grown-up, complex emotional relationship. Not like: "Ga-ga, I'm in love." It's more like: "The two of us have stuck with each other, which is lucky because we get on quite well." That's a country music sentiment, to me.'

If *Just As You Are* is a country tune, it is a predictably idiosyncratic one. It has the candour we expect of the genre, and an archetypal subject in drink and domestic disharmony. Yet the setting is not Nashville but Lincolnshire, and the opening verses are sung by Monica Vasconcelos, a singer-songwriter better known for jazz-tinged bossa nova:

> *It's that look in your eyes,*
> *telling me lies,*
> *So many promises broken*
> *What can I do?*
> *What should I do?*
> *Try to love you*
> *Just as you are?*

The theme of solitude in age also comes through on two other co-written songs: *You You* (about widowhood) and *A.W.O.L.* (about Alfie's mother's dementia). 'They're all about loss of some sort,' Alfie explained to David Toop; 'loss of trust, loss of husband, loss of memory. It's about grieving, actually. It's not anger, really. We know a lot of widows at the moment. There's a lot of people like Sheila Peel, Helen Walters, Paul Haines's wife, Jo. People who've been part of a partnership, absolutely solid, and their husbands have died. It's really horrible, tragic. So there's thinking about them in *You You* and *A.W.O.L.*'

As well as the prospect of losing a husband to quietus, however, *Just As You Are* was about a more urgent threat for Alfie: losing him to drink. When Robert joined Monica Vasconcelos, two and a half minutes in, the song developed into a painfully autobiographical account of a relationship unravelling.

> *It's that look in your eyes,*
> *I know you despise me,*

For not being stronger...
Will you leave? Will you stay?
There may come a day
When I'm weak and I'm stupid no longer

The unravelling would go still further once the record was finished. As an album, however, *Comicopera* soon shifts focus away from the domestic. *Be Serious*, a guitar-driven jazz shuffle, sees Wyatt returning to the familiar subject of religious belief. The tone is mischievous, but the sentiment – envy of Christians and Muslims and Hindus and Jews because, as an atheist, 'I got no-one to turn to when I'm sinking in the shit' – is sincere. 'I do envy people who have a cushion of religion to protect them,' Robert explains, 'like a warm coat against the cold harsh winter of reality.'

On the Town Square evokes Wyatt's favourite haunt in Louth. But the duet between saxophonist Gilad Atzmon and steelpan virtuoso Orphy Robinson was also inspired by a Miles Davis and Gil Evans masterpiece, 1960's *Sketches of Spain*. 'I wanted this sense of when a carnival is breaking up,' explains Robert. 'The sense of people all completely out of sync, rattling here, rattling there and gradually grouping up around Gilad and Orphy as they came into focus.'

Comicopera then becomes progressively darker during its middle section, *The Here and Now*, as its scope expands to take in the war in Iraq. As an Englishman whose democratically elected leader had trotted into combat behind Bush, Robert felt implicated. *A Beautiful War* is about so-called smart bombs, which even the US Air Force now acknowledges weren't quite as smart as was claimed at the time. *Out of the Blue* shifts perspective to the effect of those bombs as they fell to the ground. Alfie's lyrics were inspired by TV footage of a Lebanese woman left stupefied after her house had been blown to smithereens. From the apparently innocent opening detail, 'No need to wipe your feet, the welcome mat's not there', the track builds over jarring, jagged electronics and shards of free-jazz brass. We hear that 'something unbelievable has happened to the floor', that the stairs have gone, and finally that the house has been blown apart. The climax comes with the repeated line: 'You've planted all your ever-lasting hatred in my heart.' Robert's voice remains neutral, but it is the angriest line he has ever recorded – and one, he says, he would never have written himself.

'I rarely get that up close and personal to the world,' he explains. 'I do *Free Will and Testament* or something like that, but if I'm writing about

> Studio engineer Jamie Johnson at work on *Comicopera*.

the world, I tend to do something more abstract. But Alfie does them together, which is her contribution. Jamie Johnson, the engineer, had never heard me sing words like "hate" before. But I was very proud of it. I thought, "That's my Alfie. She tells it like it is."'

In *Away with the Fairies*, which opens the third section of the album, Robert abandons the English language for Spanish and Italian, achieving in song the migration he couldn't manage in real life. Wyatt explained at the time to *Music OMH*, 'Side 3 is, you know what? I'm fed up with English-speaking people. I'm going to go away with the fairies. I sing in Italian and I do a bit of surrealism, free improvisation, and end up with a romantic revolutionary song of the '60s, a hymn to Che

369

Guevara. Just to say, that's my generation, the kind of hope that kept us going. I'm not saying it worked or didn't, but without these little dreams and hopes, I couldn't survive.'

The lengthy *Canción de Julieta* is a high point of this final section. Powered by a lithe bass line, it is warm and approachable despite its Soft Machine-esque 11/8 time signature. The lyrics come from Federico García Lorca, the Spanish playwright and poet shot by a right-wing firing squad during the Spanish Civil War. The other highlight is *Hasta Siempre, Comandante*, written by Castroist songwriter Carlos Puebla but transformed by Robert into stop-start Afro-Cuban jazz. As with *Canción de Julieta*, the backstory was bleak – but, again, Robert approached it, without apology, from the perspective of a dreamer.

'*Hasta Siempre, Comandante* is a very poignant song that was written for Che Guevara when he left Cuba to go off and, as we know, get assassinated,' he explains. 'It's not about the political realities of Latin America, it's about evoking the dreams of the time, both in music and on record. So where these two lines meet, that's my crosshairs. That's what I aim at.'

⤙⤚ ⤙⤚ ⤙⤚

By the time *Comicopera* was finished, Rykodisc had been taken over by Warner Music Group. Wyatt couldn't see himself on a major label, especially since Andy Childs had left in the merger. And so, free to leave under the deal struck by Alfie and Geoff Travis, he looked around for an alternative home. Domino, a leading independent label, seemed the perfect option: Robert had already signed a publishing deal with the company, and they agreed to the same, artist-friendly terms he had enjoyed with Ryko/Hannibal. Andy Childs helped make the deal, just as Geoff Travis had eased Robert's transition from Rough Trade to Rykodisc; few artists in popular music inspire such loyalty.

Comicopera was released by Domino in October 2007. Like *Cuckooland*, it was a long album. 'There was a sense on the last couple of records', Wyatt explains, 'that I thought: "This may be the last thing I ever do." I'm in my sixties, things happen around us. And it's not just a question of things happening to me. I thought, "What about when Alfie's mum dies? Who's going to be able to sit around writing songs when we're going through all that?" So there was just a sense that you've got to get things done while you can. This is borrowed time, the twenty-first century. I'm a twentieth-century person.'

Comicopera was not, thankfully, the last time Robert would appear on record – but it is, to date, his last solo album. The hope is that his creative gestation period simply remains elephantine. But even if the interminable fishing trip for new melodies proves fruitless, *Comicopera* is a record of which even the self-effacing Wyatt can be proud. It was among *Mojo* magazine's top ten albums of 2007: 'It's hard to imagine a record more original or full of life, from any artist of any age, emerging this year'. *The Wire* named it their record of the year, while *Uncut* went as far as to dub *Comicopera* 'Wyatt's finest work ever'. The broadsheets loved it, too: 'It is not often that one has the chance to recommend a concept album by a 62-year-old, wheelchair-bound, Marxist songwriter with a beard,' wrote Sean O'Hagan of the *Observer*, 'but you really should

› Alfie's minimalist strip-cartoon cover for *Comicopera*.

beg, steal, borrow or illegally download a copy of Robert Wyatt's new CD, *Comicopera*, as soon as you can.'

While some might see *Comicopera* as the album of 2007, however, Alfie – who had co-written four of its songs – finds it too painful to listen to. 'It's really sad,' she sighs, 'because I now associate Robert doing music with this drunk. And I've totally gone off listening to anything he does, anything new. It's just danger.'

Despite the counselling prior to *Shleep*, Robert still required alcohol to give him what Jean Rhys, one of his favourite authors, called 'fire and wings'. 'It gave me that thing that makes alcoholics so tiresome,' he admits. 'This egomaniacal narcissism. Unfortunately, it's what I find I have to feel in order to be bothered to make music. I have to think that the next note really matters, and that nothing *else* matters. It doesn't matter if I don't eat properly, if I bugger up a relationship. I've got to get the next tune right. Objectively, intellectually, you know this is tosh. But, subjectively, that's the only way I can get the fuel hot enough to write a song.'

'Quite a few times Alfie would go out, to do something in London, and he'd be caning it before she'd get back,' recalls Jamie Johnson of recording *Comicopera*. 'But she would always know. When she got back, she'd just have to look in his eyes, and she would know. And there was a bit of secret drinking, chucking stuff in tea so that she wouldn't know. So he was obviously on the one hand saying to her, "Look, I'm stopping and I'm not doing it", but needing it to do the performance.'

Wyatt had been drinking fairly heavily since the 1968 Hendrix tour, but he had usually been able to moderate his intake when not writing or recording. This time, however, the boozing didn't drop when the tape stopped rolling. When he moved from wine to vodka, the usually empathetic Wyatt became as self-centred in his personal life, as he felt he needed to be in the studio.

Alfie was no teetotaller: when she's drunk, as we know from *Sea Song*, she's 'terrific'. 'We'd always got drunk,' she says, 'and he'd got drunk and stupid, but it wasn't secret and, in the mornings, and hidden bottles, and cross-eyed, actually, all day. I mean, he was a stupid person all day long. There was not a moment when his brain was working. And then pretending he wasn't drinking, just lying – and lying, I can't bear.'

Upset by the deviousness and deception, Alfie was also alarmed to find herself suddenly responsible for quality control – particularly since she had co-written several of the best songs. 'A lot of the time when Robert was drunk, I think he wasn't doing things well enough,' she recalls. 'I was scared of him just being careless and just not thinking about the detail enough. By the skin of his teeth he scraped through it, but there were moments where I thought, "What the fuck is he doing? This isn't going to work, it's going to rebound on him, and then he's going to be *really* destroyed." So it was touch and go.'

There were non-musical problems, too. Robert concedes that the drinking played havoc with his physical condition: 'If you're paraplegic, it's really complicated. It takes you quite a while in hospital just to learn how to get dressed and undressed. Drunk, it's just a real struggle.' He also admits that the drinking led to 'loutish behaviour, tempers and argufying'. 'The only time Robert is nasty,' confirms Alfie, 'is in response to other people's stupidity. He's had a history of absolutely ruining social occasions by anger at somebody's thoughtless, stupid remark – because he was drunk, and the inhibitions had gone.'

As well as Robert, Alfie was looking after her increasingly senile mother, Irena, by now living with them on Queen Street. 'She had had a stroke. So I had a doolally mother and a drunk. It was really lonely. I just couldn't deal with it any more. In a way it was a vicious circle, because the more he was like that, the more I obviously despised him. That song, *Just As You Are*, that's it: I look at him, I can see he's drunk, and he looks at me and says, "I can see you despise me." So that made him drink more. So our relationship just *wasn't*. It was one of hate and fear.'

Eventually, recalls Alfie, it reached crisis point. 'I thought, a) you're going to kill yourself, if not by the booze then by falling out of the chair and hitting your head on the pavement. And b) I married him – I can't go out for walks with him, can't go out dancing. There are loads of things we can't do. What have we got? Our brains. Right. But if he decides to pickle his brain, what have I got? What's the point of him? No point at all.' She's able to laugh now, but at the time, with her senile mum living with them too, it was too much to bear. 'I said he'd have to go.'

–»» «« – –»» «« – –»» «« –

Faced with Alfie's ultimatum (get sober or get out) and the chilling realisation that he had isolated his wife, Robert enrolled at Alcoholics Anonymous. He attended every Sunday from 4 March 2007: Alfie still has the date marked on the back of an envelope. He had nine relapses, also marked on the envelope. But within a year he was teetotal. 'He's done it,' says Alfie. 'He's come through. I've got Robert back. It's wonderful. I've got my pal, my best friend.'

Today, Robert regrets the amount of time he spent behaving 'like a complete idiot... All this drinking malarkey, that's childish in a bad way. I know children don't drink, but you know what I mean. Of *course* you can get a buzz having a drink, every kid on the block on a Saturday night knows that. That's not *enough*. But in my idiocy, I have let that be enough for acres of time.'

Wyatt admits to dreaming 'once in a blue moon' of a glass of wine, while listening to Motown records, but says the thought never lasts more than a couple of minutes. And, he insists, he doesn't miss the vodka at all. Staying on the wagon, however, hasn't been quite that painless. For one thing, Alfie misses the days before Robert's drinking got out of hand: 'We've had lots of jolly times drunk,' she sighs, 'especially when I was drinking as well. I miss that aspect of it. I'm really sad at the idea that we can't sit on the beach in Spain any more with a big jug of sangria, watching the waves, getting tiddly, and saying how nice life is and how much we like each other.'

Wyatt himself happens to have a stout constitution, and was for a long time even spared hangovers. But his drinking took a physical, as well as emotional, toll on Alfie. Tasked with holding the household together while Robert was in his cups, she eventually found herself unable to get out of bed for weeks on end. 'I didn't know what it was,' says Alfie. 'I was just wasted, I couldn't get up. I thought I was physically ill, but the doctor said, "No, you're depressed." I thought, "Oh shit, they always say that. I don't want to take any bloody pills." I'd had terrible flu, and that often leaves you quite vulnerable. But when one of you is going through some kind of trauma, the other one's supposed to do all the right things. Well, I never seemed to have a moment when I could actually collapse and have my own trauma. So maybe it was a result of years of just keeping going, being the grown-up.'

Alfie had seemed indomitable – but after four decades as the mainstay of Robert's personal and professional life, she had succumbed to a kind of post-traumatic stress. When she developed age-related macular degeneration, a progressive blindness aggravated by cigarette smoke, she and Robert even gave up smoking.

As well as giving up alcohol and cigarettes, what Robert calls his 'climb back to respect' within the household involved spending time with Alfie's mother, Irena. 'Although Alfie was able to take care of all the practical things,' he explains, 'she would get impatient with her mum's doo-lalliness. I've spent a lot of my life in Doo-lallyland. And so I was able to keep Irena company a lot. I'd talk to her, take her out. We'd have these bonkers conversations and I was able to follow them completely.

> Robert at the unfairground.

It was my clumsy way to try and do something for Alfie, to really be a
friend to her mum. I wasn't much practical use – I wasn't *any*. But I just
thought: "I've got a role here in this house.'"

The fag-free year ended with Irena's death in 2009: Robert and Alfie
both caved in the day before the funeral. But, though the rhythm and
ritual of cigarettes has returned, the booze has not. After three months,
Alfie came off the antidepressants – and, slowly, she and Robert began
to piece things back together. It helped that Delfina Entrecanales, the
'fairy godmother' at whose farm Robert had recorded the bulk of *Rock
Bottom*, paid for the expensive eye injections that go some way towards
treating Alfie's eye condition, until they became available on the NHS. It
helped, too, that Robert's confidence had been bolstered by the success of

his last three albums: 'Even though I was in trouble after *Comicopera*,' he explains, 'that and the two records before had got me out of this thing of my life being over. It clearly wasn't.'

Irena's death served at least to unite Robert and Alfie in grief. But the most important change was Robert's newfound sobriety. 'So then,' says Robert, 'it was just a question of, I can't help Alfie, but trying to avoid making it *harder* for Alfie in the future. And that's where we are now. We came together when I stopped drinking and have been, I think, fine ever since.'

22

WHAT'S NEW?

The eight bars Robert got right

In 2009, Wyatt's entire solo catalogue, with the exception of 1970's *The End of an Ear*, was re-released by Domino as a box set: seven studio albums, plus the *Nothing Can Stop Us* compilation, the Drury Lane live album and the collection of EPs. The media response was both passionate and panoramic, with features appearing everywhere from *Wire* magazine to the *Telegraph* and *Spectator*.

The collaborations continued, too, and were no less diverse. One minute Robert was appearing as a drummer on *Strange Overtones*, a gospel funk number by Brian Eno and David Byrne; the next he was playing piano and trumpet on Paul Weller's *Song for Alice*, a tribute to jazz harpist Alice Coltrane. He also recorded *A Season in Hell* for BBC Radio 3, singing words by Arthur Rimbaud set to music by the Bristol-based composer Elizabeth Purnell.

Wyatt – or at least the Wyattatron – featured on Kevin Ayers' first studio album in fifteen years, 2007's *The Unfairground*. With Kevin back from his self-imposed exile in France, the old friends spent 'a lovely couple of hours' in Phil Manzanera's studio. 'I was very touched by that,' Robert recalls. 'Just a little hello from the past.' Far removed from the droll and languid pop of Ayers' album was Wyatt's collaboration with Kevin's successor in The Soft Machine, Hugh Hopper. Clear Frame were a free improv group, also featuring Charles Hayward, Lol Coxhill and Orphy Robinson, who had played on *Comicopera*. Wyatt contributed 'Chet Baker meets Don Cherry' cornet to the group's self-titled album, released in 2008.

Sometimes he was repaying favours: Robert sang with Monica Vasconcelos, the Brazilian vocalist who had joined him on *Just As You Are*, on her 2008 album *Hih*. Other collaborations were serendipitous: Robert joined Billy Bragg in the studio after happening upon the punk-folk singer in Louth. Left-wing but some distance from the CPGB, Bragg's *Mr Love & Justice* record tackled extraordinary rendition and the Iraq War. *I Keep Faith*, to which Robert contributed choirboy backing vocals, was a call to stand one's ground in an age of personal and political change. 'For a Stalinist,' Bragg said later, 'he really knows how to sing like an angel.'

> Hot Chip: Alexis Taylor is standing, in the lumberjack jacket.

Invitations arrived from younger musicians, too. Wyatt doesn't say yes to everything: Alfie, in particular, is aware of the danger of his becoming the 'musician's musician', bestowing credibility on a younger generation. But it is striking that Wyatt's horizons have not narrowed with age. He sang *Camouflage*, a fragile duet with Berlin's Barbara Morgenstern, and joined Swedish singer-songwriter Jeanette Lindström on the gently shimmering *The River*, on her award-winning album *Attitude & Orbit Control*. Most significantly, perhaps, in late 2008 Robert went into the studio with electronic pop act Hot Chip.

The group had already remixed *This Summer Night*, a collaboration between Wyatt and French producer and label boss Bertrand Burgalat that featured lyrics by Alfie: in Robert's words, 'an imaginary, Philadelphia soul-inspired gay disco record from sometime in the 1970s'. Wyatt reworked three Hot Chip tracks in return. Already more thoughtful and folk-derived than the band's reputation for quirky, perky dancefloor tunes would suggest, they became, with the addition of Robert's vocal, softer and sadder than ever.

'That experience for us was fantastic', recalls Hot Chip co-founder Alexis Taylor, a Wyatt fan so committed that he had actually written the press release for *Comicopera* in 2007. 'He was so giving of himself and his time towards this music, and so quick at coming up with really good ideas', Taylor says. 'We brought a synthesiser along, thinking "Maybe Robert will like playing that." But actually he would just go quietly into the vocal booth, and add all these new percussion parts, do vocals, and then come out again. We'd all be listening to it while he was in there, just thinking: *this sounds amazing*. He invented a new counter-melody to go with *Made in the Dark*, which completely changes the feel of the song. He did cornet parts. He was working very quickly, but also working very hard, to do something for us.'

—»)(«— —»)(«— —»)(«—

The collaborations, like the box set, gave the impression that Wyatt was making new music. But, while he had always written slowly, he had *never* written sober. His muse was booze, and it just wasn't the same sitting at the piano with a cup of tea in the hand not holding a cigarette. Would he start writing safe, out-to-pasture songs? Now that he no longer had alcohol to drown the inner critic, would he be able to write at all?

At the time of writing, it is too soon to answer that question. There has been no solo album since 2007, although Robert did release a new record in 2010 as one third of a trio – alongside Gilad Atzmon and violinist Ros Stephen.

'I'd always wanted to do something with a singer,' says Stephen, best known for her tango group, Tango Siempre. 'And Robert's voice seemed absolutely perfect to work with strings, because his voice is incredibly beautiful, incredibly emotional, and there's a real honesty in there. He doesn't pretend to be an American. He is himself.'

On the whole, the finest moments on *For the Ghosts Within* turned out to be jazz standards. There had always been a jazz sensibility to Wyatt's music, but he now tackled head-on the music he had loved since adolescence. The tunes – *Laura, Wonderful World, Lush Life, What's New?, Round Midnight* – many dating from between the world wars – were almost defiantly anachronistic. But they reflected the fact that, having always been influenced by horn players more than singers, Robert was now warming to vocal jazz of an earlier era. 'Somebody said to me a few years ago,' recalls Robert, '"How would you like to end up?" I said, "Sitting in a piano bar playing old standards." I can't, but I seem to be drifting that way on my cornet. I just sit in my front room, just finding the notes, accompanying a really slow singer, to accommodate my technique – like Nat "King" Cole and Julie London. When all the other brain cells have died off, I hope to be left with enough to do that. And I'll die happy.'

Unlike most collaborations, described by Robert as 'a series of revolving dictatorships', *For the Ghosts Within* was a genuinely collective effort. The three figures on Alfie's front cover, a paper-cut reminiscent of Henri Matisse, emphasised the album's collaborative nature. Influenced by both Atzmon's Middle Eastern roots and Stephen's love of tango, this was the Real Book whirled around the world, then dipped in a warm bath of strings.

It was a risky strategy: 'This is the third project Ros and I have done together,' says the ever-unequivocal Gilad, 'and we are all the time surfing close to the wind in terms of cheesiness. We are on very dodgy territory. Tango with saxophone is a fucking disaster.' 'But,' adds Ros, 'it works when Gilad does it.' It works even better when Robert joins them. His thin voice could hardly have been further from the stereotypical crooner, but it cut through the schmaltzy strings like gin through a summer afternoon. And though he might have sounded offhand, almost distracted, as he tackled some of jazz's most imperishable compositions, Wyatt's pitching and phrasing were spot-on: the lifetime of listening had paid off.

> The jazz standards trio: Robert, Gilad Atzmon and Ros Stephen.

Gilad, who produced the album, had readied himself for six weeks at the mixing desk. In fact, the majority of Robert's vocals were laid down in just two days. 'Four bars into *Laura*,' says Gilad, 'twenty seconds into recording with Robert, it was clear that – and it's an amazing thing – he actually *owns* the music. Very few people on this planet benefit from having this capacity to own music once they touch it. In my musical career, I'd say three, maybe five people. You know, you invite them to play a twelve-bar solo, and they do something – and *my god, what's that?* This transforming moment.'

Laura, first released in 1945 and covered by Billy Eckstine, Julie London and Frank Sinatra, among others, is one of the most moving tracks Wyatt has ever recorded. His version is drenched in nostalgia for a period he was born too late to experience first hand – but which seems more and more precious and rare with passing years. 'It's like old family photographs,' explains Robert. 'The older it gets, and the fewer of us there are to whom this matters, the more poignant and important these musicians become. It's just my inner country, from which I will, of course, forever be an exile. It's my Palestine, my place, my imaginary land'.

'Nostalgia', nods Gilad, 'is the yearning for a past that has never been experienced, never been celebrated. And I think for Robert it is very clear. This is the music he loved all his life. And here he is, doing it.'

Every bit as yearning as *Laura* was Billy Strayhorn's *Lush Life*, a knowing choice for a sixty-five-year-old jazz lover who had just given up the booze. *What's New?*, another standard, was imbued with the rhythmic snap of tango, thanks to Ros Stephens' Sigamos String Quartet. Wyatt didn't like the lyrics to *In a Sentimental Mood*, written not by Duke Ellington but by manager Irving Mills and lyricist Manny Kurtz. So, with a mixture of reverence and irreverence, he hummed the melody. Equally uninspired by Bernie Hanighen's words to *Round Midnight*, he whistled Thelonious Monk's jazz perennial.

'There was actually a problem,' cackles Gilad, providing an insight into Alfie's role in the studio. 'Alfie doesn't like whistling. So we had to be

> Phil Manzanera in his home studio.

very quick, while she was making a coffee or out shopping, and we were anticipating a bit of a persuasion process. But she approved.'

Phil Manzanera, in whose studio Robert recorded his contributions to *For the Ghosts Within*, agrees that Alfie's role in the studio is 'incredibly, incredibly, incredibly important. I can't emphasise that enough... there is no Robert without Alfie. There just wouldn't have been any meaning to Robert's life. It's all there in the words – the words that he's been moved to write over the years about her, but also in her own words that he's used. And she hasn't had as much credit for that as she should have. Obviously, there's the visuals, all the covers, but it's not only that. She's the person that he bounces the ideas off. If she doesn't think it's any good,' he laughs, 'she'll tell him. And he will want to make it right.'

Concluding *For the Ghosts Within* is a track that combined Wyatt's love of jazz with his penchant for mischievous cover versions. On one level, *What a Wonderful World* was a hopelessly hackneyed choice, as well as a strange one for a self-confessed pessimist. But just as he had done almost four decades earlier with *I'm a Believer*, Wyatt compelled the listener to see the beauty – and wonder – in the overfamiliar.

Robert knew, of course, that Louis Armstrong was seen by some as a sellout, even an Uncle Tom – a reputation not much helped by releasing a song about roses and rainbows the year race riots swept America. But he also knew that, as a trumpeter, Armstrong had been jazz's first great soloist, and that there was much more to Satchmo than a raspy voice and a jovial grin. Armstrong, after all, was the man who, in 1957, had cancelled a State Department-sponsored tour of the USSR to protest against the deployment of troops at a school in Little Rock, which black students were trying to desegregate. 'Our *Wonderful World* is not sarcastic, ironic or even just sentimental,' declared Robert on the accompanying press release. 'It's social realism: not the WHOLE truth, but nevertheless the truth.'

-»)(«- -»)(«- -»)(«-

For the Ghosts Within, credited to Wyatt/Atzmon/Stephen, was released by Domino in October 2010, to four- and five-star reviews. 'There is a hole in the universe the precise shape of a record of standards – mid-century stuff from film and theater and jazz band repertory – sung by Robert Wyatt,' declared the *New York Times*. 'He is not a jazz singer in any traditional sense, though that kind of music has long inspired him for deep background. To put it otherwise, he's exactly the kind of person to be extending the usefulness of songs like *Laura*, *Lush Life*, *In a Sentimental Mood* and *What's New?*'

The album was not all standards with strings. It also found Wyatt revisiting back catalogue numbers *Maryan* and *At Last I Am Free*, and even featured Palestinian hiphop artists on a new version of *Dondestan*, retitled *Where Are They Now*. Although anomalous on an otherwise wistful album of jazz, tango and Middle Eastern folk, there was also something heartening about Wyatt's refusal to resort to sat-nav.

The album also boasted two new tracks, both featuring lyrics by Alfie. *Lullaby for Irena* was a poignant tribute to her late mother: 'From the air to your body, you gave my spirit life / You made my world / and all my wise and all my foolish ways.' *The Ghosts Within*, meanwhile, was sung not by Robert but by Gilad's wife, Tali. Gilad still remembers the first time he read Alfie's lyrics: 'We're still here, under the olive trees / When will you see, it's where we belong? / The river runs away in shame.'

'You start to sing it,' says Gilad, 'and, in my case, I really started to cry. I sung the lyrics and realised that it was about Palestine.' *For the Ghosts Within* might have found Robert indulging his inner jazz nostalgic, but neither he nor Alfie had cut themselves off from new music or contemporary politics.

Politically, Robert is remarkable in not shuffling to the right with the passing years – one of the reasons his solo albums make up such a coherent body of work. 'I haven't really changed allegiances in any important respect,' he says, reflecting on his output from *Rock Bottom* onwards. 'Some of my records may be anachronistic: I did write a song once assuming that Nelson Mandela would never be released from prison. You can't get much wronger than that. But I'm happy to be wrong and it's still a record of the feelings of the time. So on the whole, in terms of how I feel about things, I'm quite alarmingly – and, for some people, stubbornly and irritatingly – stable. I still think the same, I see the world in the same way that I have since the early 1970s, which is the period of time in which all my solo records have come out.'

Does he still consider himself a Marxist? 'I suppose if there's an -ist,' he replies, 'it's some kind of Marxist, to this day. But only by default. I can't think of anywhere, really, where a body of work or a manifesto has been brought satisfactorily to life. Absolutely not. But that doesn't make me, as a lot of my contemporaries have done, say: "Well, fuck it, then. Let's just go with the flow." On the contrary, I think: "How awful that these truths that Marxism illuminated have not been addressed."'

> Alfie's paper cut-out graces *For the Ghosts Within*.

Although no longer a Party member, Wyatt still reads the *Morning Star* in preference to any other newspaper. In one sense, this makes him a relic. But at the same time, Robert has almost waited long enough to find his political views back in fashion. Following the financial crisis of 2007–8, voices of opposition are as welcome as they were in the wake of punk, when free market ideology was first in the ascendant.

'I have an absolutely fundamental unease with the way things have gone,' Wyatt sighs. 'Sometimes what I'm uneasy about erupts in the form of farce, like the banks collapsing because the government has handed over control of the economy to a bunch of shysters. Which is sort of what I'm saying, really – but it's almost a joke version.' With all the talk of austerity and triple-dip recessions, the march of capitalism didn't look so inexorable. And it is difficult not to agree with Robert about the sheer unfairness of a world in which the wealth of the very, very rich has dramatically increased while income for the vast majority has remained static or declined, or in which taxpayers bail out banks while those responsible for the crash stay unpunished – and unrepentant.

On New Year's Day 2010, Wyatt became guest editor of Radio 4's *Today* programme. (The guest editor slot is a Christmas tradition for the BBC's flagship news show; others offered the tiller that Christmas included astrophysicist Martin Rees, artist David Hockney and Liberal Democrat politician Shirley Williams.) The BBC wanted him to discuss music, and Robert was happy to speak to Jerry Dammers of The Specials about what made a good collaboration. 'But actually,' says Robert, 'the things I wanted to get in were things about Gaza today and the recent overthrow of democracy, the return to a kind of banana republic status in Honduras, going against what are generally very exciting political movements in South America. They said, "We've got a correspondent in Mexico, he can get down to do a Honduras thing." And they did it very well. "We've got someone in Jerusalem, they can nip over the border into Gaza and do that." I was very happy with it.'

Closer to home, Robert sent socialist comedian Mark Steel to investigate the proliferation of chain stores on Britain's high streets, while the man who had introduced himself to Gilad Atzmon as an amateur musician also championed amateur choirs. 'Amateur means somebody who does something for love,' he explained, 'and I can't think of a better reason for doing anything.'

Wyatt also commissioned an alternative Thought for the Day from the Marxist writer and art critic John Berger, and brought in Tony Benn for a look, in the wake of the 2009 expenses scandal, at the unreported and unglamorous work of honest backbench MPs. 'You watch the Parliament Channel,' he explains, 'and see constituency MPs talking about safety measures for old people's homes and whether smoke alarms should be statutory and whether the owner should be replaced as a landlord and what are the legal implications. I thought, "Who amongst us really wants to sit down and think about that?" Well, they're doing it. That's real life and it's really important.'

The Marxist atheist using his BBC slot to celebrate church choirs and MPs: Robert really was, to quote one journalist, an 'awkward bugger'. His refusal to perform was another aspect of this awkwardness. Fans wanting to hear Wyatt's music played live have to make do with the various ensembles to have emerged in the wake of Annie Whitehead's Soupsongs project. Soupsongs itself continues to perform occasionally and now features Brian Hopper on saxophone, while another occasional troupe, Comicoperando, features Whitehead alongside Dagmar Krause and Chris Cutler from Henry Cow. In France, John Greaves participates in occasional ensembles, sometimes featuring

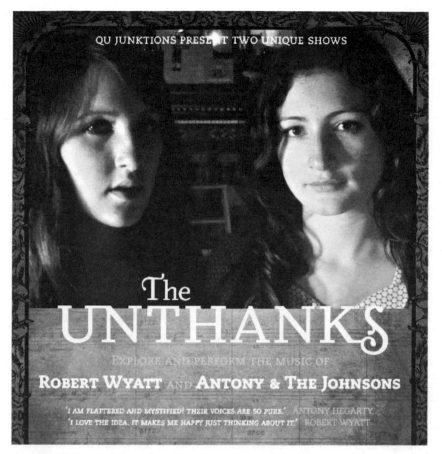

QU JUNKTIONS PRESENT TWO UNIQUE SHOWS

The
UNTHANKS

EXPLORE AND PERFORM THE MUSIC OF

ROBERT WYATT AND ANTONY & THE JOHNSONS

'I AM FLATTERED AND MYSTIFIED! THEIR VOICES ARE SO PURE.' ANTONY HEGARTY
'I LOVE THE IDEA. IT MAKES ME HAPPY JUST THINKING ABOUT IT.' ROBERT WYATT

> Geordie folk interpretations of the Wyatt songbook.

Karen Mantler. All three acts have Wyatt's blessing and at least indirect involvement: every Dondestan concert, for instance, is recorded and sent to Robert. 'And', says John Greaves, 'Robert will dutifully send his commentary on them. He's always very, very supportive. He'll say things like: "You know that version of *Trickle Down*? It's eight times better than the original." He'd obviously studied it. It was not twice as good or ten times as good. Eight times.'

In the last few years, France's Orchestre National de Jazz toured an album entitled *Around Robert Wyatt*, featuring imaginative big-band arrangements of his songs, and there have been covers albums from French leftfield rock group Mop Meuchiine and, notably, Geordie folk siblings The Unthanks, who stripped down songs like *Free Will and Testament*, *Stay Tuned* and *Sea Song* to their basics, giving them an English vocal treatment from another tradition and region.

And the list goes on. There was a 2007 album of Soft Machine covers by The Delta Saxophone Quartet, and the same year jazz musicians Max Nagl, Clemens Wenger and Herbert Pirker released *Market Rasen*, a tribute album named after the nearest railway station to Louth. In 2012, Sunderland's Peter and David Brewis included *Born Again Cretin* on their *Field Music Plays...* album, reworked as downbeat indie pop, while avant-garde jazz guitarist Mary Halvorson recorded a startling take on Philip Catherine's *Nairam*, the basis for Wyatt's *Maryan*. Most recently the Brodsky Quartet reworked Wyatt's music for strings, performing, appropriately enough, at a Canterbury festival.

That each act has taken the material in a wildly different direction is a reminder of one reason Robert's music appeals to fellow musicians: the sparse arrangements leave so much open to interpretation. Daniel Yvenic of Orchestre National de Jazz says he has been a huge fan of Robert's music since adolescence. But, he adds, 'I always thought that Robert Wyatt's music is kind of unfinished. I really like that idea. It seems as though the music he makes is ready to give to somebody else, to be taken in another direction.'

⟫⟪⟩ ⟫⟪⟩ ⟫⟪⟩

Acts like Soupsongs, Dondestan and Comicoperando are the closest most of us will now get to a Wyatt gig. But Robert did make an exception for Charlie Haden – a man as close as anyone to his musical and political hero. For a stage-fright sufferer, Wyatt had not exactly eased himself into performance by joining David Gilmour at the Royal Albert Hall; now he agreed to join Haden at the equally prestigious Royal Festival Hall. Joined by his old friend Carla Bley, Robert sang – and whistled – *Rabo de Nube (Tail of a Tornado)* by the left-wing Cuban folk singer Silvio Rodriguez. 'I think everybody was knocked out with it,' says John Cumming, today director of the jazz concert producers Serious, who had first seen Wyatt in The Soft Machine, back in 1967. 'It was an extraordinary moment.'

Robert himself compares being onstage with the bassist to being airlifted to the top of a mountain. 'Just being there, being onstage with Charlie Haden, with Carla there to hold my hand and surrounded by these brilliant youngsters – Shabaka Hutchings and Jason Yarde and so on – that was a moment in heaven for me. I have no idea what it sounded like, whether it was any good. But I don't care. Just being there, being allowed there. It was a transcendental moment.'

> Carla Bley and Charlie Haden soundcheck before their Royal Festival Hall concert in which Robert played cornet.

The compliment is returned: 'Robert's a musical genius as far as I'm concerned,' declares Haden, himself described by *Time* magazine as one of the most restless, gifted and intrepid players in jazz. 'The way that he approaches music, and the ideas that he has about his projects, are just very unique and very special.'

Joining Charlie Haden at the top of a mountain may well prove to have been Robert's last ever gig. But he continues to appear at public events. In 2009, Robert, who had dropped out of formal education early in sixth form, donned robe and sash to receive an honorary doctorship from Belgium's University of Liège. Avant-garde jazz musicians Anthony Braxton and Archie Shepp, and the Estonian composer Arvo Pärt, were honoured in the same ceremony. Wyatt won a Gold Badge songwriting award the same year, 'honouring a unique contribution to music'.

> Dr Wyatt receives his honorary doctorate from the University of Liège, in the company of Tim Berners-Lee, Dutch musician Dick Annegarn, and jazz legends Anthony Braxton and Archie Shepp.

Wyatt also shows up reasonably regularly, and unconcernedly, on the radio and as a TV talking head, and there are occasional 'in conversation' appearances, too – at the Southbank Centre and Hay Festival in 2007, at 2011's Off the Page festival and at London's Café Oto in 2012. For some reason unaffected by *le trac* if he isn't playing music, Robert is all anecdotes and jokes at such occasions: a glimpse, perhaps, of the shirtless drummer of forty years ago. 'He suddenly goes into Mr Comedian,' says Phil Manzanera, 'and he's incredibly funny. Where did that come from? The person who's incredibly nervous, who will not sing. He is an amazing raconteur, he throws in all these jokes. It's very strange, because he's so nervous about performing, even performing on the trumpet or cornet. But talking in front of a hundred or so people doesn't seem to be a problem. It's very, very weird. It's a wonderful contradiction.'

Fans, in turn, relish the physical connection: the chance to shake Robert's hand or get an album signed. Some use it as a chance to announce, publicly, quite how much Robert's music means to them. Two questions in particular tend to come up from the audience. Firstly, if he can manage such speaking engagements, will there be more gigs? 'It's not going to happen, old son,' was Robert's reply at the Southbank Centre. 'The way to approach this is just to pretend I'm dead. It makes the records such a surprise.' And, secondly, is he working on new material? 'There was a nice thing that Jean Rhys, the novelist, said,' is Robert's reply to this one. 'She wrote three novels and a few other bits and pieces, and then basically stopped. Much later, she wrote *Wide Sargasso Sea*. But her publisher got really agitated and said, "When are you going to write another novel?" She said, "Did you like the last one?" He said, "Yeah." She said, "Well, read it again."'

It is worth remembering that Wyatt, as he himself points out, is now past retirement age. That his lungs and liver have held up is remarkable, particularly given the consultant's brusque verdict following his accident, as recalled by Robert: 'It'll probably knock ten years off your life, twenty if you smoke.' Had he known he was going to live this long, Wyatt jokes, he would have taken better care of himself.

Of those that remain, many of Wyatt's contemporaries have either turned into rock dinosaurs or made embarrassing attempts to remain hip. Robert has done neither. He still sings almost as he did in The Wilde Flowers, yet he has remained protean, permeable, so determined not to become a grumpy old man that he has turned into a kind of anti-curmudgeon: the Yesterday Man who worked with Björk and Hot Chip, the Cecil Taylor fan who loves Hear'Say. 'I think we all see him as someone who's always stuck to his guns,' says Paul Weller. 'Everyone's got a tremendous respect for Robert because of that. Especially from his generation, there's very few who have done it. Most of them, as far as I'm concerned, have either copped out and done the greatest hits or they just fucking go through the same old motions. And he hasn't done that.'

Robert often mentions the fact that an Italian radio station once played his entire back catalogue back to back and it lasted only a weekend. But for someone usually seen as anything but prolific, he has made a staggering number of guest appearances: the *DiscoRobertWyatt* website lists over 200 records in its 'With Friends' discography alone. Even without his work as a band member and a solo artist, he still has the CV of a successful session musician.

As regards the releases under Wyatt's own name, *Rock Bottom* is the one that normally makes the classic album lists, but others would choose as their favourite The Soft Machine's first or second albums, or *Moon in June*, or *Shipbuilding*. And the recent trio of albums, too – *Shleep*, *Cuckooland* and *Comicopera* – contain some of Robert's finest moments. Sales may remain relatively low by rock star standards, and Robert's work-rate, never in the sprinter league, only slowing with the passing years. 'But I think the most extraordinary thing about Robert', says Alfie, 'is that he has managed to survive all this time against the odds, without doing concerts. Part of that extraordinariness has been that we've actually been able to survive financially. There were certain moments when it was really touch and go. Funnily enough, I think if he hadn't been paraplegic, there are points at which I think he would have given up, because he could have found another job.'

Yet Robert *has* achieved spectacular success by another definition: longevity without compromise. In politics as in music, he has become a byword for integrity, for sticking to one's principles. In fifty years of making music, there seems not to have been an insincere note. 'I think a lot of other artists admire him', says Brian Eno, 'because he seems to have developed a personal vision which is *intact*, somehow. The political and social part of it belongs together with what actually happens musically. He's the best example of his philosophy, and quite often that is not the case. Quite often, people are the *worst* examples of their philosophy; they sort of expect somebody else to do it when they don't. But what's impressive about Robert, I think, is that he lives his life and, as far as I can see, there aren't any glaring inconsistencies between what he claims to believe in and what he does as a person and as an artist. So that's a bit of triumph to have pulled that off.'

-»)«- -»)«- -»)«-

Perhaps it's that Old Testament beard, but Wyatt makes sense as a sexagenarian. He did recently become the reluctant owner of a mobile phone, and was pleasantly surprised to discover, thanks to his son Sam, that he has a fairly popular Facebook fan page. Due to her age-related macular degeneration, Alfie's eyes are a continuing source of concern, and Alfie's health forced them to cancel a speaking appearance at the Green Man Festival in 2013. But, with the booze now firmly behind them, the Duchess and Old Rottenhat do at least seem to be facing the future side by side.

Professionally, Wyatt has managed to gain almost universal critical respect without becoming a museum piece. Perhaps, in one sense at least, *le trac* has actually been an advantage: Robert might have struggled to remain so musically curious had he spent the last forty years belting out *Sea Song* and *Shipbuilding* and *Moon in June* and *O Caroline* night after night. 'The curse of pop music is repetition,' as Jerry Dammers puts it. 'Most pop musicians come unstuck because they just keep repeating their hits for their entire lives, just going over and over and over the same thing. If you're playing live, there's a lot of pressure to do that. It's very hard *not* to do that, and I understand that. But it does destroy people in the end. Robert is just an example to all musicians of what they should be doing, because he's never given up the creative side of trying to create new music, and be inventive.'

> Robert with his son, Sam – a photo taken by Robert's granddaugher, Beki Ellidge.

'Robert's got a very special place,' continues Dammers. 'I class him with, from that period, Nick Drake, Syd Barrett and Peter Green. And he's the survivor, obviously, of those four.'

Rather than the shooting star of a pop career, Robert's career has unfolded more like that of a jazz musician or, perhaps, the visual artist he never was. Matisse was in his seventies when he made his cut-outs, and kept going until his death at the age of eighty-four; Picasso and Miró both reached ninety, remaining feverishly creative to the last. Although more or less operating within popular music, Robert draws on jazz, folk, country, Latin and even classical composers such as Britten or Vaughan Williams, allowing him to age with dignity in an industry obsessed with youth. 'It's perfectly accepted by everyone from poets to politicians,' as Wyatt himself has said, 'that they mature as they get older. This is accepted, especially in really important things like wine and brandy – serious stuff.'

Wyatt continues to lead what he calls 'an improvised life,' and remains connected to the wider world through projects both musical and non-musical. He contributed his 'last words' to Liz Gray's 2011 book project *99 Words*, alongside a range of figures from Nelson Mandela to Yoko Ono. Robert also wrote forewords to *Bringing It All Back Home*, Ian Clayton's evocative musical memoir, and to *Red Groove*, a book of jazz essays by his friend Chris Searle. The following year, he was one of seven artists, alongside Archie Shepp, Terry Riley and Chic's Nile Rodgers, selected for *7x7*, a sound and art installation by the Belgian visual artist Jean Pierre Muller. Another artist, John O'Rourke, has been working on a four-foot-high oak sculpture of Robert's head, entitled *A Robert Wyatt Construction Kit*. And there was a kind of full-circle reconciliation with his musical roots in the award of an honorary doctorate from the University of Kent in 2014.

Those benign dictatorships continue, too. Not many months go by without a musical collaboration of some kind. In 2011, Robert joined French pianist Sophia Domancich on *Snakes and Ladders*; recorded with the Paraorchestra, a group of disabled musicians set up by conductor Charles Hazlewood; and joined the punk-jazz outfit Get the Blessing on their song *American Meccano*. Since then he has sung and read poetry on the *Cinéma el Mundo* album by Lo'Jo that combined French *chanson* with North African music; contributed to Steve Nieve's album, *ToGetHer*; recorded with his Louth musician neighbour, Ian James Stewart; sung and played tenor horn on a track by Gerald Clark; and sang on Adrian Johnston's soundtrack to Jimmy McGovern's BBC drama *Common*. He also added piano, cornet and scatted vocal to *Richardson*

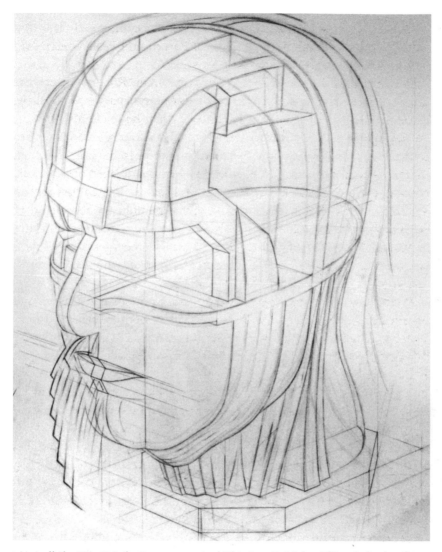

> Not all the Wyatt tributes are musical. This is artist John O'Rourke's plan for a wooden sculpture of Robert.

Road on *Unearth* by Grasscut – though little can credibly be said of this collaboration, since the name of one member of the duo matches that on the front of this book (except that, as a fee, Robert would accept only a small hamper of Sussex cheese).

Despite what he says about Jean Rhys and it being possible to simply re-read existing novels, Wyatt *is* working on material of his own, if only because he continues to put himself on the rack. 'It's not a question of enjoying it', he explains, 'so much as still feeling that I've yet to quite get it right, which stops me stopping. Every decade I think: "Got it, I understand now, that's it sorted." And then a decade later, you think, "God, what an idiot I was when I was forty. I thought I'd really got it. What did I know when I was forty?" And the same when I was fifty. And then, when I got to sixty, I thought, "I never knew anything! I didn't know anything, right up till now. But now I do.'"

Looking back over a full half-century of making music, are there *any* points when Robert himself feels he has got it right?

'There are moments,' he replies with a grin. 'I like that thing Miles Davis said: "I play in a club, I play solo after solo, and for that evening there'll be just eight bars where I just absolutely got it right." But,' Robert laughs, 'I think I'm probably the only one who knows which eight bars they were.'

FLOTSAM & JETSAM

DISCOGRAPHY, ONLINE,
NOTES AND SOURCES, PHOTO
CREDITS, THANKS, INDEX

DISCOGRAPHY

Robert Wyatt may cast himself as a minimalist but he has in fact played on hundreds of albums. At last count, the French website **Disco Robert Wyatt** (www.disco-robertwyatt.com) detailed more than 700 records in total. What follows is more selective: Robert's main albums as a band member, all his solo work, and the best of his guest spots or, as he calls them, 'benign dictatorships'.

The Wilde Flowers

The Wilde Flowers released nothing at the time but they did make recordings.

The Wilde Flowers Voiceprint, 1994

Robert Wyatt – drums, vocals; Hugh Hopper – bass guitar; Pye Hastings – guitar; Brian Hopper guitar, voice, alto sax; Richard Coughlan – drums; Graham Flight – vocals; Richard Sinclair – guitar; Kevin Ayers – vocals; Dave Lawrence – vocals, guitar, bass; Bob Gilleson – drums; Mike Ratledge – piano, organ, flute.

Impotence / Those Words They Say / Memories / Don't Try to Change Me / Parchman Farm / Almost Grown / She's Gone / Slow Walkin' Talk / He's Bad for You / It's What I Feel (A Certain Kind) / Memories (Instrumental) / Never Leave Me / Time After Time / Just Where I Want / No Game When You Lose / Impotence / Why Do You Care / The Pieman Cometh / Summer Spirit / *She Loves to Hurt / The Big Show / Memories.*

This Voiceprint CD, also issued as *Tales of Canterbury* (a booklet/CD with text from Brian Hopper, Voiceprint, 1998), does a pretty good archive job on Canterbury's Ur-band, excavating tracks from 1965 to 1969, including a few Hopper brother songs that fed into The Soft Machine. The best Wyatt moments are an early *Memories* and an original composition, *Impotence*. If this leaves you wanting more, there's a four-CD set called *Canterburied Sounds* that spans 1962–69 and also features early Soft Machine and Caravan recordings.

The Soft Machine

As well as the numbered albums, there are dozens of Soft Machine reissues – archive and live recordings – covering numerous incarnations of the band.

Jet-Propelled Photographs Piccadilly, 1971

Robert Wyatt – drums, vocals; Daevid Allen – guitar; Mike Ratledge – piano, organ; Kevin Ayers – bass, vocals.

That's How Much I Need You Now / Save Yourself / I Should've Known / Jet-Propelled Photograph / When I *Don't Want You / Memories / You Don't Remember / She's Gone / I'd Rather Be with You.*

The original Soft Machine four-piece with Daevid Allen on guitar made these recordings with Giorgio Gomelsky in 1967. They have been reissued under various titles (*Rock Generation*, *At the Beginning*, *London 1967*) and labels. Rough but charming and the basis of *The Soft Machine*. See pp.67–68.

The Soft Machine Probe, 1968

Robert Wyatt – drums, vocals; Kevin Ayers – bass, piano; Mike Ratledge, organ. (Guests: Hugh Hopper – bass; Cake – backing vocals.)

Hope for Happiness / Joy of a Toy / Hope for Happiness (Reprise) / Why Am I So Short? / So Boot If at All / A Certain Kind / Save Yourself / Priscilla / Lullabye Letter / We Did It Again / Plus Belle Qu'une Poubelle / Why Are We Sleeping? / Box 25/4 Lid. CD reissues include the Softs' first single, *Love Makes Sweet Music / Feelin', Reelin', Squealin'.*

The first official studio release – without Allen. Still fresh. CD reissues include the Softs' first single, *Love Makes Sweet Music/ Feelin' Reelin' Squealin'.* For a live version of this material, try *Middle Earth Masters* (Cuneiform, 2006), recorded at London's Middle Earth club. See pp.89–94.

Robert Wyatt 68 Cuneiform, 2013

Robert Wyatt – drums, vocals, piano, organ, bass; Jimi Hendrix – bass; Hugh Hopper – bass; Mike Ratledge – organ.

Chelsa / Rivmic Melodies / Slow Walkin' Talk / Moon in June.

Possibly the most interesting and enjoyable Softs archive release. Robert recorded these tracks largely on his own in Los Angeles and New York, following the second US tour. *Rivmic Melodies* became Side One of *Volume Two*; he sung *Moon in June* live, often, before it surfaced on *Third*; while *Chelsa* is an early version of Matching Mole's *Signed Curtain*. See pp.100–101.

The Soft Machine Volume Two Probe, 1969

Robert Wyatt – drums, vocals; Hugh Hopper – bass, alto sax, acoustic guitar; Mike Ratledge – organ, piano. (Guest: Brian Hopper – tenor sax, soprano sax.)

Rivmic Melodies: Pataphysical Introduction (Pt. 1) / A Concise British Alphabet (Pt. 1) / Hibou, Anemone and Bear / A Concise British Alphabet (Pt. 2) / Hulloder /

Dada Was Here / Thank You Pierrot Lunaire / Have You Ever Bean Green? / Pataphysical Introduction (Pt. 2) / Out of Tunes / Esther's Nosejob/ As Long As He Lies Perfectly Still / Dedicated to You But You Weren't Listening / Fire Engine Passing With Bells Clanging / Pig / Orange Skin Food / A Door Opens And Closes / 10:30 Returns to the Bedroom.

Ayers is replaced by Hopper on the Soft's second album. *Live at the Paradiso* (Blueprint, 1996), recorded in Amsterdam, features most of the songs live. See pp.103–108.

Third CBS, 1970

Robert Wyatt – drums, vocals, piano, organ, bass; Mike Ratledge – organ, piano; Hugh Hopper – bass; Elton Dean – alto sax, saxello. (Guests: Lyn Dobson – flute, soprano sax; Nick Evans – trombone; Jimmy Hastings – flute, bass clarinet.)

Facelift / Slightly All the Time / Moon in June / Out-Bloody-Rageous.

Robert gets a side to himself, on this band-splintering double album, for his largely self-recorded *Moon in June*. See pp.121–148.

Fourth CBS, 1971

Robert Wyatt – drums; Mike Ratledge – organ, piano; Hugh Hopper – bass; Elton Dean – alto sax, saxello. (Guests: Roy Babbington – double bass; Nick Evans – trombone; Mark Charig – cornet; Jimmy Hastings – alto flute, bass clarinet; Alan Skidmore – tenor sax).

Teeth / Kings and Queens / Fletcher's Blemish / Virtually, Parts 1–4.

Robert's last Softs outing. Not much Robert, not much fun. See pp.142–148.

BBC Radio 1967–1971 Hux

Disc 1: Robert Wyatt – drums, vocals; Hugh Hopper – bass, alto sax, acoustic guitar; Mike Ratledge – organ, piano. (Guest: Brian Hopper – tenor sax, soprano sax). *Disc 2:* Wyatt, Hopper and Ratledge are joined by Elton Dean (alto sax, saxello), and on the final suite by Nick Evans (trombone), Mark Charig (cornet) and Lyn Dobson (soprano sax).

Disc 1 : *Clarence in Wonderland / We Know What You Mean / Certain Kind / Hope for Happiness / Strangest Scene (aka Lullaby Letter) / Facelift|Mousetrap|Noisette| / Backward|Mousetrap (reprise) / The Moon in June / Instant Pussy / Slightly*

All The Time|Out-Bloody-Rageous. Disc 2 : *Virtually / Fletcher's Blemish / Neo-Caliban Grides / Dedicated to You But You Weren't Listening / Eamonn Andrews|All White / Mousetrap|Noisette|Backwards| Mousetrap (reprise)|Esther's Nose Job.*

Soft Machine on the John Peel show in two very different incarnations. The first disc features Robert's idiosyncratic *Moon in June* with BBC-adapted lyrics. See p.111.

Matching Mole

Short-lived though they were, Matching Mole's archive has also been foraged, resulting in several live and radio recordings.

Matching Mole CBS, 1972

Robert Wyatt – drums, voice, piano, mellotron; Phil Miller – guitar; Bill MacCormick – bass; David Sinclair – piano, organ. (Guest: Dave MacRae – electric piano.)

O Caroline / Instant Pussy / Signed Curtain / Part of the Dance / Instant Kitten / Dedicated to Hugh, But You Weren't Listening / Beer As In Braindeer / Immediate Curtain.

The three openers are essential Wyatt. The 2012 CD reissue includes out-takes (including an instrumental version of *Memories*), a 1972 Peel session (with Dave MacRae) and single edits. See pp.157–161.

Matching Mole's Little Red Record

CBS, 1972

Robert Wyatt – drums, voice. piano, mellotron; Phil Miller – guitar; Bill MacCormick – bass; Dave MacRae – grand piano, electric piano, Hammond organ and Eno's synthesiser keyboard. (Guest: Brian Eno – V.C.S.3 Synthesizer on Gloria Gloom.)

Starting In The Middle of the Day We Can Drink Our Politics Away / Marchides / Nan True's Hole /

Righteous Rhumba / Brandy As In Benj / Gloria Gloom / God Song / Flora Fidgit / Smoke Signal. CD reissue includes a Radio 1 'In Concert' and Smoke Signal (Take Four) / Flora Fidget (Take Eight) / Mutter.

Another brilliant opening followed by *Gloria Gloom* and *God Song*. The CD reissue includes alternative takes and a BBC *In Concert* session. (All Matching Mole's BBC tracks are also released as *On the Radio*, Hux, 2006). See pp.167–178.

Smoke Signals Cuneiform, 2001

Robert Wyatt – drums; Phil Miller – guitar; Bill MacCormick – bass; Dave MacRae – electric piano.

Intro / March Ides / Smoke Rings / Nan True's Hole / Brandy As In Benji /Electric Piano Solo / March Ides II / Instant Pussy / Smoke Signal /Lything and Gracing.

Predominantly radio and TV recordings, as well as snippets from the Paris Olympia concert. Another good live CD is *March* (Cuneiform, 2002): the Mole recorded at the Paradiso, Amsterdam, in March 1972.

Robert Wyatt Solo Albums

This section details all Robert's solo work. Original labels are given for releases, though almost all have been reissued (and often remastered) on Domino.

The End of an Ear CBS, 1970

Robert Wyatt – drums, voice, piano, organ. With: Elton Dean – alto sax, saxello; Mark Charig – trumpet; David Sinclair – organ; Neville Whitehead– double

bass; Mark Ellidge – piano; Cyrille Ayers – percussion.

Las Vegas Tango Part 1 / To Mark Everywhere / To Saintly Bridget / To Oz Alien Daevyd and Gilly / To Nick Everyone / To Caravan and Brother Jim / To The Old World (Thank You For the Use of Your Body,

Goodbye) / To Carla, Marsha and Caroline (For Making Everything Beautifuller) / Las Vegas Tango Part 1.

Recorded after the Softs' *Third*, this was not quite the song album CBS had expected. See pp.134–136.

Rock Bottom Virgin, 1974

Robert Wyatt – voice, keyboards, James' drum; Richard Sinclair – bass guitar; Laurie Allan – drums; Hugh Hopper – bass guitar; Ivor Cutler – voice, baritone concertina; Mongezi Feza – trumpet; Alfreda Benge – voice; Gary Windo – bass clarinet, tenor sax; Fred Frith – viola, piano; Mike Oldfield – guitar.

Sea Song / A Last Straw / Little Red Riding Hood Hit the Road / Alifib / Alife / Little Red Robin Hood Hit the Road .

The acknowledged Wyatt masterpiece. See pp.196–210.

Theatre Royal Drury Lane – Robert Wyatt & Friends in Concert, 8th September 1974 Hannibal, 2005

Robert Wyatt – voice, percussion; Dave Stewart – keyboards; Hugh Hopper – bass guitar; Laurie Allan and Nick Mason – drums; Ivor Cutler – voice, baritone concertina; Mongezi Feza – trumpet; Gary Windo – tenor sax, bass clarinet; Fred Frith – violin, viola, guitar; Mike Oldfield – guitar, Minimoog. Special guest: Julie Tippetts – voice, piano.

Dedicated To You But You Weren't Listening / Memories / Sea Song / A Last Straw / Little Red Riding Hood Hit the Road / Alife / Alifib / Mind of a Child / Instant Pussy / Signed Curtain / Calyx / Little Red Robin Hood Hit the Road / I'm a Believer

Rock Bottom and a few extras live, performed by essentially the band from the studio album. See pp.215–217.

The Peel Sessions Strange Fruit, 1987

Robert Wyatt – voice, piano, organ, marimba.

Alifib / Soup Song / Sea Song /I'm a Believer.

Tracks from *Rock Bottom*, *Ruth Is Stranger* and hit single *I'm a Believer*, stripped down for solo performance, live on the radio, in 1974.

Solar Flares Burn for You Cuneiform 2003; recorded 1974

Robert Wyatt – vocals, percussion, cornet, keyboards; Francis Monkman – synthesiser, piano, electric piano, backing vocals; Hugh Hopper – bass, loops.

Alifib / Soup Song / Sea Song /I'm a Believer / Blimey O'Riley / Solar Flares Burn for You / God Song/ Fol De Rol / Little Child / We Got an Arts Council Grant / Righteous Rhumba / 'Twas Brillig / The Verb.

The first four tracks are from Robert's solo 1974 Peel session, as above. There are also 1972 Peel Show recordings with Francis Monkman. The CD is rounded out by two more recent collaborations with Hugh Hopper, and a new song, *The Verb*.

Ruth Is Stranger Than Richard Virgin, 1975

Robert Wyatt – drums, mouth, piano, keyboards, imitation electric piano; Laurie Allan – drums; Nisar Ahmad 'George' Khan — baritone sax; Bill MacCormick – bass; Gary Windo – tenor sax; Mongezi Feza – trumpet; John Greaves – bass; Brian Eno – direct inject anti-jazz ray gun, guitar, synthetiser; Fred Frith – piano, violin.

Soup Song / Sonia / Team Spirit / Song for Che / Muddy Mouse / Solar Flares /Muddy Mouse / 5 Black Notes and 1 White Note/ Muddy Mouse-Muddy Mouth.

This tricky follow-up to *Rock Bottom* featured versions of songs by Charlie Haden, Mongezi Feza, Brian Hopper, Phil Manzanera and Fred Frith. It has aged well. See pp.227–230.

Radio Experiment Rome, February 1981 Tracce, 2009

Robert Wyatt – vocals, piano, keyboards, objects, Jew's harp, percussion.

Opium War / Heathens Havn No Souls / L'Albero Degli Zoccoli / Holy War / Revolution Without 'R' / Billy's Bounce / Born Again Cretin / Prove Sparse.

A DIY solo radio experiment, not intended for release, that emerged many years later. See p.265.

The Animals Film Rough Trade, 1982

Robert Wyatt – vocals, piano, keyboards, percussion.

Side A / Side B.

Budget soundtrack to a very bleak animal rights film. See pp.264–265.

Nothing Can Stop Us Rough Trade, 1982

Robert Wyatt – drums, voice, keyboards, percussion. With: Bill MacCormick – bass; Harry Beckett – flugelhorn (*Caimanera/Arauco*); Frank Roberts – piano; Mogotsi Mothle – double bass (*At Last I Am Free/Strange Fruit*); Peter Blackman – spoken voice (*Stalingrad*); Dishari (*Trade Union/Grass*).

Born Again Cretin / At Last I Am Free / Caimanera / Grass / Stalin Wasn't Stallin' / Shipbuilding / Red Flag / Strange Fruit / Arauco / Trade Union / Stalingrad.

The glorious Rough Trade singles (1980–81) compiled. See pp.261–264.

Work in Progress / 1982–1984 Rough Trade, 1983/1984

Robert Wyatt – drums, voice, piano, organ. With: Clive Langer – organ; Steve Nieve – piano; Mark Bedford – double bass; Martin Hughes – drums; Elvis Costello – backing vocals (*Shipbuilding*). Dave MacRae – piano, synthesiser (*Memories of You / Round Midnight*).

Work in Progress: *Biko / Amber and the Amberines / Yolanda / Te Recuerdo Amanda*. 1982–84 added *Shipbuilding / Memories of You / Round Midnight.*

Work in Progress was another singles compilation. *1982–1984* added the *Shipbuilding* EP, and was reissued in 1993 as *Mid-Eighties* (along with the *Old Rottenhat* album). See pp.279–283.

Old Rottenhat Rough Trade, 1985

Robert Wyatt – drums, keyboards, vocals.

Alliance/ United States of Amnesia / East Timor / Speechless / Age of Self / Vandalusia / British Road / Mass Medium / Gharbzadegi / P.L.A.

The first official album after a decade's pause. See pp.284–292.

Dondestan Rough Trade, 1991

Robert Wyatt – vocals, keyboards, piano, percussion, acoustic guitar, melodica.

Costa / The Sight of the Wind / Catholic Architecture / Worship / Shrinkrap / CP Jeebies / Left on Man / Lisp Service/ N.I.O. (New Information Order) / Dondestan.

Inspired by two winters in Spain and, for the first time, featuring lyrics by Alfie. Robert remixed and reordered the album in 1998 as *Dondestan Revisited*. See pp.303–310.

A Short Break Voiceprint, 1992

Robert Wyatt – vocals, percussion, piano, keyboards.

Short Break / Tubab / Kutcha / Venti Latir / Unmasked.

A little rough diamond of lo-fi, experimental recordings. See pp.310–312.

Shleep Rough Trade, 1997

Robert Wyatt – vocals, keyboards, bass, percussion, Polish fiddle, trumpet; Brian Eno – synthesiser, backing vocals, synth bass; Jamie Johnson – guitar; Evan Parker – soprano sax, tenor sax; Philip Catherine – guitar; Chikako Sato – violin; Chucho Merchan – double bass, percussion, bass, bass drum; Alfreda Benge – voice of the apparition; Paul Weller – guitar, acoustic guitar, backing vocals; Annie Whitehead – trombone; Phil Manzanera – guitar; Gary Adzukx – djembe; Jamie Johnson, Alfreda Benge, Charles Rees – chorus.

Heaps Of Sheeps / The Duchess / Maryan / Was A Friend / Free Will and Testament / September the Ninth / Alien / Out Of Season / Sunday In Madrid / Blues in Bob Minor / Whole Point Of No Return.

A cast of thousands, by Wyatt's standards, and a triumph. See pp.321–331. A re-edit was issued in 2008 with various extra tracks, including four (*Fridge/ When Access Was a Noun/Salt-Ivy/ Signed Curtain*) originally issued with an Italian limited edition book of Wyatt lyrics, *M4W*, produced by Jean-Michel Marchetti.

Cuckooland Hannibal, 2003

Robert Wyatt – vocals, keyboards, cornet, percussion, trumpet; Brian Eno – voice; Jamie Johnson – bass; Alfreda Benge – vocals; Paul Weller – guitar, acoustic guitar, backing vocals; Annie Whitehead – trombone; Phil Manzanera – voice; David Gilmour – guitar; Gilad Atzmon – saxophones, clarinet; Yaron Stavi – double bass; Karen Mantler – vocals; Tomo Hayakawa – guitar; Tomo Noro – vocals; Michael Evans – drums; Jennifer Maidman – accordion.

Part One: *Just A Bit / Old Europe / Tom Hay's Fox / Forest / Beware / Cuckoo Madame / Raining In My Heart / Lullaby For Hamza / Silence – a suitable place for those with tired ears to pause and resume listening later / Part Two '...nor there': Trickle Down / Insensatez / Mister E / Lullaloop / Life Is Sheep / Foreign Accents/ Brian the Fox /La Ahada Yalam.*

Another significant assembly of musicians, including new partner Gilad Atzmon, and Karen Mantler, daughter of Mike Mantler and Carla Bley. See pp.347–360.

Comicopera Domino, 2007

Robert Wyatt – vocals, piano, percussion, trumpet, cornet, old metronome, keyboard, karenotron (voice of Karen Mantler), Enotron (voice of Brian Eno), pocket trumpet, monicatron (voice of Monica Vasconcelos); Jamie Johnson – electrical interference; Brian Eno – keyboards, effects; Seaming To – voice, clarinet; Annie Whitehead – trombone, baritone horn; Yaron Stavi – bass violin; Monica Vasconcelos – voice; Paul Weller – guitar; Gilad Atzmon – tenor sax, clarinet; Jamie Johnson – bass guitar; David Sinclair – piano; Phil Manzanera – guitar; Del Bartle – guitar; Orphy Robinson – steelpan, vibraphone; Chucho

Merchan – bass violin; Maurizio Camardi – saxes; Alphonso Santimone – piano, keyboards; Alessandro Fedrigo – bass guitar; Paolo Vidaich – percussion; Gianni Bertoncini – drums.

ACT ONE LOST IN NOISE: Stay Tuned / Just As You Are / You You / A.W.O.L / Anachronist. ACT TWO THE HERE AND THE NOW: A Beautiful Place / Be Serious / On The Town Square / Mob Rule / A Beautiful War / Out Of The Blue. ACT THREE AWAY WITH THE FAIRIES: Del Mondo / Canción De Julieta / Pastafari / Fragment/ Hasta Siempre Comandante.

Three Acts, no less, and Robert's last solo album to date. See pp.365–373.

Wyatt/Atzmon/Stephen: For the Ghosts Within Domino, 2010

Robert Wyatt – voice, brushes, trumpet, percussion, whistling, backing vocals; Gilad Atzmon – alto sax, soprano sax, clarinet, bass clarinet, accordion, Palestinian shepherd's flute; Ros Stephen – violin, viola, backing vocals; Richard Pryce – double bass; Yaron Stavi – double bass, electric bass; Frank Harrison – keyboards; Sigamos String Quartet: Ros Stephen – violin, Tom Pigott-Smith – violin, Rachel Robson – viola, Daisy Vatalaro – cello; Julian Rowlands – bandoneon; Stormtrap (Abboud Hashem) voice; Tali Atzmon – backing vocals.

Laura / Lullaby for Irena/ The Ghosts Within / Where Are They Now? / Maryan / Round Midnight / Lush Life / What's New? / In A Sentimental Mood / At Last I Am Free / What a Wonderful World.

A trio effort rather than solo, but with some sublime jazz moments. See pp.379–384.

Compilations

Flotsam Jetsam Rough Trade, 1994

Includes appearances with Symbiosis, Lol Coxhill, Slapp Happy, Gary Windo, Unity/Hanwell Band, Claustrophobia, The Happy End, SWAPO Singers,

Slow Walkin' Talk / Moon in June [excerpt] / SYMBIOSIS: Standfast / MATCHING MOLE: No 'Alf Measures / God Song / Fol De Rol / LOL COXHILL & PHIL MILLER: Soprano Derivato–Apricot Jam / SLAPP HAPPY & FRIENDS: A Little Something / GARY WINDO: Now Is the Time / UNITY/HANWELL BAND

& ROBERT WYATT: Now't Doin / Born Again Cretin / Billie's Bounce / Locomotive / War Without Blood / Obert Tancat / CLAUSTROPHOBIA: Tu Traicion/ Obert Tancat 2 / THE HAPPY END: Turn Things Upside Down / ROBERT WYATT AND THE SWAPO SINGERS: The Wind of Change.

A wonderful collection of collaborations and obscurities, many of them unavailable elsewhere, compiled by Michael King as a companion to his *Wrong Movements* book, with the help of Andy Childs. Essential.

Going Back a Bit: A Little History of Robert Wyatt Virgin, 1994

Moon in June / To Caravan and Brother Jim / O Caroline / Gloria Gloom/ God Song / Calyx / Alifib/ Alife / Last Straw / Sea Song / Soup Song / I'm a Believer/ Memories / Yesterday Man / Sonia / Little Red Robin Hood Hit the Road/ Five Black Notes and One White Note / Team Spirit / Song for Che/ The Doubtful Guest / The Object Lesson / Arauco / A L'abattoir / I'm a Mineralist / Rangers In The Night/ All She Wanted / Left on Man / Lisp Service / The Internationale.

A decent 2-CD career retrospective that throws in a few obscurities (*Rangers in the Night, All She Wanted, The Internationale*).

EPs Rykodisc, 2004

I'm a Believer [Extended Version] / Memories / Yesterday Man / Sonia [Alternate Version] / Calyx [Live] / Shipbuilding [Remastered] / Memories of You / Round Midnight / Pigs... (In There) / Chairman Mao / Yolanda / Te Recuerdo Amanda / Biko / Amber And the Amberines /Animals' Film / Was a Friend [Remix] / Maryan [Remix] / Sunday in Madrid [Remix] / Free Will and Testament [Remix]

A beautifully packaged 5-CD box featuring versions of early/mid 1980s solo material, and remixes of tracks from *Shleep*.

His Greatest Misses Rykodisc, 2004

P.L.A. / Worship / Heaps of Sheeps / Free Will and Testament / I'm a Believer / Sea Song/ Little Red Robin

Hit the Road / Solar Flares / At Last I Am Free / Arauco / The Age of Self / Alien / Shipbuilding / Memories of You / Muddy Mouse / Mister E / Foreign Accents.

Nicely sequenced compilation from the solo albums.

Box Set Domino, 2009

All seven studio albums plus *Drury Lane* and the *EPs* box, again handsomely packaged with new artwork from Alfie.

Different Every Time Domino, 2014

CD1 'Ex Machina': *Moon in June / Signed Curtain / A Last Straw [Live at Drury Lane] / Yesterday Man / Team Spirit / At Last I Am Free / Shipbuilding / The Age of Self / Worship / Free Will and Testament / Cuckoo Madame / Beware / Just As You Are.*

CD2 'Benign Dictatorships': JEANETTE LINDSTROM: *The River* / ANJA GARBAREK: *The Diver* / HOT CHIP: *We're Looking for a Lot of Love.* / EPIC SOUNDTRACKS: *Jellybabies* / GRASSCUT: *Richardson Road* / HAPPY END: *Turn Things Upside Down* / MONICA VASCONCELOS: *Still in the Dark* / WORKING WEEK: *Venceremos* / PHIL MANZANERA: *Frontera* / STEVE NIEVE: *La Plus Jolie Langue* / CRISTINA DONA: *Goccia* / NICK MASON: *Siam* / MIKE MANTLER: *A L'Abattoir* / MIKE MANTLER: *Sinking Spell* / BJÖRK: *Submarine* / JOHN CAGE: *Experiences No. 2.*

Robert selected the tracks for this 2-CD set, issued to accompany the book. The first CD is solo material; the second guest spots.

Guest spots

Robert Wyatt has contributed to other people's records since Soft Machine days; this is a selection of those that worked best. Several feature on the *Flotsam Jetsam* and *Different Every Time* compilations (above).

Kevin Ayers: Joy of a Toy Harvest, 1969

The Soft Machine provided the backing for Ayers' debut solo recording.

Syd Barrett: The Madcap Laughs
Harvest, 1970

Robert and the Softs also played on two tracks on Syd Barrett's debut album: *No Good Trying* and *Love You.*

Daevid Allen: Banana Moon BYG, 1971

Robert drummed on all but one track of what is essentially the first Gong album. He also sings *Memories.*

Centipede: Septober Energy RCA, 1971

Big-band modern jazz – with Robert as one of three drummers in a 50-strong group.

Kevin Ayers: Whatevershebringswesing Harvest, 1972

Robert harmonises with Kevin on the title track of probably the best Ayers album.

Hatfield and The North: Hatfield and The North Virgin, 1974

Robert was a guest on early gigs by the Hatfields and, post-accident, returned on their debut album to sing *Calyx*.

Brian Eno: Taking Tiger Mountain (By Strategy) Island, 1975

Matching Mole saw the first Wyatt-Eno collaboration. This was the second, with Robert contributing vocals and percussion.

Phil Manzanera: Diamond Head Island, 1975

Debut solo album by the Roxy Music guitarist, opening with Robert's Spanish nonsense vocals on *Frontera*.

Jan Steele/John Cage: Voices and Instruments Obscure Music, 1976

Robert's performance of Cage's *Experiences No. 2* and *The Wonderful Widow of Eighteen Springs* would later inspire Björk.

Henry Cow: Concerts Caroline, 1976

Robert sings (live) on the Slapp Happy/ Henry Cow song *Bad Alchemy* and his own *Little Red Riding Hood Hit the Road*.

Michael Mantler: The Hapless Child Watt, 1976; Silence Watt, 1977

Robert is the sole vocalist on Mantler's settings of Edward Gorey's *The Hapless Child*, and shared vocals with Kevin Coyne on his adaptation of Harold Pinter's *Silence*.

Brian Eno: Ambient #1 – Music for Airports Obscure, 1978

Just as punk ran rampant, Eno devised ambient music. Robert plays piano.

Nick Mason: Fictitious Sports Harvest, 1981

The Pink Floyd drummer took lead billing but this is really a Carla Bley album, with Robert on vocals on all but one track.

The Raincoats: Odyshape Rough Trade, 1981

Robert only drums on one track – *And Then It's O.K.* – but this signalled the start of a series of fruitful collaborations with fellow Rough Trade bands.

Epic Soundtracks: Popular Classical Rough Trade, 1981

A fine EP with Epic Soundtracks (ex-Swell Maps). Robert sings *Jelly Babies*.

Scritti Politti: Songs to Remember Rough Trade, 1982

Robert helps Scritti find their way from squatland to the charts, with keyboards on *The 'Sweetest Girl'*, among other tracks.

Ben Watt: Summer into Winter Cherry Red, 1982

The debut from half of Everything But The Girl. Robert sings on *Walter and John* and plays piano on *A Girl In Winter*.

Working Week: Venceremos (We Will Win) Paladin, 1984

Another Wyatt Spanish-language vocal propels this Latin jazz 12-inch dance hit featuring Annie Whitehead and the other half of Everything But The Girl, Tracey Thorn.

Various Artists: The Last Nightingale
ReR, 1984

A miners' benefit album by Chris Cutler and other former Henry Cow members – Robert contributing vocals to *Moments of Delight* and *In the Dark Year*.

Robert Wyatt with the SWAPO Singers: The Wind of Change
Rough Trade, 1985

African optimism from a group featuring Namibian singers and Jerry Dammers.

News from Babel: Letters Home
ReR, 1986

Another almost incarnation of Henry Cow, Robert sharing vocals on several tracks, along with Dagmar Krause.

Michael Mantler: Many Have No Speech Watt, 1988

French lyrics, the Danish Radio Orchestra, Jack Bruce and Marianne Faithfull. Robert sings three numbers: *Tant de Temps*, *A L'Abattoir* and *Prisonniers*.

Ryuichi Sakamoto: Beauty Virgin, 1990

Sakamoto wanted the 'saddest voice in the world' for his take on The Rolling Stones' *We Love You*.

The Happy End: Turn Things Upside Down Cooking Vinyl, 1990

Robert excels on the title track from this left-wing, London 22-piece big band.

Ultramarine: United Kingdoms Sire, 1993

Robert sings lead on *Kingdom* and *Happy Land*, and backing vocals on other tracks.

John Greaves: Songs Resurgence, 1995

Greaves was the composer of *Kew.Rhone*, a Wyatt favourite which he reprises here, along with vocals on *The Song* and *Gegenstand*.

Phil Manzanera: Vozero Expression, 1999

Robert contributes to half a dozen tracks, singing in both Spanish and English, as well as playing trumpet, keyboards and percussion.

Cristina Donà: United Kingdoms Nido, 1999

Robert duets and plays cornet with the Italian singer on *Goccia*.

Pascal Comelade: September Song
Disques du Soleil, 2000

Comelade is a French Catalan musician who plays sparse covers of songs, often using toy instruments. This album includes *Signed Curtain*, and a vocal from Robert on Kurt Weill's *September Song*.

Michael Mantler: Hide and Seek ECM, 2001

A suite of songs from texts by Paul Auster, sung mainly by Robert, with band and orchestra.

Various Artists: MW pour Robert Wyatt In Poly Sons, 2001

Robert makes spoken-word contributions to this album of covers of his work by various French musicians, originally issued along with the Wyatt lyrics book, *M4W*.

Anja Garbarek: Smiling and Waving
Virgin, 2001

Robert sings *The Diver* on this album by the Norweigan singer-songwriter (daughter of the saxophonist Jan Garbarek). Anja, in turn, contributed to *Comicopera*.

Walter Prati & Robert Wyatt: Postcards from Italy Sonic Book, 2001

Three Variations on The Duchess – avant-garde classical/free jazz versions with voice (Robert), tape and guitars (Prati).

Bruno Coulais: Le Peuple Migrateur (Winged Migration) Virgin, 2001

Soundtrack from the film. Robert sings on *Masters of the Field*, *The Highest Gander*, *La Forêt Rouge* and *Hors Champ*.

La Tordue: Champ Libre Sony, 2001

The album's final track, *Le Pétrin*, is a protest against the French law that deports immigrants after they have served a prison sentence. It is sung in a dozen foreign languages –by Robert Wyatt and others including Lo'jo Triban, Danyel Waro and Tuvan throatsinger Yat Kha.

Sigmagtropic: Sixteen Haiku & Other Stories Tongue Master, 2003

These settings of George Seferis poems were huge in Greece and an interesting cast was assembled for this English version. Robert sings the introductions and duets with Stereolab's Laetitia Sadler on *Haiku One*.

Björk: Medulla Polydor, 2004

Bjork's voice-as-instrument album. Robert sings on *Submarine* and *Oceania*.

Gilad Atzmon & The Orient House Ensemble: Musik Enja, 2004

A new collaborator. Robert sings on *Re-Arranging the 20th Century*.

Brian Hopper: If Ever I Am Voiceprint, 2004

And a collaborator from earliest times. Robert contributes vocals and trumpet on *The Pieman Cometh* and old Soft Machine song, *Hope for Happiness*.

Bruno Coulais: Stabat Mater Naive, 2005

A composition for orchestra and voices. Robert sings on five tracks.

Max Richter: Songs from Before Deutsche Grammophon, 2006

Robert's contribution is spoken word on this album by the neoclassical composer, reading passages by Haruki Murakami as links between tracks inspired by the Japanese author's novels and stories.

Various Artists: Plague Songs 4AD, 2006

A multi-artist collection of songs based on the book of Exodus. Robert contributes atonal fly sounds to Eno's *Flies*.

Steve Nieve: Welcome to the Voice Deutsche Grammophon, 2007

Nieve's class conflict opera features Robert alongside Elvis Costello, Sting and the Brodsky Quartet. He sings on six tracks.

Robert Wyatt & Bertrand Burgalat: This Summer Night Tricatel, 2007

Bright, light electro-pop disco in two versions, one remixed by Hot Chip.

Hot Chip with Robert Wyatt and Geese EMI, 2008

One of those collaborations that makes perfect sense. Robert contributes vocals and cornet to three of the four songs on this EP – *Made in the Dark*, *Whistle for Will* and *We're Looking for a Lot of Love*.

Orchestre National de Jazz: Around Robert Wyatt Bee Jazz, 2009

France's National Jazz Orchestra rearranged fifteen songs from the Wyatt songbook to fine effect, live and on this album. Robert does vocals on *Song, Kew. Rhone, Vandalusia, Te Recuerdo Amanda, Gegenstand* and *Rangers in the Night*.

Jeanette Lindström: Attitude & Orbit Control Diesel Music, 2009

Robert contributes trumpet on the Swedish singer-songwriter's *We Would, Morning, Blue Room Yellow Tree*, and vocals to *The River*.

Get the Blessing: OCDC Naim Jazz, 2012

Robert is credited with 'voice and birdsong' on *American Meccano* – a track whose rhythm is irresistibly Wyatt.

Grasscut: Unearth Ninja Tune, 2012

Robert contributes cornet, piano and scatted vocals to *Richardson Road*.

LoJo: Cinéma El Mundo World Village, 2012

The French jazz-chanson group are a Wyatt favourite and he makes a low-key vocal contribution on *At the Beginning* and *Cinéma El Mundo*.

Steve Nieve: ToGetHer Verycords, 2013

Another multi-artist get-together from the Elvis Costello keyboard player. Robert duets with French singer and psychoanalyst Muriel Teodori on *La Plus Jolie Langue*.

Ian James Stewart: Junk DNA Dangerous Dogs, 2013

Stewart is a fellow Louth resident. Robert sings lead and plays horn on *When U Love Somebody* and contributes backing vocals to *No Water*.

Gerald Clark: The Great Divide Zube, 2014

Robert sings and plays tenor horn (his recording debut on the instrument) on *Ibrahim*.

WYATT ONLINE

There is a whole lot of Robert Wyatt (and Soft Machine) on film and online. Listed below are the most significant Wyatt-related websites, documentaries and other internet flotsam and jetsam.

Wyatt and related websites

Disco Robert Wyatt

www.disco-robertwyatt.com

This French site bills itself as 'une discographie de Robert Wyatt' but it's a lot more than that. As well as exhaustive discographies for all stages of Wyatt's career, it has archived and scanned most significant interviews and features on him, and has a wonderful mini-encyclopedia of all things Wyatt (click on 'Abecedaire'). It's mostly in English, or automatic translation.

Wyatt and Stuff

http://wyattandstuff.blogspot.com

This blogsite, actively maintained by a Norwegian enthusiast, Svenn Sivertssen, is the best source for news on contemporary Wyatt-related projects, as well as highlighting a host of archive material. It features well-written entries, in-site video links to all manner of treasures, and many diverting sideways links.

Calyx

http://calyx.perso.neuf.fr/

'The Canterbury Music Website', edited by Aymeric Leroy, features news, lyrics and discographies for anyone remotely associated with the Canterbury Scene. Leroy also moderates a Canterbury music Yahoo discussion group, *What's Rattlin*.

Strong Comet

www.strongcomet.com/wyatt/

News, discographies, lyrics and (from its 'Forum' page) some useful video links.

Noisette

www.noisette.nl

A Soft Machine/Matching Mole site packed with discographic detail and photos. Its 'Live' section has a range of embedded live videos; 'Memories' features song lyrics.

Documentaries

Free Will and Testament: The Robert Wyatt Story

Directed by Mark Kidel, 2002. Somethin' Else.

It's a shame there's no official DVD release of this terrific biography of Robert Wyatt, which charted his career from childhood and The Wilde Flowers through to life in Louth and recording *Shleep*. Kidel talks to just about everyone significant in the Wyatt story and the documentary is completed by Wyatt playing his songs with a superb band assembled by Annie Whitehead. You can watch an excerpt of the film on Calliope's website and the whole programe is generally available, in sections, on YouTube.

Little Red Robin Hood

Carlo Bevilacqua and Francesco di Loreto, 1998.

An hour-long film documentary made around the time of *Shleep* and featuring Robert recording the album in Phil Manzanera's studio with Brian Eno. There is also interesting archive footage and extensive interviews with, among others, Kevin Ayers, Andy Summers, John Peel, Nick Mason, Noel Redding, Carla Bley and Chris Cutler. A trailer lives on YouTube but the full film is a VHS rarity.

The Voices of Robert Wyatt

Produced by Alan Hall, 2012.
www.fallingtree.co.uk

This 27-minute radio documentary – just Robert talking – was made for the BBC in 2012. The producers, Falling Tree, have posted it in full on their website.

On the Internet

Some interesting clips worth a search using the keywords in our titles.

THE SOFT MACHINE

The Soft Machine Live at UFO in 1967

The original band with Daevid Allen – who recites poetry to an early Softs drone and Mark Boyle/Joan Hills lightshow.

Soft Machine Italian Documentary 1967

Scratchy but atmospheric footage from an Italian documentary, showing the band (Wyatt, Ayers, Ratledge) rehearsing at Robert's mother's house in Dalmore Road, and performing at the Speakeasy club.

Soft Machine 'Hope for Happiness' (Live television performance on Dim Dam Dom) 1967

French TV recording of the Ayers-era band performing *Hope for Happiness*.

Soft Machine – Ce Soir On Danse, 1967

Excellent, 25-minute film of the Ayers-era band playing the first album on French TV.

Soft Machine 'Moon in June' (full)

A 12-minute version of *Moon in June*, filmed for TV at the 1969 Bilzen festival.

Soft Machine 'Hibou, Anemone and Bear' Live on French TV 1969

The Softs septet –with Elton Dean, Lyn Dobson, Marc Charig and Nick Evans – performing *Hibou, Anemone and Bear* on the French TV show *L'Invité du Dimanche*.

Soft Machine – Live in Paris 1970

An hour-long concert from the Softs quintet (Wyatt, Hopper, Ratledge, Dean, Dobson) performing most of the *Third* album – though without *Moon in June*.

Soft Machine Anatomy of Pop

Search for 'G Funk' and 'soft machine documentary' on YouTube and you'll find this seven-minute documentary from autumn 1970 featuring interviews with Wyatt, Hopper and Ratledge, and footage of the band (the quartet with Elton Dean) performing live in the studio.

MATCHING MOLE

Matching Mole Paris Mai 1972

The band featuring Dave MacRae perform *Instant Pussy* at the Olympia in Paris, plus an interview with Robert playing down songs and talking of the voice as another instrument.

Matching Mole on Rockenstock 1972

Matching Mole, again with Dave MacRae, perform *Gloria Gloom* and *Part of the Dance* on the French TV program *Rockenstock* in 1972. Robert vocalises and drums in a Mexican wrestler balaclava.

Hatfield and the North with Robert Wyatt Live

Robert duets with Richard Sinclair on *God Song* and *A-Mewsing*, as part of a 20-minute medley by the early Hatfield line-up with Dave Sinclair on keyboards, from 1972.

SOLO YEARS

Robert Wyatt – I'm a Believer 1974

Robert mimes to the Neil Diamond song on *Top of the Pops*, accompanied by Dave MacRae, Nick Mason, Andy Summers, Richard Sinclair and Fred Frith.

Robert Wyatt – French TV, May 1975

Robert at the piano singing *Sea Song* and *Alifib*, and being interviewed in French wheeling around Paris. There are also clips from the same show of Robert singing *Hasta Siempre Comandante*.

Robert Wyatt – Shipbuilding (Old Grey Whistle Test 1983)

A flawless live (on TV) performance. Hunt around (*Elvis Costello & Robert Wyatt interview*) and you can also find an accompanying interview with Robert and Elvis Costello, along with the single's video.

Robert Wyatt & the SWAPO Singers – Wind of Change

Robert, Jerry Dammers and Namibian singers live on *The Old Grey Whistle Test*.

David Gilmour with Robert Wyatt – Comfortably Numb 2001

Robert sings from the wings on David Gilmour's performance at Meltdown.

David Gilmour – Then I Close My Eyes with Robert Wyatt 2006

Robert's cornet solo on the Gilmour track, live at the Royal Albert Hall.

Robert Wyatt interview at home, 1994

A 15-minute documentary for the French channel Arte. A highlight is Robert drumming and wheelie-dancing along to the Cuban band Orquesta Reve.

Charlie Haden's Liberation Music Orchestra with Carla Bley and Robert Wyatt – Tail of a Tornado, 2009

Robert's latest live performance, singing (and whistling) Silvio Rodriguez's song *Rabo de Nube* with Charlie Haden's band, at the 2009 Ornette Coleman Meltdown.

Robert Wyatt Video

robertwyattvideo.blogspot.

This work in progress site promises a 'chronological history of Robert Wyatt on film, TV and video'. It has started out from the present and clips include Robert in conversation with *Wire* editor Tony Herrington (from 2011 and 2012) and with Gilad Atzmon (from 2010).

NOTES AND SOURCES

Writing this biography, I've talked extensively to Robert Wyatt and Alfreda Benge, as well as to over seventy people who have known and worked with Robert over the years. I have also made use of Alfie's extensive cuttings archive, and a number of other books, magazines and newspapers. Where quoted directly, these sources are listed below.

I am particularly indebted to two books: Michael King's *Wrong Movements: A Robert Wyatt History* (SAF Publishing, 1994), a meticulous discography and gigography of Robert's activities up to that date, which also features several interviews and an extensive selection of photos, and Graham Bennett's fine biography of The Soft Machine, *Out-Bloody-Rageous* (SAF Publishing, 2005). I am greatly in debt to Aymeric Leroy, for his Calyx site, and to Jean-Paul of *Disco Robert Wyatt*, as well as to Mark Kidel and Jez Nelson, for their 2003 documentary *Free Will and Testament*.

Unless otherwise stated, quotes are from interviews with the author, listed below. All websites were last accessed 28.04.14. Relevant page numbers are given in brackets before each citation.

Author interviews:

Keith Albarn, Daevid Allen, Prue Anderton, Gilad Atzmon, David Bedford, Alfreda Benge, Gina Birch, Björk, Peter Blegvad, Carla Bley, Joe Boyd, Georgina Boyle, Sebastian Boyle, Andy Childs, Julie Christie, Caroline Coon, Richard Coughlan, Lol Coxhill, John Cumming, Chris Cutler, Jerry Dammers, Jeff Dexter, Lyn Dobson, Simon Draper, Sam Ellidge, Brian Eno, Delfina Entrecanales, Nick Evans, Ramón Farrán, Fred Frith, Simon Frith, Green Gartside, David Gilmour, Julian Glover, Vivien Goldman, John Greaves, Charlie Haden, Joan Hills, Brian Hopper, Hoppy, Pam Howard, Jamie Johnson, Jumbo, Adam Kidron, Dagmar Krause, Clive Langer, Bill MacCormick, Dave MacRae, Karen Mantler, Mike Mantler, Phil Manzanera, Nick Mason, Glenn Max, Louis Moholo-Moholo, George Neidorf, Jon Newey, Evan Parker, Terry Riley, Ryuichi Sakamoto, Chris Searle, Ana Da Silva, Valgeir Sigurðsson, David Sinclair, Richard Sinclair, Ellen Sipprell, Ros Stephen, Alexis Taylor, Keith Tippett, Julie Tippetts, Geoff Travis, Ben Watt, Paul Weller, Annie Whitehead, Robert Wyatt, Daniel Yvinec.

CHAPTER 1

[17] 'I do live in a dreamworld': Biba Kopf. 2011. *Local Hero*. http://www.thewire.co.uk/in-writing/interviews/local-hero

[18] 'And they possibly had an affair': Bruce King. 2008. *Robert Graves: A Biography*. London: Haus Publishing. 102.

[18] 'An Ellidge is rebellious against all rules that he has not made himself.' Honor Wyatt and George Ellidge. 1958. *Why Pick On Us?* London: Hurst & Blackett. 29

[19] 'One of the five things that make his world a better place': Charlie Gilmour. 2008. *Robert Wyatt Loves...* http://drownedinsound.com/in_depth/4135483

[20] 'Robert has described the humble, honey-loving teddy bear as his earliest role model': Kopf

[20] 'With the possible exception of the carpet-bombing of Laos': Anon. [No date, no title.] http://www.goodreads.com/author/quotes/563804.Robert_Wyatt

[20] 'The pre-eminent English example of an architectural dynasty': John Martin Robinson. 1979. *The Wyatts: An Architectural Dynasty*. Oxford: Oxford University Press. 4

[20] 'Twas dertag and the slithy Huns': Horace Wyatt. 1914. *Malice In Kulturland*. London: The Car Illustrated. 6

[22] 'Waterloo, Ypres, Agincourt, Trafalgar, Trafalgar': Jeremy Paxman. 2007. *The English*. London: Penguin. 87

[25] 'Robert told me that when he'd been a kid': Mark Boyle. 2000. *Interview with Aymeric Leroy*. 2 December, London

[26] 'George's sclerosis showed a tendency to get more and more multiple': Wyatt and Ellidge, 52

[28] 'And they never lock up a *thing*!': Wyatt and Ellidge, 115

[28] 'Like a set of 88 tuned drums': Valerie Wilmer. 1977. *As Serious As Your Life*. London: Allison & Busby. 176

[29] 'Music writers have tended to romanticise the Langton': Ian MacDonald. 1975. Looking Back. *NME*. 25 January. 32

[33] 'Saxophone colossus': Sonny Rollins. 1956. *Saxophone Colossus*. [Vinyl.] Hackensack: Prestige

[34] 'Rimbaud simply rejected every social standard that existed': Michael King. 1994. *Wrong Movements: A Robert Wyatt History*. Wembley: SAF. No pagination

CHAPTER 2

[39] 'He even describes himself as a sit-down comedian': Stephen Trousse. 2007. *Robert Wyatt*. http://pitchfork.com/features/interviews/6718-robert-wyatt/

[40] 'I had the youth ideology': *Forever Young: How Rock'n'Roll Grew Up*. 2010. [TV documentary.] Chris Rodley. dir. Various. BBC

[42] 'Graves was not averse to occasional marijuana use': William Graves. 1995. *Wild Olives: Life in Majorca with Robert Graves*. London: Hutchinson. 182-3

[43] 'To the hedonism of Federico Fellini's *La Dolce Vita*': ibid. 148

[44] 'Something we got fired from the Establishment Club because of': Daevid Allen. 1993. *Song of the Jazzman*. Daevid Allen Trio. *Live 1963*. [CD]. London: Voiceprint

[45] 'As well as being pretty damned challenging': Hugh Hopper. 1993 [recorded 1963]. Daevid Allen Trio. *Live 1963*. [CD liner notes.] London: Voiceprint

[46] 'I miss him more than I know how to say': Robert Wyatt. 1994.

Flotsam Jetsam. [CD liner notes.] Various locations: Rough Trade.

[48] 'It was at this point, according to Ayers, that the music really began to gel': King. No pagination

[49] 'The most swinging city in the world': John Crosby. 1965. *London, The Most Exciting City In The World*. In Ray Connolly (ed.). 1995. *In The Sixties*. London: Pavilion Books. 77

[49] 'Ejected from a local pub on the grounds that their hair was too long': King. No pagination

[52] 'And even church music': Edward Macan. 1997. *Rocking the Classics: English Progressive Rock and the Counterculture*. Oxford: Oxford University Press. 32

[55] 'Jimmy Somerville on valium': Kopf

[55] 'Like a poor innocent cast into a complicated world': *Free Will and Testament: The Robert Wyatt Story*. 2003. [TV documentary]. Mark Kidel (dir). London: Somethin' Else.

CHAPTER 3

[57] 'And would stand in the path of oncoming traffic to prove it': Tomás Graves. 2004. *Tuning Up at Dawn: A Memoir of Music and Majorca*. London and New York. Fourth Estate. 66

[58] 'The story is that Brunson had abducted his own daughters': Graham Bennett. 2005. *Soft Machine: Out-Bloody-Rageous*. London: SAF. 69

[60] 'Fuzzy documentary footage... still exists': Talckk. 1967 [uploaded 2009]. *Soft Machine Italian Documentary 1967*. http://www.youtube.com/watch?v=UF26wylv1Dk

[62] 'Ratledge too had stayed with the author for a brief period in New York.' Bennett. 72

[63] 'They were by far the most intelligent and educated people on the English rock scene.' King. No pagination.

[65] 'Joe Boyd suggests he was uncomfortably close to the mob world': Joe Boyd. 2006. *White Bicycles*. London: Serpent's Tail. 151

[65] 'There were rumours that Jeffery had worked for British Intelligence services': Sharon Lawrence. 2005. *Jimi Hendrix: The Man, the Magic, the Truth*. London: Pan. 55

[65] 'And later that he was responsible for the death of Jimi Hendrix': James 'Tappy' Wright. 2009. *Rock Roadie: Backstage and Confidential with Hendrix, Elvis, The Animals, Tina Turner, and an All-Star Cast*. London: JR Books Ltd. 231-4

[65] 'Jeffery was certainly one of the murkier figures in rock management': Paul Allen. 2007. *Artist Management For The Music Business*. Amsterdam etc: Focal Press. 32-3

[65] 'He can be heard on Jimi's version of the Beatles' *Daytripper*': John Lennon/Paul McCartney. 1989 [recorded December 1967]. *Day Tripper*. Jimi Hendrix Experience. *Jimi Hendrix Experience: Radio One*. [CD]. London: Castle Communications.

[67] 'The thing about Kim Fowley was, he was a complete codeine freak': Richie Unterberger. [No date.] *Daevid Allen*. www. richieunterberger.com/allen.html

[67] 'The Soft Machine have just released a hit record, *Love Makes Sweet Music*': King. No pagination

[69] 'Apparently only dipped in placebo acid': Rob Chapman. 2010. *Syd Barrett: A Very Irregular Head*. London: Faber. 117

[69] 'One of the most revolutionary events in the history of English music and thinking': Daevid Allen. 2007. *Gong Dreaming 1: From*

Soft Machine to the Birth of Gong. London: SAF. 34

[70] 'Attended by up to 10,000 revellers': Chapman. 159

[78] 'Soft Machine found themselves dubbed "the new Beatles"': Bennett. No pagination

[78] 'Let's go to my chateau': Kevin Ayers. 2003 [originally 1970]. *Clarence in Wonderland. Shooting at the Moon.* [CD]. London: EMI [originally Harvest]

[78] 'Frankly, Robert is probably the best rock drummer I ever heard': Mike Zwerin. 2002. *Interview with Aymeric Leroy.* Paris, 21 October.

[78] 'Their weird hats, long hair, shades, and their funky, bizarre garb': Mike Zwerin in King. No pagination

[79] 'A very grooooovy summer full of sunshine': Kevin Ayers. 1970. Clarence In Wonderland. Kevin Ayers. *BBC Sessions 1970-1976.* [CD]. London: Hux.

[80] 'As he notes, you've got to kill your heroes': Jaime Gonzalo. [No date, no title.] planetgong.co.uk/archives/interviews/da_ruta66.shtml

[80] 'Wyatt embraced the concept of "ubuesque mayhem"': Simon Watson Taylor. 2003. *Letter to Aymeric Leroy.* 29 September.

[82] 'They had already turned down the chance to work with producer Mickie Most': *Stuart Maconie's Freak Zone.* BBC 6 Music. 3 March 2013

[83] 'The instrument was prone to feedback': Bennett. 93

CHAPTER 4

[85] 'He thought we were terribly cute': Jonathan Glancey. 2003. You need a bit missing upstairs to play this game. www.theguardian.com/music/2003/jul/04/artsfeatures

[85] 'They arrived on top of the Pan-Am building, which still then had a heli-

pad': Zwerin. 2002. *Interview with Aymeric Leroy*

[87] '5,000 on a slow night': Bennett. 144

[87] 'Mitch Mitchell recalled Soft Machine as more than up to the challenge': Mitch Mitchell and John Platt. 1990. *The Jimi Hendrix Experience.* London: Pyramid Books. 88

[87] 'Hugh Hopper said it was a miracle any of the gigs happened at all': Bennett. 132

[87] 'This was just something that we just happened to fall into': Kevin Ayers. 2000. *Interview with Aymeric Leroy.* Montolieu, 4 June.

[88] 'Kevin Ayers, it is said, has only ever written three types of song': Nigel Williamson et al. 2008. *The Rough Guide to the Best Music You've Never Heard.* London/New York: Rough Guides. 98

[88] 'Girls lining up outside the door': Bennett. 133

[88] 'The dean threatened to cancel one college show in Colorado': Bennett. 127

[88] 'On another occasion, attempting to fly from Vancouver to Spokane': Bennett. 144

[88] 'I had short hair, and we just looked like regular passengers': Boyle. 2000. *Interview with Aymeric Leroy*

[89] 'I witnessed – outside a Hendrix concert in the US – a policeman pick up an excited Hendrix fan': Robert Wyatt. 1987. Review of Artemi Troitsky's Back in the USSR. *Soviet Weekly.* 28 November.

[90] 'All I remember about him was that he sat on the phone and called his girlfriends all day long': Mark Paytress. 1992. Kevin Ayers Interview. *Record Collector.* June. 40

[92] 'I'm nearly five foot seven tall': credited to Hugh Hopper, Kevin Ayers and Mike Ratledge, although the lyrics are in fact by Robert

Wyatt. 1968. *Why Am I So Short?* Soft Machine. *The Soft Machine.* [CD.] New York: Probe/Intersong

[92] 'It doesn't feel comfortable when I try and pump too much into the delivery': Andy Gill. 1991. Songs Remain the Same. *The Independent.* 15 August, 15

[93] 'Embarrassingly amateur': Ayers, 2000. *Interview with Aymeric Leroy.*

[94] 'You would have thought the whole nation was on fire': Bob Dylan. 2004. *Chronicles: Volume 1.* London/Sydney/New York/Toronto: Pocket Books. 113

[95] 'I could hear Robert and Mike getting very carried away': Paytress

[96] 'I went on a very strict macrobiotic diet': Glancey

[97] 'Lads-on-the-road syndrome': *Free Will and Testament: The Robert Wyatt Story*

[98] 'According to Noel, he and Robert even talked of starting their own band': *Robert Wyatt: Little Red Robin Hood.* 1998. [VHS]. Carlo Bevilacqua and Francesco Di Loreto (dir.). Italy: Polygram

[98] 'In the end you suffer from depersonalisation, loss of identity': Bennett. 132

[98] 'I was never particularly into making ugly noises': Ayers. 2000. *Interview with Aymeric Leroy*

CHAPTER 5

[99] 'According to Mitch Mitchell, their guard dogs were kidnapped and doped': Mitchell. 115

[100] 'Jimi came in and listened and whispered': Harry Shapiro and Caesar Glebbeek. 1990. *Jimi Hendrix: Electric Gypsy.* London: Heinemann. 586

[100] 'Living is easy here in New York state': Robert Wyatt. 1970. *Moon in June.* Soft Machine. *Third.* [CD]. London: CBS

[101] 'Between your thighs I feel a sensation': 1970. *Moon in June.*

[103] 'Mike Ratledge had definitely given up playing live after the American tour': Soft Machine. 2002 [recorded 1969]. *Live at the Paradiso.* [CD liner notes.] Amsterdam: Blueprint

[104] 'The official orchestra of the College of Pataphysics': Robert Wyatt. 1969. *Pataphysical Introduction Pt 1.* The Soft Machine. *Volume Two.* [CD.] London: Big Beat [originally Probe]

[104] 'Pataphysics will examine the laws which govern exceptions': Andrew Hugill. 2012. *'Pataphysics.* Cambridge, MA: MIT. 3

[105] 'The playwright was apparently consuming two litres of wine and three absinthes before midday': Hugill. 194

[107] 'A few fives to take away the taste of all those sevens': Robert Wyatt. 1969. *Pataphysical Introduction Pt 2.* The Soft Machine. *Volume Two*

[107] 'In his organ solos, he fills round the keyboard': Hugh Hopper. 1969. *Thank You Pierrot Lunaire.* The Soft Machine. *Volume Two*

[107] 'He eats brown rice and fish, how nice': Mike Ratledge and Robert Wyatt. 1969. *As Long As He Lies Perfectly Still.* The Soft Machine. *Volume Two*

[107] 'Who is that little clever-dick teenager?': Danny Eccleston. 2008. *The Godfather of Righteous Jazz-Pop Lullaby Takes MOJO's Danny Eccleston Through His Recently Reissued Back Catalogue*

[108] 'Ian and Sean fell out, so we were stuck with Sean Murphy': Bennett. 164

[109] 'Sean Murphy seems not to have been much better in terms of financial transparency': Elton Dean, for instance, speaks of 'managerial robbery' – Bennett. 238

[110] 'It was a loud fucking band, it really was': Julian Cowley. 2005.

Repeat Cycles. *Wire.* September. 259. 28–33

[111] 'I remember Robert scribbling away in the control room': Bennett. 197

[112] 'Playing now is lovely / Here in the BBC': Robert Wyatt. 1969. *Moon in June*. The Soft Machine. *BBC Radio 1967-71.* [CD.] London: Hux

[112] 'I thought they were rehearsals': Steve Lake. 1974. Wyatt: Up from Rock Bottom. *Melody Maker.* 12 October, 42

[114] 'Wyatt was inspired by The Soft Machine's new incarnation': King. No pagination

CHAPTER 6

[115] 'I should like to know on what premises I am expected to take seriously': Bennett. 217

[115] 'As far from *Top of the Pops* as Chopin is from a vaudeville act': Richard Williams. 1970. How to Succeed in Pop Without Really Trying. *Radio Times*. 6 August. 43

[117] 'It gives us a chance to bring out certain things in our music': Bennett. 180

[119] 'With seven musicians it was really becoming too much': Bennett. 183

[120] 'Nick couldn't get along with the amplified trombone': Stephen Yarwood. [No date.] Elton Dean interview. *Facelift ['the issue that never happened'.]* http://homepages.3-c.coop/facelift/facelift/elton%20dean.html.

[120] 'On another planet, but a very interesting player': Bennett 184

[120] 'Not only the best-ever line-up in the band's history': Ian MacDonald. 1975. *The End of an Ear* at the Proms. *NME.* 1 February, 31

[120] 'I was happiest in the Soft Machine when it was an all-electric trio': Richard Williams. 1972. Mole in a Hole. *Melody Maker.* 29 April. 13

[122] 'Music making still performs a normal function': Wyatt. *Moon in June*

[123] 'They did so like unwilling schoolboys': Soft Machine. 1970. *Breda Reactor*. [CD.] Breda: Voiceprint

[124] 'It's hard to work out exactly what the differences were': Bennett. 229

[125] 'Hugh, myself and Elton were pursuing a vaguely jazz-related direction': Rob Chapman. 1997. Soft Machine: A very English Trip. *Mojo*. June. 53

[126] 'John Peel's favourite drummer': John Peel. 1973. Tubular Bells by John Peel. *The Listener.* 7 June. 775

[126] 'There was a bit of a misunderstanding with the avant-garde rock scene': Richie Unterberger. 1998. *Unknown Legends of Rock'n'Roll*. San Francisco: Backbeat Books. 402

[127] 'Robert was the opposite of Mike and me': Bennett. 88

[127] 'He refused to learn to read music': John Mulvey. 2007. *The Freewheelin' Robert Wyatt*. www.disco-robertwyatt.com/images/Robert/interviews/Uncut_october_2007/

[128] 'Although the so-called conspiracy between Hugh, myself and Elton': Chapman. 53

CHAPTER 7

[129] 'Mike and I couldn't stand Robert's singing': Bennett. 221

[131] 'Six beautiful girls': Kevin Ayers et al. 1997 [recorded 1970.] *The Garden of Love*. [CD liner notes.] London: Voiceprint

[132] 'Dudu Pukwana said he was dwarfed by his own sandals': Maxine McGregor. 1995. *Chris McGregor and the Brotherhood of Breath: My Life with a South African*

Jazz Pioneer. Flint, MI: Bamberger Books. 29

[133] 'An insane travelling circus – and the happiest group he'd ever been in': Centipede. 1971. *Septober Energy.* [CD liner notes.] London: BGO Records [originally RCA]

[134] 'Most people in the company thought I was nuts when I played them that record': David Howells. 2005. *Interview with Aymeric Leroy.* London. 20 March

[134] 'Out of work pop singer': Robert Wyatt. 1970. *The End of an Ear.* [CD back cover.] London: Sony

[134] 'Casting off the corsets': Paytress. 199

[136] 'The record isn't anti-Soft Machine': Al Clark. 1972. Matching Mole: The Beginning of Another Ear. *Time Out.* 16–22 June. 14–15

[136] 'I looked up to him tremendously; he was my hero': Mike Oldfield. 2007. *Changeling: the Autobiography.* London: Virgin. 84

[140] 'Dealing with a third of all drug busts in the country': Barbara Ellen. 2000. *Still Fighting the Bad Guys.* www.theguardian.com/ theobserver/2000/jul/30/features. review17

[142] 'Both better and no better than *Third*': Bennett. 223

[146] 'He wasn't like a Keith Moon or anything like that': *Free Will and Testament: the Robert Wyatt Story*

[146] 'Storming into one dressing room at the interval': Bennett. 207

[147] 'The room vibrates with the sheer, exhilarating power of it': Steve Lake. 2005. *Email to Aymeric Leroy.*

[147] 'Robert swallowed his unhappiness a lot': Yarwood

[147] 'Because we were sort of middle class white chappies from England': *Free Will and Testament: the Robert Wyatt Story*

[147] 'Probably the last time I enjoyed what I was doing': From the Gong fanzine, trans Saverio Pechini. Re-printed in Phil Howitt (ed.). 1989. *The Mike Ratledge Interviews. Facelift.* 2. No pagination

[148] 'Someone showed me an old film of our rehearsal for Soft Machine *Fourth*': [No name or date but presumably 1971.] *Fourth Album Rehearsal.* [Youtube footage.] www.youtube.com/watch?v=P_DWKVB7riM

[148] 'Robert started to walk offstage in the middle of gigs': Bennett. 227

[148] 'There were nights when we would make fun of Robert behind his back': Chapman. *Mojo*

[149] 'Wyatt quits Softs': King. No pagination

[150] 'I was starting to get bored': Bennett. 246

[150] 'Mike couldn't say no': Bennett. 293

CHAPTER 8

[153] 'Man and wife': Robert Wyatt and David Sinclair. 1972. *O Caroline.* Matching Mole. *Matching Mole.* [CD.] London: Esoteric [originally CBS]

[154] 'Drew straws to decide which of us was going to comfort him': Linda Lewis. 2009. *The Night I Asked My Boyfriend 'Do You Mind If I Sleep with Cat Stevens?'* www.dailymail. co.uk/femail/article-1194291/Singer-Linda-Lewis-The-night-I-asked-boyfriend-Do-mind-I-sleep-Cat-Stevens.html

[155] 'Let's drink some wine': Kevin Ayers. 1971. *Whatevershebringswesing.* Kevin Ayers. *Whatevershebringswesing* [CD.] London: Harvest

[155] 'I had to put something together': Dave DiMartino. 1987. Things You Should Know About Robert Wyatt. *Creem.* January. 44

[157] 'Songs reputedly about Caroline Coon': [No author, no date, no title. www.carolinecoon.com

[157-8] 'I love you still, Caroline': *O Caroline*

[158] 'Old records are like old tattoos': Kopf

[158] 'This is the first verse': Robert Wyatt. 1972. *Signed Curtain*. Matching Mole. *Matching Mole*. [CD.] London: Esoteric [originally CBS]

[159] 'More than I'd hoped for – a song! For the first time in how long?' Lake. *Email to Aymeric Leroy*

[160] 'What we have here, ladies and gentlemen': Williams. *Melody Maker*.

[160] 'Devastates anything by the corporate cool smoothie': MacDonald. *NME,* February

[161] 'It's worse than it was in the early days of the Softs': Williams. *Melody Maker*

CHAPTER 9

[167] 'We are determined to liberate Taiwan!' King. No pagination

[169] 'Like so many of you / I've got my doubts about how much to contribute': Bill MacCormick and Robert Wyatt. 1972. *Gloria Gloom*. Matching Mole. *Little Red Record*. [CD.] London: Esoteric [originally CBS]

[170] 'What on earth are you doing, God?' Phil Miller and Robert Wyatt. 1972. *God Song*. Matching Mole. *Little Red Record*.

[170] 'Religion as the opium of the people': see Francis Wheen. 1999. *Karl Marx*. London: Fourth Estate

[173] 'For years kept a photo of Robert on his kitchen wall': John Peel and Sheila Ravenscroft. 2005. *Margrave of the Marshes*. London/Toronto/Sydney/Auckland/Johannesburg: Bantam Press. 281–2

[174] 'I've always had this problem, right from the time I started playing music': Lake. 1974

[174] '*Antimony*, the "plus–minus" central to Pataphysics': Hugill. 9–12

[178] 'It is the collected Matching Mole radio sessions': Matching Mole. 2006 [recorded 1972.] *On the Radio*. [CD liner notes.] London: Hux

[179] 'I'm a bit suicidal like that': Phil McMullen. 1992. Robert Wyatt. *Ptolemaic Terrascope*. 3(1). 9

[179] 'Outwardly at least, the two bands seemed to get on fine': Lake. *Email to Aymeric Leroy*

CHAPTER 10

[184] 'Alife my larder': Robert Wyatt. 2008 [originally 1974.] *Alifib/Alife*. Robert Wyatt. *Rock Bottom*. Wiltshire/London: Domino [originally Virgin]

[186] 'I really admired them, so I thought they must be right': Robert Sandall. 2003. *Triumph of a Late Bloomer*. www.telegraph.co.uk/culture/music/rockandjazzmusic/3603723/Triumph-of-a-late-bloomer.html

[186] 'To evade a typical party tangle': Vivien Goldman. 1980. Up from *Rock Bottom. Melody Maker*. 15 March. 32–3

[187] 'Don't worry mummy, I always was a lazy bastard': King. No pagination

[188] 'His whole philosophy as far as his accident went was "hum, bloody typical!"' Peel. 280–1

CHAPTER 11

[198] 'Dead moles lie inside their holes': Robert Wyatt. 2008 [originally 1974.] *Little Red Robin Hood Hit the Road*. *Rock Bottom*

[199] 'Oh no, no I can't stand it': Robert Wyatt. 2008 [originally 1974.] *Little*

Red Riding Hood Hit the Road. *Rock Bottom*

[199] 'Describing the mood during the recording as closer to euphoria': Jim Irving (ed.). 2000. *The Mojo Collection*. Edinburgh: Mojo Books. 359

[199] 'Burlybunch, the water mole': *Alifib/Alife*

[199] 'Alife my larder': *Alifib/Alife*

[199] 'I'm not your larder, jammy jars and mustard': *Alifib/Alife*

[200] 'Your lunacy fits neatly with my own': Robert Wyatt. 2008 [originally 1974.] *Sea Song*. Robert Wyatt. *Rock Bottom.*

[201] 'I can't understand / The different you in the morning': *Sea Song*

[201] 'You've been so kind / I know I know': *Little Red Riding Hood Hit the Road*

[201] 'A *Top Gear* session Robert recorded alone in September 1974': Robert Wyatt. 1987 [recorded 1974.] [CD.] London: Strange Fruit

[202] 'I'm not an eccentric. Everybody else is an eccentric': Ivor Cutler. 1974. Quote of the Year. *Melody Maker.* 28 December.

[202] 'Never knowingly understood': Anon. 2006. *Ivor Cutler.* www. thestage.co.uk/features/ obituaries/2006/03/ivor-cutler/

[203] 'Fierce forest of trumpets': Richard Cook. 1981. *Rock Bottom* (re-issue) review. *NME.* 18 April, 36

[204] 'Childlike visions leaping into view': Peter Mills. 2010. *Hymns to the Silence: Inside the Words and Music of Van Morrison.* London/ New York: Continuum. 296

[205] 'Equally poised between hope and despair': Mills. 296

[207] 'Virgin, Robert told a journalist at the time, was where all his mates were': Steve Peacock. 1974. Expressions of Robert. *Sounds.* 23 March. 11

[208] 'Oldfield played twenty instruments on the final album': Dave Simpson. 2013. *How We Made: Richard Branson and Mike Oldfield on Tubular Bells. www.theguardian. com/music/2013/may/20/how-we-made-tubular-bells*

[209] 'Branson's five-billion-dollar fortune': 2014. *#281 Richard Branson. www.forbes.com/profile/ richard-branson/*

[210] 'Such a deep-pile context for the music': Goldman

[210] 'Poetry in motion is what you've become': Phil Miller and Robert Wyatt. 2009 [originally 1974.] Calyx. Hatfield and the North. *Hatfield and the North.* [CD.] Oxfordshire: Esoteric Recordings [originally Virgin]

[211] 'The bugger in the short sleeves fucked my wife': Williamson et al. 98

[212] 'Naked and alone': King. [No Pagination]

[213–4] 'Robert Wyatt was probably the most creative and individual drummer in British rock': Ian MacDonald. 1974. *Review of Rock Bottom.* www.rocksbackpages. com/Library/Article/robert-wyatt-irock-bottom

[214] 'Not only is *Rock Bottom* the album': Steve Peacock. 1974. *Rock Bottom* review. *Sounds.* 10 August, 27

[214] 'It is still widely considered one of the finest albums ever made': See for instance: Al Spicer. 1999. *Rock: 100 Essential CDs.* London: Rough Guides. 197. Or Irving (ed.). Or Paul Morley. 2003. *Words and Music.* London: Bloomsbury. 318

[214] 'People think I must have problems talking about my accident': Mac Randall. 1992. *Tough Guys Don't Dance: Robert Wyatt meets Bill Nelson.* www. rocksbackpages.com/Library/ Article/robert-wyatt--bill-nelson-tough-guys-dont-dance

CHAPTER 12

[215] 'For Robert Wyatt of Twickenham, opportunity knocks!' John Peel. 1974. Introduction by John Peel. Robert Wyatt and Friends. *Theatre Royal Drury Lane 8th September 1974.* [CD.] London: Domino

[215] '*Tubular Bells* was already well on its way to selling 25 million copies': Irving (ed.). 334

[217] 'There was more genuine originality in Robert Wyatt's concert at Drury Lane Theatre': Maurice Rosenbaum. 1974. Review of Drury Lane concert. *Daily Telegraph.* 9 September

[218] 'It's amazing to hear myself saying this': Steve Peacock. 1974. *Cultured Gent Hits Rock Bottom. Sounds.* 20 July, 14

[219] 'The best single for many years': Steve Lake. 1974. Review of Drury Lane Concert. *Melody Maker.* 14 September. 17

[219] 'My doctor told me never to play faster than my pulse rate': Nick Mason. 2014, *I'm a Believer. Uncut.* February, 39

[220] 'Apparently deemed unsuitable for family viewing': Robert Wyatt. 1999. *EPs.* [CD liner notes.] Various: Domino

[221] 'Some at Virgin apparently considered it too lugubrious': *EPs*

[221] 'No, absolutely not': Lake. 1974

[222] 'Very often you will find there's a class thing in it': Peacock. *Cultured Gent Hits Rock Bottom*

[223] 'The Yardbirds getting into bed with Ligeti in the smoking rubble of divided Berlin': Jonathan Coe. 2001. *The Rotters' Club.* 2008 edition. London: Penguin. 46

[224] 'This is where our music comes from': Chris Cutler and Tim Hodgkinson. 1981. *The Henry Cow Book.* London: Third Step. 50

[225] 'I've done it a couple of times': *Front Row.* BBC Radio 4. 23 September, 2010

[228] 'Brian Eno, the self-declared non-musician': Vladimir Bogdanov et al. (ed.). 2001. *The All Music Guide to Electronica.* San Francisco: Backbeat Books. 167

[228] 'Over one hundred worthwhile dilemmas': Anon. [No date.] *Oblique Strategies.* www.enoshop.co.uk/product/oblique-strategies.html

[229] 'Direct inject anti-jazz raygun': Robert Wyatt. 2008 [originally 1975.] *Ruth Is Stranger Than Richard.* [CD liner notes.] Oxfordshire: Domino [originally Virgin.]

[229] 'Cuba in the years after the 1959 revolution': Odd Arne Westad. 2007. *The Global Cold War: Third World Interventions and the Making of Our Times.* Cambridge: Cambridge University Press. 170

[229] 'Executed in 1967 by Bolivian authorities assisted by the CIA': Westad. 178

[229] 'The revolutionary physician ready to kill or die for his ideals': Archie Brown. 2010. *The Rise & Fall of Communism.* London: Vintage Books. 306

[230] 'He even claimed to be horrified by the sound of his own voice': Allan Jones. 1975. Ruth, Richard and Robert. *Melody Maker.* 14 June, 30

[230] 'I'm the best football you have got': Robert Wyatt, Bill MacCormick, and Phil Manzanera. 2008 [originally 1975.] *Team Spirit.* Robert Wyatt. *Ruth Is Stranger Than Richard.* [CD.] Oxfordshire: Domino [originally Virgin.]

[230] 'The agony that thus far he has managed to be appearing to shrug off': Peter Erskine. 1975. *Ruth Is Stranger Than Richard* review. *NME.* 7 June, 24

[230] 'A most disturbing record': Steve Peacock. 1975. *Ruth Is Stranger Than Richard* review. *Melody Maker.* 12 July, 27

[233] 'His body apparently lying in a bare room all night before it was noticed': Gwen Ansell. 2005. *Soweto Blues: Jazz, Popular Music and Politics in South Africa*. London/New York: Continuum. 240

[233] 'Mongezi Feza died a quite unnecessary death': Bill Forman. 1998. *Avant-Pop's Elder Statesman on Hegemony, Hendrix and Heaps of Sheep*. www.disco-robertwyatt. com/images/Robert/interviews/ Pulse1998/index.htm

[233] 'A large question mark': McGregor. 164

[233] 'They had drugged him with Largactil': McGregor. 165

CHAPTER 13

[236] 'People would ask me who I thought the best vocalist I'd heard that year was': McMullen. 9

[239] 'As ignorable as it was interesting': Mark Richardson. 2002. *As Ignorable As It Is Interesting: The Ambient Music of Brian Eno*. pitchfork.com/features/ resonant-frequency/5879-resonant-frequency-17/

[242] 'Margaret Thatcher could speak of the country being "swamped" by immigrants': Andy Beckett. 2009. *When the Lights Went Out: What Really Happened to Britain in the Seventies*. London: Faber. 442

[242] 'Blair Peach could die at an anti-racism demonstration, almost certainly at the hands of the police': Paul Lewis. 2010. *Blair Peach Killed by Police at 1979 Protest, Met Report Finds*. www.theguardian. com/uk/2010/apr/27/blair-peach-killed-police-met-report

[243] 'The guitarist claimed that Britain was in danger of becoming "a black colony"': Sarfraz Manzoor. 2008. *The Year Rock Found the Power to Unite*. www.theguardian.com/ music/2008/apr/20/popandrock. race

[243] 'Eric Clapton says he loves dancing': Alfreda Benge. 1978. *Letter to Melody Maker*, printed 23 December

[245] 'Ignorant louts in hospital workers' unions': Woodrow Wyatt. 1977. *What's Left of the Labour Party?* London: Sidgwick and Jackson. 107

[245] 'Ultra-left Wing teachers who preach anarchy and the disruption of society': ibid. 135

[245] 'I think that joining the Communist Party was wanting the conversation to remain open': Brian Eno, *Free Will and Testament: the Robert Wyatt Story*

[245] 'Reagan and Thatcher ratcheted up the Cold War into something approaching an anti-communist crusade': Alwyn W Turner. 2010. *Rejoice! Rejoice! Britain in the 1980s*. London: Aurum. 97

[245] 'I decided to find out what it felt like to be "the enemy" of the time': Ryan Dombal. 2012. *Robert Wyatt*. http://pitchfork.com/features/5-10-15-20/8776-robert-wyatt/

[247] 'Oxfam and Survival International pamphlets, he says, inspired his CPGB membership as much as Marx and Engels': Neil Spencer. 1991. Rimshots Fired into the Constant Battle. *The Observer*. 8 September

[247] 'Sixteen communist states by the end of the decade': Brown. 3

[247] 'Particularly in Asia and Africa, communism was strongly linked to anti-colonialism': Brown. 334

[247] 'The Soweto Uprising of 1976 was followed by a massacre of almost 500 black South Africans, some as young as four years old': John Pilger. 2006. *Freedom Next Time*. London: Black Swan. 257

[247] 'Marxism "was invaluable in the struggle against apartheid, which was one of the reasons I got involved"': Phil Johnson. 1997.

Robert Wyatt The Only Way Is Up When You've Hit Rock Bottom. http://www.independent.co.uk/ life-style/interview-robert-wyatt-the-only-way-is-up-when-youve-hit-rock-bottom-1241992.html

[248] 'I suppose I'm a communist like Cliff Richard is a Christian': David Granville. 1999. *Morning Star.* 16 November

[248] 'Bringing to a sudden end the period of détente': Robert Service. 2007. *Comrades – Communism: A World History.* London: Pan Books. 329

[248] 'But then, I look at all the people who've been anti-communist': Graham Lock. 1980. Quiet Wyatt Breaks His Silence. *NME.* 16 August. 14

[248] 'By the time Robert joined, official British communism had for some time been dying on its feet': Service. 90

[248] 'I've always been more interested in giving nice people and nice ideas a decent funeral': Nick Coleman. 1991. *Time Out.* 11–18 September

[248] 'The problem with socialism, Oscar Wilde had it': Terry Eagleton. 2011. *Why Marx Was Right.* New Haven/London: Yale University Press. 26

[248] 'Loony left': Turner. 154

CHAPTER 14

[252] 'The archetypal indie label': 2006. Rob Young. *Rough Trade.* London: Black Dog. 10

[253] 'I look for the beautiful in people we are told to hate': John Lewis. 2001. Wyatt Riot. *Time Out.* 16–23 May. 24

[254] 'Pinochet is selling off their land to foreign big business': Lock. 14

[254] 'Wyatt found a version by Castroist singer-songwriter Carlos Puebla': Neil Taylor. 2010. *Document and*

Eyewitness: An Intimate History of Rough Trade. London: Orion. 150

[255-6] 'The apparently feel-good lyrics of Chic hits like *Le Freak, Dance Dance Dance (Yowsah Yowsah Yowsah)* and *Good Times* were in fact deeply ironic': Peter Shapiro. 2005. *Turn the Beat Around: The Secret History of Disco.* London: Faber. 154-62

[256] 'Rodgers had written the lines back when he was a Black Panther': Daryl Easlea. 2004. *Everybody Dance: Chic and the Politics of Disco.* London: Helter Skelter. 130

[256] 'He was, he later joked, still waiting for puberty': Goldman. 33

[256] 'It's a bit inappropriate, like asking a Jew to sing from the Koran': Goldman

[256] 'Then that bear smacked the Führer, with a mighty armoured paw': Bill Johnson. 2008 [Wyatt version originally released 1981.] *Stalin Wasn't Stallin'.* Robert Wyatt. *Nothing Can Stop Us.* [CD.] London: Domino [originally Rough Trade]

[256] '*Clinamen*: the slight swerve that creates an entirely new meaning': Jill Fell. 2010. *Alfred Jarry.* London: Reaktion. 131

[257] 'The evil empire': Service. 416

[257] 'Quite possibly the battle that changed the course of the entire war': ibid. 218–9

[257] 'Chris Searle: for a period perhaps the most famous teacher in England': Fran Abrams. 1995. *Sacked Radical Head Doomed to Repeat the Lessons of History.* www.independent.co.uk/news/uk/ home-news/sacked-radical-head-doomed-to-repeat-the-lessons-of-history-1527916.html

[259] 'Some, such as the American critic Greil Marcus': Taylor. 151

[259] 'I still think it was the noblest experiment in human history, the Soviet thing': Kopf

[260] 'Do not mind if I thump you when I'm talking to you': Ivor Cutler. 2008 [Wyatt's version originally 1982.] *Grass*. Robert Wyatt. *Nothing Can Stop Us*

[260] 'What people's lives mainly consist of is having families': Dombal

[261] 'These are of course entirely deliberate and reproduced as evidence of my almost painful sincerity': *Nothing Can Stop Us*. [CD liner notes.]

[262] 'The first half was apparently based on Ornette Coleman's *Peace*': King. No pagination

[263] 'Let Mandela rot in prison': Robert Wyatt. 2008 [Wyatt's original 1981.] *Born Again Cretin*. Robert Wyatt. *Nothing Can* Stop Us. [CD.] London: Domino [originally Rough Trade]

[263] '"Cretin" is actually derived from "Christian"': Anon. [No date, no title.] oxforddictionaries.com/definition/english/cretin

[265] 'What previously seemed like the wishy-washy liberal pre-occupations of vegetarianism': Sally Davison and Sue Scott. 1982. *Morning Star.* 14 May

[265] 'I was invited to go for a week just to record the actual process of my working': Robert Wyatt. 2009 [recorded 1981.] *Radio Experiment Rome, February 1981.* [CD liner notes.] Rome: Rai Trade

[266] 'I still can't see why people listen instead of doing it themselves': Hugh Hopper, arr. Robert Wyatt. 1969. *Thank You Pierrot Lunaire*. The Soft Machine. *Volume Two*

[266] 'Opening himself up to a golden age of British pop': Simon Reynolds. 2005. *Vision on.* www.theguardian.com/music/2005/apr/24/popandrock5

[266] 'I felt like a teddy bear mascot at a football match': Robert Wyatt and Tony Herrington. 2012. *The Wire Salon: An Audience with Robert Wyatt.* 12 April, Café Oto, London

[268] 'The "not nit not" lyrics on *Rock Bottom*': Robert Wyatt. 2008 [originally 1974.] *Alifib/Alife*

[268] 'Messthetics': Simon Reynolds. 2005. *Rip It Up and Start Again: Post-Punk 1978–1984.* London: Faber. 203

[268] 'Jacques Derrida or Nietzsche': Simon Reynolds. 2009. *Totally Wired.* London: Faber. 191–2

CHAPTER 15

[270] '*Shipbuilding* just arrived on my mat': *Is It Worth It?*. 2012. BBC Radio 2. 25 June, 10pm

[271] 'A new winter coat and shoes for the wife': Clive Langer and Elvis Costello. 2008 [originally 1982.] *Shipbuilding*. Robert Wyatt. *EPs.* [CD.] London: Domino [originally Rough Trade]

[271] '"Gotcha"': Turner. 110

[271] 'It was already pretty horrifying to see the glee': *Is It Worth It?*

[272] 'It wasn't that hard to imagine': *Shipbuilding*. 2013. BBC Radio 4. 17 March, 1.30pm. Soul Music series

[273] 'Costello admitted that he got choked up listening to Robert in the studio': Neil Spencer. 1982. *A Man out of Time*. www.elviscostello.info/wiki/index.php/New_Musical_Express,_October_30,_1982)

[274] 'Listeners to John Peel's show voted *Shipbuilding* the second best song of 1982': Julian White. [No year.] *John Peel's Festive Fifty 1982.* www.rocklistmusic.co.uk/festive50lists.htm

[274] 'The NME named it among their top three tracks of the year': [No author, no year.] Albums and tracks of the year (1982). www.nme.com/bestalbumsandtracksoftheyear/1982

[274] 'This time it made the top 40': Young. 176

[274] 'Here's another piece of completely escapist light entertainment': *The Old Grey Whistle Test*. 1983. BBC 2. 3 June.

[274] 'Widely regarded as a pinnacle of political pop': Daniel Trilling. 2010. *The Greatest Political Songs Of All Time*. www.newstatesman.com/blogs/cultural-capital/2010/03/greatest-political-songs

[276] 'It had even been sung by a defiant Jara': Dorian Lynskey. 2010. *33 Revolutions Per Minute*. London: Faber. 291

[278] 'Stories of the brutality of the Koevoet counter-insurgency force were legion': Christopher Wren. 1989. *Rebel Hunters in Namibia Train for Less Violent Times as Ordinary Police*. www.nytimes.com/1989/01/15/world/rebel-hunters-in-namibia-train-for-less-violent-times-as-ordinary-police.html?pagewanted=all&src=pm

[278] 'If you want to know how I view South Africa': Jack Barron. 1985. *Sounds*. 2 November

[278] 'Compromised by their interest in the country's uranium': Sheryl Garratt. 1985. *City Limits*. 18–24 October

[279] 'I am a real Minimalist, because I don't do very much': King. No pagination

[279] 'What saps my concentration is partly physical boredom I think': ibid. No pagination

[281] 'Everyone needs to feel at home': Hugh Hopper and Robert Wyatt. 2008 [originally 1984.] *Amber and the Amberines*. Robert Wyatt. *EPs*

[281] 'An EP of "secular hymns"': *EPs*. [CD liner notes]

[282] 'Biko's death "leaves me cold"': [Anon.] 1997. *Steve Biko: Martyr of the Anti-Apartheid Movement*. news.bbc.co.uk/1/hi/world/africa/37448.stm

[282] 'You can blow out a candle': Peter Gabriel. 2008 [Wyatt's version originally 1984; Gabriel's version 1980.] *Biko*. Robert Wyatt. *EPs*

[283] 'Punk on valium': Sandall

CHAPTER 16

[284] 'The very first time that I met Robert Wyatt and his wife': Granville

[286] 'Paraplegic vanity': Robert Wyatt and Tony Herrington

[286] 'Anybody who is in rock has to be interested in politics': Jack Barron. 1984. Life's a Wyatt. *Sounds*. 8 September

[286] 'Not every inhuman action of the twentieth century was perpetrated by communists': Service. 480

[288] 'Communist Party membership had doubled during the famous General Strike of 1926': Raphael Samuel. 2006 [originally 1985–7]. *The Lost World of British Communism*. London/New York: Verso. 33–4

[288] 'The longest suicide note in history': Kenneth Morgan. 2001. *Britain Since 1945: The People's Peace*. [Third edition.] Oxford: Oxford University Press. 464

[288] 'You say you're self-sufficient but you don't dig your own coal': Robert Wyatt. 2008 [originally 1985.] *Alliance*. Robert Wyatt. *Old Rottenhat*. [CD.] London: Domino [originally Rough Trade]

[288] 'I've got a couple of friends who, over the years, drifted towards the Alliance': Sean O'Hagan. 1985. Does Robert Wyatt Have the Sweetest Voice and Sharpest Brain in English Pop? *NME*. 14 December. 30

[289] 'They say the working class is dead, we're all consumers now': Robert Wyatt. 2008 [originally 1985.] *The Age of Self*. Robert Wyatt. *Old Rottenhat*

[289-90] 'Stained by its associations with apartheid South Africa': James

Vassilopoulos. 1997. *Rio Tinto: the World's Worst Company?* www.greenleft.org.au/node/15851

[290] 'The foreigners are at it again': Robert Wyatt. 2008 [originally 1985.] *The British Road*. Robert Wyatt. *Old Rottenhat*

[290] *Gharbzadegi*, which took its title from an Iranian term meaning 'Weststruckness': Jalal A-le Ahmad, trans. Paul Sprachman. 1982. Plagued by the West (Gharbzadegi). Delmar, New York: Caravan Books. xi

[290] 'Not since the golden days of Sixties protest pop': David Fricke. 1986. Review of *Old Rottenhat*. *Rolling Stone*. 4 December

[290] 'Self-proclaimed dean of rock critics': Robert Christgau. [No date.] *Dean of American Rock Critics*. www.robertchristgau.com

[290] 'Set your political statements to unprepossessingly hypnotic music': Robert Christgau. [No date.] *Old Rottenhat*. www.robertchristgau.com/get_artist.php?name=robert+wyatt

[291] 'Chomsky, to whom Wyatt attributes the phrase on Alliance, uses it too': Uploaded by Spasoje Dragicevic; interview by Danilo Mandic. 2006. *Noam Chomsky Mocks Intellectuals or 'Independent Minds'*. www.youtube.com/watch?v=ZZ0jIYPfA-s

[291] 'Perhaps 200,000 East Timorese had died': Noam Chomsky. 1999. *Why Americans Should Care About East Timor*. www.chomsky.info/articles/19990826.htm

[291] 'East Timor, East Timor, who's your fancy friend, Indonesia?': Robert Wyatt. 2008 [originally 1985.] *East Timor*. Robert Wyatt. *Old Rottenhat*

[294] 'If you're not a liberal when you're 25, you have no heart': [Anon, no year.] *Quotes Falsely Attributed*. www.winstonchurchill.org/learn/speeches/quotations/quotes-falsely-attributed

[294] 'Wyatt would later cite a couple of communist festivals in Italy, in the mid-1980s, as the happiest moments of his life': Rosanna Greenstreet. 1992. The Questionnaire. *The Guardian*. 1–2 February

[294] 'Careful people trying that bit harder': King. No pagination

[295] 'Finland was a country in which the Communist Party was a serious political force': Brown. 117

CHAPTER 17

[300] '200 miles and three decades from London': Duncan Heining. 2007. *Robert Wyatt – Human Nature*. http://www.jazzwisemagazine.com/feature-table-mainmenu-134/7172-robert-wyatt-human-nature

[302] 'I think that it has to be said that the Communist Party came about for a reason': Anon. 2008. *Robert Wyatt: Clash Q&A*. www.clashmusic.com/feature/robert-wyatt

[303] 'We'll turn things upside down when the revolution comes': Mat Fox and J. Bruce Glasier. 1990. Turn Things Upside Down. The Happy End. *Turn Things Upside Down*. [CD.] Sheffield: Cooking Vinyl

[304] 'I worked on it a lot': Randall

[304] 'After the party is over my friend': Robert Wyatt. 2008. [*Dondestan* originally 1991; *Dondestan (Revisited)* 1998.] *CP Jeebies*. Robert Wyatt. *Dondestan Revisited*. [CD.] South Thoresby: Domino [originally Rough Trade]

[304] 'Green and yellow pinky blue': ibid

[304] 'There's no such place as middle ground': 2008. [*Dondestan* originally 1991; *Dondestan (Revisited)* 1998.] *Left on Man*. Robert Wyatt. *Dondestan Revisited*

[304] 'Privatise / next / the airforce': 2008. [*Dondestan* originally 1991;

Dondestan (Revisited) 1998.] NIO. Robert Wyatt. *Dondestan Revisited*

[304] 'If you said to a Tory: let's privatise the army and the royal family': John Haylett. 1991. *Morning Star*. 19 October

[304] 'Trouble isn't my middle name': 2008. [*Dondestan* originally 1991; *Dondestan (Revisited)* 1998.] *Lisp Service*. Robert Wyatt. *Dondestan Revisited*

[305] 'Palestine's a country': 2008. [*Dondestan* originally 1991; *Dondestan (Revisited)* 1998.] *Dondestan*. Robert Wyatt. *Dondestan Revisited*

[306] 'Fierce orange of the egg-shaped fireball': 2008. [*Dondestan* originally 1991; *Dondestan (Revisited)* 1998.] *Costa*. Robert Wyatt. *Dondestan Revisited*

[308] 'Simplify, reduce, oversimplify': *Left on Man*

[308] 'In went the multifarious, multicoloured experiences; out came their unified, assimilated expression': Nicola Shulman. 2011. *Graven with Diamonds: The Many Lives of Thomas Wyatt – Courtier, Poet, Assassin, Spy*. London: Short Books. 272. Though some have speculated that Wyatt was an ancestor, Robert insists there is no connection

[308] 'Robert Wyatt's muse is back on-line': Ben Watson. 1991. *There's a Wyatt Going On*. Wire. September, 42

[309] 'The *NME* sent a self-declared Trot to lock horns with this ageing "tankie"': Steven Wells. 1991. Wheelie Saying Something. *NME*. 21 September. 12

[309] 'Popular music's best-loved unreconstructed socialist': Coleman

[309] 'Rock's last communist': Mark Sinker. 1991. *New Statesman*. 18 October

[309-310] 'The perfect way to disrupt a busy Friday night in a high street pub': Ned Beauman. 2006.

Wyatting (vb): When Jukeboxes Go Mad. www.theguardian.com/music/2006/jul/10/popandrock

[310] 'A European, a rich person, anyone not of African origin': Mark Hudson. 1989. *Our Grandmothers' Drums*. London: Minerva. 320-1

[312] 'Peel's foe, not a set animal, laminates a tone of sleep': John Greaves and Peter Blegvad. 2004. *Kew.Rhone*. John Greaves. *Songs*. [CD.] Various: Le Chant du Monde

[316] 'The right-wing triumphalism of the eighties got to me': Jonathan Romney. 1997. *The Guardian*. 10 October

[316] 'I don't want to be fossilised': *Robert Wyatt: Little Red Robin Hood*

[319] 'He had been known to burst into tears if a gig went badly': Bennett. 176

[319] 'Artists: who the fuck do we think we are?': Robert Wyatt and Tony Herrington

CHAPTER 18

[320] 'Like Alice in Wonderland': Johnson

[322] 'Had I been free, I could have chosen not to be me': Robert Wyatt and Kramer. 2008 [Wyatt's version originally 1997.] *Free Will and Testament*. Robert Wyatt. *Shleep*. [CD.] Chertsey: Domino [originally Hannibal]

[323] 'I almost forgot where we buried the hatchet': Robert Wyatt and Hugh Hopper. 2008 [originally 1997.] *Was a Friend*. Robert Wyatt. *Shleep*

[323] 'Old wounds are healing': ibid

[327] 'Beach of shapes and shingle': Philip Larkin. 1988. Here, from *Collected Poems*. 1990 edition. London: Fabor and Faber/The Marvell Press. 136-7

[327] 'Ralph Vaughan Williams had sought inspiration at *Spurn Point*':

Ralph Vaughan Williams. 1926 [this version 1992.] *Andante Sostenuto (Spurn Point)*. Janet Hilton. Bax: *Clarinet Sonata*, Bliss: *Clarinet Quintet*, Vaughan Williams: *Six Studies in English Folksong*. [CD.] Place of recording unknown: Chandos

[328] 'Oh my wife is old and young': Robert Wyatt. 2008 [originally 1997.] *The Duchess*. Robert Wyatt. *Shleep*

[328] 'Basically slightly out-of-tune nursery rhymes': Barney Hoskyns. 1999. 8 Out of 10 Cats Prefer Whiskers. *Mojo*. March. 44

[330] 'The good shepherd': Robert Wyatt. 2008 [originally 1997.] *Shleep*. [CD liner notes.] Chertsey: Domino [originally Hannibal]

[330] 'Wire magazine put Wyatt on their front cover': Photo by Michele Turriani. 1997. *Wire*. 163. Front cover

[331] 'Don't let the gringos grind you down': *Blues in Bob Minor*. *Shleep*

[333] 'A living legend': *Winged Migration*. 2001. [DVD.] Jacques Perrin (dir.). Various: Galatée Films

[335] 'It's still the same old whine': *Dondestan Revisited*. [CD liner notes.]

CHAPTER 19

[337] 'Wyatt did, however, consider a "Political Correctness Gone Mad" festival': Robert Wyatt. 2001. *Welcome to My World*. www.theguardian.com/culture/2001/may/23/artsfeatures.meltdownfestival2001

[337] 'Every single economic migrant and bogus asylum seeker': Lewis. 24

CHAPTER 20

[347] 'Solitary madam': Robert Wyatt and Alfreda Benge. 2008 [originally 2003.] *Cuckoo Madame*. Robert Wyatt. *Cuckooland*. [CD.] London: Domino [originally Hannibal]

[347] 'The witch of Salem': ibid.

[347] 'Assumed that the song was about Margaret Thatcher': Chris Jones. 2003. *Robert Wyatt Cuckooland Review*. www.bbc.co.uk/music/reviews/w5zf

[348] 'You're too bloody lonely for the likes of us': *Cuckoo Madame*

[349] 'Darwin's Rottweiler': James Randerson. 2007. 'Darwin's rottweiler' looks to round up Britain's atheists. www.theguardian.com/politics/blog/2007/apr/12/herdingathiest

[349] 'History-deniers': Richard Dawkins. 2009. *The Greatest Show on Earth: The Evidence for Evolution*. London: Black Swan. 7

[349] 'Mysteries don't lose their poetry because they are solved': Richard Dawkins. 1996. *Science, Delusion and the Appetite for Wonder*. www.positiveatheism.org/writ/dawkins2.htm

[349] 'The professor was moved to tears upon visiting the Hadron Collider': Uploaded by thiscantbeitagain. 2010. *Richard Dawkins and the LHC* www.youtube.com/watch?v=7qlmZ75hyXw

[349] 'Almost too wonderful to bear': Dawkins. 2009. 231

[351] '23,000 European Roma were transported to the death camp, of whom only 2,000 survived': Mary Sibierski. 1999. *Gypsies Remember Auschwitz Dead*. http://news.bbc.co.uk/1/hi/world/europe/410401.stm

[352] 'This is bomber country': Steven Morris. 2004. *Guardian Story Inspires Lyrics for War Lullaby*. www.theguardian.com/uk/2004/sep/09/arts.artsnews

[352] 'Largely fabricated': Andy McSmith. 2013. *West 'Ignored Evidence from Senior Iraqis' That WMDs Did Not Exist*. www.independent.co.uk/news/world/middle-east/west-ignored-evidence-from-senior-iraqis-that-wmds-did-not-exist-8538286.html

[352] '*Lullaby for Hamza* is about an Iraqi woman': Morris

[353] 'I thought about these children in Iraq having the same nightmares': Morris

[356] 'A kind of folk musician representing an unknown tribe': Frances Morgan. 2007. *Lost and Found*. www.disco-robertwyatt.com/images/Robert/interviews/Plan_B_oct_2007/index.htm

[356] 'A suitable place for those with tired ears to pause and resume listening later': *Cuckooland*. [CD liner notes.]

[356] 'Britten's almost bluesy habit of wavering between major and minor keys': Alex Ross. 2008. *The Rest Is Noise*. London: Fourth Estate. 417

[358] 'A wino's mutter': Tim Cumming. 2003. 'I've No Idea What's Next'. www.theguardian.com/music/2003/sep/22/popandrock2

[358] 'Just a bit maaaaaaad': Robert Wyatt. 2008 [originally 2003.] *Just a Bit*. Robert Wyatt. *Cuckooland*

[359] 'Add bass guitar back in': *Cuckooland*. [CD liner notes.]

[359] '*Cuckooland* feels unfinished and maybe unfinishable': Douglas Wolk. 2003. *At Last I Am Old*. www.villagevoice.com/2003-11-18/music/at-last-i-am-old/full/

[359] '*The Wire* magazine made it their record of the year': Anon. 2003. *50 Records of the Year Plus Specialist Charts*. www.thewire.co.uk/archive/2003-rewind

[360] 'The secular Christian pondered how the Ten Commandments might be dusted off for the modern age': Robert Wyatt. 2003. *The Verb*.

[360] Robert Wyatt. *Solar Flares Burn for You*. [CD.] Various: Cuneiform

[360] 'In the beginning was the Bird, and the Bird was bop': Gilad Atzmon and Robert Wyatt. 2004. *Rearranging the 20th Century*. Gilad Atzmon and the Orient House Ensemble. *Musik/Re-Arranging the 20th Century*. [CD.] London: Enja.

[362] 'As far as I'm concerned, I'm dreaming all the time': *Free Will and Testament: The Robert Wyatt Story*

CHAPTER 21

[363] 'The ultimate accolade that celebrates a unique contribution as we know it': Anon. [No date.] *The MOJO Honours List 2005*. http://web.archive.org/web/20081024084334/http://promo.emapnetwork.com/mojo/honours2005/

[365] 'That was really good': Trousse

[367] 'It's that look in your eyes': Robert Wyatt and Alfreda Benge. 2007. *Just as You Are*. Robert Wyatt. *Comicopera*. London: Domino

[367] 'They're all about loss of some sort': David Toop. 2007. *Saturday Night and Sunday Morning*. www.disco-robertwyatt.com/images/Robert/interviews/Wire_october_2007/index.htm

[367] 'It's that look in your eyes': *Just As You Are*

[368] 'I got no-one to turn to when I'm sinking in the shit': Robert Wyatt. 2007. *Be Serious*. Robert Wyatt. *Comicopera*

[368] 'Even the US Air Force now acknowledges weren't quite as smart as was claimed at the time': David Usborne. 1997. *Smart Bombs Not So Clever in Gulf War*. www.independent.co.uk/news/world/smart-bombs-not-so-clever-in-gulf-war-1258850.html

[368] 'No need to wipe your feet, the welcome mat's not there': Robert Wyatt and Alfreda Benge. 2007. *Out of the Blue*. Robert Wyatt. *Comicopera*

[368] 'Something unbelievable has happened to the floor': ibid.

[368] 'You've planted ever-lasting hatred in my heart': ibid.

[369] 'Side 3 is, you know what?': Cee Dolly. 2007. *Interview – Robert Wyatt*. http://www.musicomh.com/ features/interviews/interview-robert-wyatt

[371] 'His creative gestation period simply remains elephantine': *Robert Wyatt: Clash Q&A*

[371] 'It's hard to imagine a record more original or full of life, from any artist of any age, emerging this year': Danny Eccleston. 2007. Trebles All Round. *Mojo*. November. 91

[371] '*The Wire* named it their record of the year': Anon. 2008. *2007 Rewind: Top 50 Releases of the Year*. www.thewire.co.uk/ archive/2007-rewind

[371] 'Wyatt's finest work ever': John Lewis. [No date.] *Comicopera review*. www.uncut.co.uk/robert-wyatt/robert-wyatt-comicopera-review

[371-2] 'It is not often that one has the chance to recommend a concept album': Sean O'Hagan. 2007. *Where Are The Heirs To 'Awkward Buggers' Like Robert Wyatt?* www.theguardian.com/ music/musicblog/2007/oct/14/ wherearetheheirstoawkward

[372] 'Fire and wings': Jean Rhys. 2000 [originally 1939.] *Good Morning Midnight*. London: Penguin. 73

[372] 'Terrific': *Sea Song*

CHAPTER 22

[378] 'For a Stalinist, he really knows how to sing like an angel': Laura Barton. 2008. *'I've Said My Piece'*. www.theguardian.com/music/2008/ mar/11/folk.popandrock

[383] 'Louis Armstrong was seen by some as a sellout, even an Uncle Tom': Zenga Longmore. 2005. *Zenga Longmore On Why Louis Armstrong Was Accused of Being an Uncle Tom*. www.socialaffairsunit. org.uk/blog/archives/000283.php

[383] 'Armstrong had been jazz's first great soloist': Brian Morton and Richard Cook. 2010. *The Penguin Jazz Guide: The History of the Music in the 1001 Best Albums*. London: Penguin. 22

[383] 'The man who, in 1957, had cancelled a State Department-sponsored tour': David Margolick. 2007. *The Day Louis Armstrong Made Noise*. www. nytimes.com/2007/09/23/ opinion/23margolick. html?pagewanted=all&_r=0

[383] 'Our *Wonderful World* is not sarcastic, ironic or even just sentimental': Domino Records. 2010. *A Wonderful World Indeed*. [Press release.] www. dominorecordco.com/uk/news/25-11-10/a-wonderful-world-indeed/

[383] 'There is a hole in the universe the precise shape of a record of standards': Ben Ratliff. 2010. *Critics' Choice: New CDs*. http:// www.nytimes.com/2010/10/25/arts/ music/25choice.html

[384] 'From the air to your body, you gave my spirit life': Ros Stephen and Alfreda Benge. 2010. *Lullaby for Irena*. Wyatt/Atzmon/Stephen. *For the Ghosts Within*. London: Domino

[384] 'We're still here, under the olive trees': Gilad Atzmon and Alfreda Benge. 2010. *The Ghosts Within*. Wyatt/Atzmon/Stephen. *For the Ghosts Within*.

[385] 'The march of capitalism doesn't look so inexorable': Eagleton. xi ('You can tell the capitalist system is in trouble when people start talking about capitalism')

[385] 'The wealth of the very, very rich has dramatically increased while income for the vast majority has remained static or declined': Jodi Dean. 2012. *The Communist Horizon.* London and New York: Verso. 48

[385] 'Taxpayers bail out banks while those responsible for the crash stay unpunished – and unrepentant': Nick Cohen. 2013. *Bankers carry on Unabashed, Unscathed and Unashamed.* www.theguardian. com/commentisfree/2013/apr/07/ brtish-bankers-unpunished-unashamed

[386] 'Amateur means somebody who does something for love': Anon. 2009. *Your choir on Today.* http:// news.bbc.co.uk/today/hi/today/ newsid_8406000/8406457.stm

[386] 'An "awkward bugger"': O'Hagan. 2007

[389] 'One of the most restless, gifted, and intrepid players in jazz': Anon. [No date.] *Bio.* www. charliehadenmusic.com/bio

[389] 'Honouring a unique contribution to music': Anon. [No date.] *Gold Badge Awards.* www. goldbadgeawards.com/index.htm

[391] 'It's not going to happen, old son': Uploaded by Domino Recording Co. 2007. *Robert Wyatt - Q & A, Purcell Room, London 15th Oct 2007.* www.youtube.com/ watch?v=V9XRWkIKTYU

[391] 'It'll probably knock ten years off your life, twenty if you smoke': *Free Will and Testament: The Robert Wyatt Story*

[391] 'The DiscoRobertWyatt website lists over 200 records in its "With Friends"' discography alone' [even allowing for some repetition]: Anon. [No date.] *Une discographie de Robert Wyatt.* www.disco-robertwyatt.com/images/with_ friends/

[394] 'It's perfectly accepted by everyone from poets to politicians': *Forever Young: How Rock'n'Roll Grew Up*

PHOTO CREDITS

Most of the photogaphs and illustrations in this book come from the personal collections of Robert Wyatt and Alfreda Benge. I have also been fortunate in having access through Saffron Ellidge to archive photos by Mark Ellidge, and to the collection of Michael King who generously made this freely available. Below are credits for all images where the photographer is known; all images are copyright as listed. Apologies to any photographer who is not credited; omissions can be corrected in any future edition of the book. All the artwork from Robert Wyatt albums is copyright of Alfreda Benge and is used with her generous permission.

THANKS

This book is the result of many hours of interviews with people who have known and worked with Robert Wyatt over the years. I am hugely grateful to all those who gave up their time; they are listed at the beginning of the preceding 'Notes and Sources'. I am indebted, too, to all the journalists and authors who have interviewed Robert through his career; quotes from their work are acknowledged in the notes.

I would like to thank my agent when I began writing this book, Kevin Conroy Scott at Tibor Jones, and my agent now I have finished it, Sophie Lambert at Conville and Walsh; all at Serpent's Tail, especially Pete Ayrton, Hannah Westland, Anna-Marie Fitzgerald and, in particular, my editor Mark Ellingham; also Henry Iles for design, Nikky Twyman for proofreading, and Diana leCore for the index. I owe much to my readers, too: Aymeric Leroy, Michael King, Andy Childs, Chris Searle and Saffron Ellidge. I am particularly in debt to Aymeric for his Calyx site and for very generously giving me access to previously unpublished interviews. I would also like to thank Jonathan Coe for his introduction.

I am grateful to colleagues at Middlesex University, in particular Richard Osborne, Paul Cobley and Ben Dwyer; to Jane Beese at the Southbank Centre, John Cumming at Serious, Tony Herrington at *The Wire* and Jill Adams at Louder Than Words; and to Jonny Bradshaw, Laurence Bell, Colleen Maloney and Mathew Cooper at Domino, Ken Lower at Hermana, and Andy Childs – again – for all their work on the accompanying compilation album. Others who have helped in various capacities and at various times include John Williams, Richie Unterberger, John Trimble, Lee Brackstone, Peter Culshaw, Nat Jansz, Jean-Paul of *DiscoRobertWyatt*, Paul Sandall, Andrew Phillips and Luke McMahon. Love and thanks, as ever, to Mum, Dad, Loren and Dom; and to Charlotte, Iris and the bump.

My greatest debt, however, is to Robert and Alfie themselves – for living these lives in the first place, and for then opening them up to such scrutiny. They have been remarkably supportive and trusting throughout; I hope this book does them justice.

Marcus O'Dair, 2014

INDEX

Numbers in *italics* refer to photo captions.

Signed Prints of Rock Bottom and other artwork

To celebrate publication of *Different Every Time*, Alfreda Benge has made available unique artist print editions of her cover artwork for *Rock Bottom* and *Ruth Is Stranger Than Richard*. These have been printed on fine art paper and are numbered and signed by Alfie and Robert. For details, see www.hypergallery.com